Dick Grayson,
Boy Wonder

Dick Grayson, Boy Wonder

*Scholars and Creators on 75 Years
of Robin, Nightwing and Batman*

Edited by KRISTEN L. GEAMAN

McFarland & Company, Inc., Publishers
Jefferson, North Carolina

LIBRARY OF CONGRESS CATALOGUING-IN-PUBLICATION DATA

Dick Grayson, Boy Wonder : scholars and creators on 75 years of Robin, Nightwing and Batman / edited by Kristen L. Geaman.
    p.   cm.
Includes bibliographical references and index.

ISBN 978-0-7864-9788-1 (softcover : acid free paper) ∞
ISBN 978-1-4766-2085-5 (ebook)

1. Robin the Boy Wonder (Fictitious character)   2. Comic books, strips, etc.—History and criticism.   I. Geaman, Kristen L., 1985– editor.

PN6728.R576D53 2015
741.5'973—dc23   2015021885

BRITISH LIBRARY CATALOGUING DATA ARE AVAILABLE

© 2015 Kristen L. Geaman. All rights reserved

No part of this book may be reproduced or transmitted in any form or by any means, electronic or mechanical, including photocopying or recording, or by any information storage and retrieval system, without permission in writing from the publisher.

Front cover image of superhero © 2015 Digital Vision

Printed in the United States of America

McFarland & Company, Inc., Publishers
  Box 611, Jefferson, North Carolina 28640
    www.mcfarlandpub.com

Table of Contents

Acknowledgments viii

Introduction: The Sensational Character Find of 1940
    KRISTEN L. GEAMAN 1

Part I. Robin the Boy Wonder

Success in Stasis: Dick Grayson's Thirty Years as a Boy Wonder
    J.L. BELL 8

Outlining the Future Robin: The Seventies in the *Batman Family*
    FERNANDO GABRIEL PAGNONI BERNS and
    CÉSAR ALFONSO MARINO 28

Fashioning Himself a Hero: Robin's Costume and Its Role in
Shaping His Identity
    JOSHUA R. PANGBORN 40

The Gray(son) Area: Performing Robin the Right Way
    CARA L. MACNEIL-DONOGHUE 54

Part II. The Original Dynamic Duo: Dick Grayson and Bruce Wayne

The Child Is Father to the (Bat)Man: The Inverted Parent-Child
Dynamic of DC Comics' Dynamic Duo
    DAVID KINGSLEY 66

Dick Grayson and the Literary Tradition of Heroic Friendship
    EMILY ZINKIN 81

"The Loyal Heart": Homosocial Bonding and Homoerotic
Subtext Between Batman and Robin, 1939–1943
    CATHERINE M. VALE 94

Part III. Nightwing and Beyond: Dick Grayson Grows Up

Boy Wonder to Man Wonder: Dick Grayson's Transition to Nightwing and the Bildungsroman
    KRISTEN L. GEAMAN   112

Building Character: The Writers Who Shaped Dick Grayson's Personality
    CHRISTOPHER MCKITTRICK   130

The Heart and Soul: Dick Grayson as the Center of the DC Universe
    MOLLIE HERLOCKER   145

The New 52 (2011–present)
    JORDAN HASS *and* STAR SCHNEIDER   155

Grayson, Sex and Feminism
    TINI HOWARD   169

Part IV. Ties That Bind: Relationships with Family and Friends

Mother Alfred: The Influence of Dick Grayson's "Other Parent"
    BETHANY F. BRENGAN   178

Big Brother Dick
    YASMIN LYSAKER   197

Dick and Damian: The Second Batman and His Robin
    KALINA KEESTER   211

Titans Together
    SHELLY SPOSATO *and* PAMELA SHAH   222

Darkly Deconstructing the Dynamic Duo: Dick Grayson in Frank Miller
    ALEXANDRA SCHULZ   244

Part V. Interviews

Interview with Dennis O'Neil
    KRISTEN L. GEAMAN   264

Interview with Marv Wolfman
    KRISTEN L. GEAMAN   271

Interview with Chuck Dixon
    KRISTEN L. GEAMAN   274

Grayson on Grayson
    KRISTEN L. GEAMAN   284

Interview with Kyle Higgins
    KRISTEN L. GEAMAN   314

Conclusion. Dick Grayson: Becoming a Man
    DAN GRAYSON CORDERO   322

Bibliography   331

About the Contributors   349

Index   353

Acknowledgments

I would like to thank all the Dick Grayson fans who helped get this book off the ground—especially the crew on Tumblr. No one should doubt the power of social media to inspire, promote, and create academic work. A special thank you to everyone online who submitted interview questions for our creators, who graciously responded via email. I also want to thank and acknowledge our debt to the many websites that serve as hubs of comic-book and Batman information, including Comic Vine, the Grand Comics Database, and the Batman Universe. We couldn't have done it without these valuable resources. Finally, a huge thank you to my proofreaders, Maribeth Geaman, Brittany Koza, and Grayson Sheldon. This book is undoubtedly better because of your hard work.

Introduction
The Sensational Character Find of 1940

Kristen L. Geaman

The cover of *Detective Comics* #38 (April 1940) proudly proclaimed that Robin, the Boy Wonder, was that sensational character find. Within that issue, readers were introduced to Dick Grayson, acrobat and trapeze artist, who became Robin. For over forty years, Dick Grayson and Robin were as synonymous as Bruce Wayne and Batman, but in the mid–1980s, Robin became a legacy identity when Dick moved on to a new heroic alter ego and a new young man took his place as Batman's devoted sidekick. The year 2015 thus marks a double anniversary: seventy-five years of both Robin the sidekick and Dick Grayson, the boy who started it all.

So why a book just about Dick Grayson? For starters, Dick Grayson, the original and longest-running Robin, "the Boy Wonder," started the phenomenon of the kid sidekick, which is now a well-established and (for some) well-loved superhero motif. Simply put, no Dick Grayson-Robin means no sidekicks.[1]

But Dick is so much more than the sidekick that started it all. Robin became an integral part of the Batman mythos, from both a financial and storytelling standpoint. Robin's debut, in *Detective Comics* #38, doubled the book's sales.[2] For the next thirty years, the Dynamic Duo was virtually inseparable; even now in the cultural lexicon, Batman and Robin go together as naturally as peanut butter and jelly.

Over the years Dick matured and aged, eventually outgrowing the iconic short pants and pixie boots. Using the name Nightwing, Dick was one of the first sidekicks to mature into an independent hero. Growing up is hard to do for a comic-book character (Dick debuted in 1940 but didn't go off to college until December 1969), but Dick led the way with grace and increasing popularity among fans. In the wake of Dick's transformation,

1

other child sidekicks would take on new, grown-up superhero identities, which paved the way for new generations of heroes.

Dick reached the pinnacle of his personal growth when he served as Batman from 2009 until 2011. In the wake of his father-figure/mentor Bruce Wayne's apparent death, Dick took over the role of Batman as well as the role of guardian to his younger brother, Bruce Wayne's recently-discovered biological son Damian Wayne. Dick had come full circle. In addition, Dick's stint as Batman marks him as one of the few former sidekicks to successfully inherit his mentor's mantle.

In 2011, DC Comics rebooted their entire line of comics and Dick returned to his Nightwing identity. Given that Dick had successfully come-of-age twice, it has become somewhat of a joke among Nightwing fans that DC had to reboot their entire universe just to make Dick Nightwing again. While almost certainly untrue, the sentiment highlights Dick's extraordinary character growth: he had achieved a moral, intellectual, and social resolution that surpassed even that of the Batman.

Throughout his history, Dick Grayson has been an integral part of one of the most famous and financially successful franchises in history. Dick has also repeatedly been on the cutting edge of developments in superhero comics, starting with his inception as the first sidekick and continuing to his adoption of Batman's cowl. But the character can also serve as a lens for viewing the world outside of comics, whether it be moral development,[3] the homoerotic, or gendered readership. Dick Grayson is not simply a one-note sidekick but one of the most complex and developed characters in comics.

Surprisingly, especially given the interest in studies of popular culture, Grayson has received scant scholarly attention. Grayson has been connected with Batman for all but the Bat's first eleven months (May 1939 to March 1940), but, even if scholars are not deliberately excluding Robin from consideration, they tend to select topics of inquiry that focus on Batman alone. Those already familiar with the character will note that Grayson played a large role in a number of team books, such as *Teen Titans* and *The New Teen Titans*. Unfortunately, these books have received little scholarly attention. Dick has a large role in various encyclopedic works on these teams, but the purpose of such works has not been to engage in critical analysis.[4]

This work seeks to begin a scholarly dialogue about Dick Grayson. Dick's legacy, and the legacy of Robin, are every bit as vital and vibrant as that of Batman. It is time to give them their due.

As the first foray into scholarship devoted to the back-half of "Batman and," this book covers Dick's entire seventy-five-year career while still leaving room for future scholarly exploration. The first section is devoted to Dick's time as Robin, featuring an informative account of Dick's early history; an exploration of Robin in the 1970s, which highlights a number of developments that would bear fruit in later decades; a look at the significance of the Robin costume in the development of an individualized, fully-developed character; and an examination of what it means to be Robin through the lens of performance.

The second section examines one of the most important relationships in all of comic books: Dick Grayson and Bruce Wayne. While there is a special relationship between Batman and each of his Robins, it is undeniable that Dick and Bruce have a connection that goes beyond even that. As Bruce's closest companion in the war on crime, Dick occupies a unique niche in the Batman world. Bruce occupies pride of place in Dick's world as the man who gave him a home and taught him how to be a hero. The essays in this section explore not only how much Bruce and Dick have contributed to each other's character development, but also how these two embody important literary and historical trends.

The third section moves to a different time in Dick's life: his transition from childhood to adulthood, with a special focus on Dick's post–Robin character development (in both the pre-reboot and rebooted canon) and various coming-of-age stories.

The fourth section returns to Dick's relationships, an integral part of a character who is considered the center of the DC Universe.[5] Various essays explore Dick's interactions with some of the most important people in his life, ranging from Alfred Pennyworth, Dick's Robin brothers, and the Teen Titans. This section ends with a look at Dick Grayson in the works of Frank Miller, offering fans a chance to re-evaluate Miller's contributions and perhaps appreciate his take on Dick Grayson and his relationship with Bruce in a new way. The book continues with insightful interviews from some of the most influential writers of *Nightwing*, and ends with a moving tribute that illustrates just how deeply this character has touched fans.

With such a rich history, one book could never fully cover the many facets of Dick Grayson. Just some of the avenues open for further research include the topic of Dick and representation (he is part Romani), Dick as a leader, further exploration of Dick as Batman, and Dick beyond the pages of comic books. Dick Grayson has appeared in multiple media, including television, movies, and radio. He has also featured in both live-action and animated shows and movies. His role as a cultural icon stretches well beyond the world of comic books. Future scholarship on this character in his many guises will not only give us added understanding of the humanistic merit of comic books but also of the role this medium occupies in our wider culture.

Dick Grayson, and the entire Batman Family, are worthy of much greater consideration in both scholarship and pop culture. These characters have added immeasurably to the Batman mythos, creating stories with far greater depth and nuance than one lone avenger of the night could ever sustain on his own. It is our fervent hope that this book encourages scholarship on the Batman Family (emphasis on the Family) for decades to come.

Timeline

May 1939: Bruce Wayne debuts as Batman in *Detective Comics* #27

April 1940: Dick Grayson is orphaned and debuts as Robin in *Detective Comics* #38

- Fans traditionally hold that Dick was 8–10 when he became Robin, but the comics never give an explicit age. Dick's age is extremely fluid for 30 years; he is always "young."

1943: Alfred Pennyworth arrives in *Batman* #16 (April 1943)

1947–1952: Dick has his own solo Robin series in *Star Spangled Comics* (issues #65–130)

1964: The Teen Titans debut in *The Brave and the Bold* #54 (July 1964)

1969: Dick Grayson leaves home to attend college at Hudson University in *Batman* #217 (December 1969)

1978: The original incarnation of the Teen Titans ends with issue #53 (February 1978)

1980: Dick drops out of college and begins leading the New Teen Titans

February 1984: Dick passes on the Robin mantle to Jason Todd in *Batman* #368

July 1984: Dick debuts as Nightwing in *Tales of the Teen Titans* #44

1985: The DC-wide event *Crisis on Infinite Earths*, which reboots the DC Universe. This is the source of the continuity shorthands pre–*Crisis* and post–*Crisis*, which are used to help explain some of the many contradictions inherent in continuously-published serial works. Some backstories were also deliberately changed with this reboot. Of concern to Dick:

- Alfred has been the Wayne butler for years, meaning his arrival in Bruce's life predates Dick's (a reversal of what occurred in the 1940s).

- Jason Todd, the second Robin, receives a complete character overhaul.
- Dick's transition to Nightwing is altered.

1994: Dick leaves the Titans in *The New Titans* #114 (September 1994)

1994: Dick serves as Batman while Bruce recovers from injuries; *Prodigal* storyline from November 1994 to January 1995

1995: Dick has a solo miniseries (September–December)

October 1996–April 2009: Dick has a solo *Nightwing* series that runs for 153 issues, 2 annuals, and various specials

2009–2011: Dick Grayson serves as Batman, with Damian Wayne as his Robin

2011: DC's *New 52* reboots the entire DC Universe, creating the DCnU (new). Dick has a *Nightwing* solo series that last for 30 issues and 1 annual

2014: After Nightwing's secret identity is revealed in the miniseries *Forever Evil*, Dick becomes a secret agent working for Spyral. He has a currently ongoing series titled *Grayson*, which began in September 2014.

Notes

1. Glen Cadigan, *Titans Companion* (Raleigh, NC: TwoMorrows Publishing, 2005), 7. It is possible that Dick-Robin might simply be the best known early sidekick. See Joshua R. Pangborn's article in this volume for more.

2. Will Brooker, *Batman Unmasked: Analyzing a Cultural Icon* (New York: Continuum, 2000, 2005), 59.

3. Carsten Fogh Nielsen, "Leaving the Shadow of the Bat: Aristotle, Kant, and Dick Grayson on Moral Education," in *Batman and Philosophy: The Dark Knight of the Soul*, ed. by Mark D. White and Robert Arp (Hoboken, NJ: John Wiley & Sons, 2008), 254–268.

4. Such as Cadigan, *Titans Companion*.

5. C.F. Arnold, "Nightwing is the Centre of the (DC) Universe," *Comics Are Dead* (24 March 2010), http://comicsaredead.yolasite.com/reviews-news/nightwing-is-the-centre-of-the-dc-universe.

Part I

Robin the Boy Wonder

Success in Stasis
Dick Grayson's Thirty Years as a Boy Wonder

J.L. BELL

The cover of *Detective Comics* #38 announced "The Sensational Character-Find of 1940—Robin the Boy Wonder!"[1] That character was a joint creation of writer Bill Finger, artist Jerry Robinson, and artist and team leader Bob Kane (with possible prodding from the comic book's publisher).[2] Right away this Robin brought a happier tone to the magazine. Previous *Detective Comics* covers featured a grim Batman fighting villains or looming over a spooky mansion. This one showed him smiling as the grinning boy in a colorful costume burst through paper stretched over a hoop.

The story inside introduced that character to readers as Dick Grayson, a young circus flyer. In many ways that adventure was as dark as the solo Batman stories that came before. It starts with Dick's parents being murdered in front of him. Inker Robinson provided deep chiaroscuro night scenes—battles on unfinished skyscrapers silhouetted against full moons. During his initial fight, Robin kicks one murderous thug off a girder into thin air. The big boss kills another man, and the Dynamic Duo is more interested in capturing photographic evidence of that crime than in stopping it. That fatal violence was in keeping with the preceding Batman stories. Of the twelve tales created before Robin's arrival, five show Batman holding or using guns, and he leaves a lot of dead foes behind him.[3] But soon after Robin's arrival, the editor ordered changes, as Finger recounted: "I had Batman use a gun to shoot a villain, and I was called on the carpet by Whit Ellsworth. He said, 'Never let us have Batman carry a gun again.' He was right."[4]

That dictum was one step in how the DC Comics publishing company took creative control of the Batman franchise from Bob Kane and his little studio.[5] After 1941 or so, Whitney Ellsworth and his editorial successors steered Batman and Robin's career, assigning stories to a variety of writers and artists. That corporate approach froze the characters in place for decades. Panels from the early 1940s look almost interchangeable with panels from the early 1960s. The Boy Wonder's design remained the same; as either Dick or Robin, he had his hair combed back with small curls on either side of his forehead. Dick stopped wearing britches after World War II, but he continued to dress as any grandmother would like to see. Most important, over those decades the character functioned the same way in all Batman stories, serving as a point of identification for younger readers, a source of humor and emotional expression, and a loyal partner and family member for Bruce Wayne.

The unchanging nature of those Batman and Robin stories did not hurt their appeal to the young readers who were the main market for superhero comics. In fact, the team became one of the most popular and enduring in the genre, appearing together on every issue of *Detective Comics*, and then *Batman*, and then with Superman on *World's Finest*. Indeed, the Boy Wonder was popular enough to appear on *more* comic-book covers in the 1940s than Batman himself.[6] The Dynamic Duo were also among the small handful of superheroes who remained in print continuously. Adding Dick Grayson to the Batman saga improved the storytelling, opened new possibilities in plotting, and created a depth that the Caped Crusader's solo adventures had lacked. The partnership of the Dynamic Duo—the first of many comic-book teams featuring an adult crime-fighter and a kid sidekick—provided the emotional foundation that made their stories meaningful.

In that period the Boy Wonder's appeal did not lie in Dick Grayson's origin: a young circus acrobat orphaned by criminals, adopted by a billionaire with a similar thirst for justice. Writer Bill Finger came up with that background in 1940 to explain how an adolescent would be able to swing from tall buildings and fight with grown men, but the comics of the next three decades rarely referred back to it. Finger wrote two such tales, published in 1945 and 1960, but other Batman writers may not even have been aware of Dick's past.[7] Since it was then rare for comic-book stories to be reprinted, only a few early fans of the Dynamic Duo ever read about Dick Grayson's life in the circus or why he was living with Bruce Wayne. And that does not seem to have mattered. That first generation of readers was excited by what they saw Batman and Robin doing on the page, not by their past.

In superhero adventure series of that time, character development is limited. Stories begin with a disruption: a crime, the arrival of a monster or alien, a direct threat to the hero. Most tales pose a puzzle for readers: who committed this crime, what is that villain's next move, how can the heroes use their powers to overcome those foes without compromising their values? Most important, these adventures are emotional roller-coaster rides: just when it seems that the heroes are winning, they suffer a reversal. Just when all seems lost, the heroes triumph. The end of the adventure is almost always a restoration of the status quo ante.

Adding Robin to the Batman comics made all aspects of that storytelling easier and more effective. First of all, as writer Bill Finger explained, "Holmes had his Watson.... Batman didn't have anyone to talk to, and it got a little tiresome always having him thinking."

Although comics let readers see into characters' heads through thought balloons and captions, they are more like stage dramas than like novels. The strongest way to show what characters are thinking is through action or conversation. Thus, detective work after Robin's arrival takes this form:

> DICK: Clubfoot again! Did you hear anything about him?
> BRUCE: I was over to Commissioner Gordon's today. Found out that the man "Clubfoot" Beggs was last seen boarding a train for New York!
> DICK: There's no doubt "Clubfoot" Beggs hates the Storne family! Vengeance!
> BRUCE: Vengeance? Robin, tonight you and I are going to visit Ward, the lawyer. I want to know more about that will![8]

Paradoxically, however, Robin was just as important as someone Batman does *not* tell everything to. A thrilling adventure or puzzling mystery depends on readers *not* knowing just how things will turn out. If the audience learns who the culprit is at the same time as the detective, anything that might follow—gathering the suspects, reviewing the clues, identifying the guilty—becomes anticlimactic. If a hero anticipates the villains' next move and lays a trap, explaining that trap to readers in advance means the situation is less exciting for readers (unless, that is, the villains have also thought ahead and unexpectedly escape). Thus, the comics have many moments when Batman says he has figured out a mystery or formed a plan but does not reveal everything. Robin functions as the readers' baffled but curious stand-in:

> BATMAN: There! I've wedged these sacks of rice between the door and the first stone! Grab that water hose, Robin, and start drenching the rice bags!
> ROBIN: Gosh, I hope you know what you're doing ... I don't![9]

A different character could have become Batman's sounding board, but the industry was learning that the most avid readers of superhero comics were boys.[10] Dick Grayson was a natural stand-in for those young male readers. As artist Jerry Robinson said, "it enlarged the readership identification. The younger kids could then identify with Robin, which they couldn't with Batman, and the older ones with Batman. It extended the appeal on a lot of levels."

To allow all young boys to see themselves in Robin, the early stories were mum on his age, as well as the gap between his age and Batman's. *Batman* #10 showed Bruce celebrating Dick's birthday with a traditional spanking, cake, and gift of a small batplane. Scripter Joseph Greene had Bruce give Dick ten spanks, including "one for good measure" and one "to grow on"—suggesting Dick was as young as eight years old. But artists Kane and Robinson showed fourteen candles on his cake.[11] By not specifying how old Dick was, the Batman team let young readers of any age identify with him. Nostalgist Don Edrington (nine years old in 1940) recalled:

> My favorite superheroes were Batman and Robin. I especially liked them because I could identify with Robin—I was sure he was exactly my age. I was positive of that when I first started reading the comics at about age nine, and I was still convinced he was my age when I was fourteen or fifteen.[12]

Eventually, the magazines established that Dick is a student at Gotham High School and thus in his mid-teens, still within the aspirational sights of younger readers.[13]

Most young readers probably aspired to be Batman, the most powerful character in the series, rather than Robin. In *Manufacturing Desire*, communications professor Arthur Asa Berger (seven years old in 1940) wrote:

> Like many other super heroes, Batman provides youngsters with a young sidekick hero to identify with—Robin, though it is Batman who captured the imagination of children the most.... During the Batman rage of a number of years ago [presumably the mid–1960s], many children in my neighborhood used to tie a towel around their neck and play Batman. It was always the youngest and weakest children who were forced into the Robin role.[14]

But Robin's status as the littlest guy in the fight increases the character's appeal for some children, especially the "youngest and weakest." And when Robin performs exceptionally well—solving a case himself, rescuing Batman—the result is even more gratifying. As Bruce Wayne put it in a final panel back in 1940: "If you're as terrific as you are as a kid, I pity the criminals when you're a grown man!"[15]

Robin also changed the Batman stories by providing more humor. In his solo adventures Batman spits out a few wisecracks while beating up crooks, but even those undercut his character. In contrast, a "laughing young daredevil," as Robin was labeled from the start, can joke easily. Indeed, as writers strained for wit under deadline, they found no pun too lame to come from Robin's mouth. He particularly enjoys cracking jokes while tackling criminals, as in "Mind if I *butt* in?" while kicking a gun-toting gangster in the rear.[16] Within a few years, Batman and other characters start to comment on Robin's puns, making them an explicit part of his characterization. Dick's presence allowed for more varied moods and tones within the saga. Of the four stories in each *Batman* magazine in the early 1940s, one was often a humorous tale.

Even more important, Robin strengthened the Batman stories by broadening their emotional range. In the first "Bat-Man" story in *Detective Comics* #27, the costumed crime-fighter shows basically one emotion: grim determination. Reflecting the mid-century ideal of the American male, Bruce Wayne is in control of his feelings, not letting them overcome his judgment nor displaying them broadly. But those rules do not apply strongly to young Dick Grayson. He can express deep emotions, not only his own but Bruce's. In a 1944 story, after Batman has recovered from poisoning, a relieved Robin embraces him, saying: "Golly! I thought you ... you ... golly! Guess you think I'm a sissy bawling this way!" "Heck, I'm doing a little bawling myself!" answers Batman, not bawling.[17] When Bruce develops crippling phobias in 1963, he states grimly, "I must put away my Batman costume and retire from crime-fighting!" It is up to Dick to sob, "Oh, Batman!"[18]

Robin's emotional responses to events make the high points of each story higher, the low points lower. While Batman allows himself some pleasure at the end of a tale, Robin grins broadly and jokes about besting the bad guys. Batman can reproach himself for making a mistake, but in the same situation the Boy Wonder can fall to pieces. By the 1950s, Robin's role as an emotional cue for readers was so well established that he often appeared on a lower corner of a comic-book cover, looking on in surprise and concern at whatever threat Batman was facing that month. Fans later dubbed these tableaus "shocked Robin" covers. Like Robin, readers were supposed to gaze at Batman's predicament and be alarmed by what they saw.

When Batman was a solo hero, the most effective way to create a roller-coaster ride for readers was to show the villains getting the upper hand on him. That suggested Batman was not the physical paragon that the magazines described; as cartoonist Jules Feiffer commented, "there was some reason to believe he had a glass jaw."[19] However, it is much easier for readers to accept that villains might get the jump on little Robin. Similarly, a kid sidekick can miss a clue or make another mistake because his youth means he is still growing and learning, capable of doing better next time.

Thus, in countless Batman adventures from the 1940s through the 1960s, the Dynamic Duo are on the point of catching a gang of crooks when Robin trips over something—or perhaps over nothing at all, despite his background as an acrobat. In *Batman* #21, for example, Robin falls on his face in front of a stampeding herd of cattle.[20] At other times, he is captured and becomes, in Frank Miller's memorable phrase, "Robin, the Boy Hostage."[21] Or Robin's convenient clumsiness allows the bad guys to capture the Dynamic Duo and put them in a picturesque but inefficient deathtrap.[22] In any of these scenarios, the narrative tension rises. Writers rarely used Robin's falls for humor, just as they did not cue readers to laugh at his bafflement while Batman solves the mystery of the month. Expecting younger readers to identify with Robin, the storytellers knew better than to make fun of him.

Robin was an explicit role model for youngsters. The last panel in *Batman* #1 spells out the values that he stood for and urges readers:

> "Always be helpful to those who need help!"
> Why not become one of "Robin's Regulars?" No button or badge is needed—the world will recognize your golden acts without them! Be a "Robin Regular" by being *regular!*[23]

DC Comics was visibly trying to provide moral lessons for young readers, even forgoing the chance to sell them a "button or badge." In the summer of 1941 DC instituted a formal code for all its comics, perhaps a response to early comic book critics.[24] The company declared: "A deep respect for our obligation to the young people of America and their parents and our responsibility as parents ourselves combine to set our standards of wholesome entertainment."[25] Henceforth, Superman, Batman, and DC's other heroes would never take a life. Focusing on the market of young readers and their parents, the company did not go deeply into the horror and crime comics that outsold superheroes in the late 1940s.

In some ways, the editorial edict against Batman killing turned out to help writers to construct exciting stories. It provided an additional source of pressure on the heroes: not only must they subdue the bad guys, but they must do so without using lethal force. It also offered an easy explanation for why the Joker and other unrepentant villains survive to return in future stories. In other ways, however, DC's internal code cut off storytelling possibilities. By the mid–1940s Batman was no longer a vigilante having to hide from the authorities; the Gotham City Police Department had deputized him. Stories focused on thieves, spies, and kidnappers instead of murderers. Nonetheless, the Batman magazines remained among DC's most popular.

From the mid–1940s through the late 1960s, nearly every Batman story began and ended in the same situation, with Bruce Wayne and Dick Grayson enjoying their successes in vanquishing criminals. Yet for comic-book readers that did not become boring. For one thing, there was always a new wave of children; some DC Comics editors even recycled story ideas every few years, assuming no one would notice. Still, each month's pipeline required multiple new adventures for the Dynamic Duo, and those stories remained compelling enough for the publisher to sell millions of magazines year after year. That output was possible because Batman and Robin's regular situation, the status quo to which every tale returns, contained some inherent tensions that generated new stories.

Underlying the most gripping Batman stories from the 1940s to the 1960s was the potential conflict between the heroes' comfortable lives as Bruce and Dick and their drive to fight crime while dressed in costumes and masks. Every time Bruce Wayne's life as a playboy millionaire or Dick Grayson's as a high-school student interferes with the Dynamic Duo's work, a new plot blooms. Every story about a threat to reveal their secret identities plays off the conflict inherent in their situation. And whenever one partner or the other—or their readers—perceives something coming between them, that strikes at the saga's emotional core. In these decades, the worst trouble for Batman and Robin is not a crazy supervillain or a gang out to rob socialites at a charity ball—it is a threat to the bond between Bruce and Dick, whether in costume or not.

Among the best examples of that dynamic is "Bruce Wayne Loses the Guardianship of Dick Grayson!" Scripted by Bill Finger, the tale begins: "You must have read how Batman first took in charge a young boy named Dick Grayson.... Since that day, the mutual affection between this man and boy has been as strong as that between father and son!" The first panel shows Bruce and Dick having a pillow fight in their "happy home." But Alfred interrupts to say that a man is calling: Dick's paternal uncle George has come to demand custody of the boy.[26]

In court, Bruce expresses his feelings "In a strained voice": "Dick is like my own son! ... Your honor, I ... I love that boy! Please don't take him from me!" Dick cries on the witness stand as he testifies: "A fella couldn't want a better friend!" Nonetheless, the judge decides that a "nightclubbing, shiftless, café society playboy" like Bruce Wayne is a poor guardian for a teenager and awards custody to Uncle George. As Dick leaves Wayne Manor, Bruce waves from the porch, murmuring, "Goodbye, kid, goodbye."[27] Letterer George Roussos rendered those words in small letters inside a large balloon, showing how Bruce feels crushed—a rare early use of that graphic technique. In the following days Bruce mopes around his mansion, complaining about how unfair the situation is: "In order to cover up my Batman work, I had to pretend to be a playboy ... and now it's made me lose the person I love the most!" He tries to cheer himself up by punching crooks, but "he fights without interest or purpose." In fact, Batman is a less effective fighter without Robin, and the bad guys are on the verge of overpowering him.[28]

But then the Boy Wonder bursts back onto the page! "Reunited with Robin, Batman is his old self again!" Together the Dynamic Duo overcome the criminals. But of course those faceless foes are not the focus of this story. The major problem reappears at the end of the fight as Dick has to go back to his newfound relations. On a second visit to Bruce Wayne, Uncle George offers to let him "buy back Dick Grayson" for a mere million dollars, revealing himself as an extortionist.[29] Batman goes after him but, again without his partner, gets lured "into a man-trap!" And the Caped Crusader's only back-up now is Alfred the butler—fat, comic-relief Alfred.

Fortunately, Alfred knows where to get help: he knocks on Dick's new bedroom window, and the two of them race off and rescue Batman. On the story's last page, the judge discloses that Batman has assured him that Bruce Wayne is a fine man after all. Dick returns to Bruce's custody. "Well the mawsters are back together again!" Alfred assures readers in the final panel.[30]

Most Batman and Robin adventures were not so openly emotional, of course. Often they really were about beating back the crooks of the month. But on a regular basis *Batman* or *Detective* showed the core relationship of the Dynamic Duo to be in danger. Variations on that theme included:

- "Batman Plays a Lone Hand": Bruce kicks Dick out of Wayne Manor with no explanation in order to protect him from criminals.
- "Collector of Millionaires": Bruce is kidnapped and an abusive double takes his place.
- "The Second Boy Wonder": Dick learns Bruce is training a new boy and assumes he'll be replaced.
- "How to Be the Batman": Bruce suffers amnesia, and Robin has to retrain him.
- "A Partner for Batman": Dick is injured, and Batman starts training a new partner, leaving Dick to worry if he is being replaced.[31]

Most often those stories came from Bill Finger, co-creator of the two characters. By producing a saga with a strong relationship at its heart, he helped to make Batman and Robin stand out among the many other heroes of the early 1940s and survive into the next decade.

One recurring threat to the Batman and Robin partnership was the possibility of romance with an outsider. By the mid–1940s the saga established Bruce Wayne as a playboy, making and breaking dates with pretty women, and also established that Dick Grayson was not interested in girls. That pattern was clear at the end of the Dynamic Duo's first encounter with the Cat (later Catwoman) in *Batman* #1. Batman lets her escape. "I'll bet you bumped into me on purpose!" Robin chides. "She still had lovely eyes!" Batman replies unhelpfully; "Maybe I'll bump into her again sometime."[32] The couple does meet again in *Batman* #3, and Catwoman escapes again. "A night for romance, eh, Robin?" Batman muses. "Romance? Bah!" replies the Boy Wonder.[33] Such stories portray being able to fall in love as a weakness that keeps a man from pursuing justice.

Occasionally Dick Grayson develops a short-lived crush on a girl his own age, but those relationships all go away by the end of the story, along with the girls themselves.[34] In *Star Spangled Comics* #103, Robin meets a girl who has trained herself to be Roberta, the Girl Wonder, and during a picnic he feels tempted to reveal his real identity. But eventually he loses confidence in Roberta's ability to guard a secret, and in the end he tricks her into abandoning her fight against crime.[35] During a 1957 case, Robin falls hard for a young figure skater named Vera Lovely. Little hearts circle his head as he thinks about her. But such thinking distracts him during fights, and Dick decides, "from now on, I'm keeping my mind on criminals, not *girls!*"[36] Because love affairs disrupt the Dynamic Duo's important work, they must wait until he is older.

Dick growing older is another potential disruption to the partnership that many stories explored. In "Batman Junior and Robin Senior" a gas turns Robin into an adult and Batman into a teen.[37] In "The Grown-Up Boy Wonder" a box of "maturing gas" from outer space makes Dick's body grow to full size overnight. Bruce warns him, "You've got a lot of 'growing' to do before you're *really* a man!" But, acting "like an impulsive youngster," Dick dons a new costume and makes his debut as Owlman. Not used to his new, heavier body, Dick is even more prone to falling down and getting captured, and he realizes that Bruce was right. Owlman's career ends as soon as the extraterrestrial gas wears off. Dick runs off to play with his friends, exclaiming, "Gee, it's good to be a kid again!" The Dynamic Duo's normal partnership is restored.[38]

Even more dire, of course, was the threat of Robin not growing up at all because he is killed. In *Batman* #5, Batman finds Robin's body, apparently "clubbed to death," and the result is grim indeed:

> The Batman, man who has faced a thousand dangers, man of strength and willpower, now bends his head and weeps. Anguished sobs are torn from him!
> Slowly, his great frame straightens. Small veins stand out on his features. Muscles cord in his throat. His eyes become fires, his mouth a knife-edged line—
> For the first time, the Batman knows rage, bleak grim rage. Woe to all criminals, for now, the Batman has become a terrible figure of vengeance!

Those last two paragraphs frame a picture of Batman holding a limp and bloody Robin in his arms. It turns out Dick is not dead, but similar images would appear on the cover of Batman magazines, showing how resonant such a possibility remained.[39] The death of a partner is the ultimate threat to the Dynamic Duo.

In the late 1940s DC Comics published a series of solo Robin stories in *Star Spangled Comics*, featuring him on the cover of issues #65 through #95. In most of those adventures Batman does not appear, or appears only briefly. And without him that series lacks the compelling emotional core of the regular Batman and Robin saga. The recurring theme seems to be competence, with Robin proving his skills, but he has no ongoing connection to another character. Over time, sales drooped. In 1949 the company tried making Batman a bigger part of those stories, and then replaced Robin as the magazine's cover feature. Within a few years, Robin's *Star Spangled* series was all but forgotten.

In contrast, DC maintained the success of *World's Finest Comics* in 1954 after dropping the magazine's separate stories about Superman and about Batman and Robin and switching to one story about all three heroes working together. Those team-ups replicated the compelling emotional engine of the Batman saga: all three characters know each other's secrets and work to preserve their private identities, starting from their first adventure together.[40] Many *World's Finest* stories focused on the threat of disruptions within the trio, such as "The New Team of Superman and Robin" and "The Power That Transformed Batman."[41]

The year 1954 also brought Fredric Wertham's *Seduction of the Innocent*, an attack on comic books that at one point zeroed in on the core of the Batman and Robin saga. Wertham, a psychiatrist counseling troubled youth in New York, lumped superhero comic books among all other "crime comics" since they depicted crimes. (No matter if those crimes all involved umbrellas, or jokes, or the number two.) Crime comics led young readers to juvenile delinquency, he claimed. Wertham also warned that "a subtle atmosphere of homoeroticism ... pervades the adventures of the mature 'Batman' and his young friend 'Robin.'"[42]

Bruce, Dick, and their butler Alfred did have an all-male household. It was, as Wertham noted, nicely decorated. In their early years Bruce and Dick even shared a bedroom, sleeping in twin beds. One 1951 panel shows their beds close to each other in the middle of a "spacious room" with a huge alarm bell on the wall.[43] Other superhero teams behaved similarly, however. *Adventure Comics* shows the Sandman and Sandy also sharing a bedroom.[44] In *More Fun* #89, Green Arrow and Speedy review how they met while the younger partner takes a shower behind a clear curtain decorated with fish.[45] Such physical closeness probably reflects how most of the early comic-book creators were young men from working-class families; they were used to sharing bedrooms with relatives, probably used to sharing beds.[46]

But Dr. Wertham's interpretation of the Dynamic Duo was not just about lifestyle—it was about emotion. In his book he presented quotations from three gay patients about Batman and Robin. The longest passage was this:

> One young homosexual during psychotherapy brought us a copy of *Detective Comics*, with a Batman story. He pointed out a picture of "The Home of Bruce and Dick" a house beautifully landscaped, warmly lighted and showing the devoted pair side by side, looking out a picture window. When he was eight this boy had realized from fantasies about comic book pictures that he was aroused by men. At the age of ten or eleven, "I found my liking, my sexual desires, in comic books. I think I put myself in the position of Robin. I did want to have relations with Batman. The only suggestion of homosexuality may be that they seem to be so close to each other. I remember the first time I came across the page mentioning the 'secret bat cave.' The thought of Batman and Robin living together and possibly having sex relations came to my mind. You can almost connect yourself with the people. I was put in the position of the rescued rather than the rescuer. I felt I'd like to be loved by someone like Batman or Superman."[47]

By examining Wertham's session transcripts, Carol L. Tilley discovered that this statement was actually a composite of remarks from "two men, ages sixteen and seventeen, who had been in a sexual relationship with each other for several years." Wertham omitted their statement that they found Tarzan and Namor the Sub-Mariner (both of whom wear very little clothing) more erotic than Batman and Robin.[48]

What appealed to this young couple most about the Dynamic Duo was not their "possibly having sex relations," as Wertham claimed, but their being "loved." The teens drew the doctor's attention to a picture of "the devoted pair" in their beautiful house—a depiction of a happy same-sex household that was hard to find in popular literature. There is no mystery to why those young men found that image appealing. If a teenaged girl had described enjoying stories of being "rescued" by a handsome, loving millionaire like Bruce Wayne, Wertham might have thought such fantasizing unrealistic but he would not have called it unhealthy.

Wertham complained, "I have never seen in any of the crime, superman, adventure, space, horror, etc., comic books a normal family sitting down at a meal." Yet he immediately went on to say: "I have seen an elaborate, charming breakfast scene, but it was between Batman and his boy, complete with checkered tablecloth, milk, cereal, fruit juice, dressing-gown and newspaper."[49] Thus, the Batman stories showed Wertham what he said he wanted in comic books, except that this household was not "a normal family." *Seduction of the Innocent* warned about comics' effect of "moral disarmament ... a blunting of the finer feelings of conscience, of mercy, of sympathy for other people's suffering."[50] Yet Wertham disapproved of a panel of Dick showing sympathy for Bruce because it was too "like a wish dream of two homosexuals living together."[51]

The Batman comics of those decades did indeed depict Bruce Wayne and Dick Grayson as devoted companions, each ready to risk great danger for the other. The break-up of their partnership is the worst fate hanging over them. Many readers have drawn comfort, or entertainment, in interpreting that partnership as a metaphor for a private gay relationship, with the urgent need to protect secrets from a hostile world. But it is inconceivable that DC Comics wanted its writers and artists to depict a gay relationship in a comic book for children, even in coded fashion.

The teen-aged couple whom Wertham amalgamated and quoted may have drawn hope and inspiration from the little household in Wayne Manor, but they were not representative of the hundreds of thousands of Batman readers at the time. As critics of *Seduction of the Innocent* noted immediately, an overwhelming majority of American children of the 1940s read comic books, and Wertham based all his conclusions on the small number he met for psychological counseling, often after they had committed crimes; his "study" had no control group.

The sociologist David J. Pittman faulted Wertham further for failing to view comics stories through readers' eyes since a "child isn't a little man with the adult's emotions, feelings and reasoning in miniature."[52] Most young fans perceived Bruce and Dick through the lens of their own experiences. They saw the characters behaving like devoted pals, like brothers, and at rare times like father and son. (When Bruce tries to give Dick parental discipline, as in "Robin Studies His Lessons!," it actually disrupts their normal relationship.)[53] One of the few contemporaneous reviewers to address Wertham's analysis of the Dynamic Duo, Robert S. Warshow in *Commentary* magazine, simply dismissed the idea: "his discussion of the supposedly equivocal relation between Batman and the young boy Robin ... seems to me a piece of utter frivolity."[54]

Wertham's charges about comic books, concurrent congressional hearings on juvenile delinquency, and consumer boycotts caused a crisis for many publishers in the 1950s.[55] That attack coincided with the rise of television in American households, and studies found that children who could watch television read fewer comic books.[56] DC Comics weathered those challenges much better than many of its once-formidable competitors, including Fawcett, Quality, EC, and Charlton. By the mid–1950s DC stood head and shoulders above all other publishers in the superhero genre. Superman clearly remained the company's biggest property, helped by his television show, but Batman and Robin were second.

Some observers have assumed that DC Comics introduced Kathy Kane as Batwoman into the Batman comics in 1956 as a response to Wertham's criticism two years before. No interviews or documents have been published to confirm that—though of course the company would not have acknowledged its characters needed such fixing. In fact, many of the stories featuring Batwoman ended with Batman fending off her hints about making their relationship more intimate—in other words, they showed Batman acting *more* like a closeted gay man. Indeed, John D. Cochran's 1965 article "Batman and Robin Were Lovers..." in the satirical magazine *The Realist* used the story "The Marriage of Batman and Batwoman" as evidence that Wertham's interpretation was correct.[57] That story was built around romance as a threat to the Dynamic Duo's partnership—one which turns out merely to be Dick's bad dream, preserving the status quo again.[58]

Batwoman was just one of several recurring characters introduced into the Batman comics in the late 1950s and early '60s, expanding the Dynamic Duo and their butler into a larger "family." But only Ace the Bat-Hound is actually let into Wayne Manor to learn the partners' secrets. Bruce and Dick keep Kathy and her niece Betty, introduced in 1961 as Bat-Girl, at arm's length, just as they have behaved toward journalist Vicki Vale since the 1940s. The pattern is sexist, not sexual. What matters most, those stories say, is the fundamental friendship between Batman and Robin.[59]

By the 1960s, Batman comic books had become monotonous—not because the saga's emotional foundation had weakened but because of unimaginative presentation. Four *Detective Comics* covers in 1960 showed Robin looking shocked in one corner as Batman or Batwoman rears back in surprise at a strange creature and/or a ray. On three of those four covers Batman shouts, "Great Scott!" On three his figure is posed in the exact same way.[60] Even for young readers, those magazines would not seem fresh. The Batman comics still performed better than any other DC title not featuring Superman, but sales were drooping. The newsstand sell-through rate appears to have been especially troubling.[61] The company also faced higher costs from paying Bob Kane to supply pages at a rate set before the 1950s shakeout had lowered every other artist's asking price. DC therefore told Kane that it would cancel the magazine unless he made some concessions. Reluctantly, he agreed.[62]

DC took the Batman comics away from long-time editor Jack Schiff and assigned them to Julius Schwartz. Back in 1956, Schwartz had started to reintroduce some superhero trademarks the company had stopped using in the late 1940s: Flash, Green Lantern, and others. His *Justice League of America* and *Flash* magazines had grown to overtake *Detective Comics* in sales. Schwartz brought his top artist, Carmine Infantino, over to the Batman franchise with the understanding that they had to turn the magazine's performance around. He told Kane that his pages would now have to conform to Infantino's style, and Kane passed the word down to his ghost artist, Sheldon Moldoff. In the spring of 1964, Batman and Robin took on what DC loudly proclaimed was a "New Look."[63]

In those issues Dick Grayson no longer has the two side curls on his forehead. Some artists even drew his hair parted on one side. Previous stories showed Dick making music with a harmonica, an accordion, and bagpipes; *Batman* #164 starts with him taking up the more fashionable guitar.[64] There is a new Batmobile, designed like a sports car. The "New Look" was intended to make the Batman magazines more appealing to the youth of the mid–1960s. Despite the cosmetic changes, however, the heroes' personalities and relationship remained much the same as in the preceding years. The most emotional stories continued to arise from the bond between Batman and Robin. They still have to guard their secret identities from outsiders, and now also from Dick's previously unknown Aunt Harriet, who moves into Wayne Manor.[65] That new situation clearly had dramatic possibilities, but it erased the heroes' "happy home" and thus part of the series' appeal. DC Comics bowed to fan pressure and restored the household to its former state in 1968.

In 1964, DC Comics also pursued teen-aged readers by teaming Robin with newer kid sidekicks in a group called the Teen Titans. In that team's tales writer Bob Haney tried to reflect the decade's youth culture. He had Robin call Batman "definitely un-round" (i.e., square) for not appreciating new pop music.[66] Haney's slapdash stories centered on teen interests—pop-music idols, hot rods, mod fashions—though his teen slang was like nothing ever heard. DC even sent the Titans to San Francisco's Haight-Ashbury District a year after the Summer of Love.[67] In contrast to how Robin behaved with Batman, he is usually this team's serious leader, a step toward taking on more responsibilities as a young adult. Eventually new writers edged the stories into social concerns. Still, when compared to the teen-aged characters in Marvel comic books, *Teen Titans* showed how "definitely un-round" DC, and Robin, still were.

In 1966 ABC aired the *Batman* television show, giving the Dynamic Duo their biggest audience yet. The early episodes were good translations of the "New Look" comics to the screen with an overlay of camp; young viewers enjoyed the adventure while adults caught the winks about the whole enterprise. As Batman, Adam West slyly underplayed while Burt Ward as Robin emoted enough for both partners. With West in his late thirties and Ward playing a teenager, the show presented Bruce as more parental toward Dick. Otherwise, they behaved much as they did in the comic books, but the twice-weekly broadcast soon made the lack of character development more obvious.

The *Batman* television show burst into American culture like a fireworks display and then fizzled out over three seasons. The series had made Batman and Robin more prominent than ever in the DC Comics line, appearing in six magazines between them.[68] But when the show ended, sales of the magazines plummeted: *Batman* fell from over 500,000 copies an issue to about 350,000 in 1969. The upstart Marvel Comics line now posed serious competition; its *Amazing Spider-Man*, featuring a hero who went to college when not fighting crime, outsold *Batman* for the first time.

That led to another shift for the Batman comics—and real change this time, not just a new drawing style. For Dick Grayson, this period produced the most momentous transition since the character's introduction. In 1969 DC Comics steered sharply away from the type of story that had fed into the *Batman* television show, shelving the comical villains and the bright daylight colors. Batman became a creature of the night once more, working murder cases and facing gothic villains. And he did that *alone*.

On the cover of *Detective Comics* #393, Robin tearfully announces, "The team-up is finished! This is good-bye for Batman and Robin!" Inside readers receive hints that Dick has decided to go to college—at Hudson University, in a small town upstate.[69] That means leaving Wayne Manor, no longer working every night with Batman. DC Comics had prepared readers for this independence with a retelling of Robin's origin and some new solo stories in the back of *Detective Comics*.⁷⁰ Robin was still supposed to appeal to youth, but now DC was seeking the high-school and college-aged comic-book readers that Marvel had developed. Dick Grayson therefore had to do what those older teens were doing and aspiring to do: leave home and act independently.

In the first scene of the next issue of *Batman*, Dick rides off in a taxicab, a tear on one cheek, as Bruce and Alfred stoically look on. Frank Robbins's story went on to show Bruce closing up Wayne Manor and the Batcave.⁷¹ That ended the era in the Batman mythos that began in the 1940s: Batman and Robin would team up again, of course, but their relationship had changed. In April 1970 DC Comics would update Dick Grayson's billing to "Robin the Teen Wonder."⁷² He would appear in solo stories set in his college town. After thirty years of stasis, the saga made way for new possibilities.

Notes

1. [Bill Finger,] Bob Kane, [and Jerry Robinson], "Introducing Robin the Boy Wonder," *Detective Comics* #38 (New York: DC Comics, April 1940). Most of the earliest Batman stories were written by Bill Finger and drawn by Bob Kane with assistance from Jerry Robinson, George Roussos, and other artists. Until 1964, however, all Batman stories were credited to Kane alone. Credits to writers and other artists in this essay are based on what DC Comics has stated in more recent reprints or on the crowdsourced data at comics.org. In this essay, all citations are to the *first* volume of each comic-book title.

2. Finger's description of how Robin was created, quoted elsewhere in this essay, appears in Jim Steranko, *The Steranko History of Comics* (Reading, PA: Supergraphics, 1970), 44. Robinson's appears in "Jerry Robinson: Been There, Done That," interview with Gary Groth, *The Comics Journal*, 271 (2004), 72–111. Bob Kane's appears in Kane with Tom Andrae, *Batman & Me* (Forestville: Eclipse, 1989), 46. Kane's stories are not reliable; coauthor Andrae discussed Kane's habit of taking credit for others' ideas in a 2014 interview with Marc Tyler Nobleman: noblemania.blogspot.com/2014/03/interview-with-co-author-of-bob-kanes.html. See also Gerard Jones, *Men of Tomorrow: Geeks, Gangsters, and the Birth of the Comic Book* (New York: Basic Books, 2004), 149–54.

3. *Detective Comics* #32, #33, #35, and #36, and "Professor Hugo Strange and the Monsters," in *Batman* #1, originally meant to run in *Detective* #38. See *The Batman Chronicles Volume 1* (New York: DC Comics, 2005).

4. Steranko, *Steranko History of Comics*, 44.

5. The publisher of *Detective Comics* and subsequent magazines had several corporate names over the years; for convenience this essay refers to the company as "DC Comics."

6. In addition to all the comic-book covers that showed Batman and Robin *together*, Batman appeared without Robin on *Detective Comics* #35–37 and #153, *Batman* #47, and *All-Star Comics* #36 (six in all). Robin appeared without Batman on *Star Spangled Comics* #65–87 and #95 (a total of twenty-four).

7. Bill Finger and Dick Sprang, "Dick Grayson, Boy Wonder!" *Batman* #32 (New York: DC Comics, December 1945–January 1946), and Finger and Sheldon Moldoff, "The Man from Robin's Past," *Batman* #129 (February 1960). A 1943 pilot for radio portrayed Dick's doomed parents as both trapeze artists and FBI agents, but that was never broadcast; Les Daniels, *Batman—The Complete History* (San Francisco: Chronicle Books, 1999), 59. In "The Batwoman," *Detective Comics* #233 (July 1956), Batman deduces the identity of Batwoman by hearing her speak circus slang; scripter Edmond Hamilton evidently did not know or remember that Robin had the background to do that. Showing how few people remembered Robin's backstory, in *Stuntman* #1 (April 1946), Joe Simon and Jack Kirby gave their adult hero the same origin: he is the sole survivor of a three-person trapeze act attacked by extortionists.

8. Bill Finger, Bob Kane, and Jerry Robinson, "The Case of the Clubfoot Murders," *Batman* #2 (Summer 1940) in *The Batman Chronicles Volume 2* (New York: DC Comics, 2006), 76.

9. Bill Finger et al., "The Secret Life of the Catwoman!" *Batman* #62 (December 1950–January 1951), 11.

10. For evidence of the comic-book industry's market research in late 1939, see the 1997 interview with publishing executive Roscoe K. Fawcett by P. C. Hamerlinck, reprinted in *The Fawcett Companion: The Best of FCA* (Raleigh: TwoMorrows, 2001).

11. Joseph Greene, Bob Kane, and Jerry Robinson, "The Isle That Time Forgot!" *Batman* #10 (April–May 1942) in *The Batman Chronicles 6* (New York: DC Comics, 2008), 33. Michael L. Fleischer commented on this scene: "it seems absurd to suggest that Grayson was only eight years old at this time"; *The Encyclopedia of Comic Book Heroes: Volume 1, Batman* (New York: Collier Books, 1976), 318.

12. Don Edrington, "Comic Books, Milton Berle, and Holloway Milk Duds," www.pcdon.com/page451.html.

13. See *The Robin Archives, Volume 1* (New York: DC Comics, 2005), which collects *Star Spangled Comics* from the late 1940s.

14. Asa Berger, *Manufacturing Desire: Media, Popular Culture, and Everyday Life* (New Brunswick, N.J.: Transaction Publishers, 1996), 104.

15. Finger, Kane, and Robinson, "[A Master Murderer]," *Detective Comics* #41 (July 1940) in *The Batman Chronicles 2*, 44. This was one of three stories which featured Dick as lead investigator shortly after his debut. The other two are "[The Cat]," *Batman* #1 (Spring 1940), and "The Crime School for Boys!" *Batman* #3 (Fall 1940). See *The Batman Chronicles, Volumes 1* and *2*.

16. Finger, Kane, and Robinson, "The End of Two-Face!" *Detective Comics* #80 (October 1943) in *The Batman Chronicles Volume 10* (New York: DC Comics, 2010), 96.

17. Jack Schiff and Dick Sprang, "The Streamlined Rustlers!" *Batman* #21 (February–March 1944) in *The Batman Chronicles Volume 11* (New York: DC Comics, 2012), 101.

18. Finger, Moldoff, and Charles Paris "Robin Dies at Dawn," *Batman* #156 (June 1963), 14.

19. Jules Feiffer, *The Great Comic Book Heroes* (New York: Dial Press, 1965), 27.

20. Schiff and Sprang, "The Streamlined Rustlers!" 97.

21. Frank Miller, *Batman: The Dark Knight Returns* (New York: Warner Books, 1986), 82–83. The covers of *Detective Comics* #43, #45, #51, and #56–58 all show Robin in danger and Batman coming to the rescue.

22. For example, Finger, Kane, and Ray Burnley, "The Penny Plunderers," *World's Finest Comics* #30 (New York: DC Comics, September–October 1947).

23. Finger, Kane, and Robinson, "The Joker Returns," *Batman* #1 (Spring 1940) in *The Batman Chronicles 1*, 190.

24. In the same spring that saw Dick Grayson's debut, literary critic and novelist

Sterling North lambasted comic books in "A National Disgrace," *Chicago Daily News*, 8 May 1940.
  25. Quoted in Dale Jacobs, *Graphic Encounters: Comics and the Sponsorship of Multimodal Literacy* (New York: Bloomsbury, 2013), 77.
  26. Finger, Kane, and Robinson, "Bruce Wayne Loses the Guardianship of Dick Grayson," *Batman* #20 (December 1943–January 1944) in *The Batman Chronicles Volume 11* (New York: DC Comics, 2012), 43.
  27. Finger, Kane, and Robinson, "Bruce Wayne Loses the Guardianship of Dick Grayson," 44–45.
  28. Finger, Kane, and Robinson, "Bruce Wayne Loses the Guardianship of Dick Grayson," 46.
  29. Finger, Kane, and Robinson, "Bruce Wayne Loses the Guardianship of Dick Grayson," 48–49.
  30. Finger, Kane, and Robinson, "Bruce Wayne Loses the Guardianship of Dick Grayson," 53.
That story was successful enough for Finger to write a variation on it in Finger, Sprang, and Paris, "The Trial of Bruce Wayne!" *Batman* #57 (February–March 1950).
  31. Kane, Robinson, George Roussos, [writer unknown], *Batman* #13 (October–November 1942) in *The Batman Chronicles 7*; Joe Samachson, Dick Sprang, and Norman Fallon, *Batman* #19 (October–November 1943) in *The Batman Chronicles 10*; Kane et al., *Batman* #50 (December 1948–January 1949); Finger et al., *Detective Comics* #190 (December 1952); and Finger et al., *Batman* #65 (June–July 1951).
  32. Finger, Kane, and Robinson, "[The Cat]," *Batman* #1 (Spring 1940) in *The Batman Chronicles 1*, 177.
  33. Finger, Kane, Robinson, and Roussos, "The Batman vs. the Cat-Woman!" *Batman* #3 (Fall 1940) in *The Batman Chronicles 2*, 206.
  34. Don Cameron and Dick Sprang, "Damsel in Distress!" *Batman* #23 (June–July 1944); David Vern, Sheldon Moldoff, and Stan Kaye, "The Boy Wonder Confesses!" *Batman* #81 (February 1954).
  35. Writer unknown and Jim Mooney, "Roberta, the Girl Wonder!" *Star Spangled Comics* #103 (April 1950) in *The Robin Archives Volume 2* (New York: DC Comics, 2010), 219–228.
  36. Finger, Moldoff, and Paris, "Robin Falls in Love," *Batman* #107 (April 1957), 8.
  37. Finger, Moldoff, and Kaye, "Batman Junior and Robin Senior," *Detective Comics* #218 (April 1955).
  38. Finger, Moldoff, and Kaye, "The Grown-Up Boy Wonder," *Batman* #107 (April 1957), 2, 7, 8.
  39. Finger, Kane, Robinson, and Roussos, "The Case of the Honest Crook!" *Batman* #5 (Spring 1941) in *The Batman Chronicles Volume 3* (New York: DC Comics, 2007), 161. Similar images appear on *Batman* #156 (June 1963), *Detective Comics* #574 (May 1987), and the collection *Batman: A Death in the Family* (New York: DC Comics, 1988).
  40. Alvin Schwartz, Curt Swan, and Stan Kaye, "Batman—Double for Superman!" *World's Finest Comics* #71 (July 1954).
  41. Finger, Swan, and Kaye, *World's Finest Comics* #75 (March 1955); Jerry Coleman and Jim Mooney, *World's Finest Comics* #128 (September 1962).
  42. Fredric Wertham, *Seduction of the Innocent* (New York: Rinehart & Company, 1954), 189–90.
  43. Finger, Sprang, and Paris, "The Robberies in the Bat-Cave," *Detective Comics* #177 (November 1951). By *Batman* #156 (June 1963), they had separate bedrooms.
  44. Jack Kirby and Joe Simon, "Dreams of Doom," *Adventure Comics* #77 (August 1942).

45. Joe Samachson, Cliff Young, and Steve Brodie, "Birth of the Battling Bowman," *More Fun Comics* #89 (March 1943).

46. In addition, during World War II hundreds of thousands of young Americans, many of them comics readers, were sleeping and showering together in military service.

47. Wertham, *Seduction of the Innocent*, 192.

48. Carol L. Tilley, "Seducing the Innocent: Fredric Wertham and the Falsifications That Helped Condemn Comics," *Information & Culture*, 47:4 (2012), 394. Tilley also notes distortions and omissions in Wertham's portrayal of another teen-aged boy who had engaged in a more violent form of same-sex activity. That patient stated, "I have read Batman. I liked it once but not any more." Wertham changed that to "he was a special devotee of Batman: 'Sometimes I read them over and over again….'" Wertham's unedited transcripts leave the impression that he quizzed this patient about Batman comics instead of waiting to see if the teenager would bring them up on his own.

49. Wertham, *Seduction of the Innocent*, 236. Wertham also acknowledged a similar scene in *Wonder Woman* with the title character and a young girl.

50. Wertham, *Seduction of the Innocent*, 91.

51. Wertham, *Seduction of the Innocent*, 190. The panel is from Alvin Schwartz (?) and Jim Mooney, "The Confession of Batman," *World's Finest Comics* #44 (February–March 1950). Another of the lines Wertham quoted appears in David Vern et al., "The Man Who Wrote the Joker's Jokes!" *Batman* #67 (October–November 1951).

52. David J. Pittman, "Mass Media and Juvenile Deliquency," in *Juvenile Delinquency*, Joseph S. Roucek, editor (New York: Philosophical Library, 1958), 240.

53. Joe Samachson, Kane, and Robinson, "Robin Studies His Lessons!" *Batman* #18 (August–September 1943) in *The Batman Chronicles 10*.

54. Robert S. Warshow, "Paul, the Horror Comics, and Dr. Wertham," *Commentary* (June 1954), reprinted in Warshow, *The Immediate Experience: Movies, Comics, Theatre & Other Aspects of Popular Culture* (Cambridge, Mass.: Harvard University Press, 2001), 70.

55. David Hadju, *The Ten-Cent Plague: The Great Comic-Book Scare and How It Changed America* (New York: Macmillan, 2009), examines this period in American comics history.

56. Wilbur Schramm, *Television in the Lives of Our Children* (Palo Alto, Cal.: Stanford University Press, 1961), 17–8, 70, 261–71, measured the effect of television on children's comics-reading habits.

57. John D. Cochran, "Batman and Robin Were Lovers…" *The Realist* #57 (March 1965), 29–30.

58. Finger, Moldoff, and Burnley "The Marriage of Batman and Batwoman," *Batman* #122 (March 1959). This story inspired a series of further tales positing a future in which Bruce and Kathy marry, and Dick takes on the role of Batman II with young Bruce, Jr., as Robin II. All these adventures are collected in *DC's Greatest Imaginary Stories, Vol. 2: Batman and Robin* (New York: DC Comics, 2010).

59. Finger, Moldoff, and Paris, "Bat-Girl!" *Batman* #139 (April 1961). In 1963 there were hints that Dick was becoming more interested in a girl. Finger, Moldoff, and Paris, "Prisoners of Three Worlds," *Batman* #153 (February 1963), shows Robin enjoying his first serious kiss with Bat-Girl; at the end the two of them walk off hand in hand. During Betty Kane's next visit to Gotham, Dick shows special concern for her; Finger, Moldoff, and Paris, "The Great Clayface-Joker Feud," *Batman* #159 (November 1963). If Finger planned to develop the characters' relationship further in 1964, he never got the chance; the series' new editor retired the characters of Batwoman and Bat-Girl for the rest of the decade.

60. *Detective Comics* #284 through #287 (October 1960 through January 1961). Batman's exclamation on #287 reads like a summation of this period: "Another bizarre creature with another fantastic weapon!"

61. All sales figures and comparisons cited in this essay are based on the numbers reported by DC Comics and Marvel Comics in their magazines and collected at comicchron.com. On sell-through, Carmine Infantino recalled only "32 percent sales" for a Batman comic: dialbforblog.com/archives/204/.

62. Kane with Andrae, *Batman & Me*, 134. On Kane's contract, see Jones, *Men of Tomorrow*, 246–7.

63. John Broome, Carmine Infantino, and Joe Giella, "The Mystery of the Menacing Mask!" *Detective Comics* #327 (May 1964); France Herron, Sheldon Moldoff, and Giella, "Two-Way Gem Caper!" *Batman* #164 (June 1964).

64. At first Dick's practicing pains Bruce's ears, but soon playing guitar would become another of the Boy Wonder's many skills—see Mike Friedrich, Ross Andru, and Mike Esposito, "The Teen-Age Gap," *Detective Comics* #386 (April 1969).

65. In Gardner Fox, Carmine Infantino, and Sid Greene, "The Cluemaster's Topsy-Turvy Crimes!" *Detective Comics* #351 (May 1966), Aunt Harriet finds the entrance to the Batcave and even installs hidden cameras to spy on her nephew and his guardian.

66. Bob Haney and Bruno Premiani, "The Thousand-and-One Dooms of Mr. Twister," *The Brave and the Bold* #54 (New York: DC Comics, June–July 1964), 2. Haney and Nick Cardy, "The Return of the Teen Titans," *Showcase* #59 (New York: DC Comics, November–December 1965), 3.

67. Haney, Lee Elias, and Nick Cardy, "Captain Rumble Blasts the Scene!" *Teen Titans* #15 (New York: DC Comics, May–June 1968).

68. *Detective Comics, Batman, World's Finest Comics, Justice League of America, Teen Titans*, and *The Brave and the Bold*.

69. Frank Robbins, Bob Brown, and Joe Giella, "The Combo Caper!" *Detective Comics* #393 (November 1969), 1, 4, 15.

70. E. Nelson Bridwell, Ross Andru, and Mike Esposito, "The Origin of Robin!" *Batman* #213 (July–August 1969). Mike Friedrich wrote the Robin back-up stories in *Detective Comics* #386, #390, and #391 (April, August, and September 1969).

71. Frank Robbins, Irv Novick, and Dick Giordano, "One Bullet Too Many!" *Batman* #217 (December 1969).

72. Robbins, Gil Kane, and Vince Colletta, "Moon-Struck," *Detective Comics* #398 (April 1970), 1.

Outlining the Future Robin
The Seventies in the Batman Family

Fernando Gabriel Pagnoni Berns
and César Alfonso Marino

In the 70's, Dick Grayson is reformulated through a series of stories which try to take him away from the shadow of a mentor who was capturing the entire scene. In those years, Batman was gradually returning to his deep roots as a "creature of the night" while shaking off the image created by the 1960's TV show.[1] In this new scenario, Robin, became "more of a liability than an asset,"[2] so he was sent to attend the fictional Hudson University in New Carthage (New York).

Robin ends his tenure as a sidekick in *Batman Family*, a comic-book that runs for twenty issues through 1975–1978. It is in this magazine that Robin gets his first "mature" solo adventures.[3] We will argue that the character of Robin in the seventies was framed by two complementary matrices. First, Robin experiences drafts of future changes that will be developed later. It is in *Batman Family* where changes of costume as a way to begin building an identity of his own appear for the first time (and it is interesting to note that it was the readers who polemicize on this idea, while offering designs for the new uniform). Second, a romance with Batgirl/Barbara Gordon starts to bloom. Thus, *this book is seminal* for years to come.

The second matrix responds to the cultural and socio-historical changes that teenagers underwent throughout the seventies. The decision to shield Robin from the kind of danger that Batman undertakes corresponds to the end of the Vietnam War, a time when young people were supposed to return to matters more in line with their age. Also, the seventies was the decade in which teenagers, increasingly distrustful of adults, felt very uncertain about what the future would hold for them. These were the years in which teenagers, now less naive and somewhat disillusioned, worked more strongly than ever before to craft an identity for themselves among a wide array of "identity prisms," as Robin starts to do.[4] Identity was often obtained through a completely new wardrobe, which responds to the period's locus; this is reflected in the changes of wardrobe suggested for Robin.[5] Finally, this decade had an increase in the number of teenyboppers. Not coincidentally, Robin has his own club of (mostly) female fans, the Robin-rooters, and he recognizes that he needs the cheering from people as if he were a teenage idol.[6]

Researching and analyzing this overlooked series, we will work through the representation of Robin in what we consider a critical moment in his career. We will start with a close reading of the first issue and then we will analyze the subsequent issues grouped in sections dedicated each one to a different topic.

Batman Family # 1: *Youth as the Heart of America*

By the seventies, "the level of worry among young people 21 to 39 years old climbed from 36 percent in 1967 to 50 percent in 1976."[7] Robin and Batgirl, as young heroes of the time, had to engage somehow with this way of thinking, especially considering that the purpose of this series was to narrate the adventures of two teenagers while briefly looking at their intimate world. Issue 1 of *Batman Family* was dated October 1975. The cover depicts Batman presenting the origin of the "new dynamic duo" of Batgirl and Robin. The presence of Batman is important because he is legitimating this new duo which had come to replace the previous one formed by Batman and Robin. *Batman Family* will comprise stories focusing on the new dynamic duo as well as stories with each of the members in solo adventures. Since this series follows the format of an anthology, each issue of *Batman Family* will have five or six stories per issue, carried by people connected with Batman's world such as Commissioner Gordon, Alfred, or Man-Bat.[8]

The story that opens the first issue is the publicized debut of the new duo. Written by Elliot Maggin and drawn by Mike Grell, the story titled "The Invader from Hell" pitted Barbara Gordon/Batgirl and Dick Grayson/Robin against an undead Benedict Arnold, a military man from a bygone era somehow resurrected.

The motif of Batgirl and Robin as guardians of the soul of America is given from the first page. Clearly, the editors and the writer tried to establish a dichotomy between an old and corrupted America and the hope represented in the youth. In the third vignette of page two, Congresswoman

Barbara Gordon laments that many of her peers are not interested in hearing her speech: two old congressmen play cards while she gives her speech. This way, the creators were looking to attract empathy from teenage readers in two ways: first, with the notion that mature people are not interested in listening to youth (at least, female youth) and second, that young people are right to mistrust politicians since they are not interested in change. Hence, General Benedict Arnold, a military figure from old, is the perfect foil for our heroes. He represents "old generations" in a literal way. After coming to life within the congress in which Gordon is giving her speech,[9] Arnold explicates his goal of conquering America,[10] and only Batgirl and Robin (who was in the crowd listening to the speech as Dick Grayson) will get in his way.

While marching to the Pentagon with an army made of entranced civilians, Arnold takes prisoner both heroes.[11] His intention is to show the decadence in which America has fallen; therefore both Batgirl and Robin are placed upon a mechanism composed of two very tall poles to which both are loaded upside down, tied at the ankles. Each have a free hand so they can reach a latch that will free the other while sacrificing him/herself. The meaning of this complicated ruse is to show to the whole of America the egotism of youth, since Arnold presumes that neither of his prisoners will make the sacrifice.[12] But both the heroes pull the latch, to Arnold's fury. After saving themselves from a sure death thanks to trapeze maneuvers, Batgirl and Robin defeat Arnold, who turns out to have been resurrected by the devil himself to prove that America's soul is rotten.[13] But because both young heroes chose self-sacrifice rather than self-preservation, it is the devil who is defeated since America's spirit is "strong as ever."[14] After fleeing, the devil angrily exclaims that the spirit of these "young crusaders" will be "models of heroism everywhere."[15]

The story is silly, but the purpose is clear: establish Batgirl and Robin as the new generation of heroes in an America slightly lost in the seventies, years traversed by "failing economies, corrupt governments, failed wars,"[16] and a generation gap increased by mistrust in politicians.[17]

Of both heroes, Batgirl is the better prepared: she was not a teenager anymore but rather a young adult, a woman with a job (congresswoman) that requires a great deal of responsibility. Unlike Robin, she never really was under Batman's cape, so she was considered a strong character with independence before *Batman Family*. Robin is the one who must prove his valor as an autonomous agent acting without Batman's help. In this first story both heroes were actively configured as a new generation that had proven their bravery and moral values. But it is Robin who is under the microscope since the writers had to create for him a universe entirely of his own to make him complex as a character.

Drafting Robin as a Leader

When approaching this series, readers get a feeling of uncertainty generated by the constant changes because the writers are continually testing something new (a duo, a romance, and a leader).

Robin's first steps are taken in parallel with those of Batgirl, who works as some sort of reflection of the young male hero. If Batgirl gets rid of the garments of her public identity to display her costume, the sequence is matched for one in which Robin does the same. If until now Batman was the big mirror that served to orient Robin within the superhero world, from now on the adult Barbara Gordon will try to fulfill the role of mentor. But it will be a problematic relationship since what Robin lacks in maturity, he has in experience shared with Batman—experience that is lacking in Batgirl. Furthermore, Robin will try to shake off his identity as sidekick to gain confidence as a hero, assuming a leading role in this new dynamic duo.

Both as an action hero and as detective finely attuned by Batman, Robin surpasses Batgirl, especially in the latter since Barbara never was trained by the Dark Knight himself. But again, Batgirl gains in life experience. Since the comic is about the two of them and must appeal to their respective fans, a truce must be established, and for that, the skills of both parts of the new dynamic duo are put to the test.[18] "Isle of a Thousand Thrills" in *Batman Family* # 3 ends with both of them revealing that they have guessed the secret identity of the other partner.[19] In this simple way, they are established as equals and neither of them is diminished in the other's eyes.

In the fifth issue of *Batman Family*, the parallel vignettes multiply: we will see Batgirl riding elevator cables while criminals shoot her, then Robin swinging on a rope to reach a girl thrown by a mechanical shovel, then Batgirl escaping from a building mounting the ball of a wrecking machine, and thereafter Robin mounts a moving car using his batarang.[20] To put it simply, the readers are seeing both characters in these scenes competing for a place of enunciation, although it should be asked: what could be this place for which they are competing? The answer to this question will be delayed until issue 7. Batgirl and Robin are subjected by the villains Sportsmaster and Huntress to a series of challenges which are nothing more than a way of talking about the background problem: the battle for who should lead the duo.[21] For example, Robin chooses to cheat in the first challenge[22] apparently because he is more prepared to face whatever comes at the end of the competition.[23] Thus, Robin thinks of himself as someone above Batgirl. For the next challenge, both of them try to defeat the other with no discernible reason other than to prove superiority.[24] On page 19, the subtle tension within the duo comes to light when Batgirl mocks Robin's young age, something that the young wonder does not care for: "Can't say I appreciate Batgirl's sense of humor."[25] The competition is an excuse to underline the tension for leadership which frames the duo. Moreover, the names of the villains metaphorically recall the ferocity of competition.

However, it was not until *Batman Family* #13 that the rupture is formalized. In the third chapter of this issue, titled *Explosive end of the dynamite duo!*, Robin says: "I'm a big boy now and I have to say something you might not want to hear" and then proceeds to declare his love for Batgirl for the very first time (see more below).[26] This confrontation takes place within the Titans Tower (where Robin is a leader) and with the background of two gigantic images of another duo always in tension: Batman and Superman. The possibility of a romance between Robin and Batgirl was later developed in subsequent years in diverse publications, but in *Batman Family* the declaration of love serves as a point of inflection which marks that both heroes must go their separate ways to avoid further tensions (developed by sexual attraction and/or problems about leadership).

Robin's Maturity

Dick Grayson was not a kid anymore but he was far from being an adult. Only 18 years old, Robin was mature enough to get his own series but not adult enough to get involved with the horrors of crime-fighting—at least, not to his mentor's level. Robin had fought crime before in the dangerous streets of Gotham as Batman's sidekick, but America in the seventies was framed within "post–Vietnam War nonviolent sensibilities," especially when engaging with works made for kids and teenagers.[27] The idea was to get adolescents as far away as possible from the horrors of battle and the defeat that transpired in the Vietnam War; to achieve this, the comics adapted heroes to nonviolence.[28]

Robin was in need of cutting himself away from Batman's shadow to create his own persona capable of sustaining his own comic-book. The series oscillates between giving Robin independence as a character with agency of his own and Robin as eternally linked with the Dark Knight. Readers acknowledged this question, if we take the letters published in the series into account. In a letter published in *Batman Family* # 3, Robin "has been overshadowed by his masked mentor" while T. E. Pouncey, in the same issue, addresses an important point: Robin has emerged finally from Batman's shadow ... "to be placed under Batgirl's shadow!"[29] Readers are grateful that Robin had acquired independence from Batman, but fearful that that independence means that he will be under the cape of another bat-person.

Robin will change his costume and acquire a new persona in the eighties, when he changes his vigilante persona to that of Nightwing. *Batman Family* was seminal in this aspect. It is in this comic-book where the idea of a change in Robin as a way to mark his maturity and independence appears for the first time. In issue 3 concerns about the possibilities of the character as an autonomous actor were raised, while in issue 4 there appears a significant double-page spread (pages 10–11) in which different drafts of potential new costumes for Robin are displayed, to a total of nine sketches. Two things are interesting to note in this respect: first, that the drafts were made by the readers themselves[30] as a response to their concerns about Robin's independence. A change of costume was needed if the character was to grow up and make a name for himself.

The second point is that of the nine sketches, only two represent Robin with naked legs. For the readers, Robin cannot continue his adventures using only green briefs and pointed shoes. This image may have permeated popular culture since Robin's inception, but with Grayson now a teenager, readers ask for a more proper costume for their hero. So much discussed was the need (or not) of a change of costume that new drafts made by readers were displayed again in issue 13, page 45, under the title "A new look for Robin?" highlighting that the topic of Robin's maturity was an important one in *Batman Family*.

Furthermore, fashion and wardrobe was a very important item for teenagers in the seventies, so a new costume for the hero was not only related to independence for the character but also to the social context. Fashion was a way of self-expression in which youth could mark a difference from older generations.[31] This issue came to its peak in *Detective Comics* #481[32] in which Robin, by request of the Robin-rooters, had to choose between three different costumes designed by the hero's fan club (in truth, the three designs that Robin uses in that issue were sketched by readers). During this adventure, Robin effectively changes his costume three times, but at the end he states "from now on, the old look Robin is the only look

Robin."[33] DC Comics opens the way for two possible future paths: Robin's maturity will be embodied in a more "serious" costume if enough readers want Dick to change his heroic persona or he will continue using his traditional outfit if this is the decision most readers want. The final decision, if not explicitly stated, lies in readers' hands and their reactions. Since issue #1, DC and the editors encouraged readers to express their opinions about the future of the series and the future developments of the characters. In no way was it stated that the opinions would be taken into account, but clearly DC wanted to please the fans. This is why *Batman Family* featured new costume sketches made by readers, even if those ideas were not explicitly requested. The series just took and incorporated within itself the concerns of the readers. In retrospect, this opened the possibility of a future change of Robin's costume, a change which would take place many years later.

Robin's Secondary Cast

Besides a change of costume and name, the independence of Robin required his own supporting cast, one that helps to establish him as a grown up. For that reason, secondary characters were needed to show Dick Grayson as someone capable of sustaining his own world. Romantic relationships, family, friends, and foes must help sustain Robin as an interesting and exciting "new" character with independence from Batman.

Robin's girlfriend Lori Elton[34] is helpful in a twofold way: first, because she established Dick Grayson's maturity since he is now dating a girl and getting serious with her. Lori is Dick's official girlfriend and this image helps in the idea that DC Comics wants so desperately to convey to the readers: Robin is not a kid anymore.

Furthermore, Lori, and by some extent, Batgirl, were helpful to underline Robin's (hetero)sexuality and manliness. Now that Robin was flying alone, the time was right to depict him not only as a heterosexual teenager, but also as a hot-blooded one. Robin flirts with Batgirl even during Dick's romance with Lori,[35] forming a sort of "love triangle" in which Barbara is the lover while Lori the official girlfriend. Thus, Robin's manliness was sustained by these love affairs. Furthermore, while it is true that nothing implies that Dick and Lori slept together, nothing implies the contrary either.

Eventually, Dick breaks with Lori and immediately starts a brand new romance with a girl called Jennifer Anne (*Detective Comics* # 488). This way, Dick remains romantically active and the headaches that women give him are an attempt to mirror those in the real lives of the young adults and teenagers reading Robin's adventures. In this respect, Robin's investigations and cases almost never take him out of Hudson University. As *Batman Family* progressed and Robin started to get only solo adventures, without the involvement of Batgirl, the stories related more to his life as a student. Murders, robberies, dope traffic, and felonies take place within the campus, so Dick must integrate his life as a (mediocre)[36] student and his nocturnal job as vigilante.

The villains that Robin faces during his years in *Batman Family* were in accordance with the scenario that the writers have created for the hero, since they are not costumed supervillains but crooks. With the exception of an appearance of Scarecrow in *Detective Comics* #486, Robin never faces arch-villains or many costumed criminals, but rather "normal" thieves, murderers, and a criminal organization named Maze.

The foe most related to the idea of an arch-enemy for Robin will be the Joker's Daughter in *Batman Family* # 6, a criminal who presents herself as the offspring of the Joker and makes Dick's life miserable through some issues. In each appearance, she shows up as the Scarecrow's Daughter, the Penguin's Daughter, the Riddler's Daughter and so on, always committing petty crimes.[37] She finally will be stopped and her identity revealed as that of Duela Dent, daughter of Two-Face. Her crimes were committed to call Robin's attention since she wanted to be part of the Teen Titans, the group commanded by Robin.[38]

Joker's Daughter and her personalities as female offspring of villains (including "catgirl," a youthful version of Catwoman),[39] paradoxically, does not connect Robin with maturity but with inoffensiveness. Robin seems incapable, following this idea, of taking on by himself the gallery of villains of his mentor and must have to engage in battle with "lesser" versions. Rather than arch-villains, he takes down younger and feminized clones of the criminals who dominate Gotham. Again, this scenario configures Robin as a sort of "son" of Batman, a kid eagerly following the steps of his father rather than a figure capable of taking within his hands business of his own. Within this line of thinking, Robin tackles minor versions of Batman's rogues so that, after maturing, he can assume the mantle of the bat and confront the "real" foes. This way, Robin would not have characteristics of his own or enemies of his own, but rather he is in a stage of preparation to assume his role as future Batman, an idea that contradicts the work done in other aspects, such as his maturity or possible change of costume.

To add to this contradiction, when Robin fights Scarecrow in *Detective*

Comics # 486, even when the hero deciphers the different clues and brings down Jonathan Crane, he does so in the last minute by faking an apparition of Batman, which fills Crane with fear, thus paralyzing him.[40] Again the intention of fleshed out Robin is contradicted with the notion that, when fighting a real Batman foe, the foe can only be stopped by Robin if he fakes Batman's help. Thus, Robin's maturity and capacity as crime-fighter are inadvertently diminished in this particular story.

Writers seem to understand this, and after Duela Dent, they leave Dick Grayson to fight criminals of his own within the campus, which helped establish his identity even when these criminals rarely involved costumed villains.

Last, the Robin-rooters. They appear for the first time in *Batman Family* #12 but return intermittently during the whole run. Directed by Margie Spratt, the Robin-rooters were a fan club of the hero that were always cheering him up and looking for his heroic appearances. For his part, Robin is clearly glad to have people applauding him,[41] a love for recognition probably born in his years as a player in the circus. Robin-rooters were a way to engage with the adolescent readers of the comic in a decade full of teenage idols. In fact, the editors will address the readers on the mail section of *Batman Family* #12 calling them "Robin-rooters."

In this aspect Robin as a textual character and the social context again intersect. For many, the seventies were a decade of selfishness in which everything was "me, me, me"; a decade of superficiality in which everyone wanted to be the center of attention.[42] Thus, in Robin's fictional adventures and his need of popular recognition and fame, the real life of his readers as Robin-rooters and the culture of the seventies intersect one more time.

Conclusions

Batman Family, with its format of various stories per issue, allows readers the chance to enjoy adventures of characters such as Robin and Batgirl in their first solo adventures. With Batman getting back to darker traits, and with the word "family" in the title, it is easily understood why this particular collection was and is still overlooked by academics. But even with its ingenuities, this comic allows us to analyze first how the character of Robin was passing through a series of changes that oscillate between keeping him as a sidekick or making him a hero with his own personality and second, how all these changes were related to adolescence in the seventies.

These oscillations were made by DC Comics' attempts to interpret Robin as a hero mature enough to be interesting, with problems of his own with which any teenager in the seventies could relate. Thus, Robin coming out of the shadow of both Batgirl and Batman provoked tensions over leadership when the male hero interacts with Barbara Gordon. These tensions were born from the very idea that now Robin was the one who must be the leader since he was trained by Batman himself, while Batgirl did not let an occasion pass without mentioning her status as "older sister." Meanwhile, Dick Grayson battled problems with girlfriends and bad grades in an attempt to have Robin relate to the experiences of many of his readers.

But many times *Batman Family* contradicts these implicit intentions when diminishing the abilities of Robin as an independent character. The only time in which Robin battles a Batman foe is when he faces Scarecrow, but he defeats him using his intelligence and the shadow of Batman. Leaving this battle aside, Robin faces a criminal organization and common criminals without super-powers or psychotic traits. This contradicts Robin's capability to take on dangerous criminals, but the Vietnam War was still a shadow upon America and youth must be kept away from violence in a decade sick of horrors. If Batman was returning to more violent stories, the logical conclusion was to keep Dick Grayson away from him, mature enough to tackle criminals, but safe from psychos.

Among all these complexities some future changes start to appear here, for the very first time, as seminal moments: readers start to question Robin's name, costume, and his relationship with the bat-people. If Robin really was to start a career of his own, he must leave behind his past, including his alias and physical appearance. While this idea is merely discussed in *Batman Family*, these changes will eventually take place in Robin's life.

In one of the last issues of *Detective Comics* merged with *Batman Family*, issue 495, the legendary *The New Teen Titans* team of Marv Wolfman and George Pérez were announced for the first time. If an era was closing for Robin with the cancellation of *Batman Family*, a new era was also beginning for our hero, one that would establish him forever as a character capable of sustaining his own universe, whether as Robin, as Nightwing, or just as Grayson.

Notes

1. Will Brooker, *Batman Unmasked: Analyzing a Cultural Icon* (New York: Continuum, 2005), 175.
2. Roberta Pearson and William Uricchio, eds, *The Many Lives of the Batman: Critical Approaches to a Superhero and his Media* (New York: Routledge, 1991), 201.

3. We underline "mature" since Robin had his first solo adventures, as a kid, in the pages of *Star-Spangled Comics*, a series published by DC Comics which ran for 130 issues from October 1941 to July 1952. Stories featuring Robin, the Boy Wonder began in issue #65 (February 1947) and continued through the end of the title, and primarily featured Robin solo adventures, but also included some occasional cameos by Batman (See Randy Duncan and Matthew Smith, eds, *Icons of the American Comic Book: From Captain America to Wonder Woman*, Volume 1(California: ABC-CLIO, 2013), 607. The Robin adventures that take place within *Batman Family* have a teenage Dick Grayson as protagonist.

4. Stephen Miller, *The Seventies Now: Culture as Surveillance* (Durham: Duke University Press, 1999), 19.

5. Anne-Lise François, "Fashion as Compulsive Artifice," in *The Seventies: The Age of Glitter in Popular Culture*, edited by Shelton Waldrep (New York: Routledge, 2000), 155.

6. Bob Rozakis, Irv Novick, and Vince Colletta, "Rally Round Robin," *Batman Family* (1) #12 (New York: DC Comics, July–August 1977), 35.

7. Neil Hamilton, *The 1970s* (New York: Infobase, 2006), xi–xii.

8. The series also featured characters not related to Batman, such as Black Lightning and the Demon, without much explanation of why.

9. Elliot S! Maggin and Mike Grell, "The Invader from Hell," *Batman Family* (1) #1 (September–October 1975), 3.

10. Maggin and Grell, *Batman Family* #1 (Sept–Oct 1975), 8.

11. Maggin and Grell, *Batman Family* #1 (Sept–Oct 1975), 11.

12. Maggin and Grell, *Batman Family* #1 (Sept–Oct 1975), 11.

13. Maggin and Grell, *Batman Family* #1 (Sept–Oct 1975), 15.

14. Maggin and Grell, *Batman Family* #1 (Sept–Oct 1975), 15.

15. Maggin and Grell, *Batman Family* #1 (Sept–Oct 1975), 16.

16. Thomas Hine, *The Great Funk: Styles of the Shaggy, Sexy, Shameless 1970s* (New York: Sarah Crichton Books, 2007), 102.

17. Miller, *The Seventies Now*, 4.

18. Issue #3. This is their second adventure since issue two was a reprint.

19. Elliot S! Maggin, J.L. Garcia Lopez, and Vince Colletta, "Isle of a Thousand Thrills," *Batman Family* (1) #3 (Jan–Feb 1976), 20.

20. Elliot S! Maggin et al., "The Princess and the Vagabond," *Batman Family* (1) #5 (May–June 1976), 7, 9, 18, 19.

21. Elliot S! Maggin, Curt Swan, and Vince Colletta, "Thirteen Points to a Dead End," *Batman Family* (1) #7 (September–October 1976).

22. This first challenge is a chariot race and Robin decides to win it by splintering the wheels of Batgirl's chariot. Maggin, Swan, and Colletta, *Batman Family* #7, 15.

23. Maggin, Swan, and Colletta, *Batman Family* #7, 15.

24. Maggin, Swan, and Colletta, *Batman Family* #7, 17.

25. Maggin, Swan, and Colletta, *Batman Family* #7, 20.

26. Bob Rozakis et al., "The Man Who Melted Manhattan," *Batman Family* (1) #13 (September 1977), 18.

27. Christopher Lehman, *American Animated Cartoons of the Vietnam Era: A Study of Social Commentary in Films and Television Programs, 1961–1973* (North Carolina: McFarland, 2007), 184.

28. Lehman, *American Animated Cartoons*, 171.

29. Maggin and Lopez, *Batman Family* #3, 61.

30. Each design has the name of the reader who designed it at its side.

31. Kelly Boyer Sagert, *The 1970s* (Westport, Connecticut: Greenwood Press, 2007), 97.

32. After *Batman Family* 20, the title merged with *Detective Comics* (beginning with *Detective Comics* #481), which for twenty issues changes into an anthology book, with stories starring Batman, Robin, Batgirl, or the Human Target. *Detective Comics* #496 marks the return to a magazine with just one story starring Batman. Robin and Batgirl solo stories were discontinued.

33. Rozakis "Does the costume make the hero?" *Detective Comics* #481 (New York: DC Comics, Dec–Jan 1978–79), 30.

34. Lori appears in *Batman Family* already as Dick's girlfriend, without much previous history, which indicated that the editors and writers were anxious to sexualize Grayson.

35. See for example, in the last panel of their combined adventure in *Batman Family* #11, in which Robin makes a move on Batgirl, and also *Batman Family* #13, page 8.

36. Dick's inability to turn in an academic paper on time is mentioned a few times in *Batman Family* (for instance, see issues #12 and #14). Moreover, he is also chastised because of his inability to attend classes or give full attention to the lectures. This way, Dick's life as a student can relate to those readers who felt that they do not fit in college or who have troubles in concentration or in study. Writers try to recapture the relationship that characters such as Spider-man had with his readers; Peter Parker's troubles mirrored those of the readers in school.

37. Bob Rozakis, Irv Novick, and Vince Colletta, "Startling Secret of the Devilish Daughters," *Batman Family* (1) #9 (January–February 1977).

38. Rozakis, Novick, and Colletta, *Batman Family* #9, 22.

39. Rozakis, Novick, and Vince Colletta, "The Copycatgirl Capers," *Batman Family* (1) #8 (November–December 1976).

40. Jack Harris, "Fear times four," *Detective Comics* # 486 (Oct–Nov, 1979), 54.

41. For example, in "The League of Crime" written by Rozakis (*Detective Comics* #482), Robin, while saving innocents from an aerostatic balloon that is falling down, thinks "be nice if somebody on the ground is getting this on film. I love playing the hero for the crowds" (56).

42. For example, the famous dance of John Travolta in *Saturday Night Fever* (John Badham, 1977) can be seen, in this perspective, as a sort of attention-seeking: a person starts to display his or her skills in dance while everybody else is just around him or her cheering. It must be noted that almost everyone in the seventies tried to imitate Travolta's moves in the disco. See Sagert, *The 1970s*, 204.

Fashioning Himself a Hero

Robin's Costume and Its Role in Shaping His Identity

Joshua R. Pangborn

Robin's costume. With its distinct color pattern and flashy style, it's as iconic as that worn by his mentor. If W.J.T. Mitchell's *Picture Theory* is to be believed, then we exist in a period of the "pictorial turn," a "world of images" that construct and define our social reality.[1] Images, then, have begun to form our identities, colored our lives, and given meaning to our actions. Justice and heroism are no longer abstract terms, but rather ideas taken shape as images of uniformed soldiers or costumed vigilantes, all at once cartoonish and realistic. And the word "hero" is no longer just a four letter word on a page, but a term which conjures depictions of capes, cowls, and costumes. In this world of media, our imagination is colored by the visual examples our minds are flooded with. Robin, a character born in 1940, has entered the collective consciousness of not just the United States of America, but of the world at large. And alongside Batman's, Superman's, and Wonder Woman's costumes, Robin's costume stands out as one of the most memorable costumes of all superhero comics' characters. Yet, he is unique amongst these iconic costumes in that he was primarily conceived to be nothing more than a sidekick. However, as a sidekick, Robin—Dick Grayson—has created a long-lasting visual memory for our society, and on multiple levels has surpassed original intentions. And though Dick Grayson was not the first sidekick in comics,[2] he has arguably had the most significant impact on the role and served as a model for all the sidekicks which debuted after. Dick Grayson—Robin—The Boy Wonder—he has served as the epitome of what it means to be a sidekick, but even more than that, what it means to be a hero in one's own right. Through Dick Grayson, the reader is allowed to grow up, to find his own voice. And, if we are to believe we exist in Mitchell's "pictorial turn," then this all stems from one iconic image: Robin's costume. Through the varied origins of Robin's costume, the colors of the costume, and even the theatrical and Renaissance inspirations for the costume and how this serves as a basis for a feminine, harmonious balance to Batman's more masculine costume, I will endeavor to show how Robin represents hope and a chance for anyone, no matter how old, to fashion their own destiny.

Origins: Laying Out the Pattern and Choosing the Colors

Artist Jerry Robinson, in an interview with *The Comic Journal*, states he based the costume of Dick Grayson's Robin on a memory of N. C. Wyeth's Robin Hood drawings.[3] At first glance, this is very hard to see, given Wyeth's Robin Hood was depicted in a brown tunic with green leggings. Certainly there are character traits in Robin which are reminiscent of Robin Hood—the vigilante living outside the law and fighting corruption, the traditionally jovial nature of both Robins, whether it is during an adventure or at rest—but visually they do not seem to have much in common. Then again, Robin, the Boy Wonder does not seem to have much in common visually with his own mentor, Batman. While in *Picture Theory*, W.J.T. Mitchell certainly reminds his reader "man is created *in the image* of his maker," he could not be further from the truth in this case.[4] Yes, Batman is Robin's creator in a sense, but Dick Grayson's original costume, that bright red, green, and yellow look with the pixie boots and exceptionally short shorts, stands in stark contrast to the darker colors of Batman's costume. Frankly, it doesn't make much sense at all for Dick to be dressed as he is, especially not as Batman's companion and partner. For a character who primarily operates at night, Dick Grayson's Robin costume is a walking traffic light amidst the shadows, someone who stands out when he, seemingly, should be blending in with his surroundings. Well, unless his goal is to attract bullets, which has been a reoccurring joke heard around comic book conventions. Though Dick's Robin costume, like Wyeth's Robin Hood's, does have a tunic, Wyeth's character almost has more in common with Batman than Robin—Robin Hood's costume, like Batman's, permits the hero to blend in with his surroundings (in Wyeth's case, Sherwood Forest, and Batman's, the urban landscape), something Dick's not only prevents, but seems to reject outright. This alteration is significant. When Dick's costume eschews the color scheme of Wyeth's earthier tones, he truly begins to take ownership for his own identity. Dick's costume is not one of practicality, as Robin Hood's, or designed to instill fear, as Bruce Wayne's. His is meant to honor the memory of dead loved ones (but more on this later). Of course, like all early superheroes, Robinson's character also adopts a cape. He also trades Wyeth's leggings for bare legs. In so doing, Robinson created a costume which became a symbol, and dressed a character that would eventually become both sidekick and hero.

Dick's costume defines his character for those writing him—Mitchell's "pictorial turn" at work. Yet, it's also Dick's character that defines the costume. In Chuck Dixon's *Robin: Year One*, Alfred Pennyworth—trusted butler and confidant of Batman and Robin—notes how Dick is Dick, both in and out of costume: "He's had no need to develop the masquerade that master Bruce felt necessary. He has not divided his entire life into two aspects. His personality remains the same with or without the mask and boots."[5] Dick is Dick, costumed or otherwise, and this is inherently a part of who he is, as opposed to Bruce who is one man in the cape and cowl and an entirely different one without it. Despite the tragedy in his life, the loss of his parents, Dick's still been able to find joy and revel in who he is. As Alfred says in *Robin: Year One*, "He's never the brooder his mentor was as a child."[6] DC is—was, as the post–*Flashpoint* DC Universe has somewhat done away with the concept—celebrated for its inherent sense of legacy, and in keeping with this, Dick eventually dons the cape and cowl of Batman. Yet even in that persona he retains his joie de vivre. As he says to Alfred, "Don't ever let me forget the golden rule, Alfie. The show must go on."[7] Dick Grayson is, essentially, who many heroes strive to be. Superman may represent the epitome of alien heroes, Wonder Woman may represent the epitome of magical heroes, and Batman may represent the epitome of non–powered heroes, but Dick Grayson represents something else entirely: he is the character who can embrace the darkness within himself without getting lost in it. More importantly, he can embrace the joy within it. As Tim Drake says: "[Dick] likes to free-fall. To him, this is fun. He handles the pressure—the responsibility—all of it, so ... effortlessly. I wish I could be so comfortable in my own skin."[8]

All this is reflected in Dick's costume from the beginning of his existence. Dick Grayson's costume is the costume of a performer, of someone who experiences pain, love, joy, hate, fear, anger, suffering, and the full spectrum of emotions, each and every night, for the catharsis of others, and yet still goes on living his own life day in and day out, willingly returning to the role again for the betterment of others. Dick is a performer; this is at the core of his being, as he is reminded time and again by those around him.[9] While in several incarnations Bruce tried to discourage the costume

Dick chose for himself—"Long leggings would be more practical"[10] and "You might want to rethink the yellow cape"[11]—Dick's costume remained how *he* wanted it, not Bruce. Of course, there is a scientific basis for the yellow and red colors which made up the vast majority of Dick's costume. Yellow is the color "that captures our attention more than any other color" while red is "one of the most visible colors, second only to yellow."[12] For a performer like Dick Grayson, these colors are made for him. He relishes in an audience, even while keenly aware this is something Bruce does not need and never did.[13] With red and yellow as his signature colors, Dick's capable of drawing attention to himself, of capturing the attention of villain and bystander alike. Perhaps more importantly, however, is the joy it brings to Dick to wear this costume, a joy noticeable even to young children like Tim Drake, who, in *A Lonely Place of Dying* recounts his first meeting with Dick Grayson, when neither were costumed heroes, but merely young boys: "I kept staring at your circus costume. It was bright red and green and you seemed so happy in it."[14] That circus costume formed the basis for his Robin costume, and that joy Dick felt under the big top as an acrobat he continued to feel under the night sky as Robin.

More than just capturing attention, however, Dick's choice to incorporate the colors he did—the yellow specifically—is born from a sense of legacy, true to form for pre–*Flashpoint* DC Comics. And while that legacy is not the obvious legacy of Batman, it is Dick's way of honoring the death of his parents just as Batman is the way Bruce found to honor the death of his: "Those were the colors *my parents* wore in the circus," Dick tells Bruce in *Dark Victory*.[15] And, years later when Alfred redesigned Dick's Nightwing uniform, he incorporated yellow feathering to further both the legacy of Dick's family and the legacy Dick created for himself in the role of Robin.[16] Dick has since gone on to wear several variations on his original Nightwing costume, not to mention his own version of the cape and cowl during his run as Batman. As the focus here is on Dick's Robin costume, not all of his costumes, there will be no discussion of his later Nightwing costumes, or his Batman. What is mentioned already has only been done to emphasize Dick's consideration of the role of legacy and the reason for the presence of so much yellow in Dick's Robin costume.

In December 1955, DC retconned the origin of Robin's costume in *Detective Comics* #226 where Bruce explains to Dick how he created the costume for Robin himself, before he became Batman, to learn the art of crime fighting from Detective Harvey Harris—who also coined the moniker "Robin" for his young pupil.[17] By doing this DC reinforced the concept of legacy, as Dick was then following in Bruce's shoes by being finally understand Bruce ... I'm finally thinking like Batman."²⁷ Tim's identity as Robin isn't his own, not at this point, but neither is he playing the role of Dick's Robin. He is Bruce's, with Bruce's alterations to the costume, with Bruce's identity swallowing Tim's with the loss of his father. As Catwoman says to Batman in *Dark Victory*, "A father's love can be a terrible thing."²⁸ Bruce is Tim's father, as he is the father to so many young heroes, and Tim's quest to find out who he is at heart leaves him at a loss for an identity of his own as he allows Bruce's to overshadow him. Yet, for all his confusion, Tim at least understands the role he assumes. He understands the need for it, even if it means he is left with questions about himself. As he says to Bruce in the pages of *A Lonely Place of Dying*, "I don't know why you decided to wear that costume—but it makes you a symbol. Just as Robin was a symbol. Or Superman, or Nightwing, or the policeman who wears his uniform. And this isn't just a symbol of the law, it's a symbol of Justice. When one policeman is killed others take his place because justice can't be stopped."²⁹ Tim's Robin, then, may be influenced by Batman, may just be the next in a series of Robins, may never be completely original, but at least his Robin understands the need to maintain something that works. His Robin understands sacrifice, perhaps greater than any other Robin. His Robin understands the need to walk the shadows, like Bruce, yet find joy in life, like Dick. And when Tim's greatest fears come true and he finds he starts thinking like Batman, it isn't to Batman he turns, it is to Dick's greatest legacy: the Teen Titans. With them he shares his tears and his pain and opens up in ways only someone who has learned from Dick Grayson can.³⁰ Tim's Robin is the truest reflection of his mentors, and, like with any Robin, this is clearly reflected in his costume—particularly by its black cape and yellow lining.

When to Step Back: The Mentor's Role

Dick's Robin does not want to become Batman. No Robin seems to want this. Robin represents justice, yes, but they also represent life. They dress in colors reflecting joy and happiness.³¹ They do not want to succumb to the darkness they see Bruce living in, day in and day out. They do not want to be alone. Bruce, as surrogate father, adoptive father, and literal father, likely recognizes this—perhaps even fears their descent into darkness even more than they do (for who better knows the loneliness and pain of being the Batman than the master of brooding himself). This, then, is perhaps Batman's greatest gift to Robin: his costume. While Dick's insistence that his costume reflects his desires, not Batman's, is so important for his retention of his individuality, it doesn't change the almost ridiculous fact of Batman electing to place his partner, the person he will trust with his life, in what amounts to a costume version of a neon-glowing sign. Yet—consider Batman's greatest fear for Robin, perhaps even greater than his dying (for if he were most afraid of this, Bruce would never allow any child to take up the mantle, especially not after the death of Jason Todd). No, Batman is probably more afraid of Robin following in his footsteps, of becoming him. If this is true, then Batman, in his role as both mentor and father to Robin, allows Robin the chance to deal with his rage and anger, the same feelings he felt as a suddenly-orphaned Bruce Wayne, by becoming his partner. Yet, Bruce ensures his ward maintains some brightness and sense of life throughout his youth—ensuring, essentially, his rage will be tempered by a sense of light and hope, and thus a potential for a better life, a different life, than what Batman must face. Batman cannot change. Robin doesn't have to be Batman, though. And this further explains Batman's motivation not to create a legacy sidekick, as his colleagues have, but to create someone who will carry on his work rather than his mantle. Here, then, in Dick Grayson's costume is the evidence of Batman's love for his partner, his son—Robin's costume gives him the chance Bruce himself never had.

Bruce's contemporaries in the Justice League are not like him; they are not consumed by chaos and darkness from early childhood, and thus the characters they choose to take on as their partners should seemingly not run the risk of succumbing to the darkness. This, of course, is actually the opposite of what happens in many cases, as the lives of the sidekicks of the Justice League are dark and riddled with pain—Roy Harper's Speedy with his drug addiction, for instance—pain they were not prepared for because their mentors didn't live in it the way Bruce Wayne did. This also accounts for why Dick Grayson is the outright leader of the Teen Titans, whereas the Justice League is an ensemble team, rarely with a distinct leader: Dick is the most capable of the teenage heroes because he has been allowed to come into his own by his mentor. He's not Aqualad, or Kid Flash, or Wonder Girl; he's not Speedy, unique in name but nearly identical in costume to his mentor. He is Robin. He looks and behaves nothing like his mentor. He has shown himself capable of leading himself, and thus the Titans trust him to lead them. Later, when Dick moves out on his own and becomes Nightwing, he serves as an example for his teammates. The other Titans, inspired by Dick, eventually paved their own paths and changed their own monikers, costumes, and identities (save for Kid Flash

Wally West, who—in true pre–*Flashpoint* fashion, honored the legacy of his mentor by assuming his mantle and becoming the new Flash after Barry Allen's apparent death). Nevertheless, it was Dick Grayson who did it first and who, by this point, is as recognizable for his work as Nightwing as he is for his time spent as Robin.

With Dick's transformation into Nightwing, the mini–Justice League that was the Teen Titans became an entity entirely separate from the League—it became a family. But, Dick's transformation itself was an organic reaction to the cast of *The New Teen Titans* by Marv Wolfman and George Pérez. Rather than play host to a cadre of Mini-Me Justice League clones, as the original Titans did, Wolfman and Pérez filled the reformed Titans with entirely new characters without mentors, characters who were individuals: Starfire, Raven, Cyborg, and Beast Boy (or Changeling as he was known at this time). At this point, the Titans did not need their mentors—and this is where stories about their mentors needing *them* begin (such as *A Lonely Place of Dying*). It's worth noting Starfire, Raven, Cyborg, and Beast Boy, these non-legacy characters, alongside Dick Grayson's Robin, are the cast of the animated *Teen Titans* series. Likely this was done to differentiate this series completely from the *Justice League* series also airing at this time. Also worth noting, then, is the fact they chose to include Dick Grayson/Robin in this run, because he is not a clone of Batman. Tim Drake, currently possessing the mantle of Robin when the series came out, was too similar to Batman, too much of a potpourri of identities struggling to coalesce into something entirely unique to himself. Dick did not come with this baggage, Dick was the original Robin, and as has been explained, the original Robin is not Batman and never would be (well, only in a non-literal sense of course, as he does eventually don the cape and cowl). And while he can, and does, manifest darker traits, like Batman, he does not need him to exist with his own identity.

Balance: A Renaissance Homage

Undeniably Dick manifests some of the darker traits of Batman, yes—but more often he serves to complement him. For instance, while Dick Grayson's costume is an homage to his parents, it can't be ignored that there is something decidedly feminine about Robin's lower half. Had he been drawn wearing tights, he would have had more in common with Wyeth's Robin Hood and it would have been more evocative of characters like Peter Pan. As it is, with the bare legs and almost bikini bottom short shorts, it is easy to see the female in the Boy Wonder. This, like the life of

Bruce Wayne, creates yet another sense of homage, in this case to that which so inspires Batman's method of fighting crime: the theatre. Christopher Nolan's Batman films constantly repeat the phrase "Theatricality and deception are powerful agents" and at its heart, Batman and his tools are the tools of a performer, what with his costumes and his attempts at instilling emotion in his "audience" (specifically fear).[32] Batman's world is reminiscent of Renaissance drama, particularly when combined with the almost Shakespearean tragedy which are Bruce Wayne's and Dick Grayson's lives. But if Batman is cast as the male Shakespearean hero, then Dick Grayson, in his earliest incarnation, is a boy performer, and the roles these young actors typically played in Renaissance drama were roles of women.

Connecting Dick Grayson to the boy performers of Renaissance English theatre is not meant to demean him in anyway. But he *is* smaller, and as he has yet to physically mature, less masculine than Bruce, though this depiction is in keeping with typical manifestations of sidekicks as physically distinct, possibly weaker, than their heroic counterpart.[33] As Bronwyn T. Williams states in "Action Heroes and Literate Sidekicks: Literacy and Identity in Popular Culture," "the action hero usually embodies traditionally masculine characteristics such as physical strength, calmness under pressure, stoicism, and so on, [so] the [...] sidekick is often played as a character that is decidedly less masculine."[34] And so if Robin's costume evokes something of the theatrically feminine, then this is to be expected, even typical. Such a distinction appropriately resonates with later writers of Robin, too, as we see in the 1995 Annual of *Robin* where Mary Grayson, Dick's mother, is the source for the Robin name.[35] It is appropriate for a figure like Dick Grayson, who embodies something of the feminine, that he be named by his mother and thus ensure he carries something of her with him always, particularly since so little emphasis is generally placed on mothers in the world of Batman.[36] And, if we consider the male-female fusion of Robin through the lens of speculative nostalgia (which is the authorial use of a classical element, either real or fictional, to comment and critique the current society in which he lives),[37] then, if anything, Robin's feminine elements cement him as Batman's partner even more so. During the Renaissance, it has been argued the notion of being a boy was not a matter of age, but of being almost an entirely different gender (at least as we measure gender today). As Will Fisher explains in "The Renaissance Beard: Masculinity in Early Modern England," there was even a sense of "erotic interchangeability of boys and women" coming from an "expectation of [...] submissiveness" from them.[38] So if Dick Grayson is playing the role of the boy performer to Batman's Shakespearean hero, then he is, in some ways, playing the role of Batman's female counterpart. Unlike Superman's female counterpart, Lois Lane, who debuted in the same issue as Superman, Batman does not have any traditional female companion. Yes, there was Julie Madison, Bruce Wayne's first girlfriend, but she disappeared a year after Dick Grayson's debut. There were other women after her, but none consistent, none who were a match for Batman, a perfect counterpart. They came and went; Dick remained. This is not to suggest Dick and Bruce have or had a sexual relationship; rather, at his youngest, Dick reflected the feminine which balanced the masculine Batman, allowing for a harmonious partnership. In the fight for justice, there was no room for romance, not for an ordinary human like Bruce Wayne—even if he does represent the heights to which "ordinary" heroes can soar. This revolving door of potential girlfriends for Bruce does not, however, mean there was not a need for the presence of the feminine alongside the masculine in his nightly adventures. In the 1940s, America was slowly, ever so slowly, recognizing the existence, even need, for a fusion between the distinctly masculine and the distinctly feminine, with the eventual emergence of such figures as the Canadian Ronnie, the Bren Gun Girl in 1941, and the iconic Rosie the Riveter in 1942. Such a fusion led to pictorial depictions of women behaving in many ways as men, for the greater success of the country. It is natural artists and writers living in this turbulent period would respond to this growing realization and, intentionally or otherwise, hearken back to a period when a fusion between the masculine and the feminine not only existed, and did so to immense success. In Renaissance England, Shakespeare and his company still stand as the pinnacle to which all subsequent theatre strove to match—and thus the theatrical Batman would, too. This was the reign of Elizabeth I, the Virgin Queen, who was both mother and father to the kingdom and in whom manifested both traditionally masculine and traditionally feminine traits—a figure Shakespeare and his contemporaries used as an inexhaustible source of inspiration, and remains a source for artistic inspiration today.[39] During the Great Depression and World War II, it would be natural, through speculative nostalgia, to turn to a similar period of turmoil and strife, when the spirit of the world was recognizing a need for a harmonious relationship between the masculine and the feminine, and recreate it through figures like Rosie the Riveter, or what would eventually become the epic partnership of Batman and Robin. Through this harmonious relationship, a sense of hope was achieved, both at home and abroad, and this is precisely what Batman and Robin strive for, that greater world, in the pages of Gotham City.

"The image is always sacred" begins Jean-Luc Nancy's *The Ground of the Image*,[40] and Robin's image becomes synonymous with justice, both in the world of the comics and in the world we live in. His place in the world is more than just a caped crusader; he has become elevated to a higher status, one where his very image is greater than any one individual who wears the costume (and thus this accounts for the ability for several individuals to slip on the Robin costume). Robin's costume is an iconic representation of justice, but more than that, hope. For while the wearing of the costume raises Dick Grayson—and those who follow—to something greater than boy or man, he is not created in the image of his maker, as Mitchell claims. Instead, he is capable of creating himself into the person he wants to be. He may carry baggage with him, but this baggage is a part of who he is, and he proves he is able to rise to the challenge of accepting this baggage, even dealing with it, and growing into something greater. This is what Robin signifies, more than anything—Robin is the potential we all have within ourselves to take from the past and fashion something of our own, something that reflects who we are, without anyone else telling us who to be. Robin is potential. And this potential all stems from one thing: Robin's costume.

Notes

1. W.J.T. Mitchell, *Picture Theory* (Chicago: University of Chicago Press, 1994), 41.
2. This honor may be due to the sidekick of Mr. America, Bob Daley—aka Fatman—who debuted in *Action Comics #2*. ["List of comic book sidekicks," *Wikipedia*, http://en.wikipedia.org/wiki/ List_of_comic_book_sidekicks.]
3. Gary Groth, "Jerry Robinson: Been There, Done That," *The Comics Journal*, 271 (2004): 86.
4. Mitchell, *Picture Theory*, 24.
5. Chuck Dixon et al., "Robin: Year One, Book 2," *Robin: Year One* #2 (New York: DC Comics, November 2000), [12].
6. Dixon et al., *Robin: Year One* #2, [11].
7. Grant Morrison and Frank Quitely, "Batman Reborn, Part Two: The Circus of Strange," *Batman and Robin* (1) #2 (New York: DC Comics, September 2009), [18].
8. Fabian Nicieza, Marcus To, and Ray McCarthy, "7 Days of Death, Part One: Little Triggers," *Red Robin* #23 (New York: DC Comics July 2011), [6].
9. Batman in *Batman #615* (Jeph Loeb, Jim Lee, and Scott Williams, "Hush (Part VIII of XII)—The Dead," *Batman* #615 [New York: DC Comics, July 2003], [16]), and Alfred in *Batman and Robin* (1) #2, [17] (see note 7 for details) are two examples of characters recognizing Dick is more than a hero, he is a performer.
10. Chuck Dixon et al., "Nightwing: Year One, Chapter One: Only Robins Have Wings" *Nightwing* #101 (New York: DC Comics, early March 2005), [19].
11. Jeph Loeb and Tim Sale, "Peace," *Batman: Dark Victory* #13 (New York: DC Comics, December 2000), [47].
12. J.L. Morton, "Color Matters," last modified 2011, http://www.colormatters.com.
13. Dixon et al., "Nightwing: Year One, Chapter Three: Deadman Talking" *Nightwing* #103 (early April 2005), [13].

14. Marv Wolfman, Jim Aparo, and Mike DeCarlo, "A Lonely Place of Dying (Part III): Parallel Lines," *Batman* #441 (November 1989), [8].

15. Loeb and Sale, *Batman: Dark Victory* #13, [47].

16. Dixon et al., "Nightwing: Year One, Chapter Six: First Flight," *Nightwing* #106 (late May 2005), [21].

17. Joe Samachson, Dick Sprang, and Joe Certa, "When Batman was Robin," *Detective Comics* #226 (New York: DC Comics, December 1955). This legacy theme continues with Thomas Wayne as the first Batman at a costume ball. See Bill Finger, Sheldon Moldoff, and Joe Certa, "The First Batman," *Detective Comics* #235 (September 1956).

18. Unfortunately it appears DC Comics has decided to once again make Batman the designer of Robin's original costume, as is shown in *Grayson: Future's End* (Tom King and Stephen Mooney, "Only a Place for Dying," *Grayson: Future's End* #1 [November, 2014].) Batman, not Dick, is the one to make the costume bright and colorful. Dick wants to dress more like Batman, not less. This decision by King and Seeley (helped plot the story) is regrettable and indicates they have little, if any, understanding of what, exactly, Dick Grayson stands for in the world of the DC Universe—not to mention contradicts events as established in *Nightwing* #0 only two years earlier; through narration Dick explains how he assembled his Robin suit (which looks nearly identical to the one in *Grayson: Future's End*) from discarded elements of Batsuits, without Bruce's knowledge.

Furthermore, Dick is the independent free spirit Bruce can never be. He does not, as Barbara Gordon says in *Grayson: Future's End*, want someone sour and dark and like Batman for a lover. Dick's two great loves, Starfire and Batgirl, are anything but sour and dark, and represent exactly what Dick Grayson embodies: a love of life. Taking away his autonomy takes away everything Dick Grayson represents and turns him into Batman-light.

19. Loeb and Sale, *Batman: Dark Victory* #13, [48].

20. From Alex Ross' realistic image of the two characters to the silhouettes of Dick and Bruce on the wall of the Batcave in an animated episode of *Teen Titans*, this image is the defining moment of Dick and Bruce's relationship, when Dick was officially recognized as Batman's partner.

21. Dixon et al., *Robin: Year One* #2, [15].

22. Marv Wolfman, George Pérez, and Bob McLeod, "A Lonely Place of Dying (Part II)—Roots," *The New Titans* #60 (New York: DC Comics, November 1989), 24.

23. Geoff Johns, Mike McKone, and Mario Alquiza, "War and Peace," *Teen Titans* (3) #6 (New York: DC Comics February 2004), [20].

24. Geoff Johns et al., "Wednesday," *Teen Titans* (3) #7 (March 2004), [11].

25. Brad Meltzer, Rags Morales, and M.R. Bair, "Chapter Six: Husbands and Wives," *Identity Crisis* #6 (New York: DC Comics, January 2005), [4].

26. Geoff Johns, Mike McKone, and Mario Alquiza, "Titans Tomorrow (Part I of III)—Big Brothers and Sisters," *Teen Titans* (3) #17 (December 2004).

27. Geoff Johns, Tom Grummett, and Nelson, "Hiding," *Teen Titans* (3) #20 (December 2005), [3].

28. Loeb and Sale, *Batman: Dark Victory* #13, [47].

29. Wolfman et al., "A Lonely Place of Dying (Part V)—Rebirth," *Batman* #442 (December 1989), 15.

30. Johns, Grummett, and Nelson, *Teen Titans* (3) #20, [3].

31. Morton, "Color Matters," http://www.colormatters.com.

32. *The Dark Knight Rises*, directed by Christopher Nolan (2012, Los Angeles: Warner Brothers, 2012), Blu Ray.

33. Examples range from the overweight and mentally simple Sancho Panza or Samwise Gamgee to more modern ones like Hermione Granger.

34. Bronwyn T. Williams, "Action Heroes and Literate Sidekicks: Literacy and Identity in Popular Culture," *Journal of Adolescent and Adult Literacy* 50, no. 8 (2007): 683.

35. Chuck Dixon, Jason Armstrong, and Robert Campanella, "Year One," *Robin Annual* #4 (New York: DC Comics 1995), [29].

36. Thomas Wayne often gets dialogue and action sequences in both comics and animation/live action, while Martha is typically relegated to the background. Similarly, characters like Zatanna place such emphasis on their fathers, with little mention of their mothers. Even Tim Drake's step-mother disappears from comics once Jack Drake is killed in *Identity Crisis* (not to mention how little his mother's death seems to have affected him as compared to his father's).

37. Speculative nostalgia, as outlined in my dissertation *Speculative Nostalgia and Its Role in Shakespeare and Renaissance Literature*, espouses the idea the author/artist living in a turbulent time looks backwards to some element of historical or fictional past, which he then utilizes in his contemporary project to provide some commentary, and potentially advice, to his audience. In the case I outline here, the artists and writers responded to the tumultuous period of World War II and the years prior, and recognized a need for a greater contribution by all members of society, male and female, working together to achieve a better life; also, given Batman's theatrical nature, speculative nostalgia allows for the audience to reflect on the natural union of Batman and Robin and attribute its success to the success of the male and boy actor of the Renaissance, bringing to life timeless masterpieces like *Romeo and Juliet* and *King Lear*. Joshua R. Pangborn, "Speculative Nostalgia and Its Role in Shakespeare and Renaissance Literature" (DA diss, St. John's University, 2014).

38. Will Fisher, "The Renaissance Beard: Masculinity in Early Modern England," *Renaissance Quarterly* 54, no. 1 (2001): 175–176.

39. Elizabeth I most recently appeared in a 2013 episode of *Doctor Who*, played by Joanna Page.

40. Jean-Luc Nancy, *The Ground of the Image* (New York: Fordham University Press, 2005), 1.

The Gray(son) Area
Performing Robin the Right Way
Cara L. MacNeil-Donoghue

> "One is not born ~~a woman~~ Batman, but rather becomes one."
> —~~Simone de Beauvoir~~ Cara L. MacNeil-Donoghue

Oftentimes when we think about Batman (as a genre), we think about action. Movement, fighting, kitschy little "KAPOW" signs signifying a devastating blow. Action defines superheroes, doesn't it? One correlation that isn't studied with enough frequency is assessing *action* as *performance*. Judith Butler is a feminist scholar whose focus is on redefining gender/sex categories by looking at performance. She quoted Simone de Beauvoir when opening her book *Gender Trouble* in which de Beauvoir famously said "One is not born woman, but rather becomes one." Butler wants to offer an alternative to a binary way of thinking about gender—instead of gender being only defined as "man" and "woman" in which "man" and "woman" act as opposites without a gray area.

Judith Butler was frustrated with how limited terms like "woman" and "man" were. After all, I might not be the same type of woman as Wonder Woman, Angelina Jolie, Harley Quinn or Mother Theresa—but we all get called a woman. When you say "woman" there is also a problem—who made up the term? Judith Butler says that your society is what defines "woman"—so my view of "woman" is influenced by my family, my city, my state and my country. Butler identifies an institutional problem—she believes that these are all institutions dominated by sexist ideology. So she wanted to get away from using terms with definitions that were inherently sexist and instead be able to see gender as a performance that you can perform any way you choose.[1] This is useful in that it allows for men to perform feminine behaviors (like doing dishes or raising children) and women to perform masculine behaviors (like being the primary breadwinner, wearing pants). It makes a safe space for people who don't fit "traditional" (read: rigid) gender roles—not just gays, lesbians and transgender people but also little girls who run around in Batman capes pretending to be masked vigilantes that roam the streets of Gotham seeking justice. We perform the role we want to be, and we don't have to worry about "not fitting in"— because we've altered the way we see the categories.

How is that useful when talking about Batman and the Boy Wonder? Glad you asked.

Batman and Philosophy[2] did a great job outlining the many different ways we can interpret Batman, but nobody really talked about interpreting Robin sans the Caped Crusader. In celebrating 75 years of Dick Grayson, it's important to talk about what it means when we say "Robin." What makes a good Robin? How do we understand what a Robin is? Who makes a good Robin? Why do they make a good Robin? Using performance as the way we define "Robin" makes it possible to view the behaviors of various Robins and decide what consistently happens that makes someone a Robin. From there we can compare it to other "Robins" and decide who is the best.

For the sake of argument, let's limit our primary discussion of Robins to just the first two: Dick Grayson and Jason Todd. There's a lot to be said for Carrie Kelly, Stephanie Brown, Tim Drake, and even Damian Wayne, but this is one chapter, not the whole book so they will have to go to the sidelines. Dick and Jason are worth considering separately because many readers feel they exemplify two rather different ways of being Robin.

Performance is comprised of repeated action—one action doesn't "make" you anything, but rather what you repeatedly do defines who you are. So what does Robin do repeatedly? *First of all, Robin performs physical acts of bravery alongside the Dark Knight. Secondly, he maintains a sense of justice that (like Batman's) is devoid of personal involvement and permits the supremacy of an impartial system. Third, Robin maintains absolute loyalty to the Bat and is willing to take Batman's place for the sake of Batman, not for personal gain.* In the wide world of Batman comics and graphic novels we can probably find exceptions to every rule, but remember—isolated incidents do not define us. Since Robin is a category, a type of performance, we assess how our "Robins" perform even when they might not be labeled as "Robin." Performance isn't a title, it's a set of repeated actions so we can look at characters who aren't called "Robin" and assess them as a Robin if they behave the way a Robin would. For example, we can judge Dick and Jason as "performing" Robin even while they are Nightwing and Red Hood (respectively). Performance exists as long as we take part in performing it, even if we call it something different, so the behaviors of Dick and Jason before, during, and after their tenure in tights as the "Boy Wonder" are all parts of how we determine who best fits the role of Robin.

Performing Robin: Physicality

Action defines Batman and Robin. Repetitive, physical acts of valor and skill are performed routinely in these books, and the Dynamic Duo take a lot of time to prepare. One of the great unsaid portions of Batman and Robin's written history is the great amount of time devoted to becoming physically fit enough to even *kind of* keep up with the demands of the criminal class of Gotham City. Beyond just physical fitness, both Batman and Robin are master fighters, so masterful that they can disable without killing in hundreds of different ways. If we say that "Robin" is its own category that can be defined by performance, how is it being defined? Even beyond wearing the costume, Robin can physically keep up with the Batman. Considering he is the Boy Wonder, that makes him doubly impressive—he doesn't have the mass or muscle of Batman and yet never falls behind. How do the different Robins perform these physical roles?

Dick Grayson notably was a circus performer for years before becoming the ward of Bruce Wayne. He was a trapeze artist in Haly's Circus—in fact one so accomplished that only three people in the world could perform his moves.[3] The conditioning it would take to make a prepubescent boy that accomplished is tantamount to the training Olympic gymnasts undergo. A key feature of Robin is that he keeps up with a physically demanding role—if you can't, you can't be Robin. Dick has always shown an aptitude for the physical aspect of being Robin that pre-dates Batman—Dick Grayson always has an acrobatics background, even in the various creation stories he has undergone over the years. His physical abilities are set from childhood and the development of them never ceases. He brings a grace to the role that Frank Miller might have been referencing when he said, "I'd never intended to use Robin. But then, one day, I pictured a little bundle of bright colors leaping over buildings, dwarfed by a gray-and-black giant ... and there she was. Robin."[4] There is a juxtaposition between Robin and Batman—the hulking, black shadow and the bright, bird-like jumping bean. This comparison fails if Robin is trailing behind, panting for breath, unable to stand beside the Bat.

Why is Dick Grayson physically superior to other Robins? As previously mentioned, Dick comes to the role of Robin already physically gifted—more so than other boys his age and other Robins (if we consider a pre–New 52 Tim Drake). This perhaps set a standard for physical achievement that others couldn't ever hope to equal. Consider Dick's performance as Robin compared to Jason Todd. In the post–*Crisis* timeline, Jason Todd is scrappy, street-smart and ballsy when he meets Batman after attempting to steal the wheels off the Batmobile. He is from a broken home, destined for a life of crime without Batman's interference—something Batman repeatedly thinks about when he is frustrated with Todd's rebellious attitude. Batman admits that Todd lacks Grayson's physical skills but hopes that Todd's rage will act as a replacement. Todd was purposely set up as rebellious—as unlike Dick—in this timeline which provides an excellent opportunity to study whether people that aren't like Dick can really *be* Robin.[5] Interestingly, the original version of Todd was nearly identical to Grayson—the orphaned son of circus parents who had raised him as an acrobat.[6] The second, more widely accepted version of Todd puts him in stark contrast to the original Robin as opposed to making him a carbon copy. Jason Todd was the anti–Dick Grayson—he swore, he smoked, he didn't take orders and never apologized for misbehaving.

When we listed our traits of performing Robin, we said that Robin performs acts of bravery beside Batman. The physical feats that Grayson performs are undoubtedly more spectacular than the ones that Todd performs, but that doesn't mean that Todd fails to keep up with Batman. Todd is not as athletic nor is he as refined, even artistic, as Grayson but certainly he keeps up with Bruce. In fact, we might say all versions of Robin keep up with Bruce Wayne, or they wouldn't make the preliminaries. So in terms of performing Robin, they can all perform the physicality—Jason Todd performs this physical role well enough even if we might say that Dick does the same role with a bit more flair.

Performing Robin: Blind Justice

Among the most notable traits of Batman and the Bat family is that they do not kill the criminals they are up against. We all know the driving force behind Bruce Wayne's transformation into Batman: the brutal murder of his parents in front of him as a young boy. This creates an unrelenting need in Bruce to clean up Gotham's streets—but he does not see himself as Judge and Jury. Rather Batman functions like a bail bondsman or a bailiff—it's his job to see that these criminals are given their day in court. It is fundamental to Batman that he not kill, that he not become God.[7] Even the "goddamn Batman" might be fueled by rage, by a cutting sense of injustice, but he does not believe it is up to him to decide who lives and who dies—famously, Batman never kills The Joker despite the atrocities that the Joker commits and the seemingly revolving door at Arkham Asylum that allows the Joker to escape to commit further atrocities.[8] Because of this ironclad value system, Batman requires a like-minded Robin. If Robin cannot maintain devotion to an impartial system of justice *despite personal feelings of rage or injustice* then he will fail as a Robin. Part of Robin's performance is to maintain the system of catch and imprison, even if this becomes a game of catch-and-release because the prison system fails. This is a great performance assessment for Robin—who plays this role loyally despite the frustrations one might incur in the performance?

Dick Grayson and Batman share a common origin—they are orphaned when violence causes them to watch their parents die. This shared bond seems so strong that it is almost archetypal for Robin's to share this connection to Batman; a bond that Jason Todd shares in only one version. However, in performing the role of Robin, both Dick and Jason have to face the rage (and sometimes the criminals) of their pasts and act as agents of justice devoid of personal motives.

This is where the performance aspects of Todd and Grayson really diverge.

In the recent run *Court of Owls* we got to see Batman, Dick, and Jason all confront killers that were using personal motives against them. Batman was able to maintain his code of honor—but how do Dick and Jason measure up? When Dick is faced with such dark family history, the lies of those he trusted, the revelation of Haly's trickery, and Batman's cold reception of these traumatic events, we might forgive Dick for losing his cool—which he does. He yells at Batman, screaming about being overwhelmed with negativity and not understood. Batman's reaction is to hit Dick in the face knocking out a tooth that reveals, once and for all, that Dick was in line to be the Court's chosen assassin.[9] Dick Grayson is confronted with the ghost of his great-grandfather William Cobb who comes in the form of a Talon assassin for the Court. Cobb is relentless in his wish to kill Dick because he sees Grayson as a disgrace because Dick was destined to become a Talon and managed to avoid that fate. Dick is then finally faced with his great-grandfather and has a choice: he can kill him—or he can choose the impartial system. Given the emotional strain of the situation the impartial system seems impossibly far off—and yet Dick manages to incapacitate and restrain the Talon without killing him.[10]

Jason Todd, when faced with a Talon, is less forgiving. He doesn't have the personal connection that Dick does but he is surprised (and even a bit emotional) about being confronted with another person who was trained to be a killer, who died, and who was resurrected. Given that Jason was even in Gotham because he was following up (read: killing) a crime boss from his past, he was already in a vulnerable place emotionally—he actively avoids Gotham, he doesn't want to be associated with the Bat Family at this time, and this particular criminal had him reliving the harrowing moments of putting himself together post–Lazarus pit. When the Talon falls on his knees and begs Jason to kill him, Jason does not hesitate—he pulls the trigger.[11]

If an essential part of being Robin means being impartial, being able to separate your feelings from your actions so that criminals are brought to court fairly, then we see clearly that Jason fails. The entire basis of his Red Hood persona is that he does what the Batman won't—he will kill to accomplish his goals, which are mercurial. Jason sometimes fights on the side of purely good, and sometimes he fights for a gray area that Batman cannot condone.

Dick, however, is the perfect son. Just in the *Court of Owls* arc he could have done several things differently: he could have killed Raymond for murdering Mr. Haly—he didn't. He could have murdered William Cobb—he didn't. He could have abandoned Bruce for callously ignoring the emotional toll this arc had on him—but he didn't.[12] Dick may have had a crisis of identity when he got too big for the Robin costume and wanted to be Nightwing (more on that decision in the next section) but he never has a crisis of faith with the Batman—he remains loyal to Bruce Wayne's methods, especially regarding keeping your personal feelings out of the verdict.[13] Jason Todd simply couldn't hold up that mantle—he thinks Wayne is weak and selfish both for not killing when it is called for and also for not taking things a little more personally. When Jason is resurrected he is stunned that Batman wouldn't kill the Joker out of love for Jason—and hurt by the revelation.[14] He diverges from the Bat Philosophy and this is part of the reason we do not read him as a good Robin. Of course, Jason's frustration with Bat Philosophy doesn't come purely from his own death as we see just before *Death in the Family* when he may (or may not) have killed a rapist.[15] That's not to say that Dick is a *perfect* Robin—remember, we don't have to ALWAYS perform the role the same way but we need to be as consistent as possible. Notably Dick strayed from the path by beating the Joker in *Joker: Last Laugh*.[16] Performance theory tells us that we need to look at what consistently happens or what reoccurs—if Dick and Jason have both strayed from the Bat Path we need to consider how each man consistently acts. Jason's indiscretions may have started with the death of

Felipe Garzonas (the rapist) but they only grow over time. Dick may have beaten the Joker but he tends to remain loyal and steadfast to Bruce's ideals of justice, which shows that he performs Robin better and more consistently than Jason. In addition, Dick is devastated he beat Joker to death and feels really guilty, despite Joker being revived and everyone telling him to get over it.[17] Jason doesn't feel guilt.

Performing Robin: All for the Bat

The last notable feature of Robins, perhaps the hardest one to achieve, is that the existence of Robin, and any development or promotion Robin undergoes, is only for the benefit of Batman and Gotham, not for any personal gain. This is something even Dick Grayson struggles with as he undergoes the notable growing pains that lead him to Blüdhaven as Nightwing. The training that it takes to be Robin, the daily toll, does not stop the children and teens who perform the role of Robin from becoming adults ... and it is hard to be an adult Robin. Robin is a sidekick, a secondary character, but expected to maintain the same standards as Batman ... to be able to stand in for Batman at a moment's notice, or take over when he dies. However, taking over the Bat Cave cannot be done selfishly, and Robin's most vital quality is that he never lets his own excellence go to his head, he never questions the authority of the Bat, and he never, ever uses his powers for personal gain. Everything remains for the greater good because without that drive Robin would be no different than the criminals he fights.

Dick Grayson is remarkable among the members of the Bat Family because he is the only person to accept the responsibility of the cowl without changing the essential qualities of the cowl—being an impartial judge in a corrupt system, being a selfless act in a world of selfishness, being the light in the darkness. This is a hard task—one that even Bruce Wayne struggles with passing on and why the role of Robin must be so difficult to perform well—because, to paraphrase *Henry IV*, heavy is the head that wears the crown. Bruce Wayne gets to choose an heir, really vet one, but this creates a severe tension because Bruce understands the potential of his heirs to misuse the cowl.

The problem with Nightwing and Red Hood is that both have been prepped to be Batman, but only one is prepared to fully surrender himself to the *Bat* and leave his new identity behind. Ultimately, the best Robin must be prepared to become Batman—not become sort-of like Batman but with an edge. We know that taking on the cowl is hard and that people have been overwhelmed by the power and responsibility and begin to alter the Code. Notably, Jean-Paul Valley (Azrael) was asked to step in as Batman while Bruce Wayne recovered from a broken back but lost control—and the cowl promptly passed to Nightwing.[18]

In *Battle for the Cowl* and *Batman Reborn* Dick takes up the cowl despite there being confusion about whether or not Bruce wants an heir.[19] Dick returns not out of personal motivations, but out of a sense that Batman *needed* to be in Gotham—he abandons his post as Nightwing in order to fulfill this need. And this is why Dick Grayson will always be the ultimate Robin—despite building up a whole life for himself he can, has, and likely will again leave it all behind to return to Batman *because Batman needs it*, not because Dick feels that he's earned it. Dick feels he has earned the right to Nightwing, but the cowl is something that you *serve*, not something that can be gotten by desire alone. This is where Grayson rises above Todd—Todd cannot wear the cowl for the sake of Batman, because his death irreversibly alters his motives and he is forever wearing the mask for *himself*, to prove a point to a mentor he is disappointed in. In *The New 52* Nightwing is constantly re-aligning himself with the Bat Family—he brings Haly's Circus to Gotham, he keeps looping back to see what Bruce and Damian might need, and he is always the first to come during a crisis. *Red Hood and the Outlaws* does interact with the major Batman arcs, but Jason is always torn—he feels he *has* to help the family but he wants to do it on his terms, in his own way. This is the inevitable difference between them: Dick performs this self-sacrificing behavior more than any other Robin.

The Nightwing or the Red Hood: Who Is the Better Boy Wonder?

If we buy into performance theory, the role of Robin is defined by continuous and repetitious acts performed by whoever is wearing the mask. These continuous and repetitious acts are associated with being a "good" or "bad" Robin—and lead us to an important question: who is the better Robin?

There is a reason we are celebrating 75 years of Dick Grayson—he is simply a character that endures because of his persistent and consistent performance as Robin. Characteristics of this Robin performance continue when he becomes the Teen Wonder and, later, Nightwing. Dick Grayson has the physical ability to stand next to Batman, a dedication to an impartial system of justice, and the loyalty to Batman that is unparalleled. Despite how varied the different arcs have been over the last 75 years, many of Dick Grayson's qualities that established what a "Robin" was have never left him, and other characters simply have not been able to perform at his level.

Notes

1. Judith Butler, *Gender Trouble: Feminism and the Subversion of Identity* (London: Routledge, 1989).
2. Mark D. White, Robert Arp, and William Irwin, eds, *Batman and Philosophy* (Hoboken, NJ: Wiley, 2008).
3. Marv Wolfman, Jim Aparo, and Mike DeCarlo, "A Lonely Place of Dying Chapter Three: Parallel Lines!" *Batman* #441 (New York: DC Comics, November 1989), 14–15.
4. Frank Miller, introduction to *Batman: The Dark Knight Returns*, explaining his use of Carrie Kelly. See Frank Miller, Klaus Janson, and Lynn Varley, *The Dark Knight Returns*, Tenth Anniversary Edition (New York: DC Comics, 1996), 7.
5. These are the post–*Crisis* books, notably leading to *Death in the Family*. See especially Max Allan Collins, Chris Warner, and Mike DeCarlo, "Did Robin Die Tonight?" *Batman* #408 (June 1987).
6. Check out the pre–*Crisis* books for this timeline, specifically his intro in Gerry Conway, Don Newton, and Ed Hannigan, "Deathgrip," *Detective Comics* #524 (New York: DC Comics, March 1983).
7. People may argue *but Batman kills* as recently as *Court of Owls*. Batman sent a few Talons down to their dusty graves—interestingly this is defended by saying that the Talons were resurrected dead bodies, which meant Batman wasn't killing them because they were already dead. This is covered in Scott Snyder et al., *Batman Vol. 2: The City of Owls*, The New 52 (New York: DC Comics, 2013).
8. Perhaps the most notable example is he never kills the Joker for killing Jason Todd, something Red Hood holds against Batman in the "Under the Hood" arc (*Batman* #635–641, #645–650, and *Batman Annual* #25, all written by Judd Winick).
9. Kyle Higgin et al., "Turning Points," *Nightwing* #7 (New York: DC Comics, May 2012), [17–18] and Scott Snyder, Greg Capullo, and Jonathan Glapion, "The Talons Strike!" *Batman* #7 (New York: DC Comics, May 2012), [15–17].
10. Kyle Higgins, Eddy Barrows, and Andres Guinaldo, "The Gay Son," *Nightwing* #9 (July 2012).
11. Scott Lobdell and Kenneth Rocafort, "Who are You?—Hoo Hoo?" *Red Hood and the Outlaws* #9 (New York: DC Comics, May 2012), [18].
12. For some of the tough times Dick faced see Higgins et al., "Haly's Wish," *Nightwing* #2 (December 2011). For Dick and Bruce, see Scott Snyder, Greg Capullo, and Jonathan Glapion, "Face the Court," *Batman* #4–5 (February 2012 and March 2012) and Scott Snyder, James Tynion IV, and Rafael Albuquerque, "The Call," in *Batman* #8 (June 2012), [29].
13. Higgins et al., *Nightwing* #7 (May 2012), [16–18] and Snyder, Capullo, and Glapion, *Batman* #7 (May 2012), [11–18].
14. Both the book and animated movie versions of "Under the [Red] Hood" include this moment. Judd Winick was the lead on the graphic novel run and a writer of the film; Brandon Vietti directed the film.

15. Jim Starlin, Mark Bright, and Steve Mitchell, "The Diplomat's Son," *Batman* #424 (October 1988).

16. Chuck Dixon et al., "Part Six: You Only Laugh Twice," *Joker: Last Laugh* #6 (New York: DC Comics, January 2002), 23.

17. Chuck Dixon, Trevor McCarthy, and Karl Kesel, "Red, Fright and Blue," *Nightwing* #63 (New York: DC Comics, January 2002).

18. *Batman* #500 (October 1993) during *Knightfall* is when Valley becomes unstable; his instability continues in "Knightfall: The Crusade," prompting Robin to question Valley's appropriateness for the role. Valley has the cowl taken away in *KnightsEnd*.

19. There was a will that suggests Bruce doesn't want an heir, but isn't that just counter intuitive to the aims of Batman Inc? I think it was Bruce thinking Nightwing and Robin were enough. When he returned from time and saw how much Batman was needed, he did the Batman Incorporated thing.

Part II

The Original Dynamic Duo: Dick Grayson and Bruce Wayne

The Child Is Father to the (Bat)Man
The Inverted Parent-Child Dynamic of DC Comics' Dynamic Duo

DAVID KINGSLEY

In 1939, Bob Kane and Bill Finger created the character of Batman to capitalize on the success of Superman.[1] Batman's grim and solitary nature offered an inverse to Superman's colorful and affable characterization. However, where Superman served as a relatable surrogate for young readers—with meek, bookish Clark Kent secretly able to leap over skyscrapers and bend steel girders—Batman and Bruce Wayne proved unrelatable. Early appearances describe Batman as an "eerie figure of the night," a "weird figure of darkness" who fights a "lone battle against evil."[2] Consequently, *Batman*'s writers introduced Robin: The Boy Wonder (Dick Grayson), in 1940, to make Bruce Wayne's lonely and cheerless existence more appealing for younger audiences. A circus acrobat orphaned by mobsters and fostered by Bruce Wayne, Grayson provided a bombastic and colorful viewpoint character that was the same age as many readers of *Detective Comics*. Much of Robin's early characterization and critical interpretation regard Wayne as a father figure to Grayson. I argue, instead, that Dick Grayson serves as a Freudian father figure for Bruce Wayne, in that Dick Grayson creates the opportunities for Bruce Wayne to transition from an unhealthy, pseudo-childhood to healthy adulthood and attain catharsis for his parents' murder.

Trauma theory provides the best critical lens for analyzing Wayne and Grayson's relationship, as both characters are orphaned by violent crime. Trauma theory provides a psychoanalytic framework for reading and interpreting literature, and extends back to Sigmund Freud's arguments that trauma was a psychological impediment caused by an unexpected, external event.³ Bruce Wayne and Dick Grayson both incur trauma in their childhoods. Bruce Wayne watches an anonymous mugger shoot his parents to death; Dick Grayson witnesses his acrobat parents plummet to their deaths after a gangster, Tony "Boss" Zucco, weakens their trapeze ropes with acid. Freud further wrote that traumatic events, such as those suffered by Grayson and Wayne, become buried in the subconscious until the sufferer resolves the traumatic experience through psychoanalysis. Freud believed this resolution recurs in literature, and, contemporarily, it can be found in Batman and Robin's simultaneous character arcs.⁴

Recent psychoanalytic criticism further facilitates the reading of Batman's fictional history with trauma theory. Cathy Caruth and Sandra L. Bloom both define trauma as an "unclaimed experience." Bloom defines unclaimed experiences as inexpressible terror.⁵ While traumatized individuals may not have words to articulate their trauma, Caruth contends that traumatic experiences can be tacitly understood by survivors of similar traumatic experiences.⁶ Before Robin, Batman lacked a supporting cast to which to talk and relate the trauma of his murdered parents.⁷ Robin functions as the figure through which Bruce can process his trauma and loss. Since Bruce's confrontation of his loss leaves him a more balanced and adjusted adult, Dick fills a parental role in Bruce's life. Dick is a Freudian father figure who aids Bruce's transition from childhood to adulthood.

The trauma of the Wayne murders traps Bruce in a damaged, childlike stasis that he externally symbolizes through the identity of Batman. In her overview of trauma theory, "Trauma Theory Abbreviated," Bloom concludes that traumatized children often lack a "developed sense of self" and thus Bruce invents a separate self to fulfill his childhood promise, modeled after a bat that flies through his window.⁸ Recognizing that criminals are a "superstitious cowardly lot" Bruce aims to use the symbol of the bat to traumatize those whom, as a child, traumatized him, by "strik[ing] terror into their hearts."⁹ For Bruce Wayne, then, Batman becomes what Lenore Terr refers to as "post-traumatic play."¹⁰ Terr and Caruth both write that this play constitutes "repetitive actions," what Bloom describes as externalizing in "violent acting-out" "anger as a problem-solving strategy, hypervigilance, and absolutstic thinking" that, especially for children, marks itself as "revenge that will be exacted either upon themselves, upon others, or both."¹¹ Both Bloom and Caruth accurately describe the traumatized behavior of Batman, who seeks revenge on criminals. Both writers also accurately define the traumatized behavior of Bruce Wayne, who seeks revenge on himself by waging an unwinnable, one-man war.

Despite being a child himself, Robin helps break Batman of this endless cycle of childish, self-destructive behavior and models adult behavior for Bruce Wayne to follow. In 1969, Dick Grayson's character moved out of Wayne Manor to attend college. Grayson later fostered strong interpersonal connections by moving in with and becoming engaged to his longtime girlfriend Koriand'r, the superhero Starfire, with whom Grayson served on the (Teen) Titans, in the position of team leader. He later developed his own superhero identity, Nightwing, distinct from Batman, before assuming then rejecting the Batman mantle, in 1994's "Prodigal." While these life events define Dick Grayson's maturity and development, I argue that they force a similar development in Bruce Wayne's character and foster his growth into adulthood.

Dick and Bruce struggle for the father role in their relationship. Lawrence Jay Dessner typifies the Freudian father as occurring in trauma fiction as it relates to orphaned characters through father figures that "terrorize, ... succumb to, and lovingly pardon..." their adopted sons who "love, and fear, and [figuratively] kill" their father.[12] Both Dick and Bruce occupy the role of orphan, and, in 1994's "Prodigal" storyline both enact the father figure as well. In "Prodigal," Dick assumes Batman's identity and dresses in the character's cape and cowl. This artistic decision literally illustrates Dick Grayson as the transformative father figure who may finally pardon Bruce. Bruce seeks to be pardoned for being unable to express his frustration that Dick overcame his trauma to grow and develop into Nightwing, a healthy, functioning adult identity, while he remained in a childlike pattern of behavior as Batman. Bruce achieves catharsis by expressing his previously unclaimed and inexpressible feelings. As a result, Bruce grows into an adjusted and balanced adult, like Dick.

Secret Origins and Reclaimed Origins

More recent creators and filmmakers, such as Frank Miller, Tim Burton, and Christopher Nolan, have downplayed, denigrated, or deleted Dick Grayson's presence in Bruce Wayne's life, regarding the character as a child who reduced the potential to tell more serious and mature stories. As a result, many creators have chosen to advance Grayson's age at the time of his parents' deaths. This decision is reductive to both Bruce's and Dick's characters. Bruce offers catharsis to Dick at approximately the same age Bruce was when he lost his parents, and this extension of catharsis to Dick alternately facilitates catharsis for himself. This mutual relief reflects Cathy Caruth's previously mentioned sentiment that wounded people best overcome their trauma through help from a similarly wounded person. Dick Grayson was deliberately provided to find this voice, as Batman co-creators Bill Finger and Bob Kane both acknowledged that Robin was designed to give Batman somebody "to talk to."[13]

Specifically, Robin provides Batman with the first character that Batman can talk and relate to about the shared trauma of witnessing the murder of his parents. Batman confides to Grayson, in Robin's first appearance: "My parents too were killed by a criminal. That's why I've devoted my life to exterminate them."[14] Creators had not given Batman an origin until November, 1939, though the character had debuted in May. In Batman's first printed origin, "The Batman Wars against the Dirigible of Doom," only two panels span the years between young Bruce's vow to avenge his parents' deaths and Bruce Wayne, as an adult, committing to become a "weird figure of the dark."[15] Gardner Fox, author of "Dirigible of Doom," writes, "[a]s the years pass, Bruce Wayne prepares himself for his career. He becomes a master scientist. Trains his body to physical perfection until he is able to perform amazing athletic feats."[16] Fox delivers this brief origin as exposition outside of the story's events, as Batman yet has no supporting character to relate the information.

Grayson's introduction not only gave Batman a character to whom he could talk but to whom he could emotionally relate. In Robin's first appearance, Batman relents to Dick, "[w]ell, I guess you and I were both victims of similar trouble. All right, I'll make you my aid."[17] The senseless murder of the Graysons, therefore, allows Bruce to contextualize the senseless death of the Waynes. By offering Grayson justice for the murder of his parents, Bruce achieves catharsis for the murder of his parents. In Batman's earliest origin, set fifteen years earlier, Gardner Fox gives no indication the Wayne's killer was ever identified or apprehended.[18] Indeed, young Bruce Wayne swears, "by the spirits of [his] parents" that he will "avenge their deaths by spending the rest of [his] life warring on all criminals," and that sentiment clearly indicates that Bruce has been denied closure.[19] Bruce's vow, again, complements Bloom's research that traumatized children exact a mutual revenge on themselves and others. Furthermore, Bruce's actions as Batman complement the trauma theory findings of Lenore Terr. In *Too Scared to Cry: Psychic Trauma in Childhood,* Terr writes that children often respond to trauma with anger, and this anger manifests aggressive behavior and a desire to inspire fear.[20] The psychological profile of a traumatized child frames Bruce Wayne's Batman and his goal to strike terror into criminals' "cowardly" hearts through physical intimidation.

Terr's and Bloom's research, however, fails to frame Dick Grayson, whose brightly clad costume exists to inspire hope, rather than fear, and who overcomes the trauma to which Bruce succumbs. Terr writes that children rebound from trauma through the act of post-traumatic play. Children often play by imagining themselves to be someone or something else. The more traumatic the event, the more likely these imaginary role plays will become obsessive attempts to master the assumed identity, resembling Bruce's obsessive devotion to Batman's identity.[21] Indeed, Terr describes the post-traumatic play of damaged youths as "grim," in much the same way Bruce Wayne's early activities as Batman were described.[22] Furthermore, where Bruce's grim role play is to obsessively assume the identity of a bat, Terr describes the case study of Timmy Donnorio, a traumatized child who sought relief from his trauma by role playing as Batman.[23] Dick Grayson's play as Robin, however, is described as joyful and dynamic, with early appearances defining him as "a laughing, fighting young daredevil" in contrast to Batman's previously mentioned, earliest descriptions.[24]

Robin's first appearance also indicates that Dick can cease his play as Robin, at his leisure, while Bruce cannot terminate his play as Batman. Bruce has Robin photograph Tony Zucco knifing a henchman at the end of Robin's first appearance, and the picture sends Zucco to the electric chair. Bruce gives Dick closure and permission to return to the circus, suggesting that Dick's play as Robin can end, where Bruce's cannot. Dick refuses to return to the circus and comments that he loves adventure and looks forward to his and Batman's next case, suggesting that Dick derives a joy from costumed play that Bruce does not.[25] Bruce's behavior as Batman echoes Terr's study that "traumatically inspired" play "is obsessively repeated," and Bruce grimly repeats his play as Batman because his earliest origins imply the Wayne murders, unlike the Grayson murders, were never solved.[26]

Bruce, however, undergoes a character shift and achieves catharsis by helping Dick achieve catharsis. Les Daniels, author of *Batman: A Complete History*, remarks that "the solitary and sinister Batman of the early days" disappeared and was tempered by Robin's "brightness."[27] Daniels also remarks that Robin's introduction transformed Batman from a "lone avenger" to a "fatherly big brother," but this remark contradicts Bloom's hypothesis that children "cannot soothe themselves until they have been soothed by adults."[28] Bruce Wayne engineers the circumstances that allow Robin to avenge the Grayson's death, but he is more soothed by Robin than Robin is by him, as evidenced by Bruce's less absolutistic, angry, vigilante, and violent characterization following Robin's introduction. Dick Grayson fills, then, the role of "fatherly" and soothing adult that Batman lacks, and this characterization continued for two decades.

Leaving the Nest

Until 1969, few milestones marked any chronological or emotional progression in Dick Grayson's life. In 1964, Grayson joined and became leader of the Teen Titans, a crimefighting group rostered by analogues and sidekicks of popular, adult superheroes, such as Aqualad, Kid Flash, Speedy, and Wonder Girl. Grayson's maturation from boy to teen was reflected in Robin's 1969 status change from "Boy Wonder" to "Teen Wonder." 1969 also found Dick moving out of Wayne Manor to attend Hudson University. Dick's move allowed him to construct an adult life for himself, rather than stay in his childhood home, dress in costume, and "play" in a self-destructive, unwinnable war, as Bruce does. Dick's decision provokes Bruce to grow and make a similar change in his life. Bruce confesses to Alfred that "Dick's leaving brought home the stark fact that our private world has changed! We're in grave danger of becoming—outmoded! Obsolete dodos of the mod world outside! Our best chance for survival is to—close up shop here," and Bruce, inspired by Dick, decides to leave his childhood home for a life that he has constructed.[29] Bruce makes his new home in the penthouse of the Wayne Foundation, a corporation that Bruce changes to suit his more adult goals.

In "One Bullet Too Many," Bruce Wayne reconfigures the Wayne Foundation to fight crime in a more mature, more effective fashion than he has been fighting crime as Batman. Sandra L. Bloom writes that traumatized children often react to their trauma through violence and terrorizing behaviors, such as those Bruce performs as Batman.[30] "For healing to occur...," Bloom writes, "people often need to put the experience into a narrative, give it words, and share it with themselves and others," which is what Bruce reconstructs the Wayne foundation to do.[31] Bruce tells Alfred that he and Dick "were in the fortunate position to claim justice for ourselves—but what of the less fortunates? Precisely what the Wayne Foundation intends to correct![32] Children who play through traumatic experiences often create "dangerous game[s]," in which they enlist non-traumatized children to engage in reenactments of their traumatic experiences in an attempt to "'undo'" the inciting event, much as Bruce, as Batman, enacted with Grayson.[33] Bruce's new goal suggests that he is no longer playing as Batman but working as Bruce Wayne. His new goals express a desire to use his resources to listen to other victims and thereby provide catharsis, rather than use his resources to finance weaponry to terrorize criminals. This new direction suggests Bruce's trauma has been lessened, and he no longer seeks comfort through role-playing and misdirected violence.

Bruce learned how to offer compassion to others by the sympathy he provided to Dick years earlier, and now learns how to find catharsis through non-violent means by following Dick's example to construct a non-superhero identity. For these reasons, Dick continues to represent the adult and father figure, in that he demonstrates the mature, healthy behavior that contributes to the alleviation of Bruce's trauma and Bruce's evolution into adulthood. Dick Grayson, too, continued to evolve and would, fifteen years after "One Bullet Too Many," develop Nightwing, an identity distinct from Batman.

Flying Solo

Dick Grayson revealed a maturity beyond that of his partner by proving himself as an effective team leader, capable of making and maintaining deep and sincere relationships, in contrast to Bruce Wayne's earliest depictions as a joyless, solitary figure. Sandra Bloom writes that people who have been traumatized require the support of others in relationships "that are not based on terror."[34] Bruce's relationships with others—such as his fellow superheroes in the Justice League, Commissioner Gordon, or the multiple Robins—largely center upon Batman's obsession with terrorizing criminals. Indeed, Bruce bases his relationship with Dick on a mutual desire to terrorize Gotham City's criminal element. Dick, however, surpasses Bruce when he creates relationships with his teammates on the Teen Titans that allow him to confront his loss through healthier means. Issues such as "Loving You," *The New Teen Titans* #39 (January, 1988), in which Grayson and Starfire decide to cohabitate as a show of commitment, and "Something Old, Something New, Something Borrowed, Something ... Dead!," *The New Titans* #100 (August, 1993), which opens with Grayson and Starfire's wedding invitation, reveal levels of intimacy and complexity lacking in many of Batman's interactions with the Justice League of America.

For decades, writers characterized Batman as externalizing Bruce Wayne's childlike desire to terrorize; Marv Wolfman characterized Nightwing as externalizing the relationships that Dick Grayson formed that were not based on terror. In 1987, Batman asserted his leadership of the Justice League of America by sucker-punching Guy Gardner, an obnoxious teammate who challenged Batman's authority.[35] Conversely, Dick openly expresses both his romantic and platonic love for his teammates Starfire and Raven, in 1989's "Loving You." Marv Wolfman wrote the 1984 story in which Dick assumed the identity Nightwing, a superhero identity formerly used by Superman. Nightwing exists as a rejection of Batman's self-destructive cycle and a celebration of the support Dick received from characters like Raven and Starfire. Wolfman's Grayson explains:

> And Superman. I grew up in your shadow, too. You taught me honor, selflessness, and the true meaning of the word "hero"! A long time ago you used the name I've been thinking of. It was a name from your Kryptonian heritage. I'm the sum of so many people who have influenced me, shaped my thinking, and given me love.... I gave up being Robin because that tied me to Batman. But now I've become someone new who commemorates all those people who made me someone special. Are you people ready? Say hello to—Nightwing!³⁶

Nightwing's connections to Superman show Grayson's rejection of Batman's endless trauma and darkness and create an identity in relation to others, such as his parents, teammates, and friends.

Nightwing's identity also facilitated the means by which Dick could be judged as an adult, rather than as a child sidekick. Dick had rejected Batman's partnership and methods following a shared mission where Bruce had attempted to usurp Robin's command of the Titans. This incident forced Dick to recognize that he "ha[d] to become someone—an adult. Whoever Dick Grayson decides to be."³⁷ When Dick asserts his leadership to Bruce and rejects Batman's style of coercive camaraderie, Bruce recognizes that Robin has surpassed him. Bruce then verbalizes how Robin has inverted the dynamic to become Batman's instructor: "I guess even the teacher can learn from his pupil ... his former pupil."³⁸ These sentiments affirm five decades of subtext and confirm that Dick Grayson has taken the instructive adult role in the dynamic duo.

(Bat)Manhood and Beyond

Marv Wolfman characterized Dick Grayson's assumption of the Nightwing identity as a mature and enlightened rejection of Bruce Wayne's childlike stasis, but future authors revised Grayson's decision. These stories, "Did Robin Die Tonight?" and "Prodigal," both reimagine Bruce as the adult / father and Dick as the child. In "Prodigal," Two-Face, a politician disfigured by acid, hangs both Batman and the district attorney who replaced him. Dick severs the noose, but the district attorney drowns, and Two-Face brutalizes Grayson until Batman intervenes and subdues Two-Face.³⁹ "Did Robin Die Tonight" reveals that Batman fired Grayson as Robin for similar helplessness. In that story, the Joker shoots Dick and Batman declares, "[i]n what I do, there is no place for a child," an admonishment that retracts Grayson's adulthood.⁴⁰ Both stories reduce Dick's agency to elect Batman as the figure who controls Dick's progression into adulthood.

These stories appear to delete decades of Grayson's growth and development to keep Dick Grayson as a child, but for the sake of the characters' arcs, Bruce must be repositioned as an adult so that Dick can confront and overcome him. Homans argues that orphans rewrite the past to create a sense of identity, and the changed origins for Grayson's adoption of Nightwing rewrites Batman's narrative so he, rather than Dick, is the adult.⁴¹ In "Prodigal" Bruce, recovering from a broken spine, offers the role of Batman to Dick Grayson. Bruce's offer reduces Dick's agency in his own adulthood by repositioning Bruce as the figure capable of making Dick a (Bat)man.

For decades, writers characterized Batman as a child in a contrast to Dick Grayson's growth and maturity; making Dick Batman allowed Grayson to rehabilitate Batman's identity as an adult's identity. As Batman, Grayson has his own Robin (Tim Drake) who comments, "[a]wesome—you [Dick] can cook and do the laundry? ... Blimey—does Alfred ... know you've mastered all his domestic secrets? ... Since ... Bruce relies on Alfred, it looks like you can teach a trick or two the other Batm[a]n couldn't."⁴² Drake's comments highlight how Grayson possesses the skills to care for himself and care for a child, which Bruce lacked and for which Bruce necessitated an adult caregiver. Furthermore, Tim is kidnapped by Two-Face and suspended with a rope along with a second hostage, recreating Dick's trauma from the revised Robin origin and allowing Grayson an opportunity to rewrite his own traumatic event. Dick realizes that "[h]e has to make the game his own," and saves both the hostage's and Tim Drake's life.⁴³ Upon reflecting about the first time Two-Face hanged a hostage, Two-Face's psychiatrist remarks, "[o]bviously the murder of [the district attorney] was a symbol. Dent meant to kill himself—his past life."⁴⁴ By that logic, Dick Grayson saving Robin is a symbol of Dick saving himself by overcoming the trauma Two-Face emblematized.

Two-Face's impossible challenge to Dick offers a small-scale recontextualization of Bruce Wayne's unbeatable war on crime. Bruce uses Batman to terrorize the criminals who terrorized him and thus endlessly relives the trauma that wounded him; Grayson "makes the game his own" by using Batman to end his traumatic event by creating a happy ending.⁴⁵ Following these events, Dick has no reason to be Batman. He thinks, "[n]ow that Two-Face is down, I may not need or want the Bat."⁴⁶ Later, he considers, "[i]t never stops, never ends ... how does that one man, alone in an eternal night of violence cope? By being more driven, more than a normal man ... and a lot more than I'm prepared, or able, to be. There's only one Batman.... And it isn't me."[47] Dick rejects Batman's identity, as he once rejected Robin's identity, and this rejection represents his character's purpose to define and develop Bruce Wayne. Robin recognizes Batman's campaign to eliminate all crime is destructive, childish, and futile, and he makes the adult decision to walk away from it.

Dick Grayson returns Batman's cape and cowl to Bruce at the conclusion of "Prodigal," and, since Dick has redefined Batman's garb as an adult identity, Dick now becomes the father figure who can arbitrate adulthood for Bruce. "Prodigal" rewrote Dick's backstory so that Bruce could act as the adult and usher Dick into (Bat)manhood, but Dick rewrites and overwrites his own trauma to act as the adult that ushers Bruce into manhood. Phil Jiminez, the penciler of "Prodigal's" climactic confrontation confirms this thematic reversal by illustrating Robin's costume superimposed over Bruce's body as Dick is clad in Batman's costume. Dick, then, offers Bruce the opportunity to confront the father figure he represented at the beginning of the storyline. As the father, Dick chastises Bruce's childish behavior, telling him, "[y]ou never need words. You never question. You never examine yourself or the people around you."[48] This excoriation echoes Bloom's notion that "the traumatized person is cut off from language, deprived of the power of words, trapped in speechless terror," until they find a similarly traumatized partner.[49]

Dessner refers to this fatherly punishment as a necessary, "symbolic, purifying death...," and Bruce lays his trauma to rest, here, by finally finding the words to voice his trauma.[50] "A distance grew between us," Bruce acknowledges, "I left so many things unsaid. I handled it all wrong. But that's the way it always is, isn't it.... Between fathers and sons."[51] This panel appears to affirm the reading that Bruce is Dick's father figure, but this reading is complicated by the previous illustration of Robin's costume superimposed on Bruce's body and Dick being dressed as Batman. Jiminez purposefully presents Bruce in this exchange as the child and Dick as the father. This panel and this storyline instead affirm fifty years of subtext and confirm the notion that Dick Grayson's ability to grow and mature mark Dick as the adult figure who teaches Bruce how to grow and mature. Both Bruce and Dick rewrite their history to confront their trauma, a characteristic Homans cites as consistent with trauma fiction, and then both characters lay that trauma to rest through dialogue, a characteristic Lenore Terr cites as consistent with trauma resolution. Terr writes that Timmy Donnario, the child who played as Batman to alleviate trauma, no longer needed to enact Batman after talking through his trauma.[52] Dick no longer needs to be Batman after verbally rejecting Batman's identity and the trauma it represents. In "Prodigal," Dick acts as the Freudian son who kills his father by killing, via rejection, Batman's identity, to become the Freudian father who lovingly pardons the child, by returning Bruce's Batman costume and forgiving him. Dick Grayson, therefore, proves the transformative character of Bruce Wayne's story arc. He models how to transition from a traumatized childhood to a healthy adulthood, and ultimately becomes Bruce Wayne's father; he offers catharsis by replacing Bruce Wayne's murdered father and by teaching Bruce how to be a father himself.

Why Batman Needs a Robin

"Prodigal" serves as an effective conclusion to Batman's story, but, since Batman serves as the cornerstone of a multimillion-dollar, multimedia conglomerate, ending his story proves impractical. "Prodigal" acknowledges the ongoing nature of Batman's publication. When Bruce emerges as Batman, on the story's concluding page, Tim Drake exclaims, "[y]our costume … it's…."[53] Bruce's costume remains unseen, but, based on the thematic implications "Prodigal" creates, Bruce's costume is different because Dick transformed Batman into an adult's identity. Indeed, Bruce interjects that Batman's costume is "just the start of changes I'm going to make," which suggests that Bruce's changed Batman is more well-balanced.[54] Bruce has learned to grow from Dick Grayson. He has confronted the Waynes' killer through helping Dick confront the Graysons' killer. He has learned to use Wayne Enterprises to help victims by observing Dick Grayson move from Wayne Manor and the Batcave. He has learned how to be a father to Tim and Dick by observing Dick be a father to him. Indeed, "Prodigal" concludes with Dick Grayson as Nightwing once more. This decision does not undo Grayson's character development, since orphan literature, Homans and Dessner write, often concludes with the past being revisited and with the orphan, as an adult, returning to a recreated childhood by a reinvented family.[55]

Batman and Robin write mutual happy endings for one another and recreate the family that each has lost, and any deviation from this dynamic does a disservice to both characters. However, most recent Batman stories have detrimentally altered this dynamic. Creators and audiences still regard Robin as an avatar of previous era's adolescence who unnecessarily mitigates Batman's maturity, rather than regard Dick Grayson as the impact character who concludes Batman's character arc. "If Robin crops up in one of the new Batman films," Christian Bale, star of Christopher Nolan's *Dark Knight* trilogy, declared, "I'll be chaining myself up somewhere and refusing to go to work."[56] Bale's denigration of Dick Grayson displays the tendency for filmmakers to deemphasize Robin in all media adaptations of Batman, post 1989, though the character had appeared in all media incarnations of Batman since 1943. Tim Burton was admittedly "happy" that Robin was cut from his 1989 *Batman* film.[57] Chris O'Donnell was cast in *Batman*'s sequels *Batman Forever* and *Batman and Robin*, directed by Joel Schumacher. O'Donnell's age, 25 and 27 at the dates of release, substantially alters Bruce's and Dick's shared trauma of losing their parents at an early age. The idea of Bruce Wayne adopting an adult ward is absurd, and the movies catered to this absurdity. *Batman and Robin*, the final film in Warner Brothers' initial Batman franchise, instigates conflict between Batman and the adult Dick Grayson by having the duo compete with each other, at auction, to purchase sexual favors from the villain Poison Ivy.

Writers fundamentally altered and assassinated Dick Grayson's character in comic books, as well. Frank Miller famously visited Batman's future and his origins, in the storylines *The Dark Knight Returns* (1986) and *Year One* (1987), neither of which featured Dick Grayson. Miller, however, featured Dick Grayson in *The Dark Knight Strikes Again* (2001–02), a story set further in Batman's future. In *The Dark Knight Strikes Again*, Miller posits that Dick Grayson becomes a genetically-altered, shapeshifting government assassin. Miller's Grayson also obsesses after Bruce Wayne, who openly despises and professes never to have liked Grayson. *The Dark Knight Strikes Again* concludes with Bruce hurling Dick into a volcano.

Miller's Batman served as an inspiration for both the first Warner Brothers 1989 Batman franchise and Christopher Nolan's *Dark Knight* trilogy, Warner Brothers' second Batman franchise, begun in 2005, which incorporated numerous characters and elements from Miller's *Year One*.[58] Despite Bale's comments on Robin, Nolan introduced the character in *The Dark Knight Rises* as Gotham City police officer, John "Robin" Blake. Blake possesses no formal training but assumes Batman's identity after Bruce fakes his death and flees to Europe with a burglar who helped physically disable him and with whom he becomes romantically involved. *The Dark Knight Rises*, *The Dark Knight Strikes Again*, and *Batman and Robin* all attempt to reposition Batman and Robin outside the traumatized parent/child roles established in the characters' earliest days. These adaptations fail to include the formative trauma-based relationship that has contributed to the dynamic duo's growth over decades. The noted narrative difficulties of those stories illustrate the impossibility of concluding Batman's story with any ending other than Bruce finding recognition, reconciliation, and redemption from a fellow, traumatized child.

The redemption Bruce receives from Dick provides Bruce Wayne with the only logical endpoint of his story. By adopting Dick Grayson, Bruce Wayne overcomes the trauma of his parents' murder that he was unable to surmount on his own. When writers age Dick Grayson from an adolescent to an adult, Bruce lacks a recognizable voice of shared trauma; when writers remove Dick from the dynamic entirely, Bruce Wayne is denied catharsis and Batman's story becomes incomplete. Tim Drake, in his first appearance as Robin, tells Batman, "Batman has to have a Robin. ... Batman needs a Robin."[59] The complications of stories that seek to resolve Batman's narrative without Robin show that Bruce Wayne has to have Dick Grayson. Batman needs Dick Grayson.

Notes

1. Gerard Jones, *Men of Tomorrow: Geeks Gangsters, and the Birth of the Comic Book* (New York: Basic Books, 2004), 149.

2. Gardner Fox and Bob Kane, "The Batman Meets Doctor Death," *Detective Comics* #29 (July 1939), in *The Batman Chronicles Volume 1* (New York: DC Comics, 2005), 18; Bill Finger and Bob Kane, "The Case of the Ruby Idol," *Detective Comics* #35 (January 1940), in *The Batman Chronicles Volume 1*, 87; Bill Finger and Bob Kane, "The Case of the Chemical Syndicate," *Detective Comics* #27 (May 1939), in *The Batman Chronicles Volume 1*, 4.

3. Daniel S. Schechter and M. Cevdet Tosyali, "Posttraumatic Stress Disorder," in *Anxiety Disorders in Children and Adolescents: Epidemiology, Risk Factors and Treatment*, eds. Cecilia A. Essau and Franz Peterman (London: Routledge, 2002), 288.

4. As Batman and Robin's character arcs have both been in constant publication and constant flux for seventy-five years, I have limited this paper's scope to the ongoing (continuously published) DC Comics' titles published between 1939, with Batman's introduction, through the 1994 "Prodigal" storyline.

5. Sandra L. Bloom, "Trauma Theory Abbreviated," *Final Action Plan: A Coordinated Community-Based Response to Family Violence* (Philadelphia: CommunityWorks, 1999), 11.

6. Cathy Caruth, *Unclaimed Experience: Trauma, Narrative and History* (Baltimore: Johns Hopkins University Press), 8.

7. Writers did not establish Alfred Pennyworth as Bruce's adoptive parent and legal guardian until Frank Miller's and David Mazzucchelli's "Year One" story arc, published between 1986–87. Prior to "Year One," Alfred entered Bruce's employ well after Bruce and Dick had established themselves as Batman and Robin. Bruce's uncle Philip was introduced as Bruce's legal guardian and Mrs. Chilton, Joe Chill's mother, was introduced as Bruce's primary caregiver, in 1969. For the first thirty years of his existence, however, no writers specified who cared for young Bruce in the years following his parents' murders.

8. Bloom, "Trauma Theory Abbreviated," 8.

9. Gardner Fox and Bob Kane, "The Batman Wars Against the Dirigible of Doom," *Detective Comics* #29 (July 1939) in *The Batman Chronicles Volume 1*, 63.

10. Lenore Terr, *Too Scared to Cry: Psychic Trauma in Childhood* (New York: Harper & Row, 1990), 238.
11. Terr, *Too Scared to Cry*, 239; Caruth, *Unclaimed Experience*, 4; Bloom, "Trauma Theory Abbreviated," 9, 5.
12. Lawrence Jay Dessner "The Ghost of a Man's Own Father," *MLA* 91.3 (1976): 439, 442.
13. Jones, *Men of Tomorrow*, 153; Bob Kane and Tom Andrae, *Batman & Me* (Forestville: Eclipse, 1989), 46.
14. Bill Finger and Bob Kane, "Introducing Robin the Boy Wonder," *Detective Comics* #38 (April 1940), in *Batman Chronicles Volume 1*, 127.
15. Fox and Kane, "Dirigible of Doom," 63.
16. Fox and Kane, "Dirigible of Doom," 63.
17. Finger and Kane, "Introducing Robin," 127.
18. Fox and Kane, "Dirigible of Doom," 62.
19. Fox and Kane, "Dirigible of Doom," 63.
20. Terr, *Too Scared to Cry*, 61–3.
21. Terr, *Too Scared to Cry*, 238–9.
22. Terr, *Too Scared to Cry*, 238.
23. Terr, *Too Scared to Cry*, 314–5.
24. Finger and Kane, "Introducing Robin," 125.
25. Finger and Kane, "Introducing Robin," 136.
26. Later Batman writers contradicted the idea that the Waynes' murder was never solved. Beginning in 1948, writers characterized Joe Chill as the Waynes' murderer. Like Robin and Zucco, Batman later engineered the circumstances precipitating Chill's execution. Writers further complicated Batman's origin by revealing that the Waynes' murder was not random but a deliberate execution engineered by a gangster, Lew Moxon, who hired Chill as revenge on Thomas Wayne, Bruce's father, who aided in Moxon's conviction. Writers have continued to alternate between identifying an anonymous mugger and Chill as the Waynes' killer for decades, making Batman's origin maddeningly inconsistent. To resolve the numerous, contradictory origins writers have provided for Batman over the years, I have chosen Batman's earliest origin, in which the Waynes' killer was never identified. I further argue that identifying the Waynes' killer is detrimental to Batman's character. Bruce's behavior becomes exponentially more childish and self-destructive when he continues to engage in childish and self-destructive behavior after receiving closure. Furthermore, definitive closure robs Bruce of the shared catharsis Bruce achieves through providing Dick's catharsis.
27. Les Daniels, *Batman: The Complete History* (San Francisco: Chronicle, 2004), 37–8.
28. Daniels, *Batman: The Complete History*, 46; Bloom, "Trauma Theory Abbreviated," 4.
29. Frank Robbins, Irv Novick, and Dick Giordano, "One Bullet Too Many!" *Batman* #217 (New York: DC Comics, December 1969), 4.
30. Bloom, "Trauma Theory Abbreviated," 4.
31. Bloom, "Trauma Theory Abbreviated," 6.
32. Robbins, Novick, and Giordano, *Batman* #217, 7.
33. Terr, *Too Scared to Cry*, 241.
34. Bloom, "Trauma Theory Abbreviated," 10.
35. Batman's one-punch victory over Guy Gardner may represent Batman's first defining moment as a Justice League member, which, for twenty years, had been characterized as undistinguished and unremarkable. Later comics emphasized Batman's uneasy relationship with his fellow Justice Leaguers. This tension climaxed in "The

Tower of Babel" (2000) whose author, Mark Waid, revealed that Batman had invented lethal deathtraps to destroy his Justice League's teammates, should he ever deem it necessary.

36. Marv Wolfman et al., "The Judas Contract Book 3—There Shall Come a Titan," *Tales of the Teen Titans* #44 (New York: DC Comics, July 1984), 21–2.

37. Marv Wolfman and George Pérez, "Crossroads," *The New Teen Titans* #39 (February 1984), 21.

38. Mike W. Barr and Jim Aparo, "Psimon Says...," *Batman and the Outsiders* #5 (December 1983), 24.

39. Chuck Dixon, Tom Grummett, and Ray Kryssing, "Brothers in Arms," *Robin* #0 (October 1994), 15–18.

40. Max Allan Collins, Chris Warner, and Mike DeCarlo, "Did Robin Die Tonight?" *Batman* #408 (June 1987), 6.

41. Homans, "Adoption Narratives," 13, 16, 23.

42. Doug Moench, Mike Gustovich, and Romeo Tanghal, "Double Deuce," *Batman* #513 (December 1994), 10.

43. Chuck Dixon at al, "Twice Told Tale," *Detective Comics* #680 (New York: DC Comics, December 1994), 21.

44. Dixon, Grummett, and Kryssing, *Robin* #0, 7.

45. Dixon et al., *Detective Comics* #680, 20.

46. Doug Moench, Ron Wagner, and Joe Rubinstein, "One Night in the War Zone," *Batman* #514 (January 1995), 7.

47. Moench, Wagner, and Rubinstein, *Batman* #514, 22.

48. Chuck Dixon et al., "Wings over Gotham," *Robin* #13 (January 1995), 7.

49. Bloom, "Trauma Theory Abbreviated," 11.

50. Dessner, "A Man's Own Father," 447.

51. Dixon et al., *Robin* #13, 19.

52. Terr, *Too Scared to Cry*, 314–5.

53. Dixon et al., *Robin* #13, 22.

54. Dixon et al., *Robin* #13, 22.

55. Homans, "Adoption Narratives," 5; Dessner, "A Man's Own Father," 447.

56. SpinMedia, "Batman Bale Says No to Robin," *Starpulse*, July 2, 2008, http://www.starpulse.com/news/index.php/2008/07/02/batman_bale_says_no_to_robin_

57. "The Gathering Storm" in *Shadows of the Bat: The Cinematic Saga of the Dark Knight*, directed by Constantine Nasr (2005; Burbank, CA: Warner Brothers, 2005), DVD.

58. Daniels, *The Complete History*, 164.

59. Marv Wolfman et al., "A Lonely Place of Dying Chapter Five: Rebirth," *Batman* #442 (December 1989), 13–15.

Dick Grayson and the Literary Tradition of Heroic Friendship

Emily Zinkin

The heroic friendship is a reoccurring trope found throughout history, from as early as the Assyrian epic *Gilgamesh*, and is still a common staple found in modern literature. This warrior duo seems to be a lasting symbol, recognized by most civilizations, even those thousands of years apart; it speaks of brotherhood, of a friendship stronger than love, forged by hardship. In the age of superheroes, the superhero-sidekick have become the very pinnacle of the heroic friendship in the modern day, with Batman and Robin, particularly Bruce and Dick, being the best example of this. To examine the Bruce-Dick dynamic in the context of the heroic-friendship, it is instructive to compare them to two other historical pairs; Achilles and Patroclus from the *Iliad* and Sherlock Holmes and Doctor Watson. All three are unique in that they usually had a long canon, as multiple writers would tackle and develop the same material and characters, and are well known literary examples of the heroic friendship in their historical context.

The Iliad *and the Hetairos/Therapon relationship*

The *Iliad* was written in the eighth century BCE; it covers two weeks in the Trojan War, and is attributed to Homer. While there are multiple characters in the epic poem, Achilles is the main focus, the poem focusing in the first line on the "rage of Achilles." Whilst Patroclus may be a relatively minor character in terms of line space and rank, he holds a special place at Achilles' side, and his death is the turning point of the Trojan War, as well as the cause of Achilles' rage.

The most common terms used to describe Achilles and Patroclus' relationship through the *Iliad* are therapon and hetairos, often interchangeable terms that refer to a heroic companion within the Greek army. However, it is generally accepted during the Trojan War therapon described a close subordinate companion, hence why it can be so readily applied to Patroclus and Achilles. The prevailing opinion is that the hetairos relationship is reciprocal, differentiating it somewhat from the term therapon, which is particularly demonstrated because Achilles is the hetairos of his own hetairos Patroclus. Furthermore, it is also generally accepted that therapon and hetairos are similar in role, despite possibly having different connotations.

This essay uses the accepted definition that hetairos meant "attendant" or "comrade-in-arms"[1] and the interpretation that a therapon is the preferred, closest hetairos to the hero in question. Patroclus, when fully identified, is both the therapon[2] and hetairos,[3] thus showing him to be not only companion and comrade of Achilles, but his chosen and particular friend.[4] Patroclus is the therapon of Achilles because he was chosen to be the particular companion of Achilles in the narrative. To quote Sinos: "the Patroklos figure provides the most valid solution to the artistic problem of finding for Achilles a genuine compliment, an omega for Achilles' alpha."[5] Therefore, in a literary context, being Achilles' therapon ultimately boils down to being his bosom companion and right-hand man.

The epithet "Dear friend" which Achilles uses in Ancient Greek is "hetairos" qualified by "philos" which connotes a mutual, sentimental affection shared by the two, showing Patroclus as a close and trusted companion above all others.[6] King Peleus tells his son Achilles "to be the bravest and best and excel above all others"[7] whereas Menoetius advises his son Patroclus, "My child, by birth Achilles is superior to you, but you are older. He is far stronger than you but your proper task is to give him words of wisdom and advise him and guide him—and he will listen to you for the best."[8] Achilles position as superior to Patroclus is explicitly dictated, but so is Patroclus' role as an advisor and whetstone for Achilles. Therefore Patroclus fulfills the role of right-hand man not only through his actions, but also through his advisory role, which he is allowed because of Achilles' trust and reliance on him.

The Batman/Robin relationship is slightly different, in the sense that Robin is actually younger than Batman, and Batman is seen as the mentor figure of their relationship. However, Dick establishes in his capacity as the first Robin that he acts as assistant and right-hand man in Batman's crime-fighting endeavors, much like the therapon/hetairos relationship.

Whilst Dick does not often offer advice he does temper Batman at his most extreme and is often the only person Batman listens to. When Batman claims proving Superman's guilt is his "whole life's mission" and slaps Dick in the face, Dick stands his ground and replies "Your grief has obsessed you with this idea of vengeance. I beg you ... give it up!" and later "In a plan of vengeance like this, I *can't* be with you!"[9]

In this sense, Dick is specifically Bruce's right-hand man because he is not only willing to confront and challenge Batman, but because he also ultimately continues to have faith in him, stating he could rely on him always in multiple issues and multiple ways. As Bruce states in the Hush comic arc, "Dick always spoke to me without fear. No matter what else had happened through the years, he has earned that right."[10] This mimics Patroclus' devotion to Achilles, in that he continues to appeal to Achilles when everyone has failed and is in turn rewarded for his loyalty. It is in this devotion that the two relationships cross time and place and resonate with one another. When describing his relationship to Bruce, Dick says,

> And me and Batman, we had an arrangement ... if he was in trouble, I got him out. If there was a death trap he couldn't handle on his own, I was there to get him free. He knew he could count on me. That's how we worked. He was my brother, my best friend.[11]

Both Dick and Patroclus are time and time again the only people who can and will stand up to Bruce and Achilles, and they are also often the only people who succeed in getting through to them, as well as the companion who they rely on utterly.

The Adventures of Sherlock Holmes *and Romantic Friendship*

Sherlock Holmes and Doctor John Watson were created by Sir Arthur Conan Doyle and first appeared in print in 1887 in *A Study in Scarlet*; Doyle would later go on to write 4 novels and 56 short stories about them. The consulting detective and his partner and biographer immediately captured the public's attention, to the extent that even after Doyle killed the character of Holmes off, public demand was so great he was forced to bring him back. Even after Doyle's death Holmes and Watson continued and have had countless books, films, television and radio shows—official and unofficial—made about them. The international popularity of the BBC's recent show *Sherlock*—a modern adaptation of Holmes and Watson's adventures—

and the 2009 blockbuster film starring Robert Downey, Jr. show that Holmes and Watson's appeal has not diminished.

Romantic friendship is a phenomenon common of the Victorian era, and has been described as "primarily a heterosexual ideal accessible to both genders."[12] It was considered a higher love than the sexual, an intimacy so great that Eve Sedgewick (queer studies scholar) said that if it existed in the same form today, it would be described as homosexual, despite its nonsexual condition.[13] The Victorian world was one of heavily divided gendered spheres, the public and the private, and full of highly scripted social interactions, both of which separated the sexes and kept their interactions very formalized at least until marriage. In this environment, close friendship and intimacy was often only to be found in persons of the same gender and, with the lack of public homosexual scandal and fear of accusation until the rise of sexology, combined with the need for separation of the sexes, romantic friendship was born.[14] There is a case for Holmes and Watson having a romantic friendship, which, due to its nature of domestic companionship and weighty emotional bond, is often seen as a valid alternative to a heterosexual love affair.

A heterosexual love affair is a wide and encompassing experience, but one of the main points of it is that if successful it is expected to culminate in cohabitation. Ironically enough, this is where Holmes and Watson's relationship begins; when Watson, having been recently honorably discharged from the Army, begins the search for a roommate. He soon finds Holmes through an old acquaintance, and the two of them soon meet and agree to live together in *A Study in Scarlet*. They then proceed to live together in happy harmony until 1888, where Watson meets and becomes engaged to Mary Morstan.[15] Despite his marriage and the pair's separate living arrangements, however, in the stories dated between 1888 and 1891, the year *The Final Problem* is set, Watson continues to follow and accompany Holmes' adventures. Nevertheless, in one of the few stories Holmes himself narrates, he speaks of Watson's new living arrangements, saying "the good Watson had at that time deserted me for a wife, the only selfish action which I can recall in our association. I was alone."[16] This shows that Holmes at least rated their domestic companionship equal, or above even that of marriage; sees Watson's "desertion" as a betrayal of their association; and he views it as an alternative to a heterosexual love affair.

This domestic association is also very much present between Batman and Dick as Robin, meaning that if we take this to be an element of romantic friendship, then it may be possible to apply this society-specific term to these other literary relationships. Batman adopts Robin when he too is orphaned around the same age Batman was, and whilst he later becomes Batman's sidekick, they, much like Holmes and Watson begin their relationship as a living arrangement, when Bruce Wayne takes in Dick Grayson as his ward. Their relationship then becomes both a domestic and warrior one, with Dick considering Wayne Manor his home, and Bruce claiming Dick enriches his domestic sphere and has become such a part of it "it feels emptier around here without you."[17] Much like Watson, Dick eventually moves out to attend college, and then to set himself up as Nightwing when he stopped being Robin; and, much like Watson he continued to be an important figure in Batman's adventures. When Bruce is thought to be dead in *Batman R.I.P* Dick even goes one step further than Watson and picks up the cowl, taking Bruce's place as Batman, though both Holmes and Bruce eventually returned.

This idea that the romantic friendship relationship can be just as meaningful, if not more so, as the heterosexual love affair and partnership continues with the other pairings as well. Batman and Robin even continue to refer to each other as partners, as they have done for the 75 years of their publishing history.[18] This is particularly noteworthy when considering that neither have had a love affair that has lasted nearly as long, thus making them the most enduring partnership in both their lives. Therefore whilst romantic friendship is a Victorian specific societal term, elements of it exist in even the Bruce and Dick dynamic, implying a connection throughout literary history in the heroic friendship.

Batman and Robin and the Superhero and Sidekick

Originally created in 1939 by Bob Kane during the golden age of comics, Bruce Wayne became "the Caped Crusader." Another common pastiche of the superhero trope is the sidekick; a daring, usually younger companion that aids the superhero on their quest for justice. The sidekick was a popular concept during both the golden and silver ages of comics and there are plenty of famous examples from both major publishing houses; with Marvel sending Captain America and Bucky to fight the Nazis and DC pairing Green Arrow with Speedy and giving the Flash his own Kid Flash. Yet none have been as popular or as enduring as Batman and his Robin. Bursting onto the comic book stage in 1940 in one of Batman's most shocking stories yet, Dick Grayson's parents fall to their deaths in front of both the young boy's and Batman's eyes. This gripping turn of events would leave the talented young acrobat orphaned with nowhere to go, and an immediate connection with Batman, who had also witnessed his parents' murders at a young age. Deciding to take the boy in and offering him the chance to avenge his parents' death, Batman began a partnership that has endured for the rest of his publishing history.

It is easy to begin to see parallels between Batman and Achilles; they are both fighting a war, though one on Troy and the other on crime, and are considered above their contemporaries in both skill and mythological weightiness.[19] In a classification of five types of fictive heroes, it is the Type II hero that we concern ourselves with when it comes to the superhero. The definition of Type II states that "If superior in degree to other men and his environment, the hero is the typical hero of romance, whose actions are marvelous but who is himself identified as a human being … [though] the ordinary laws of nature are slightly suspended."[20] When it comes to being human, though somewhat above the ordinary laws of nature and having a "semi-divine aura," we can clearly see this in Batman who, despite being one of the few supposedly ordinary humans in the superhero community, nevertheless displays an almost preternatural intelligence, including a knowledge of seemingly everything, and the martial arts skills to rival Bruce Lee. We can also see this in Achilles; whose divine heritage allows him to be "the best of the Achaeans" and in Sherlock Holmes whose deductive powers are almost omniscient (he is referred to as "masterful" at least once every three stories). Yet despite all of these strengths, Type II heroes are still "capable of error … and ultimately vulnerable."[21] And this is where the sidekick comes in.

It has been argued that what Dick as Robin ultimately stood for is Batman's own loss of innocence, and that by taking him in, he is seeking to ease the suffering he himself has felt by not being able to see justice done to his parents' killer and prevent further loss of innocence until adulthood.[22] However, much as with the therapon and hero, it is a mutually beneficial relationship, with Dick injecting empathy, positive energy, and stability into the Dark Knight's ultimately gloomy life. Whereas the hero is the dominant figure, as well as the better fighter, who often had to cover his sidekick in battle, he is offered a companion on his quest.

Batman only existed alone for an editorial year before Dick was added, and the short periods without a Robin have been particularly dark parts in his history since; Dick set a precedent of stability which Bruce tries to recreate with the other Robins. Whilst the assumed identity aspect of the superhero genre allows identities to be discarded and picked up by other people, Dick, as both Robin and himself is nevertheless an important part of Batman's and Bruce's identity, and his story. Dick encapsulated and set the modern baseline for the enduring literary traits of the sidekick; the less skilled assistant who learns from their mentor and in many ways aspires to be him; whether that means fighting super-villains, solving mysteries or conquering Troy. Furthermore, the sidekick in the heroic friendship is meant to become a necessity in the superhero's life, and his loss or absence anathema and destabilizing, making it an interesting reciprocated relationship where both need the other, though for different reasons. Dick Grayson, by creating the role of Robin, the most enduring sidekick, has become an important character in the heroic friendship, as well as adding to its long historical narrative.

Wider Relationship Context

Whilst all three pairings are a product of their society, the heroic friendship as a relationship is more than just the societal specific role it has been assigned. It is this which connects the relationships through time and demonstrates that heroic friendship is a narrative trope that transcends individual societies, as Dick and Bruce well demonstrate.

THE SECOND SELF

The concept of the second self in the heroic friendship has several parts to it; firstly, that the companion is so necessary to the hero's identity, that they themselves are part of it, both from a personal sense, and a meta-textual sense. Secondly, that this is shown through their behavior paralleling the hero's so much that they almost become a second version of the hero; acting as they would do. And finally, that they aspire to be, or even manage to achieve becoming the hero themselves, though this ascension never lasts that long before the natural order of the narrative is reasserted.[23]

As Achilles' counterpart in the *Iliad*, Patroclus is responsible for Achilles' heroic identity and this is recognized in a number of ways; when Achilles refuses to fight, it is Patroclus' appeal which seems to move Achilles the most, and he immediately capitulates to Patroclus' suggestion he return to the fight in Achilles' armor. In doing this Patroclus is trying to protect both his fellow Achaeans but also Achilles' heroic reputation, which he does when his death spurns Achilles into re-joining the battle, thus meta-textually saving Achilles' heroic identity amongst the Achaeans, but also to the readers in the context of the *Iliad*. However, by donning Achilles armor he has "taken upon himself not only the armor but also the heroic identity of Achilles."[24]

This is similar to the *Battle for the Cowl* plotline in the *Batman* comics, where, after Bruce Wayne's supposed death, two past Robins—Dick Grayson and Jason Todd—both don the cowl and assume Batman's costume and superhero identity to continue his work. Whilst the identity could technically be assumed by anyone, there seems to be a literary tradition whereby it is right and proper for the companion to do so, as they seem to "deserve" it, as someone who has learnt from and been close to the hero. This may explain why Achilles is so enraged when he sees Hector in his armor, as it was given to Patroclus, his chosen companion, and has been stolen by his enemy, and by wearing it Hector has become a false second self of Achilles. Jason, using guns as Batman and extreme violence goes against Bruce's ideals and thus makes himself the false second self of Batman. Dick, on the other hand, having been asked by the current Robin to take up the mantle and, living by what Bruce has taught him, becomes the true second self. This includes giving up the mantle once Bruce returns and returning to their previous status in the heroic friendship.

Furthermore, Dick in-part considers himself a reflection of Bruce, stating,

> You taught me, you showed me, you encouraged me—you never lied to me and you never demanded that I be anything I'm not. I didn't imitate you because you insisted that I do so, but because I wanted to. Of all the men I knew, you were most worthy of imitation.[25]

Ultimately, the scholar Van Nortwick best concludes what the second-self is, when he describes it as "a figure who represents parts of the hero that he is denying or has lost touch with, usually through arrogance and pride."[26] To be the hero's second self, the companion must also be their link to humanity.

Link to Humanity

The heroic friendship is a balancing act of the companion acting as both an emotional guide and empathetic link between the brilliant but detached hero and the rest of the world.[27] The hero believes himself to have risen above humanity but the companion thrives in it, and often has many social links and enjoys others' company. Watson appears to enjoy friends at his Rugby club and to have kept in contact with people from his medical training and army days, whereas Holmes only connects with acquaintances through the series when they have a case for him. Similarly, Dick is shown to have friends both in school and within the superhero community, such as the Teen Titans, whereas Batman only connects to people through his work.

The *Iliad* opens with a statement about the "wrath of Achilles" and he displays little pity or remorse until the very end when he is confronted by Priam. The only real divergence of this is at Patroclus' death, when his emotions finally override his pride in the face of his loss. But for the companion to act as this link, he must also remain loyal and sympathetic to his hero, as we can see when Patroclus claims he must return to Achilles swiftly despite not being told to do so.[28] This shows special attention to Achilles' moods and wants, and may explain how he came to be his chosen companion above others. Such loyalty can also be seen in the Batman comics, particularly during the *Bruce Wayne: Murderer?* story arc, where Batman is accused of murder and framed so convincingly that even his companions begin to believe it, except for Dick Grayson, who continues to believe in Batman's innocence even with mounting evidence to the contrary and little reason to think otherwise apart from his long history of loyalty. Even when Bruce tells him to abandon him, Dick replies "Just abandon you? Sorry, I wasn't raised that way. You've been set up and you need all the friends you can get."[29]

Bruce, especially as Batman, often appears so detached and above everyone else, that many are too scared to even try appealing to his humanity, and it is often only Dick who dares to question him or take him to task about his behavior. In the *Bruce Wayne: Fugitive* plot-arc where Batman declares Bruce Wayne only a mask and Batman the true identity, it is again Dick Grayson who challenges this, and attempts to humanize him once again by using their relationship. Before Batman can leave Dick stops him by saying "If there is no Bruce Wayne, then who IS Dick Grayson the adopted son of? Who raised me? Can you answer that?"[30] This role as the hero's link to humanity is true for the companion in all heroic friendships, and why they occupy their exalted place in the hero's life.

Social Microcosm

The true test of the heroic friendship that goes beyond society-specific descriptions and even verges into the pathological is the social microcosm; the fact that the hero and his companion seem to have a friendship that transcends all others, and even seems to be capable of replacing them. They display characteristics of only needing each other, and thus existing in their own social microcosm.[31]

The previously discussed domesticity is a large part of this; in the *Iliad* the special, synchronic parallelisms of Patroclus' to Achilles's actions and vice versa are constantly presented in their scenes together. Patroclus and Achilles present a homely picture in Book 9 with their relay performance when the embassy arrives, and Patroclus cooking,[32] and Achilles intervening and arranging the final apportionment of food in symbiosis. The happy equilibrium leaves the impression of a necessity to the relationship within the displayed harmony, which in turn foreshadows the collapse of control of the survivor should one be removed from their microcosm, as both people are necessary for this harmony to be achieved. Homer strives to present the connection between them as intense, and does this through the extraordinary complementarity and self-sufficiency of the couple. When Achilles declares "Oh father Zeus and Athena and Apollo, if only none of the Trojans would escape death, and none of the Argives, but only you and I could survive destruction, so that we alone could break Troy's holy crown of towers,"[33] it is shocking. But it is also a genuine desire, and if Patroclus and he could defeat the Trojans by themselves and share the glory whilst everyone else died, Achilles can see no happier circumstances. As Johannes Haubold summarizes, Achilles and Patroclus are "a circle which gives the impression of being self-contained precisely because Patroclus replaces Achilles' other social bonds."[34]

This state of affairs is mimicked by Holmes and Watson, as Watson, despite pointing out Holmes' detachment from most people fairly frequently, describes their relationship as: "Holmes was a man of habits ... and I had become one of them ... a comrade ... upon whose nerve he could place some reliance ... a whetstone for his mind."[35] Thus showing that to Holmes, notorious for his drug habits, Watson has become another addiction within his life. This explains why Holmes' growing obsession with Moriarty only really takes off after Watson leaves him for domesticity with Mary Morstan. Holmes' claims in *The Final Problem* in his farewell note to Watson that "no possible conclusion ... could be more congenial to me than this," show that, with Watson removed from their social microcosm, his world has been destabilized enough that he considers his life satisfactorily fulfilled if he can bring Moriarty down with him.[36] With the necessary social microcosm disrupted, dying in the attempt to gain glory is the only solution Holmes and Achilles can see, as it allows them to retain their heroic status, without having to live without their stabilizing other half.

Dick, as the first Robin, provides Bruce with a companionship that brings him great contentment, to the extent where he does not seem to seek out any further. After Dick vacates the Robin position, Bruce continues to fill it with others, trying to regain the companionship that he has lost with Dick moving away. After Jason dies Bruce gives it up as a failure and both Tim and Stephanie, and even Damian, have to convince him of their worthiness of taking up the Robin mantle. Dick is the ideal that all other Robins must live up to, him and Bruce being seen as the ideal heroic friendship within Batman comics.

Bruce states "I miss those days" when talking about Dick's time as Robin, as he has never managed to reach that level of companionship with any other partners, where any other company is unneeded.[37] After being fired and replaced by Jason, Dick eventually confronts Bruce about the matter, and Bruce replies that he asked Jason to join him because he was lonely.[38] Since Dick's departure as Robin, Bruce has cut himself off and isolated himself much more than he did as Dick's partner while simultaneously trying to recreate the connection he initially had when Dick was Robin. Furthermore while Dick and Bruce made their own social microcosm of two and were, for a while all the other needed, Bruce has never had that relationship with another Robin, because he has considered Nightwing a partner as well as them, rather than them being his only partner.

The same can be said for Dick, as even as Nightwing, a supposedly solo superhero, Dick has always been quick to reply to Bruce's calls for aid, and the two have regained much of their closeness as their relationship slowly mended over the years. Dick still considers Bruce responsible for who he has become, even as an independent adult, as he himself says, "You're a part of me, Bruce. I can't deny it. And I don't want to any longer. I just wanted you to know that. That, and one other thing—I'm proud to have been Robin."[39] The hero Dick has become is reliant on the hero who shaped him and continues to shape him, despite what difficulties they have had; Dick states,

> The effect Bruce has had on my life is profound. There's no question that knowing him had changed me, changed my relationship to the world, profoundly. I'll admit that there were times when I felt restrained somehow.... More often though, this work that I've done with Bruce has felt like an avocation, a perfect expression of everything I've ever been capable of becoming.[40]

Conclusion

The heroic friendship is a literary tradition that goes back as far as the written word, and though each society will create its own version of it, and its own characters to fulfill it, it is nevertheless a continuing narrative. Starting with the ancient epics, we can still see traits of the epic hero and companion in Dick Grayson and his relationship with Bruce Wayne. A heroic friendship has many of the same traits throughout history, despite societal specific definitions for the relationship. Ultimately Dick Grayson and Bruce Wayne are the definitive modern heroic friendship in that they not only fulfill the traits of a heroic friendship, but all societal specific versions of it as well. When it comes to our most modern version of the heroic friendship, the superhero and sidekick, they are who we think of, and they have so dominated our culture that we now project this version of the heroic friendship back through time as well. Dick and Bruce may have traits of the therapon/hetairos relationship and romantic friendship, but Achilles and Patroclus and Holmes and Watson are now commonly referred to as hero and sidekick. The creation of Dick Grayson in the Batman ethos has not only been an effect of our continued fixation with the heroic friendship in literature, but has also added to it, and brought that fixation to multiple new generations. In Dick Grayson's own words "The Batman taught me, guided me, trained me. What I am I owe to him. What more can I say?"[41]

Notes

1. D. Sinos, *Achilles, Patroklos and the Meaning of Philos* (Washington: H. Kowatsch, 1980), 30.
2. Homer, *The Iliad* (Oxford: Oxford University Press, 2008), 17.255.271, 23.90.
3. Homer, *Iliad*, 11.602, 24.416.
4. G. Nagy, *The Best of the Achaeans: Concepts of the Hero in Archaic Greek Poetry* (Oxford: John Hopkins, 1998), 159–60.
5. Sinos, *Achilles, Patroklos*, 29.
6. Homer, *Iliad*, 1.345.
7. Homer, *Iliad*, 11.784.
8. Homer, *Iliad*, 11.786–9.
9. Edmond Hamilton, Curt Swan and George Klein, "The Clash of Cape and Cowl," *World's Finest Comics* #153 (New York: DC Comics, November 1965), 5.
10. Jeff Loeb, Jim Lee, and Scott Williams, "Hush (Part VIII of XII)—The Dead," *Batman* #615 (New York: DC Comics, July 2003), [12].
11. Grant Morrison et al., "Blackest Night, Part One: Pearly and the Pit," *Batman and Robin* (1) #7 (New York: DC Comics, March 2010), [19–20].
12. C. Oulton, *Romantic Friendship in Victorian Literature* (Hampshire: Ashgate, 2007), 3.
13. L. Faderman, *Surpassing the Love of Men* (London: HarperCollins, 1998), 22.
14. E. Sedgwick, *Between Men: English Literature and Male Homosocial Desire* (New York: Columbia University Press, 1985).
15. A. C. Doyle, "The Sign of The Four" from *The Case-Book of Sherlock Holmes* (Oxford: Oxford University Press, 2009).
16. Doyle, "The Adventure of the Blanched Soldier" from *The Case-Book of Sherlock Holmes*, 64.
17. Len Wein et al., "Color Me Deadly!" *Batman #316* (October 1979), 6.

18. Devin Grayson et al., "Sibling Rivalry," *Batman: Gotham Knights #14* (New York: DC Comics, April 2001).
19. R. Rollin, "Beowulf to Batman: The Epic Hero and Pop Culture," in *College English* Vol 31, No. 5 (February 1970), 4.
20. N. Frye, *Anatomy of Criticism* (Princeton: Princeton University Press, 2000), 33.
21. Frye, *Anatomy*, 33.
22. J. Black, "Robin: Innocent Bystander" in *Batman Unauthorized* (Dallas: BenBella Books, 2008), 15.
23. M. Fantuzzi, *Achilles in Love* (Oxford: Oxford University Press, 2012).
24. G. Nagy, *Homer the Classic (Hellenic Studies)* (New York: Harvard, 1979), 34.
25. Dennis O'Neil, Greg Land, and Mike Sellers, "Dead Simple" *Nightwing miniseries* #4 (New York: DC Comics, December 1995), 21.
26. T. van Nortwick, *Imagining Men: Ideals of Masculinity in Ancient Greek Culture* (Stanford: Praeger Publishers, 2008), 84.
27. G. Zanker, *The Heart of Achilles* (Michigan: University of Michigan Press, 1997), 138–40.
28. Homer, *Iliad*, 11.649.
29. Chuck Dixon et al., "Bruce Wayne: Murderer?, Part Three: Bustout!" *Nightwing* #65 (New York: DC Comics, March 2002), [13].
30. Ed Brubaker, Scott McDaniel, and Andy Owens, "The Scene of the Crime," *Batman* #600 (April 2002), 17.
31. Fantuzzi, *Achilles in Love*.
32. Homer, *Iliad*, 9.204–17a.
33. Homer, *Iliad*, 16.97–100.
34. J. Haubold, *Homer's People: Epic Poetry and Social Formation* (Cambridge: Cambridge University Press, 2000), 78.
35. Doyle, "The Creeping Man" from *The Case-Book of Sherlock Holmes*, 50.
36. Doyle, "The Final Problem" from *The Case-Book of Sherlock Holmes*, 554.
37. Judd Winick, Doug Mahnke, and Tom Nguyen, "Under the Hood, Part 2: First Strike," *Batman* #636 (March 2005), [13].
38. Jim Starlin, Jim Aparo, and Mike DeCarlo, "White Gold and Truth," *Batman* #416 (February 1988), 18.
39. Michael Reaves, Stan Woch, and Rodin Rodriguez, "Night of the Dragon," *Teen Titans Spotlight* #14 (New York: DC Comics, September1987), 22.
40. Devin Grayson et al., "The Ride's Over," *Nightwing #100* (February 2005), [3–4].
41. Marv Wolfman et al., "The Judas Contract Book 3—There Shall Come a Titan," *Tales of the Teen Titans* #44 (New York: DC Comics, July 1984), 21.

"The Loyal Heart"
Homosocial Bonding and Homoerotic Subtext Between Batman and Robin, 1939–1943[1]

Catherine M. Vale

Since his debut in *Detective Comics #27* in 1939, Batman has enchanted Americans of all ages. In contrast to Superman, the original superhero, Batman embodies the darker side of "truth, justice, and the American way."[2] While Batman's grim perspective has come to define his character, the addition of a child sidekick in 1940 provided both levity and controversy to Gotham City. Robin's role in the Batman mythos is as recognizable as his mentor's, and his historic origins reveal much about the culture of 1930s and 1940s America.

Popular culture does not exist in a vacuum—thus, the basis of this analysis is drawn from *The Batman Chronicles: Volumes 1–7*, a collection of all Batman comics in chronological order, in conjunction with scholarly commentary on Batman and Robin in relation to historical events and issues of the 1930s and 40s.[3] Original creators Bill Finger and Bob Kane based the character and plots of early Batman comics on cultural norms and styles dating back to the traditional masculine American heroes of 19th century dime novels and early 20th century pulps. Like these predecessors, Batman appealed to early male readership as a strong, individualistic, and violent character who acted both above the law and outside a society on the brink of chaos. Americans keenly felt this chaos in their own lives as they struggled to recover from the Great Depression. However, World War II drastically changed the tone and audience of comic books in the United States. Readership by adolescents and servicemen quickly grew, pushing Batman publisher Detective Comics to change the character's narrative style. DC created the altogether wholesome Robin, the Boy Wonder, specifically to appeal to children and their wary parents. Robin's addition is significant not only for his demographic pull, but for the role he played in changing the hypermasculine environment of superhero comics, in which father-son bonding became more central to Batman's homosocial world than antagonistic relationships with other adult males. While Batman's early creative teams did not intend to create a homoerotic relationship between Batman and Robin, the early comics featuring the Dynamic Duo present a relationship between the two that reflects a homosocial setting that is, on occasion, homoerotic in nature.

Scholars use homosociality to examine a wide range of intense nonsexual bonds in male-dominated environments, from pirates and medieval knights to college fraternities. Homosocial environments often reinforce stereotypical hypermasculine traits, such as physical prowess and violent dominance. While a few women might exist on the fringe, their primary function is to serve male relationships as prizes, sexual favors, and child bearers. Because these environments lack female participants and center on male bonding, mentorship, and rivalry, they can also mirror or produce homosexual relationships. The popular term "bromance" is a prime example of how these relationships become conflated.[4]

The relationship between Batman and Robin in particular serves as a callback to the father-son bonds of an idealized paternalistic America. In this fantasy, according to historian Dan Backer, "many men want to feel both 'wild' and strong yet emotionally open and vulnerable with other men." This fantasy also celebrates emotional and psychological separation from the women in their lives, whose only purpose is served through fulfilling sexual desires, as seen in Batman's lack of a serious female romantic partner post–Robin.[5] Ultimately, Batman and Robin's relationship blurs parental, collegial, and romantic bonds that simultaneously recall and challenge previous iterations of homosocial frontier fiction in America.

The Origins of Hypermasculine Superhero Comics

Although sequential art and comics began as early as the Middle Ages and were popularized through the creation of the printing press and the Protestant Reformation, the comic *book* in American culture did not become popular until the creation of the superhero in 1938.[6] Superman graced the newsstands on the cover of DC Comics' *Action Comics #1* and became "the ideal that spawned an industry."[7] Superman was an instant hit, selling 900,000 copies per month of *Action Comics* compared to the

1930s comic book standard of 200,000 to 400,000.[8] This unprecedented turn of events spawned a superhero craze in which readership among youth reached as high as 95 percent by the World War II era.[9] Naturally, DC sought to capitalize on Superman's popularity and turned to young cartoonist Bob Kane to create another superhero for the company. Kane accepted, eager to make more than the meager salary of most anonymous assembly line comics' artists and writers. With the help of writer Bill Finger, the two created a character that was a combination of popular culture characters and historical information, including *The Mask of Zorro*, a film called *The Bat Whispers*, a radio show featuring the great pulp hero *The Shadow*, and the inventions of Leonardo Da Vinci.[10] This character, known as "The Bat-Man" in his earliest days, would later become Batman, a character recognized nationwide on insignia alone.

Despite their heavy popularity, artistic circles derided comics as vulgar and low class. Nevertheless, many young artists and writers pursued careers in comics as a way to rebuild economically during the Great Depression, whose shadow lingered over the late 1930s even as World War II approached.[11] Batman's "dark outsider" identity seemed in many ways to counter the disillusionment that clouded the era.[12] Batman acted as fantasy fulfillment for his young creators through both of his personas. Kane and Finger designed Batman to "strike terror" as a "weird figure of darkness," something decidedly different from Superman's bright red and blue suit soaring above the gleaming City of Tomorrow.[13] While Superman was known to friends as bumbling Clark Kent, Batman operated in Gotham City high society as Bruce Wayne, a rich and charming playboy with little regard for others. Despite the character's contemporary timeliness, Batman's darker side and individualist mentality also stemmed from earlier dime novel and pulp figures that had proven popular in past decades.

Dime novels, the first mass-produced story-paper popular fiction in the United States, are the original late 19th century incarnation of popular masculine norms and frontier fantasy in American literature. Dime novels stressed the fantasy of frontier life as a "lurid adventure" steeped in violence. Police figures were oftentimes portrayed as "stupid louts" while lone male heroes killed their way to victory and independence in the Wild West.[14] Dime novels mirrored comic books in significant ways. Most popular amongst Americans from lower socioeconomic classes, publishers cheaply produced dime novels in mass quantities on low quality paper stock for maximum profit. Just as comics' readers would struggle under the financial uncertainty of the Depression in the 1930s, dime novel readers suffered economically under the corrupt regimes of robber barons.[15] Despite high sales, highbrow critics feared that young wayward boys would be influenced by such stories to commit crime.[16] However, as urban living populations overtook traditional rural American lifestyles, popular tastes shifted to the spell of the city. Popular American literature changed in response to these cultural and geographic shifts with the creation of pulps.

Like dime novel protagonists, pulp heroes were dark, brooding characters with single-track minds bent on solving crime; however, they differed in focusing on the new urban frontier of the twentieth century. Pulps gained their highest popularity in the 1920s and had the same readership as early dime novel and comic book readers; in fact, many pulp and comic book publishers would later share writers, editors, and illustrators. Characterization and plot between the two mediums tended to overlap not only due to shared talent but because comic book publishers pushed for storylines and characters that were proven sellers. Comics frequently functioned as an extension of action and mystery pulp stories.[17] Kane and Finger listed popular pulp heroes Zorro, Green Hornet, the Shadow, the Phantom, Doc Savage, and even comic strip pulp hero Dick Tracy as inspirations for Batman.[18] These men embodied the masculine image that Batman would continue to portray in the comics medium—one of physical strength, solitude, and self-reliance.

Like earlier dime novel and pulp protagonists, Batman represents the masculine hero of the frontier, a place lacking any semblance of law or reason. Batman's frontier is Gotham City, a quintessentially urban imitation of New York City. Kane and Finger designed Gotham as a place where both old and new money ideals of "high civility" fused with "lower-class" violence.[19] Brutal, dark Gotham City is filled with crime, incompetent cops, and notorious criminals. This mirrored the environment of Depression-era America's limiting policies, like the Volstead Act, and mob violence, like Al Capone.[20] In this environment, Batman is driven to fight violence with violence, exacting his own brutal brand of justice. As a singular figure, he represented the desires of Depression-era men who longed to be the ultimate symbol of justice in an unjust world.[21] This justice, however, could only be attained through violence, the most stereotypical act of masculinity, an activity by which white males claimed and conquered the frontier.[22]

In dime novels, pulps, and Batman's earliest issues, violence is the primary representation of homosocial relationships in frontier fiction, chiefly between the detective and the criminal or the detective and law enforcement. In both dime novels and pulps, women are used as both prize and unattainable ideal, yet both of these functions serve to reestablish the "morally contaminating bond" between male antagonists while also emphasizing a "heroic masculinity unhinged from the demands of heterosexual coupling and reproduction."[23] In these early issues, Batman comics oozed pulp. Like the cowboys who roamed the Wild West, Batman traversed Gotham City alone.[24] A detective like the many hardboiled pulp heroes who came before him, Batman is serious, violent, and single-minded in the pursuit of justice. He kills opponents on multiple occasions, an action that would be forever taboo after Robin's addition.[25] These traits continued to symbolize the hypermasculine strength of the pulp hero. Vigilante status, from cowboys to private eyes, continued in Batman's early antagonistic relationship with Gotham City Police Commissioner James Gordon.[26]

In his earliest appearances, Batman uses makeup and costume regularly to navigate the urban environment. Bats themselves often featured in pulp stories because they were "nocturnal, secretive, [and] dark cloaked," thus creating an atmosphere of mystery and intrigue.[27] Bruce Wayne is characterized as a wealthy playboy and "bored young socialite" in the vein of Green Hornet, the Shadow, and the Phantom.[28] As the quintessential rich playboy, he is simultaneously bored with life and content to coast on his wealth while enjoying the pleasures of upper class entertainment and women.[29] While Batman represented stereotypical masculine traits of the 1930s and 1940s, Bruce Wayne's wealthy and self-indulgent persona closely resembles that of an 18th and 19th century dandy or 20th century fop.[30] Like Zorro's alter ego Don Diego de la Vega, Bruce acts as "frivolous, effeminate, [and] apolitical" so that no one will suspect him of being the hypermasculine Batman.[31] The playboy persona not only represents a case of false identity, but the conflict between masculine and feminine. However, Batman is ultimately a quintessential masculine hero in the homosocial world of the frontier. While these two personas eventually coalesce in a third "true" identity to commiserate with Robin, Batman alone emerges as the "true" identity of the character in these early issues.

Despite their primary focus on a solitary hypermasculine hero, dime novels and pulps provided a few possible inspirations for Robin in Chick Carter and Junior Tracy. Young wards of dime novel hero Nick Carter and pulp detective Dick Tracy respectively, both boys came from humble origins and were not the biological children of their mentors. Chick and Dick Jr. are shown as highly capable of the same level of deductive reasoning and fortitude as their role models, and at some points even surpass them.[32] Like the later Robin, the two sidekicks directly address the child reader and participate in the learning process of becoming a detective, focusing particularly on a father-son relationship in which burgeoning manhood was a key factor. While these relationships were minor appendages in relation to the borderline-homoerotic hostile relations between their mentors and the criminal element, father-son bonding would become paramount for Batman and Robin in the context of a new social order.

"The Sensational Character Find of 1940: Robin—The Boy Wonder"[33]

The Caped Crusader only patrols Gotham City solo for eleven months before the addition of his ward, whose inclusion greatly changed the stories' tone and character.[34] Before Robin, Batman was his own primary conversational partner. Artist depictions rarely gave the character any semblance of joy, and even his smile was described as "grim."[35] Story panels were almost always set at night in back alleys, rooftops, and criminal hideaways in dark hues of brown, blue, and black. In addition to stoically killing or maiming criminals, Batman was also oftentimes on the run from the authorities.

Kane and Finger's liberal use of dime novel and pulp influences implies that DC originally catered Batman to adult men. Like their predecessors, comics' cheap price and printing material implied that comic literature was neither highbrow nor memorable.[36] While the books' violent illustrations and salacious storylines initially achieved high levels of popularity among adult males of lower socioeconomic class, the onset of World War II brought two significant reader demographics to the genre in children and servicemen.[37] Robin was added to the Batman mythos to draw and maintain the new profitable child demographic.[38] Instead of gritty and morally ambiguous pulp figure Batman, readers would soon come to embrace a Batman who, with his new adolescent sidekick Robin, would exemplify "the purest expression of dominant social values" in American society during the 1940s, a culture that would include continued celebration of hypermasculinity.[39]

DC Comics' attention to Batman and Robin's adolescent readers is most notable in its shift in marketing.[40] Unlike earlier tales, Batman and Robin often spoke directly to the reader with advice ranging from warning against the dangers of criminality to suggesting that children see the 1940 World's Fair.[41] Letters signed by the duo mentioned the high volume of correspondence received from loyal young readers. In addition, a paper cutout Batplane insert readers assembled to reenact Batman and Robin's comic adventures allowed children to interact with the material in new ways.[42]

Within the stories themselves, Robin enabled Batman to connect with comics' fast growing young audience and made them feel as if they too could fight alongside the Caped Crusader. Throughout these early stories, Robin is frequently portrayed as a David versus multitudes of Gotham City Goliaths.[43] Robin is oftentimes overcome by bands of criminal foes, but if one giant brute is up against the Boy Wonder, a flick of his mighty slingshot brings the imposing criminal down. Crooks are often surprised by Robin's fighting prowess in relation to his slight stature and age, highlighting Robin's role as wish fulfillment for child readers.[44]

Unlike Batman's Bruce Wayne persona, Dick Grayson appears genuine both in and out of costume. Dick oftentimes acts "undercover" as a shoeshine boy on the street to gather information but almost never uses makeup to disguise his looks, while Batman continues to liberally use disguise well into Robin's tenure. Outside of his duties as Robin, Dick's life revolves around spending time with Bruce and completing homework assignments. This implies that Robin attends school somewhere, but the reader is never shown Dick's school life.[45] While this seems relatively odd for a character meant to appeal directly to the child reader, it ultimately shows that Dick's and Robin's lives are one and the same (minus the physical violence). In direct contrast to the major character split between Batman and Bruce Wayne, Robin often appears as a more well-adjusted character.

Like Batman, Robin's identity is tied to economic class conflict. However, unlike Bruce, Dick's less economically fortunate background leaves him without financial support and makes him dependent on Bruce's generosity.[46] His introductory story seems to follow these lines when the creators state that his superhero name honors the legendary Robin Hood, friend of the poor. However, the writers' reasoning for this connection is because Dick is "a laughing, fighting, young daredevil who scoffs at danger like the legendary Robin Hood," rather than the assumed character trait in which one would steal from the rich to give to those in need.[47] Like other legendary pulp heroes, Robin's primary concern is hypermasculine in nature, focusing on aggression and violence in the alluring dregs of urbanity.

While some early Batman themes remained intact, notable new themes arose after the Boy Wonder was added to the series. Like earlier Batman issues, Batman and Robin stories had a decidedly economic and urban crime focus while remaining mystery and detective stories. However, more stories featured child victims and criminals, oftentimes ending with moral platitudes for young readers instead of death and grim satisfaction.

Whenever Batman and Robin partake in any crime fighting spree, the lines are rife with puns and other bad jokes, and both characters smile and jokingly converse as they fight.[48] Even when fighting alone, both Batman and Robin make light of the situation as they punch a criminal's face or kick him to the ground.[49] The end for many criminals may be much less severe than the death sentence that Batman's earliest foes received, yet the comical portrayal of violence acts as a desensitizing tactic used by creators to make Batman and Robin's antics seem like good clean fun instead of brutal beatings. In essence, this style minimizes the antagonistic relationship between the detective hero and the criminals he seeks to apprehend.

Robin's addition also brought cooperation with the Gotham City police force where previously there had been none.[50] Newer stories showed Batman and Robin venturing outside of Gotham City to protect citizens from crime as approved by the federal government. In these tales, Batman and Robin become state-sanctioned representatives of the entire nation.[51] Rather than sticking with the anti-law enforcement stance that had permeated dime novels and pulps, Batman stories sought to connect the reader with the benefits of cooperation with the American state. This was usually marketed as blatant advertisement for the war effort.

Instead of continuing as an illustrated version of the pulps of the previous decade, the Batman and Robin comics evolved into what DC hoped would appeal to children and servicemen alike. The colors were brighter and Batman and Robin fought crime with a smile.[52] As a result, the two primary antagonistic relationships that defined the homosocial environment of Batman comics were reduced, leaving Batman and Robin alone as the primary focus. In time, however, this focus began to raise concerns over the boundaries of male companionship.

Homosocial Bonding and Homoerotic Subtext

While Robin's introduction to the Batman mythos clearly marks a shift in demographic, the resulting relationship between the Caped Crusader and his ward became more complex and controversial than creators anticipated. Batman comics' homosocial setting as gleaned from pulps and dime novels greatly blurred the lines between father and son, adult and child, and partner and lover. As a result, Batman and Robin's relationship in these early years shared paternal, collegial, and romantic bonds.

Instead of branching out into new serious romantic interests with female characters after adopting Dick, Bruce becomes firmly ensconced in his pseudo-father role. Bruce's paternalistic relationship with Dick is clear both inside and outside the duo's fighting personas. This ranges from Bruce forcing Dick to stay home and finish schoolwork rather than fight crime to Batman scolding Robin in the field on his pun choices in the midst of crime fighting.[53] While rarely shown, domestic life in the Wayne household still sheds light on the familial bond creators sought to portray between Bruce and Dick. The two initially lived in an upper-middle class suburban home and neighborhood despite the implausibility of such an arrangement for a millionaire crime fighter.[54] Within the home, domestic life mostly involved relaxing activities like reading or doing homework by the fire.

Despite these domestic depictions, from Robin's perspective (which, as noted earlier, is essentially interchangeable with Dick's), Batman and Robin are both partners and "pals." Whenever this friendship is broken or threatened, creators show Robin taking great offense.[55] Bruce also regularly refers to Dick as his friend and, judging by the amount of responsibility given to Robin, treats him as a colleague.[56] Throughout the stories, Robin flies the Batplane, drives the Batmobile, completes undercover solo missions, and is out all hours of the night fighting grown men with Batman.[57] Because DC sought to appeal to children, this focus allowed readers to view themselves as Batman's friend and equal while simultaneously seeking parental guidance and love through Batman's leader- and mentorship. Like Chick Carter and Junior Tracy, the hope that one could be both respected and cared for by one's father figure falls in line with homosocial frontier ideals.

In addition to paternal and collegial depictions between Batman and Robin, the Boy Wonder also often filled the "damsel in distress" role in many Batman comics. In almost every Batman story from Robin's inclusion to 1943, Robin is captured by criminals and thought to be dead. When this occurs, Batman exhibits a "rare" loss of composure distinct from his typical cold poise in earlier stories.[58] In contrast to Superman's Lois Lane, Batman and Robin's relationship allowed creators to exclude female characters and romantic relationships from Batman storylines. A member of the duo is often shown waiting in the manner of a domestic partner for the other to return home from either a day of work, school, or secret mission.[59] By using Robin in the role of romantic partner, the Dynamic Duo's relationship becomes further muddied.

Ultimately, creators intended for the reader to see Batman and Robin as much more than comrades in arms against evil. This unusual relationship points an idealized view of a father from the specific viewpoint of a son with "a loyal heart."[60] Yet, regardless of intention, Batman and Robin's relationship contained both homosocial and homoerotic elements elevated by the reduction in antagonism between Batman and other male figures. These elements would both become demonized by Cold War–era critics and embraced by readers searching for representation in popular literature.

From the moment dime novels stepped into the American consciousness, citizens questioned the role of frontier fiction in adolescent male delinquency.[61] However, in the forcibly sanitized cultural environment of Cold War America, Fredric Wertham's *Seduction of the Innocent* (1954) became the first to posit a new and potentially threatening relationship between Batman and Robin—homosexuality. The implication that children who read comic books were either homosexual or socially stunted in regards to both platonic and romantic relationships came in large part from the lack of fulfilling heterosexual relationships in superhero stories and the substitution of homosocial relationships in their stead.[62] Wertham states that the relationship between Bruce Wayne and Dick Grayson "is like a wish dream of two homosexuals living together" that threatens the very fabric of society by corrupting young boys into leading deviant lives.[63] Despite the denials of later Batman creators, countless observers have questioned the purity of the relationship between Batman and Robin. In addition, multiple scholars have written about Batman as a queer figure as a result of Wertham's writings despite the fact that most soundly denounce *Seduction of the Innocent* for misleading quotations and insufficient evidence.[64] As Andy Medhurst states,

> Denied even the remotest possibility of supportive images of homosexuality within the dominant heterosexual culture, gay people have had to fashion what we could out of the imageries of dominance, to snatch illicit meanings from the fabric of normality, to undertake a corrupt decoding for the purposes of satisfying marginalized desires.[65]

For many, Batman and Robin exist as gay cultural icons despite the nonexistence of a canonical romantic relationship. Nevertheless, creators of the comic did not intend the Dynamic Duo to be viewed in this light. Gotham City meant to represent a homosocial hypermasculine environment reminiscent of dime novels and pulps where women only exist in a sexual function unworthy as colleagues and companions. Batman co-creator Bob Kane's analysis of Catwoman's creation illustrates this role perfectly:

> We came up with the idea of associating her with cats because they were kind of the antithesis of bats. I felt that women were feline and men were like dogs. While dogs are faithful and friendly, cats are cool, detached, and unreliable. I feel much warmer with dogs around me—cats are hard to understand, they are erratic, as women are. Men feel more sure of themselves with a male friend

than a woman. You always need to keep women at arm's length. We don't want anyone to take over our souls, and women have a habit of doing that ... I do feel that I've had better relationships with male friends than with women.[66]

Catwoman's rare appearances in early Batman stories show how women exist in homosocial environments merely as "adjuncts to man's remasculinization, providing emotional supports and physical targets" rather than as psychologically and intellectually equal companions. Despite Catwoman's criminal status, Batman's true rivalries lay with male criminals like the Joker and the Penguin.[67] Batman lets Catwoman escape on multiple occasions because her femininity prevents him from considering her a true threat. Kane defines Catwoman's moral ambiguity as a specifically feminine trait, in which "she was never a murderer or entirely evil like the Joker"; instead, Catwoman existed to "give the strip sex appeal."[68] The fact that Catwoman's ambiguousness is based entirely upon her gender implies that women do not represent a real threat to the superhero and the masculine world over which he rules, and are consequently not considered his equal.[69]

Although Bruce Wayne initially only has one romantic interest—fiancée Julie Madison—he later goes on to have relationships through both personas with multiple women like Catwoman and Linda Page, a socialite turned nurse.[70] In these early issues, Batman attempts to save Julie's life many times; however, she eventually breaks it off because of his inability to commit to anything substantial in his flighty playboy persona. Batman does not have relationships with any other women until the inclusion of Robin.[71] In comparison to Bruce's earlier monogamous relationship with his fiancée, he now continues his relationship with Madison while also having relationships with Catwoman and Page until Madison disappears from the comic as if she had never existed.[72] Oftentimes, Batman's relationships during this time are used as plot devices, with women "relegated to minor roles ... and presented in ways that give priority to men and the idea of adventure" rather than focusing on the romantic relationship itself.[73]

Robin's negative reaction to Batman's romantic entanglements is noteworthy here. Creators continually contrast Catwoman's ability to escape Batman's clutches through sex appeal to Robin's disapproval.[74] On one level, Robin's moral high ground identifies with child readers who would view the situation similarly, as opposed to adult males who would presumably understand letting the law slide for a chance at romance with an attractive woman. However, Robin's negative reaction also places him in the role of competitor with these women for Batman's affection. From this viewpoint, Robin always wins because he maintains a deeper and "truer" connection with his mentor than female characters can hope to have in the narrative world of superhero comics.

DC's focus on hypermasculinity and homosocial relationships extended outward to readers past the storylines contained within comics pages. While the percentage of children comics' readers during the late 1930s and early 1940s was abnormally high among boys and girls alike, DC Comics rarely marketed to female readers.[75] Ads in superhero comics featured "body building, bicycles, toy cars, and guns" and creators' reluctance to focus on romantic relationships or female characters in-story cemented adolescent boys as comics' primary target audience.[76] Themes of hypermasculinity and homosocial bonding in superhero comics continue to make it difficult for women to interact with storylines and characters in the same ways male readers do.[77] The dwindling of comic book readers from its World War II heyday can be attributed in part to this focus both in-story and in marketing initiatives by comic book companies. Many women still do not feel welcome in current comic book environments both in comic book stores and on the internet for reasons that lie both with continued gender-specific marketing by comic book publishers and a generally sexist "fanboy" culture.[78]

Early Batman creators' fictional all-boys club of vigilantes, law enforcement, and criminals is a gender-exclusive homosocial environment that recalls the worlds of rural frontier legends and urban pulp detectives. Robin's inclusion makes male father-son bonding central to this environment, where women appear solely as secondary characters and sexual objects to advance the stories and legends of men. As a result, hypermasculinity and its homoerotic implications are still alive and well in the Dynamic Duo's relationship, and thus in the wider domain of superhero comics.

Notes

1. The phrase "the loyal heart," is taken from Bob Kane (p), Jerry Robinson (i), George Roussos (i), and [writer unknown], "The Batman Plays a Lone Hand!" *Batman* #13 (October–November 1942) from *The Batman Chronicles* 7 (New York, NY: DC Comics, 2009), 115.

2. This quote originated from the 1950s *Adventures of Superman* television series introduction sequence.

3. These years cover both Batman's time solo and the Dynamic Duo before the addition of trusted butler Alfred Pennyworth.

4. Literary critic Eve Kosofsky Sedgwick's *Between Men: English Literature and Male Homosocial Desire* (New York: Columbia University Press, 1985) and *Epistemology of the Closet* (Berkeley, CA: University of California Press, 1990) provide further exploration of homosociality in literature.

5. David Leverenz, "The Last Real Man in America: From Natty Bumppo to Batman," *American Literary History* 3, no. 4 (Winter 1991), 754.

6. Dan Backer, "A Brief History of Political Cartoons," *Uniting Mugwumps and the*

Masses, Part 1, University of Virginia (Aug 1996) http://xroads.virginia.edu/~MA96/PUCK/part1.html#christi.

7. For more on Superman's origins, see Bradford W. Wright, *Comic Book Nation: The Transformation of Youth Culture in America* (Baltimore and London: The Johns Hopkins University Press, 2001), 1–5.

8. Wright, *Comic Book Nation*, 14.

9. Matthew Pustz, *Comic Book Culture: Fanboys and True Believers* (Jackson, MS: University of Mississippi, 1999), 26.

10. Bob Kane, *Batman & Me* (Forestville, CA: Eclipse Books, 1989), 39.

11. Danny Fingeroth, *Disguised as Clark Kent: Jews, Comics, and the Creation of the Superhero* (New York and London: Continuum, 2007), 19.

12. Fingeroth, *Disguised as Clark Kent*, 55.

13. Bill Finger, Bob Kane, and Sheldon Moldoff, "The Case of the Ruby Idol," *Detective Comics* #35 (January 1940) from *The Batman Chronicles* 1 (New York, NY: DC Comics, 2005), 86.

14. Alan Trachtenberg, *The Incorporation of America: Culture and Society in the Gilded Age* (New York: Hill and Wang, 1982), 199.

15. For more information on the impact of well-known "captains of industry" like J.P. Morgan, John D. Rockefeller, and Andrew Carnegie, see Alfred Chandler, *The Visible Hand: The Managerial Revolution in American Business* (Cambridge, MA: Belknap Press, 1977) and Jonathan Hughes and Louis P. Cain, *American Economic History*, 8th edition (Upper Saddle River, NJ: Prentice Hall, 2010).

16. Trachtenberg, *The Incorporation of America*, 198.

17. Sabin, *Comics, Comix and Graphic Novels* (London: Phaidon Press Limited, 1996), 54.

18. Wright, *Comic Book Nation*, 15–17.

19. Leverenz, "The Last Real Man in America," 773.

20. Roberts, *Dick Tracy and American Culture*, 61.

21. Sabin, *Comics, Comix, and Graphic Novels*, 54.

22. Leverenz, "The Last Real Man in America," 766.

23. Pamela Bedore, *Dime Novels and the Roots of American Detective Fiction* (New York, NY: Palgrave Macmillan, 2013), 106–107 and Daniel Worden, *Masculine Style: The American West and Literary Modernism* (New York, NY: Palgrave Macmillan, 2011), 20–21.

24. Bill Finger and Bob Kane, "The Case of the Chemical Syndicate," *Detective Comics* #27 (May 1939), from *The Batman Chronicles* 1 (New York, NY: DC Comics, 2005), 4.

25. Finger, Kane, and Moldoff, "The Case of the Ruby Idol," from *The Batman Chronicles* 1, 86.

26. A few examples of this relationship include "Frenchy Blake's Jewel Gang," *Detective Comics* #28 (June 1939), 16; "The Return of Doctor Death," *Detective Comics* #30 (August 1939), 38; and "The Case of the Ruby Idol," *Detective Comics* #35 (January 1940), 97 from *The Batman Chronicles* 1 (New York, NY: DC Comics, 2005).

27. Gerard Jones, *Men of Tomorrow: Geeks, Gangsters, and the Birth of the Comic Book* (New York: Basic Books, 2004), 150–153.

28. Jones, *Men of Tomorrow*, 150.

29. This is best illustrated in Batman's introductory issue, Finger and Kane, "The Case of the Chemical Syndicate," from *The Batman Chronicles* 1, 9.

30. Catherine Williamson, "'Draped Crusaders': Disrobing Gender in *The Mask of Zorro*," *Cinema Journal* 36, no. 2 (Winter 1997), 3. Queer theory scholars have evaluated the role of superhero secret identity as a way for individuals who identify as homosexual

to hide behind "clothing and performance to signify an ironic relationship between gender and sex" as a metaphorical closet before "coming out" to friends and family.

31. Williamson, "Draped Crusaders," 8.

32. See Bedore, *Dime Novels*, 168–175 and Garyn G. Roberts, *Dick Tracy and American Culture: Morality and Mythology, Text and Content* (Jefferson, NC: McFarland and Company, Inc., 1993), 66–67 for more on Chick and Junior.

33. This line is taken from the cover page for Robin's debut in the Batman mythos. Bill Finger, Bob Kane, and Jerry Robinson, "Introducing Robin, The Boy Wonder," *Detective Comics* #38 (April 1940) from *The Batman Chronicles* 1 (New York, NY: DC Comics, 2005), 124.

34. From "The Case of the Chemical Syndicate," (May 1939) to "Introducing Robin, The Boy Wonder," (April 1940).

35. Finger and Kane, "The Case of the Chemical Syndicate," from *The Batman Chronicles* 1, 6.

36. The various covers within the *Batman Chronicles* 1–7 show ten cents as the standard price during this era.

37. Pustz, *Comic Book Culture*, 26.

38. In Alan Donald's online panel question, "Is Batman Gay?" *The Panel: Silver Bullet Comic Books*, http://www.comicsbulletin.com/panel/106070953757230.htm, former Dark Horse publicist Lee Dawson states that, "the boy sidekick trend was created and appealed to a generation of kids whose fathers had gone off to war," which may explain part of what made Robin so appealing to child readers during the World War II era.

39. Bongco, *Reading Comics*, 33.

40. Whitney Ellsworth and Jerry Robinson, "The Batman Says," *Batman* #3 (Fall 1940) from *The Batman Chronicles* 2 (New York, NY: DC Comics, 2006), 207.

41. Finger, Kane, and Roussos, "Batman and Robin Visit the New York World's Fair," *New York World's Fair Comics* (1940 Issue) from *The Batman Chronicles* 2 (New York, NY: DC Comics, 2006), 111.

42. "Batplane." 1943. *The Batman Vault: A Museum-in-a-Book with Rare Collectibles from the Batcave* (Philadelphia, PA: Running Press, 2006).

43. Kane, Robinson, and Roussos, "The Wizard of Words!" *Batman* #12 (August–September 1942) from *The Batman Chronicles* 7 (New York, NY: DC Comics, 2009), 39.

44. Finger, Kane, Robinson, and Roussos, "The Secret of the Iron Jungle," *Batman* # 6 (August–September 1941) from *The Batman Chronicles* 4 (New York, NY: DC Comics, 2007), 110.

45. Edmond Hamilton, Bob Kane, and Jerry Robinson, "Bandits in Toyland," *Batman* #11 (June–July 1942) from *The Batman Chronicles* 6 (New York, NY: DC Comics, 2008), 140.

46. Finger, Kane, and Robinson, "Introducing Robin, The Boy Wonder," from *The Batman Chronicles* 1, 127. While Robin's origin story may seem odd to the modern reader, former Batman writer Alan Grant in Alan Donald's "Is Batman Gay?" states that loose and informal adoption regulations in the 1930s and 40s made this development an acceptable story device. See Alan Donald, "Is Batman Gay?" *The Panel: Silver Bullet Comic Books*, http://www.comicsbulletin.com/panel/106070953757230.htm.

47. Finger, Kane, and Robinson, "Introducing Robin, The Boy Wonder," from *The Batman Chronicles* 1, 125.

48. Jack Schiff, Bob Kane, and Jerry Robinson, "The Case of the Costume-Clad Killers," *Detective Comics* #60 (February 1942) from *The Batman Chronicles* 5 (New York, NY: DC Comics, 2008), 118.

49. Finger, Kane, and Robinson, "The Three Racketeers," *Detective Comics* #61 (March 1942) from *The Batman Chronicles* 5 (New York, NY: DC Comics, 2008), 186.

Part II: The Original Dynamic Duo

50. Finger, Kane, Robinson, and Roussos, "Public Enemy #1," *Batman* #4 (Winter 1941) from *The Batman Chronicles* 3 (New York, NY: DC Comics, 2007), 70.

51. Finger, Kane, and Robinson, "The Cross Country Crimes," *Batman* #8 (December 1941–January 1942) from *The Batman Chronicles* 5 (New York, NY: DC Comics, 2008), 72.

52. Finger, Kane, Robinson, and Roussos, "The Case of the Laughing Death!" *Detective Comics* #45 (November 1940) from *The Batman Chronicles* 2 (New York, NY: DC Comics, 2006), 221.

53. Finger, Kane, Robinson, and Roussos, "The Trouble Trap," *Batman* #7 (October–November 1941) from *The Batman Chronicles* 4 (New York, NY: DC Comics, 2007), 186 and Finger, Kane, and Robinson, "The White Whale," *Batman* #9 (February–March 1942) from *The Batman Chronicles* 5 (New York, NY: DC Comics, 2008), 146.

54. Finger, Kane, Robinson, and Roussos, "Victory for the Dynamic Duo," *Batman* #4 (Winter 1941) from *The Batman Chronicles* 3 (New York, NY: DC Comics, 2007), 74 and Kane, Robinson, and Roussos, "The Wizard of Words!" from *The Batman Chronicles* 7, 34.

55. Finger, Kane, Robinson, and Roussos, "The Strange Case of the Diabolical Puppet Master," *Batman* #3 (Fall 1940) from *The Batman Chronicles* 2 (New York, NY: DC Comics, 2006), 166 and Kane, Robinson, Roussos, [writer unknown], "The Batman Plays a Lone Hand!" *Batman* #13 (October–November 1942) from *The Batman Chronicles* 7 (New York, NY: DC Comics, 2009), 113.

56. Finger, Kane, Robinson, and Roussos, "Clayface Walks Again!" *Detective Comics* #49 (March 1941) from *The Batman Chronicles* 3 (New York, NY: DC Comics, 2007), 105.

57. Finger, Kane, Robinson, and Roussos, "The Secret of the Iron Jungle," from *The Batman Chronicles* 4, 107 and Finger, Kane, Robinson, and Roussos, "Public Enemy #1," from *The Batman Chronicles* 3, 65.

58. "Hook Morgan and His Harbor Pirates," *Detective Comics* #54 (August 1941) from *The Batman Chronicles* 4 (New York, NY: DC Comics, 2007), 70, "The Case of the Honest Crook!" *Batman* #5 (Spring 1941) from *The Batman Chronicles* 3, 161, and "The Joker's Advertising Campaign," *Batman* #11 (June–July 1942) from *The Batman Chronicles* 6 (New York, NY: DC Comics, 2008), 120–124 show the abnormally high levels of emotion Batman displays when fearing for Robin's life.

59. Finger, Kane, and Robinson, "The Joker," *Batman* #1 (Spring 1940) from *The Batman Chronicles* 1 (New York, NY: DC Comics, 2005), 144.

60. Kane, Robinson, Roussos, [writer unknown], "The Batman Plays a Lone Hand!" from *The Batman Chronicles* 7, 115.

61. Worden, *Masculine Style*, 18.

62. Pustz, *Comic Book Culture*, 208–9.

63. Fredric Wertham, *Seduction of the Innocent* (New York: Rinehart, 1954), 190.

64. Wright, *Comic Book Culture*, 162.

65. Andy Medhurst, "Batman, Deviance, and Camp," in *The Many Lives of Batman: Critical Approaches to a Superhero and his Media*, ed. Roberta Pearson and William Uricchio (New York: Routledge, 1991), 152.

66. Kane, *Batman & Me*, 108.

67. Leverenz, "The Last Real Man in America," 770–772.

68. Kane, *Batman & Me*, 107.

69. Bongco, *Reading Comics*, 110.

70. Gardner Fox with Bill Finger, Bob Kane, and Sheldon Moldoff, "Batman Versus the Vampire, Part One," *Detective Comics* #31 (September 1939) from *The Batman Chronicles* 1, 41 and Finger, Kane, and Robinson, "The Cat," *Batman* #1 (Spring 1940) from *The Batman Chronicles* 1, 177.

71. Finger, Kane, Robinson, and Roussos, "Clayface Walks Again!" from *The Batman Chronicles* 3, 100.

72. Finger, Kane, Robinson, and Roussos, "The Secret Cavern," *Detective Comics* #48 (February 1941) from *The Batman Chronicles* 3 (New York, NY: DC Comics, 2007), 87.

73. Bongco, *Reading Comics*, 111.

74. "The Cat," from *The Batman Chronicles* 1, 177, "Joker Meets Cat-Woman," *Batman* #2 (Summer 1940) from *The Batman Chronicles* 2 (New York, NY: DC Comics, 2006), 58, and "The Batman vs. the Cat-Woman," *Batman* #3 (Fall 1940), 206 are just a few examples of Robin's distaste at Batman's soft spot for the jewel thief.

75. Bongco, *Reading Comics*, 126.

76. Bongco, *Reading Comics*, 114.

77. Pustz, *Comic Book Culture*, 8.

78. Pustz, *Comic Book Culture*, 208.

PART III

Nightwing and Beyond: Dick Grayson Grows Up

Boy Wonder to Man Wonder

Dick Grayson's Transition to Nightwing and the Bildungsroman

Kristen L. Geaman

In 1984, after serving as Robin for over forty years, Dick Grayson emerged as a new hero—Nightwing. Nightwing represented, in Dick's own words, "someone new who commemorates all those who made me someone special."[1] Dick's protracted childhood had finally ended as Batman's first sidekick came of age.

The initial narrative saw Dick willingly passing on the mantle of Robin, but the scenario underwent revision in short order. DC's universe-wide *Crisis on Infinite Earths* (1985) reset continuity, although the event's effect varied across properties. *The New Teen Titans*, for instance, in which Dick was a star player, was relatively unaffected. *Batman* experienced moderate changes. Most notable was the complete revision of the origins and character of Jason Todd. Jason's alteration seemingly went hand-in-hand (the stories appeared in the same issue of *Batman*) with a new version of how Dick became Nightwing. This Bat-centric version was largely ignored by *The New Teen Titans* writers, but it sowed the seeds of a darker coming-of-age story.[2]

Those seeds had their fullest flowering in *Nightwing: Year One*, a six-part story from 2005. In this rendition, Dick suffers from a gamut of growing pains: alienation from his father-figure, deep uncertainty about his future, and apprehension over his place in the world (both physical and metaphysical). These specific changes signal a shift in genre. What was once a coming-of-age tale based on mutual respect and acknowledged character growth has morphed into a more fraught story that is better termed a bildungsroman, a specific subset of the coming-of-age genre.

The Original

The short answer to when Dick Grayson became Nightwing is *The New Teen Titans'* "The Judas Contract" (*Tales of the Teen Titans* #42–44 and Annual #3). In reality, it is a much longer saga. The trade paperback includes issues #39–41, but even that is only a portion. Dick's original coming-of-age spanned two editorial desks (Batman and Teen Titans), multiple books (*Batman, Detective Comics, The New Teen Titans,* and *Tales of the Teen Titans*), multiple issues, and seventeen months.

From the beginning of *The New Teen Titans*, Dick separates himself from Bruce. Despite spending ten happy (real time) years in university, Dick drops out of college after a semester.[3] Ostensibly college interfered too much with Robin's crime fighting and higher education could not teach Dick anything germane to his calling (superheroism) that he didn't already know. But the decision also freed Robin for full-time crime fighting with a new group, provided a reason for him to be on the outs with Bruce (and thus desire other vigilante pastures), and firmly established Dick as a teenager—either still 18 or a very young 19.

Bruce, of course, did not approve of Dick's decision to quit college. The seeds of discord that this sows between the Dynamic Duo created the perfect condition for Dick to branch out with a new team in order to find his confidence as a hero. As Dick notes in the inaugural issue of *The New Teen Titans*, Bruce still regards him as a child, although Dick feels relatively confident in his abilities. Still, he thinks, "Maybe this new Titans coming up right now is a good idea ... I can use a place where I can prove myself."[4]

From the very beginning of the series, Dick's character arc was one based on developing maturity and a desire to prove himself to his father figure. This was an important theme for the entire *New Teen Titans* book, which, at its most basic level, was about young vs. old, children vs. parents. According to Marv Wolfman, "These universal conflicts, understood by all teens as they grow up and separate from their parents, could be revisited time and time again."[5] Within the first few years of the series, Dick revisited the theme multiple times as he grew more confident in his abilities and developed his own leadership style that clearly separated him from Batman.

Just as it happens for the non-heroic teenager, Dick's distancing from his parent took years of development. Ultimately, when Dick stepped out from the shadow of the Bat, it was a bittersweet moment, rather like when a child graduates from college and lives independently. Parent and child are separated, but it is a separation born of mutual respect and pride. There is generally no violent rupture with and subsequent alienation from the parents, which is more of a hallmark of the bildungsroman and a feature of later versions of Dick's transition to Nightwing.

For Dick, one subtheme of the first seven issues of *The New Teen Titans* was personal growth. Dick was eager to find a place for himself that wasn't college and wasn't alongside Batman; leading the Teen Titans gave Dick a sense of purpose and self-worth. At the end of the first arc, after an early victory over Trigon, Dick comments that being with the Titans has been a "lifesaver" and given him direction.[6] The first arc thus ends with Dick committed to the Titans, yet still tied to Batman through the Robin identity.

Dick's growing pains did not return in full force until a couple of years later in *The New Teen Titans* #28 from February 1983. As Kory (Starfire) frets to Donna (Wonder Girl) that Dick has been pulling away lately, the two compare Dick to his mentor and conclude that he can never be Batman because "he hasn't got the same *fanatical obsession*." When Dick arrives on scene, he reveals that he has been doing some work with the circus, which lays the initial foundations for one of the biggest shake-ups in the history of the Dynamic Duo.[7] Within a year, February 1984, Dick would pass on the mantle of Robin to Jason Todd and debut his Nightwing identity a few months later in July 1984.

Over the ensuing year, Dick undergoes a time of personal growth and reflection as he evaluates his place at Batman's side and his role in the Teen Titans. While Dick contemplates quitting as leader of the Teen Titans, a sign of his personal struggle with growing up, he ultimately decides to quit being Batman's sidekick and remain leader of the Titans.[8] Dick therefore chose to grow up rather than remain stuck in his kid-sidekick pattern of the past.

Bittersweet though it can be, part of growing up involves carving out an identity for oneself and reducing one's tie to parents or guardians. As Dick matures as a hero, he and Bruce come to realize their ways of fighting crime are no longer as compatible as they once were. After Jason's mother Trina Todd accidentally discovers the duo's secret identities (*Detective Comics* #524), Bruce expresses doubt she's trustworthy. When Dick vouches for her, claiming Bruce doesn't want to trust anyone, Batman dismisses Robin as "still young." Although Bruce agrees to work with the Todds to bring down Killer Croc, it is abundantly clear that he is doing this as a sop to Dick and against his own better judgment. Bruce thinks to himself, Dick's "still an idealist ... doesn't understand human nature ... I've learned you never trust anyone especially not the ones you love!"[9] This exchange reveals a fundamental divide in the way the two halves of the duo go about their business. Dick is much more inclined to trust people, although it is important to note that he does not do so willy-nilly; he has interacted with Trina Todd, the two have mutual circus friends in common, and Trina's perceptive ways remind Dick of his mother.[10] Bruce, on the other hand, has a basic objection to trusting people, based on his perception of human nature. Bruce doesn't distrust Trina because he doesn't know her; he distrusts Trina Todd because he has a fundamentally more suspicious nature.

This dichotomy is again showcased in *The New Teen Titans* #37. Dick is at Wayne Manor, discussing with Bruce that "my ideas of justice and yours have become radically different," when both the Teen Titans and Outsiders (a superhero team led by Batman) are called into action. While the Titans called the Manor asking for Dick, the Outsiders contacted the Batcave. Dick is shocked Bruce hasn't revealed his identity to his team, but Bruce is cavalier: "when they *need* to know, they'll know."[11] This is in marked contrast to the Teen Titans, who knew each other's alter egos from the beginning. Dick's fundamental willingness to trust was displayed from the moment of the group's founding when he followed Raven, someone he had never met but who needed his assistance.

Bruce and Dick thus suit up to lead their teams on a joint mission. Despite Dick having just expressed his desire to no longer be Batman's kid partner, Batman falls into some old habits on the mission, which leaves Robin resentful and Starfire and Kid Flash unhappy with the way Batman treats his sidekick.[12] Eventually, after Batman attempts to assign some heroes to roles unsuited to their skill sets, Robin asserts himself to reassign the Titans because "I know more about the Titans than you, and I know more about running a *team* than you!"[13] Robin's assertion is proven correct not only when his strategy wins the day but when Batman admits his protégé has surpassed him and is now his *former* pupil.[14] Not only does Batman acknowledge Dick's skills, but he also recognizes that Dick has moved beyond his tutelage.

Despite ending their crime-fighting partnership, Dick and Bruce do not undergo a total break. In *The New Teen Titans* #37, just before receiving their call to action, Dick told Bruce he no longer wanted to be a duo. Bruce initially overreacted, thinking Dick wanted to end their friendship! Dick clarified, clearly stating he only wanted to end their partnership "as in Batman and Robin. Not our *relationship* as Bruce Wayne and Dick Grayson."[15] Even as Dick takes this important step, he also still clings to the past. Recently-orphaned Jason Todd hears Dick severing his partnership with Bruce and immediately asks to become the new Robin. Dick quickly squashes that idea because he is not ready to give up the role he has been "playing" since he was eight.[16]

Yet a scant two issues later, Dick gives up the Robin identity for good. Both *Batman* #368, in which Dick passes on the Robin costume to Jason, and *The New Teen Titans* #39, in which Dick explains his decision to his teammates, place heavy emphasis on the theme of growing up. In Gotham City, Jason and Bruce are trying to come up with a suitable heroic identity when Dick appears. The narration highlights Dick's coming-of-age, noting "…the unexpected visitor, now a handsome young man, slowly strides from the cavern shadows of his childhood…."[17] As Dick briefly reminisces with Jason, he expresses how much he loved being Robin "even though it's time to put that phase of my life behind me."[18] Dick acknowledges that Robin belongs in Gotham City (he shares a similar sentiment with the Titans when he admits that "Robin will always be the back half of 'Batman and—'"[19]) and passes the mantle on to Jason. As Dick elaborates to the new Dynamic Duo, he has stopped trying to be Batman and is now ready to be the leader of the Titans "in *name* as well as fact."[20] Creating a new identity is thus an important way for Dick to express his commitment to this new phase of his life.

Sad as it makes Bruce, he recognizes that Dick needs to do this. As tears cloud Bruce's eyes he thanks Dick; according to the narration, the past also flashes before Bruce's eyes as he "speaks to the boy, looking at the man…."[21] Bruce experiences classic parental emotions as his youthful ward moves firmly into the adult phase of his life; proud as Bruce is of everything Dick has become, he still tears up as he acknowledges the bittersweet passage of time. Dick has grown into a man Bruce is proud of, but it is sad when a son no longer needs his parent.

When Dick informs the Teen Titans of his decision to give up being Robin, he explains that he had outgrown the role of "happy-go-lucky kid partner."[22] The short pants and pixie boots had to go in order for Dick to fully commit to adulthood and his responsibilities as a Titan. In addition, Dick expressed his maturity by passing on the Robin identity before he had created a new moniker and costume for himself. Nightwing was still a few months in the future, so Dick had to drop not only his alter ego but also his public acts of heroism. Dick's ability to leave the limelight took maturity and confidence.

Finally, the Teen Titans helped Dick mature in multiple ways. Aside from helping Dick develop as a leader, the Teen Wonder's romantic relationship also signaled his maturity as he moved away from his guardian and became closer to his long-term partner, Koriand'r (Starfire). In addition,

Dick's relationship with Kory allowed him to open up emotionally as he moved beyond Batman's influence. The Dark Knight is one of the more emotionally-repressed superheroes, whereas Dick is much more comfortable expressing his feelings. This, however, was something he cultivated more-or-less without Batman, who had "always taught me [Dick] to be guided by my *head*, not my *heart*."[23] Dick's maturity manifested itself in an increasing ability to express his emotions. Almost from her first moments on Earth, Kory was attracted to Dick, but it took some time for Dick to come to terms with his own feelings, largely a result of his upbringing in which logic was emphasized over emotions. As mentioned previously, during the year (real time) in which Dick was sorting out his place in the world and dealing with Bruce obtaining a new ward in Jason Todd, he was pulling away from Kory. Kory frequently fretted about this, but the situation showed marked improvement once Dick came to terms with growing up. In *The New Teen Titans* #38, just after Dick has severed his partnership with Batman but before he has given up the Robin identity, Dick mentions that he should apologize to Kory for "being such as ass to her these past months."[24] This is a moment of self-awareness that Dick has not shown in previous issues, and it marks the beginning of a new state of greater emotional maturity and openness. At the end of the issue, Dick calls Kory and asks to see her, something he has not done in some time. Not long thereafter, Dick casually calls Kory "m'love" out in the field and openly admits that she has helped him mature more than she knows—"but not more than you *will* know."[25] As Dick becomes his own man, he is more open to expressions of affection and more in tune with his emotions, something which also sets him apart from his mentor. Although Dick would never completely abandon Batman's lessons of logic and duty to the mission, he also took the time to develop his emotions. Along with his new identity, Dick's growing emotional openness expressed his independence from Batman and his successful coming of age.[26]

The Bat Version

Such was Dick's original, *New Teen Titans* influenced, transition to Nightwing. In post–*Crisis* continuity, however, a new version appeared, one more focused on the Batman side of things and more negative. As George Pérez noted, the "only problem that happened after that [original transition] is when the *Batman* group went and did their version of Dick Grayson's leaving Batman, they made it seem like Batman fired him, as opposed to our take which was that he grew out of it [and] decided he needed to dedicate his time to the Titans...."[27]

Pérez's quote aptly highlights what are probably the two main differences between the original version (which largely remained the Teen Titans version[28]) and the saga's subsequent development: Batman now fired Robin (reducing Dick's agency) and the new story altered the timeline of Dick's personal growth. The change in which desk was responsible for the story also had profound implications. The tale of Nightwing's origin went from being a Teen Titans story, in which team comradery and Dick's leadership role allowed him to grow into a person who no longer needed the Robin identity, to a Batman story which emphasized the breakup of the Dynamic Duo and Bruce's increasingly controlling tendencies. In addition, Dick's coming-of-age no longer culminated in him leaving Batman's side; rather that became the act that started Dick down his new path.

This new version debuted in *Batman* #408, which also introduced the post–*Crisis* version of Jason Todd. In the new rendition, the Joker gets off a lucky shot that hits Robin in the shoulder, causing him to lose his footing and topple over the edge of a skyscraper. Robin's fall is stopped by his fortuitous entanglement in his Bat-rope, but the damage is done. A film crew records Robin's fall, runs with the story "Did Robin Die Tonight?" and Bruce reacts badly. Unable to bear the thought of losing Robin and plagued by guilt that it would have been his responsibility had Joker slain his partner, Bruce summarily decrees that Robin should stay dead. Dick vehemently protests and the ensuing exchange highlights Dick's liminal state—on the threshold of childhood and adulthood—and Bruce's convoluted thinking. Bruce claims that Dick can no longer be Robin because "in what I do, there is no place for a child."[29] Never mind that Dick is in his late teens and has been working with Batman for years![30] When Dick protests (especially the child part), Bruce responds, "And you *are* a man now. Man enough to accept my decision."[31] Bruce thus imposes his will on Dick in a manner many frustrated teenagers can sympathize with, taking advantage of Dick's relative youth while simultaneously appealing to his maturity as a way to forestall a scene. It works. Dick grumpily accepts Bruce's decision, but warns him "you can't keep me from pursuing my own destiny" as readers get a shadowy glimpse of Nightwing.[32] Despite Dick clearly telling Bruce he will remain a costumed hero, and thus will not be out of danger, Bruce smiles and encourages Dick.[33] Although the firing ends on a positive note, Bruce is not shown in a particularly charitable light—something which is further developed in subsequent retellings. Batman summarily fires Robin, claiming he is doing it to protect Dick, but it truly seems Bruce is doing it to protect himself. Bruce cannot bear the responsibility of Dick getting hurt on his watch, but he is comfortable with Dick continuing to put himself in danger. In his desire to ease his own conscience, Bruce causes Dick pain by stripping him of an intrinsic part of his life. It might be an understandable response, but it also showcases Bruce's flawed, very human side.

The scene in issue #408 does not elaborate on when and how Dick took up the Nightwing identity. *Batman* #416, although written by a different author and so slightly altered, basically picks up where #408 left off and fills the reader in on the Batman version of how Dick became Nightwing. The tale is told as a flashback; in the main action, Dick has returned home for the first time since the demise of the original Dynamic Duo and confronts Bruce about how hurt he was about being fired. According to Dick, when Bruce fired him, he left his "life in ruins"; Dick clearly still feels this pain because he tells Bruce during their confrontation, "[i]t didn't matter to you that I *didn't* have any life other than the one we shared."[34] Feeling rejected by Bruce, Dick left home, tried and left college, wandered the country, and then fell in with the Teen Titans. After spending some time as the group's leader, Dick cast aside his Robin identity and became Nightwing.[35] In this version of events, Dick was fired from the Dynamic Duo but retained the Robin identity until he decided to change. Nevertheless, Bruce still gave Jason the Robin identity (presumably after Dick had become Nightwing although that is never stated), which is a stark contrast with what came before. In the closing panels of *Batman* #416, Dick passes one of his old costumes on to Jason, but the meaning is not the same as it was in the original version. Here Dick giving Jason his old costume shows acceptance of what had already come to pass; Jason was Robin whether or not Dick approved. In the original version, Dick passes on the identity of Robin willingly and of his own volition. Dick not only personally delivers a costume to Jason, he overrides any qualms Bruce might have, saying Jason's "not 'stealing my identity'—I'm giving him permission."[36] Dick's agency has been drastically reduced. Instead of coming of age on his own terms, Dick's hand is forced. Dick still comes-of-age, but he is no longer the master of his own circumstances. He is reacting to Bruce's actions.

Since this new narrative appeared in the Batman comics, it is not surprising that Batman takes on a much larger role. As a consequence, the role of the Teen Titans is drastically reduced. It might just be a continuity error, or the result of post–*Crisis* confusion, but *Batman* #416 indicates that Dick was not a part of the Teen Titans until after he was fired.[37] While the Titans and his new leadership role still helped Dick mature, his reduced agency diminished his coming-of-age. Before Dick had been both a sidekick and a leader, and chose to leave his guardian's tutelage both to make way for a new pupil (who needed Batman more) and to better direct the course of his own life. Those choices displayed a great deal of maturity and highlighted just how far the Teen Wonder had come. After being fired, Dick did not have the chance to make those choices, which somewhat lessens the impact of his coming-of-age.

Batman #408 and #416 were both relatively short versions of Dick's transition to Nightwing. Their exact narrative would later be replaced by *Nightwing: Year One*, a version that blended elements from both pre- and post-*Crisis* continuity. Most notably, this would be Bruce firing Dick, a grimmer tone, and the Bat-centeredness of the tale. In *Nightwing: Year One*, these elements would come together in a new way, one filled with greater alienation, greater conflict between generations, and greater difficulties for our young hero. Nightwing's origins moved from a coming-of-age story that highlighted Dick's agency and maturity to a bildungsroman that focused increasingly on the trials and tribulations Dick underwent on his path to a new identity. This essay has mentioned the bildungsroman before without defining the term. This is partially because the bildungsroman is an exceedingly difficult genre to define. As far as literary scholars are concerned, there "is virtually no agreement on either what constitutes a Bildungsroman or which novels belong to this tradition."[38] At its most generic level, the bildungsroman is a novel that charts the growth and development of a young person from late adolescence to adulthood. It is thus similar to, but different from, the coming-of-age novel—it is a subset of that broader genre.[39] Although the bildungsroman resists an easy definition, it has distinctive features which separate it from coming-of-age stories such as a greater emphasis on self-cultivation, learning outside formal education, alienation, generational conflict (beyond the usual), soul searching, and reaching an accommodation with the outside world (and family).[40] This is, of course, not a perfect definition but it is important to distinguish between the two.[41] Everyone comes of age but not everyone must undergo the added trials and tribulations of the bildungsroman. In comic fandom terms, the bildungsroman requires angst. Through great angst comes great wisdom. After reading a variety of scholarship that aimed to define the bildungsroman, this essay has decided to rely most heavily on Anniken Iversen's dissertation, supplemented by Jerome's Buckley's *Seasons of Youth*, for its concept of the bildungsroman.[42] Rather than rely on a definition designed to classify works as either bildungsromans or not, Iversen developed an index of 96 characteristics designed "not so much to define the bildungsroman as to pinpoint and describe typical features of novels that are generally recognized as bildungsromans."[43] This index allows readers to place literature on a continuum in which works might possess more characteristics of the bildungsroman than others. This has proven immensely helpful in understanding Dick Grayson's journey from Robin to Nightwing. Dick's journey is clearly about a young man growing up and leaving the cave, but that story has undergone changes over time. These changes, especially those between the original *The New Teen Titans* version and the *Year One* version, move Dick's story increasingly into the bildungsroman sub-genre, as reflected by *Year One* possessing a greater number of characteristics from Iversen's Bildungsroman Index. Since all versions of Dick's transition to Nightwing focus on the young hero's development from a youth to an adult, this examination of *Year One* will focus on the differences between this version and the original that mark the 2005 tale as being more of a bildungsroman that what came before.

Even before opening the cover of *Nightwing: Year One*, readers receive a signal that this is a bildungsroman. The title includes both the main character's name and the word year, which are two things often found in the titles of bildungsromans.[44] In addition, the narrative scheme in *Year One* is different and more in line with the bildungsroman.[45] In *Year One*, Dick's narration has a retrospective flavor; for instance, right after Bruce fires him, Dick mentions "This time it was for good," which is something he would not necessarily have known in the moment.[46] Furthermore, readers clearly knew the *Year One* story was a flashback. It appeared in 2005, after Dick had been Nightwing for more than twenty years. The tale also initially ran as issues #101–106 of the *Nightwing* solo title, interrupting the already ongoing story. It thus had both internal and external marks of retrospective narration, whereas the original version took place in "real time."

In *Year One*, Dick's break with Bruce is immediately precipitated by a fight with Clayface. Readers are not privy to the long lead-up, but Dick's narration offers a hint: he was in college, leading the Titans, and attempting to have a life, all while being Batman's partner.[47] On the night in question, a Titans mission to defeat Brother Blood (a cult leader and serious adversary) made Dick late for his second-shift as Batman's back-up. Although the Dynamic Duo was ultimately successful, Batman snaps at Robin on their return to the Batcave. "This is a *war*, Dick. Robin is my second ... my lieutenant. Anything less than *total* devotion to this cause is simply *wasting* my time." This culminates with: "You're fired, Dick. **Get out of my cave**."[48] Adding insult to injury, Bruce also demands that Dick leave behind a new uniform that Alfred had given him only moments before.[49] The implication is clear: Dick is fired not only from the Dynamic Duo but also from the very identity of Robin.

As noted previously, Bruce firing Dick takes away Dick's agency. No longer does Dick decide when he has grown up and express his maturity by willingly passing down his sidekick identity. Dick has had the decision made for him. This act ties into the bildungsroman in two ways: male bildungsroman heroes are often somewhat passive in that life happens to them, and other people play a vital role in making the protagonist grow up.[50] Passive is not the best way to characterize Dick throughout *Year One*, but he is passive in the beginning. His firing happens to him. He has no say. Furthermore, Bruce's actions force Dick to start his journey to becoming Nightwing. In the original version, Dick came to his own decision that it was time to leave Batman and the Robin identity behind, but this time Bruce initiated the change.

Year One is also the harshest and most alienating version yet. Bruce does not fire Dick out of concern for his safety (or even out of guilt) but out of anger that Dick can no longer devote his time exclusively to assisting Batman. In a way, Bruce is upset that Dick is growing up and pushes him away, which alienates Dick from his parent figure.[51] It is also worth noting that by the time *Year One* came out in 2005, Dick's Robin origin had also been altered. The name and costume were Dick's own creation, designed to memorialize his circus roots and commemorate his mother's nickname for him.[52] It was an especially cruel act for Bruce to strip Dick of his alter ego, but it is one that emphasizes the parent-child conflict so often present in the bildungsroman.[53]

Following his rejection by Bruce, Dick goes on a literal and figurative journey of self-formation. He visits Superman and hears the inspirational story of the Kryptonian Nightwing, then returns to Haly's Circus and the trapeze.[54] After being fired, Dick felt lost; as he revealed to Superman, he always thought he would grow up to become Batman.[55] Being cast aside by Bruce caused Dick to call all of that into question. Dick is thus on a journey of personal discovery and working to find his place—in his case, whether he wants to return to his pre-superhero life.[56] After realizing that he cannot stop helping people and being a hero (thereby determining his place in life and exemplifying learning and soul-searching outside the confines of formal education), Dick returns to Gotham City (his childhood home in terms of heroing). While Dick ultimately returns to the Teen Titans, going home to show off how far he has come is an important aspect of the bildungsroman.[57] It is also something notably absent from previous versions of this story. Back in 1984, Dick visited Gotham to pass on the

Robin mantle to Jason, but he did not need to return as Nightwing and show off the man he had become because Bruce already knew and respected Dick as an adult.

The basic outline of *Year One* is thus more in the mode of a bildungsroman (generational conflict, journey of self-discovery, returning home to show off one's new self) than the original version. It is Dick's relationships, however, that offer the most fascinating change, particularly that of the former Dynamic Duo. Bruce/Batman is a much darker figure, which serves to alienate Dick and heighten generational conflict. This change plays into the general idea that the bildungsroman showcases parent-child difficulties (especially those shaped by loss or alienation), as well as what might be a theme mainly prevalent in English-language bildungsromans: "the hero's need to come to terms with his father."[58]

Bruce is generally portrayed negatively. Aside from cruelly firing Dick, he behaves callously towards Alfred and Jason Todd. When Bruce returns to the Batcave to find Alfred cleaning a glass case with Dick's Robin outfit inside, he snaps at Alfred that is it neither a memorial nor a trophy. While Bruce might not want to see the outfit because it causes him pain, he ignores Alfred's feelings. Given the way Alfred carefully maintains the case, it holds therapeutic value for him.[59] After all, Alfred was Dick's other parent; consequently, he is suffering deeply as well. A more egregious example, however, is Bruce's initial treatment of Jason Todd. One day Alfred enters the Batcave to find a young man gagged and tied to a chair! This is Jason, brought back after Batman caught him trying to steal the tires from the Batmobile.[60] Batman abducted Jason and kept him captive in the cave for hours, a huge contrast to Jason's earlier origins in which Batman first attempted to find Jason a good home.[61] In addition, Bruce keeps Jason at arms' length; on overhearing Alfred refer to Batman as "Master Bruce" Jason asks, "Bruce? Is *that* your real name?"[62] All of this serves to highlight and justify the alienation Dick feels from Bruce. This Bruce Wayne is a much less appealing father-figure, which makes the conflict between the generations understandable.

Bruce does have some redeeming features, which helps the readers to see in him what Dick saw in him, as well as make us hope for a reconciliation between the two. Deadman, a ghostly superhero who communicates with the living by possessing people's bodies, visits the Batcave to let Bruce know that Dick is at the circus "just like you thought." Bruce then asks if Dick is coming back, revealing that despite his cold exterior Bruce has been concerned about Dick's welfare.[63]

The climax of *Year One* comes when Dick meets and partners with

Jason Todd, the new Robin. Jason is participating in the "gauntlet," which is what Batman has termed the final exam for his Robins. Unbeknownst to Dick, he has a role in the gauntlet Bruce constructs for Jason. Dick's role is both a testament to Bruce's faith in Dick's abilities and an instance of Bruce taking advantage of Dick's nobler qualities. Even though Bruce has a shock in store for his former partner, he knows that Dick will teach Jason a few important lessons.

Even before the gauntlet began, Bruce had Jason studying footage of Dick in action as Nightwing (footage Bruce had obtained from video cameras around the city).[64] Bruce knows there are things Dick can teach Jason, that Dick has moves Jason would do well to imitate (if he can). Consequently, Bruce sets up the gauntlet so that Dick and Jason will meet, through the assistance of Batgirl/Barbara. Barbara coordinates a fake stakeout with Dick, who, on seeing another youngster in his old costume, initially thinks it is a tasteless joke. After a few scuffles, Dick and Jason do end up working together. Although the mission they ultimately embark on (rescuing a disguised Alfred from Killer Croc) was not the one planned, the two work together fairly well as a team.[65] In fact, Dick begins to wonder, "Is the gauntlet meant to forge a partner? Or to build a team? You remember teamwork, don't you?"[66] This quote marks the second time Dick's inner monologue has asked Bruce if he remembered teamwork, suggesting that this is what Bruce wanted Jason to learn from Dick.[67] As Tim Drake, a youth who would eventually become the third Robin, noted back in 1990, "Bruce told me to see you. He said *he* could teach me ... all the *skills* a *Robin* needs.... But only *you* could teach me how to be his *partner*."[68]

The gauntlet, however, also showcases Bruce's flaws. He wants to test Dick and unfairly springs Jason on him without warning, while simultaneously taking advantage of Dick's willingness to help. Bruce knows that Dick will work with Jason, and he has planned for that. Batman tells Alfred, who has been disguised as Two-Face for the purposes of the test, that he will "have an audience of *two*."[69] Since Bruce has his own role to play and Barbara is not involved beyond setting up Dick, the audience of two can only mean Dick and Jason. This makes Bruce's choice of Two-Face particularly interesting. Dick has a fraught history with the villain, who attempted to beat him to death in his early days as Robin.[70] When confronting the disguised Alfred, Dick has a flashback to this beating, although it quickly dissipates when Two-Face turns out to be Alfred. Nevertheless, Dick can sense that this situation was more than just a test for Jason: "You [Batman] designed the gauntlet as the final test to prove my worthiness to become Robin. So what were you testing this time?"[71]

Perhaps Bruce was testing Dick's ability to move on and let go (despite Dick having created the Robin identity). If so, Dick passed with ease. Only hours after meeting him, Dick yelled for Jason to get down during a fight, but Dick called him "Robin." As Dick noted, "I called him by name. My name."[72] While Dick does claim ownership of the name, he also has already begun to apply it to Jason. Dick might not be thrilled that Bruce has passed on his identity so soon after firing him, but he has displayed the maturity to accept that which he cannot change.

By the end, Dick has also accepted his place in the world and the failings of his father figure, Bruce. At the end of the night, Bruce requests that everyone, including Dick, return to the Batcave for debriefing. This is a natural reaction for a concerned guardian who has not seen his child in many months. Bruce wants to see Dick. Dick, however, has reached a level of acceptance in which he realizes that seeing Bruce right now is not what is best for him. As Dick tells Barbara, "There comes a time when every son has to leave the nest and take wing for the first time." For Dick, that time is now. Instead of visiting Bruce, he records a message for him, letting Bruce know that he is "as committed to your crusade as the night you made me swear the oath." Dick's final show of wisdom comes when he also assures Bruce that, "You were the best father you could be. Given the circumstances."[73] At the very end, Dick returns to the Teen Titans in his new identity. He has thus completed his bildung and reached accommodation with the world. He has accepted Bruce and his flaws and made strides to protect himself (rather than keep the relationship on Bruce's terms). Dick has also found his place in society, as a crimefighter who leads a team of young people.

Although the Titans are where Dick finds his place in the world, they are notably absent from his *Year One* coming-of-age. The reader knows that Dick is a member of this team because he mentions it, before being summarily fired, as one of the things reducing his time with Bruce. The *Year One* timeline is thus consistent with the original version. No Titans' member, however, appears until the third issue (*Nightwing* #103) and that is only a brief phone call between Dick and Donna. Donna's voice appears again when she calls Alfred for laundry advice later in the issue, but only Alfred's side of the phone conversation is shown.[74] This time Dick's journey is largely a solo one; he meets various people along the way, but they serve fleeting functions—they are there to briefly impart wisdom to Dick and disappear. This is unlike the original version, in which Dick's coming-of-age was a part of a larger story and his Titans comrades were fully realized characters. This change also marks *Year One* as a bildungsroman because the focus is almost exclusively on Dick and the other characters serve as guides to further his development.[75]

As his circumstances have changed, Dick's journey from childhood to adulthood has changed right along with it. By 2005, Dick's years as a Teen Titan were long in the past, but he was intimately tied to the Batman Family. Perhaps as a consequence of that, his transition to Nightwing reflected the importance of the Bat-Family. This new focus was darker and granted Dick less agency, tying in with the grimmer tone of the Batman books. Depending on taste, the *Year One* version can be aggravating and emotionally trying, but its literary merit grants it recognition as a classic alongside Dick's original *New Teen Titans* coming-of-age.

Notes

1. Marv Wolfman et al., "The Judas Contract Book 3—There Shall Come a Titan," *Tales of the Teen Titans* #44 (New York: DC Comics, July 1984), 21.

2. "Marv Wolfman: Titans Twice a Month as Crisis Looms [interview with Marv Wolfman by Glen Cadigan]" in *Titans Companion* (Raleigh, NC: TwoMorrows Publishing, 2005), 137–148, at 137.

3. This is in "The Gotham Connection," *Detective Comics* #495 (October 1980), written by Jack C. Harris. This was the same month that DC ran a test of the New Teen Titans in *DC Comics Presents* #38 (October 1980).

4. Marv Wolfman, George Pérez, and Romeo Tanghal, "The Birth of the Titans," *The New Teen Titans* (1) #1 (New York: DC Comics, November 1980), 7.

5. Marv Wolfman, "Foreword," in *The New Teen Titans Omnibus, Vol. I* (New York: DC Comics, 2011), 8.

6. Wolfman, Pérez, and Tanghal, "Assault on Titans' Tower," *The New Teen Titans* (1) #7 (May 1981), 2–3.

7. Wolfman, Pérez, and Tanghal, "Terra in the Night," *The New Teen Titans* (1) #28 (February 1983), 9 (quote), 10. Dick is shown arriving at the circus in a few panels in February's *Detective Comics* #523. That same month, the letter column in *Batman* #356 (page 24) prepared fans for the coming changes in a reply announcing, "You fans of Dick Grayson can also rejoice, 'cause we've got plans afoot for everyone's favorite Teen Wonder. Hoo boy, have we got plans ... and we guarantee they're gonna knock your socks off...."

8. Dick thinks about quitting in *The New Teen Titans* (1) #31 (p. 3), #32 (p. 4), and #36 (p. 2).

9. Gerry Conway, Curt Swan, and Rodin Rodriguez, "Don't Mess with Killer Croc!" *Batman* #358 (New York: DC Comics, April 1983), 12. The "ones you love" is mainly a reference to Vicki Vale and Selina Kyle, Bruce's then-current love interests.

10. Coway, Swan, and Rodriguez, *Batman* #358, 12 for mother comment.

11. Wolfman, Pérez, and Tanghal, "Lights, Out, Everyone!" *The New Teen Titans* (1) #37 (December 1983), 15.

12. Mike W. Barr and Jim Aparo, "Psimon Says..." *Batman and the Outsiders* #5 (New York: DC Comics, December 1983), 5 and 10.

13. Barr and Aparo, *Batman and the Outsiders* #5, 19.

14. Barr and Aparo, *Batman and the Outsiders* #5, 24.

15. Wolfman, Pérez, and Tanghal, *The New Teen Titans* (1) #37, 15.
16. Wolfman, Pérez, and Tanghal, *The New Teen Titans* (1) #37, 15.
17. Doug Moench, Don Newton, and Alfredo Alcala, "A Revenge of Rainbows," *Batman* #368 (February 1984), 2.
18. Moench, Newton, and Alcala, *Batman* #368, 6.
19. Wolfman and Pérez, "Crossroads," *The New Teen Titans* (1) #39 (February 1984), 19.
20. Moench, Newton, and Alcala, *Batman* #368, 7.
21. Moench, Newton, and Alcala, *Batman* #368, 7.
22. Wolfman and Pérez, *The New Teen Titans* (1) #39, 20.
23. Wolfman, Pérez, and Tanghal, "Runaways Part 1," *The New Teen Titans* (1) #26 (December 1982), 2.
24. Wolfman and Pérez, "Who is Donna Troy?" *The New Teen Titans* (1) #38 (January 1984), 12.
25. Wolfman and Pérez, *The New Teen Titans* (1) #39, 5 and 21.
26. As Dick noted in *Tales of the Teen Titans* #44 (July 1984), 21: "I gave up being Robin because that tied me to Batman."
27. "George Pérez: New Teen Titans and Crisis Conundrums [interview with George Pérez by Glen Cadigan]" in *Titans Companion*, 149–158, at 151.
28. According to Marv Wolfman, "I ignored it. I don't care about that stuff. I think the line I've used for many, many years is that continuity holds the best writer hostage to the worst writer. Just because somebody comes up with something doesn't mean it's a good idea, and that includes myself." See *Titans Companion*, 137.
29. Max Allan Collins, Chris Warner, and Mike DeCarlo, "Did Robin Die Tonight?" *Batman* #408 (June 1987), 1–7 (involve Dick), 6 (quote).
30. Dick's age is not specified but he is clearly a teenager. Given that he was originally 19 when he became Nightwing, Dick is surely in the 17–18 age range. In the related but slightly different version given in *Batman* #416, Dick goes to college shortly after his break with Batman, which confirms he is about 18. Later Dick mentions that Batman couldn't handle having a nineteen-year-old partner (p. 14), yet still made Jason Robin, so perhaps Dick was as old as 19 when he was fired.
31. Collins, Warner, and DeCarlo, *Batman* #408, 6.
32. Collins, Warner, and DeCarlo, *Batman* #408, 7.
33. Collins, Warner, and DeCarlo, *Batman* #408, 7.
34. Jim Starlin, Jim Aparo, and Mike DeCarlo, "White Gold and Truth," *Batman* #416 (February 1988), 12 and 15.
35. Starlin, Aparo, and DeCarlo, *Batman* #416, 13.
36. Moench, Newton, and Alcala, *Batman* #368, 7.
37. *Batman* #416 uses a post–*Crisis* timeline. For instance, Dick mentions he was Robin for six years, which indicates he became Robin at 12, rather than 8 as was established in pre–*Crisis* continuity.
38. Susan Ashley Gohlman, *Starting Over: The Task of the Protagonist in the Contemporary Bildungsroman* (New York: Garland Publishing, 1990), 228.
39. Some scholars are quite testy over the relatively broad use of the term. For instance, James Hardin has termed a "...serious problem ... the imprecise use of the word to categorize virtually any work that describes, even in the most far-fetched way, a protagonist's formative years." See Hardin, "Introduction" in *Reflection and Action: Essays on the Bildungsroman*, ed. James Hardin (Columbia: University of South Carolina Press, 1991), x.
40. This brief criteria is based on Jerome Hamilton Buckley, *Seasons of Youth: The Bildungsroman from Dickens to Golding* (Cambridge, MA: Harvard University Press,

1974), 17. He lists the major characteristics of English-language bildungsromans but does not contrast them with more general coming-of-age stories.

41. As Iversen, *Change and Continuity*, notes (see note below), "How we define a genre is therefore dependent on what we have read" (13). I was struck by how much additional suffering the protagonists of works commonly termed bildungsromans endure as opposed to those who come of age. Dick Grayson's transitions to Nightwing, especially the original version and *Year One*, are an apt comic book example of this difference.

42. Buckley, *Seasons of Youth* and Anniken Telnes Iversen, *Change and Continuity: The Bildungsroman in English*, PhD Dissertation (University of Tromsø, 2009), 51–67 (for index and explanation).

43. Iversen, *Change and Continuity*, 51.

44. Iversen, *Change and Continuity*, 63.

45. Iversen, *Change and Continuity*, 56. Bildungsromans tend to have retrospective narration.

46. Chuck Dixon et al., "Year One, Chapter One: Only Robins Have Wings," *Nightwing* #101 (New York: DC Comics, early March 2005), [20].

47. Dixon et al., *Nightwing* #101, [1].

48. Dixon et al., *Nightwing* #101, [20].

49. Dixon et al., *Nightwing* #101, [21].

50. Iversen, *Change and Continuity*, 57–8.

51. Although the Bruce-Dick relationship is difficult to define, *Nightwing: Year One* situates it as father-son. As Dick comments on the duo's return to the cave, "at least the *other* parent [Alfred] was glad to see me." (Dixon et al., *Nightwing* #101, [18]).

52. Chuck Dixon, Jason Armstrong, and Robert Campanella, "Year One," *Robin Annual* #4 (New York: DC Comics, 1995) and Jeph Loeb and Tim Sale, *Batman: Dark Victory* (New York: DC Comics, 1999–2000, 2001).

53. Buckley, *Season of Youth*, 17–18.

54. Dixon et al., "Year One, Chapter Two: Friends in High Places," *Nightwing* #102 (late March 2005), [12–13], [15].

55. Dixon et al., *Nightwing* #102, [14].

56. Buckley, *Season of Youth*, 17–18; Iversen, *Change and Continuity*, 59.

57. Buckley, *Season of Youth*, 17–18; Iversen, *Change and Continuity*, 61.

58. Buckely, *Season of Youth*, 17–19, 65 (quote, contention common in English bildungsromans).

59. Dixon et al., *Nightwing* #102, [17].

60. Dixon et al., "Year One, Chapter Three: Deadman Talking," *Nightwing* #103 (early April 2005), [9–10].

61. See *Batman* #408 (June 1987) and #409 (July 1987).

62. Dixon et al., *Nightwing* #103, [21].

63. Dixon et al., *Nightwing* #103, [20].

64. Dixon et al., "Year One, Chapter Four: Night in the City," *Nightwing* #104 (late April 2005), [22].

65. Dixon et al., *Nightwing* #105, 106.

66. Dixon et al., "Year One, Chapter Six: First Flight," *Nightwing* #106 (late May 2005), [17–18].

67. See Dixon et al., *Nightwing* #106, [11], [18].

68. Marv Wolfman, Tom Grummett, and Al Vey, "Dejavu," *The New Titans* #65 (New York: DC Comics, April 1990), 1.

69. Dixon et al., "Year One, Chapter Five: Like Killing Two Birds…" *Nightwing* #105 (early May 2005), [3].

70. See Chuck Dixon et al., *Robin: Year One* (New York: DC Comics, 2000, 2002), which develops from Dixon, Tom Grummett, and Ray Kryssing, "Brothers in Arms," *Robin* #0 (New York: DC Comics, October 1994).
71. Dixon et al., *Nightwing* #106, [10].
72. Dixon et al., *Nightwing* #106, [16].
73. Dixon et al., *Nightwing* #106, [20].
74. Dixon et al., *Nightwing* #103, [1–3], [9].
75. On the function of secondary characters, see Iversen, *Change and Continuity*, 58.

Building Character
The Writers Who Shaped Dick Grayson's Personality

CHRISTOPHER MCKITTRICK

Despite being one of the most famous characters in comics, for the first forty years of his existence the original Robin, Dick Grayson, lacked a clearly defined personality. In the beginning this was intentional. Robin was created as the "everykid" who would serve as the audience surrogate for the young readers of Batman comics. However, the character's longevity eventually led to writers expanding the characterization of Robin from Batman's junior partner to his adult alter ego Nightwing, a leader of superhero teams and a protector of his own city. While creating a personality for Dick Grayson decades after his creation posed challenges, creators such as Marv Wolfman, George Pérez, Chuck Dixon, and Devin Grayson each shaped Nightwing and created a character that developed a dedicated fan base. Although, editorial interference and some controversial narrative choices made the process inconsistent at times, each of Dick Grayson's primary writers saw the character differently and their dedication to the character greatly added to Dick Grayson's enduring popularity.

When Robin was introduced in *Detective Comics* #38 in April 1940 by Bob Kane, Bill Finger, and Jerry Robinson, it was not an era of strong characterization in comic books. In the Golden Age of Comics, stories were driven by plot rather than character. In fact, even the characters were often interchangeable—for example, several Batman stories were rewritten as Green Arrow stories.[1] In addition, Robin's role as the "everykid" prevented writers from fleshing out Dick Grayson. Even when Robin received his own solo feature in *Star-Spangled Comics* (which ran from 1947 through 1952), Robin showed little personality beyond being a good-natured youth who could occasionally be mischievous. Robin only veered from his straight-laced personality when he was playing practical jokes on Batman, or in numerous stories in *World's Finest* when he teamed up with Superman's pal Jimmy Olsen to trick Batman and Superman.[2]

It wasn't until the "New Look" era ushered in by editor Julius Schwartz with 1964's *Detective Comics* #327 that Robin received an updated appearance. Robin began to be drawn older and he was consistently portrayed as a high school student.[3] While Robin solo stories would periodically appear in the Batman comics beginning with "The Boy Wonder's Boo-Boo Patrol" in *Batman* #184 (September 1966), these stories did little to expand on Grayson's personality except for adding an occasional Burt-Ward-style pun in his dialogue in line with the popular Batman TV series. Similarly, at the same time in *Teen Titans*—a superhero team-up title for sidekicks that featured Robin—writer Bob Hanley had Robin and his teammates speak in "hip" phrases in an attempt to appeal to young readers. These different approaches to dialogue were the most significant changes in character that Robin had since his creation, but they did little to define his personality.

A major narrative change in the Batman titles came with December 1969's *Batman* #217 "One Bullet Too Many!" In an attempt to distance the Batman comics from the TV series, which had been canceled the previous year, the creators limited Robin's role in Batman's adventures by sending Grayson to college. Furthermore, the writers finally acknowledged Robin's advancing age in *Detective Comics* #398 (April 1970) when Robin was billed as "The Teen Wonder" instead of "The Boy Wonder" he had been for the previous thirty years. Robin had his own solo back-up feature in Batman comics in which he primarily solved crimes around the campus of the fictional Hudson University. The back-up stories were written by several writers including Frank Robbins, Dennis O'Neil, Mike Friedrich, Elliot S! Maggin, Bob Rozakis, and Jack C. Harris, who all portrayed Robin essentially as Batman as a college student. By the end of 1976, Robin solo stories became increasingly infrequent and Robin was usually portrayed in team-ups with Batgirl, occasionally alongside Batman in the main Batman titles, and in *Teen Titans* (though that series ended with February 1978's *Teen Titans* #53). The stories that teamed Robin with Batgirl often depicted a flirtatious relationship between the pair. For the most part, between 1977 and 1980, like every year since his creation, Robin was handled by several writers over multiple titles a month, which meant that no creator had the opportunity to create a distinct personality for Dick Grayson.

By 1980, the Marvel Comics style of character-driven stories—highlighted by Chris Claremont's acclaimed run on *Uncanny X-Men*—dominated the market. A character with a thin personality like Robin seemed increasingly anachronistic among far more popular characters. Robin's personality woes started on the path to a solution in 1980 when the *Teen Titans* book was revived under the name *The New Teen Titans* by writer Marv Wolfman and artist George Pérez. Robin was depicted as the leader of the revived team, which was DC's counterpart to Marvel's popular X-Men.

Despite Robin being one of the most recognizable and oldest characters in comics, Wolfman and Pérez were essentially working with a blank slate. The two realized that Robin would need a strong personality if his team was going to compete with the X-Men. From the beginning of his tenure Wolfman wanted to distance Robin from his traditionally juvenile portrayal. As he recalled in a 2006 interview, "I wanted to do away with the childish puns and the silly Robinisms that had existed. They were great for eight-year old readers, but we weren't going there. I wanted to make him a competent older teenager on the verge of adulthood."[4] A month after the first issue of *The New Teen Titans* was released, Wolfman also began a short run on *Batman* with December 1980's issue #330. Wolfman's run was preceded by the last Robin college back-up story in *Detective Comics* #495 (October 1980) written by Jack C. Harris, which mentions—with no foreshadowing—that Grayson is failing a course for missing too many classes because of his activities as Robin. The first issue of *The New Teen Titans* confirms that Grayson had dropped out of Hudson University and is now living with Bruce Wayne again. Meanwhile, the cover of Wolfman's first issue of *Batman* teases dissension between the Dynamic Duo. On the cover, Robin is arguing with Batman over his relationship with Talia, daughter of Batman's nemesis Ra's al Ghul. Robin says to Batman "Either she goes—or I do!" to which Batman replies, "The door is that way, chum—GOODBYE!" The bottom right corner of the cover features the phrase "The beginning of the END?"[5] While the contents of the issue are less dramatic, a subplot of Wolfman's five-issue run on *Batman* is Batman's unhappiness over Robin dropping out of college, which causes tension between them. What was teased on the cover of #330 was exactly what would lead to the Dick Grayson character coming into his own. As Wolfman would later point out in an interview with *Amazing Heroes*, "Dick Grayson had no identity other than being the other part of Robin, and Robin was nothing but the bottom half of Batman."[6] In order for Grayson to become his own character, Wolfman believed that the character had to be distanced from Batman.

Nevertheless, Wolfman and Pérez were unable to entirely separate Robin from Batman in the early years of *The New Teen Titans*. Wolfman left *Batman* with issue #335 and Gerry Conway, in the revived Robin back-up feature in subsequent issues of *Batman* and *Detective Comics*, portrayed

Robin differently. Conway depicted Robin going on the road with the circus and did not mention his activities with the Titans. Then, almost as abruptly as Grayson quit college less than a year and a half prior, the Robin back-up feature ended. Robin returned to Batman's side full-time in Conway's *Batman* #344 (February 1982), telling his mentor, "I learned a LOT these past few months on the road. Mostly I learned I NEED your friendship. We're a team, Batman, no matter what happens in the future—that's something I won't EVER forget again."[7] In the same month's *Detective Comics* #511 (also written by Conway), Grayson registers to continue college at Gotham University, though this was quickly forgotten. Obviously this depiction of Robin contrasted greatly with the depiction of Robin in *The New Teen Titans*, in which Robin spent most of his time at Titans Tower in New York City. While Wolfman and Pérez established Grayson as a confident, level-headed hero who was a beloved leader of the Titans—particularly by the alien Starfire, with whom Robin was developing a romantic connection—Conway continued to portray Robin as Batman's junior partner. Because the writers of Batman comics had priority use of Robin, Wolfman and Pérez were unable to alter his characterization in any significant way outside of their own title. As long as Grayson was appearing as Robin in the Batman titles, any attempt by Wolfman and Pérez to create a non-sidekick version of the character would be stifled.

Conway's quick return to the sidekick status quo reflected his belief that an adult, independent-minded Robin was not ideal for the dynamic between the Dynamic Duo. Referring to both Robin and Captain America's sidekick Bucky in a 1981 interview with *The Comics Journal*, Conway explained,

> Bucky ideally should be about 15 years old, just as Robin ideally should be about 15 years old. They should be on the verge on manhood, they should be on the verge of taking on responsibility for their own lives, and they should be looking toward Captain America or Batman or whoever as the model on which they want to build their own lives. [...] Robin is now almost a college graduate in his early 20s, I would guess, or late teens; at the very earliest he'd be 19. So you've lost that essential connection.[8]

It was not until the Batman editors and writers decided to compromise by replacing Grayson with a younger Robin named Jason Todd that Wolfman and Pérez were given carte blanche to develop the Dick Grayson character as they preferred. As Pérez remarked at the time, "Dick Grayson, since he had no real identity before we got to him, now belongs to us."[9]

In July 1984's *Tales of the Teen Titans* #44 (*The New Teen Titans* series had been renamed with issue #41), Grayson adopts the identity of

Nightwing, a name taken from a minor Superman character. As Nightwing, Grayson develops a deeper relationship with teammate Starfire, which was portrayed far more maturely than his flirtatious relationship with Batgirl in their 1970s adventures. Pérez would continue to work on *Titans* as co-plotter and artist through mid–1985, and though Pérez returned for some issues from 1988 through 1989 Wolfman became the primary writer for Dick Grayson. In Wolfman's hands, Grayson became the confident leader that Wolfman always envisioned he could be, just now in the guise of Nightwing. Many years later when he was writing Nightwing's solo title, Wolfman assessed his view on Grayson's personality and popularity, saying:

> To me, Dick is the one hero who simply decided being a fighter for justice was the right thing to do. The murder of Dick's parents was solved almost immediately so there was never a feeling he needed revenge. Even back when he was created he was someone who made bad jokes and seemed to have fun doing what he did. He wasn't the sole survivor of a doomed planet. He didn't feel responsible for the death of his parents. He wasn't appointed an intergalactic cop. When Batman put his parent's killers behind bars he saw that stopping crime was something worth believing in. Dick is the only one I know who is like that. And he does it without having been given any special powers. To me Dick is the best kind of character there can be; he's dedicated to his cause for all the right reasons. Plus he's human, so Dick has to work hard to be good. Unlike Superman he has no natural powers. Shoot him and he will be hurt. That makes his stories more interesting.[10]

Aside from depicting Nightwing as a respected leader and a beloved teammate, Wolfman also explored Nightwing's love life and emotional side. Nightwing and Starfire had a tumultuous relationship and were nearly married, and Nightwing became emotionally torn apart by the trauma and death faced by him and his Titans teammates.

Wolfman ceased being the primary writer behind Nightwing in 1994 when Nightwing left the series in September's *The New Titans* #114. The character had already returned to the Batman titles, which were in the midst of the famed "Knightfall" storyline in which Bruce Wayne's back is broken and he is replaced as Batman by another character, Jean Paul Valley. It was at this time that Nightwing was first written by Chuck Dixon, who was one of the co-writers of "Knightfall."

Dixon had become a fan favorite on the Batman titles in part because of his writing of the third Robin, Tim Drake, in three *Robin* mini-series, the ongoing *Robin* monthly series, as well as *Detective Comics*. Though Drake was created by Wolfman, it was Dixon who made the character popular. Dixon's first experience writing a story entirely about Grayson came with October 1994's *Robin* #0, which retold the origin of Grayson as Robin. Over the next year and a half, Nightwing would periodically appear in the Batman titles (most notably during crossover issues written by Dixon) and had his own four-issue mini-series written by Dennis O'Neil, then editor of the Batman titles. In issue #1 of the mini-series, O'Neil gave an in-story reason for Grayson's lack of personality over his decades as Robin. Nightwing says of his time as Robin,

> It wasn't all fun. I was on call twenty-four hours a day and you subjected me to discipline that would make a marine boot camp look like a Girl Scout cookie-fest. I was able to handle schoolwork but there was no time for anything else. No football games, no dances, no proms, no girlfriends. Just Robin, laughing boy daredevil. Batman's faithful shadow. And where was Dick Grayson? Nowhere. Nowhere at all.[11]

When Nightwing finally received his own ongoing series, which launched in October 1996, Dixon was the natural choice to write the character. Dixon would write the series for almost six years. The *Nightwing* series moved Nightwing from Gotham to Blüdhaven, a city not far from Gotham but plagued by similar crime issues. By setting Nightwing in his own city, Dixon gave Nightwing the opportunity to grow as a solo character without having a parade of Batman-related guest stars every issue.

However, Dixon did not follow O'Neil's angst-ridden portrayal of post–*Titans* Nightwing. Though Dixon's Nightwing dealt primarily with his Bat-family rather than his Titans family, Dixon portrayed Nightwing as the same approachable ally as he was when written by Wolfman. In fact, Dixon often defined the main difference between Nightwing and Batman as this approachability. Oddly enough, a character that had lacked a personality for decades was now well-loved by his fans for having such an affable, sincere temperament and for his spirit of swashbuckling fun.[12] While Wolfman portrayed Nightwing as being uncomfortable with Batman's harsher methods of crimefighting, Dixon portrayed Nightwing as uncomfortable with trying to live up to what he perceived were Batman's impossible expectations for him. Nonetheless, Dixon's Nightwing was portrayed as much more confident in his abilities, which was arguably the natural progression of his character. During Batman's guest starring stint in *Nightwing* #13–15, Dixon put any lingering confidence issues between Nightwing and Batman to rest when, after taking on Blockbuster together, Batman tells Nightwing, "You've got a handle on things down here. I'm proud of you" when Nightwing expects a lecture.[13] Dixon wrote Nightwing in multiple titles and crossovers and consistently portrayed Nightwing as confident and having Batman's full support.

Dixon's view of Nightwing as a character was similar to Wolfman's. In a 1997 interview with *Wizard* magazine, Dixon reflected on the differences between Batman and Nightwing as characters. He explained,

> He grew up seeing this brooding, self-tormented guy all the time. Sometimes you see things your parents did and you go, "I'm not going to be like that." I think Dick made a conscious effort to say, "I'm not going to let it eat me alive the way Bruce has." He's not as uncomfortable being Dick Grayson as Batman is being Bruce Wayne. Dick Grayson is not that much of a masquerade, whereas Bruce Wayne is a complete sham. Dick Grayson can let off steam. He can lighten up a little bit. Dick knows that you gotta take the costume off once in a while and just go to a movie.[14]

Despite Dixon largely maintaining Wolfman's characterization, the new *Nightwing* series was firmly established as a Batman spinoff and was not affiliated with any *Titans* titles. Nightwing's past with the Titans was rarely referenced in the Batman books, and Dixon's use of the various Batman-related heroes as Nightwing's primary allies and Barbara Gordon as Nightwing's love interest separated Nightwing from his Titans connections. In January 1999, Dixon also launched the *Birds of Prey* series, which featured a female team lead by Barbara Gordon, who was now the wheelchair-bound superhero tactician Oracle. August 1999's *Birds of Prey* #8 became a fan-favorite issue that guest-starred Nightwing that left the romantic relationship status between Nightwing and Oracle ambiguous. Like Nightwing's prior romance with Starfire in *New Teen Titans*, his relationship with Barbara continued to differentiate him from Batman/Bruce Wayne, a character known for having trust issues. Even though he dated fellow superheroes, it still gave Nightwing much more of a social life than Batman.

In the latter half of Dixon's run on *Nightwing* Grayson becomes a police officer in Blüdhaven and Dixon largely wraps up his long-running storyline about Nightwing's archenemy Blockbuster, the crime kingpin of Blüdhaven. In *Detective Comics* #725 (also written by Dixon), Nightwing gives the rationale for become a police officer as, "Blüdhaven's so rotten I don't think it can be corrected by what we do."[15] Using a police officer as his cover identity created tension between Dick and Batman because Batman disliked that Dick would be carrying a gun. Having Dick become a police officer created significant narrative potential for the character. He would be far more skilled in crimefighting than his fellow officers, but his code against using guns and lethal force would naturally create conflict. It also showed that Dick was now willing to sacrifice his non-superhero personal life to combat criminal activity in Blüdhaven, demonstrating his deepening commitment to eliminating crime in the city.

Dixon's replacement on *Nightwing* was Devin Grayson, who would write the title from September 2002's issue #71 through April 2006's #117. Like Dixon before her, Devin Grayson was the natural choice to write the series because of her previous experience with the character.[16] She also had personal affinity for the character: she was introduced to superheroes by *Batman: The Animated Series*, and her favorite character from the show was Robin (Dick Grayson).[17]

Based on her prior work, Grayson demonstrated a similar understanding of Nightwing as Wolfman and Dixon. In *Nightwing and Huntress* #1 she established Nightwing's independence from Batman when Huntress accuses Nightwing of following Batman's methods and he responds, "If that were true, I wouldn't have spent so much time with the Titans. I'm open to different methods of problem solving."[18] At the same time, Grayson portrayed Nightwing as being overly trusting—particularly of the women in his life—which would carry over to her run on *Nightwing*. For example, in *Nightwing and Huntress* #3, when he tells Barbara that he is working with the Huntress, a vigilante that she disproves of, Barbara tells him during a phone call, "But for all your talents, you are not the world's best judge of character. You grew up thinking Bruce was normal."[19]

Initially, Grayson followed the foundation laid by Dixon. Nightwing remained a police officer and Blockbuster returned to pursue Nightwing with a vengeance. However, there were two major changes that Grayson introduced. First, she focused more on Nightwing's relationship with Barbara, portraying Nightwing as much more affectionate toward her (while Grayson was the writer of *Titans* she depicted Nightwing and Starfire having difficulty being friends based on their past relationship, which essentially wrote Starfire out as a love interest for Nightwing).[20] Second, Grayson introduced former FBI agent Catalina Flores in her very first issue. By the second page she appears on Flores is already asking Dick for his phone number after knocking him down in a self-defense class that he is teaching, establishing Flores as an aggressive, dominating personality. Flores would later become the violent vigilante Tarantula that Grayson extensively featured in much of her run.

When Grayson's second year on *Nightwing* began she embarked on a lengthy arc that is very reminiscent of Frank Miller's classic "Born Again" story in Marvel Comics' *Daredevil*.[21] Nightwing's intent on pushing himself despite a gunshot injury causes tension between Nightwing and the Bat-family, but most notably with Barbara. Over the next several issues their relationship deteriorates because Barbara becomes jealous that Nightwing begins working with Tarantula. Barbara interprets this partnership with

Tarantula as a surrogate of the old Batgirl and Robin partnership. This culminates in Barbara breaking up with him in *Nightwing* #87, accusing him of living too much in their past and also of trying to be as driven as Batman, which was in contrast to Wolfman and Dixon's more even-tempered portrayal of Nightwing.[22]

Blockbuster also learns Nightwing's secret identity and his revenge on Nightwing includes blowing up Dick's apartment building. This kills off almost Nightwing's entire supporting cast, most of whom had been part of the series since the first dozen issues. Furious and depressed, Nightwing is reduced to sleeping on fire escapes and only seeks support from the unproven vigilante Tarantula, whom he knows is not averse to murdering criminals. Curiously, for someone who had such extensive experience writing Nightwing teaming with his allies in *Gotham Knights* and *Titans*, Grayson kept the character at arm's length from his allies in this story. Nightwing had never been depicted as a loner since his creation in 1940, yet in this storyline he completely isolated himself from his longtime allies, which was a major personality shift.

Grayson's plot reached its climax in the most controversial issue of her run, July 2004's *Nightwing* #93. In the issue, Nightwing confronts Blockbuster over the murders of his supporting cast and Blockbuster tells the hero that he will kill everyone he knows, threatening "I'll take out the people you care about—hell, even strangers you stand next to on the street—you won't be able to shake someone's hand without marking them for death! Do you like being ALONE, Dick? I'll make sure you can't save any of them."[23] This is naturally a distressing threat for a character with so many close allies. As Nightwing is torn about what to do, Tarantula arrives with a gun and murders Blockbuster. With his mind broken over not stopping Tarantula, a distraught Nightwing retreats to the building's roof. Tarantula follows him and has sex with him despite Nightwing saying "Don't … touch me."[24]

There was considerable uproar among Nightwing fans who questioned if Tarantula was in fact raping Nightwing while he was in a fragile state of mind and whether or not Nightwing, who had been portrayed by Wolfman, Pérez, and Dixon as an extremely level-headed hero, would have ever been pushed to these physical and emotional limits. When she was asked about the scene in a 2004 interview with Comic Boards, Grayson responded, "For the record, I've never used the word 'rape,' I just said it was nonconsensual."[25] In an interview with The Batman Universe website in May 2014, Grayson expressed remorse for her words and the scene, saying,

I was wrong. I messed that one up and I apologize. My interview comments were uninformed and ignorant and I'm grateful for the chance to revisit the issue. [...] I used a literal rape as a metaphorical nadir, and I know better. Or, at least, I should have known better and certainly do now. I was concentrating so hard on other elements of that scene which felt so much more narratively significant to me (Blockbuster's murder, primarily) that I totally lost sight of the power and non-symbolic consequence of the gesture I was using. By the time I realized the severity of the mistake and how harmful it might have been to actual survivors of sexual abuse and assault (myself included), I had run out of time to make it right. I'm not sure I could have made it right, mind you, but I did at least have the intention of bringing the story back around to it so that the act didn't exist completely devoid of consequence or analysis. But it does, and I regret that more deeply than I can say.[26]

The following issues portray Tarantula leading a disoriented Nightwing as fugitives running off to Atlantic City, with Nightwing written in a state of shock and subservient to Tarantula even to the point that she pushes him to marry her in issue #95. At best, Grayson's storyline took Nightwing to a narrative place that he had never been before. At worst, Grayson took a fan favorite character and made him subservient to a character that she created while removing the optimistic, devil-may-care swashbuckling aspect of the character and replacing that with a paranoid, broken, and depressive character.

The Nightwing/Tarantula marriage issue ends with the paperwork at the Atlantic City courthouse being interrupted by a call from Batman requesting Nightwing's assistance. Curiously, after ignoring his allies throughout this entire storyline, Nightwing essentially "snaps out" of his depression the moment he receives a call from Batman, suggesting that all along what Nightwing needed was the support of his allies even though he refused to acknowledge them since Barbara broke up with him in *Nightwing* #87. While Wolfman had previously depicted Nightwing as becoming distant from his allies when he was in times of great emotional stress,[27] this storyline took this trait to the extreme before this rapid reversal. The next three issues of Nightwing are part of the "War Crimes" crossover with all of the Batman titles and depict Nightwing's state of mind inconsistently. For example, despite being led by her as fugitives for the past several issues, Nightwing refers to Tarantula as "my stalker" to Batman in *Nightwing* #96.[28] He is also portrayed as afraid to tell Batman about Blockbuster's murder because he is convinced that because he didn't stop Tarantula he is more responsible for Blockbuster's murder than she is. But in issue #98 he is once again unhinged and reckless, even using a supervillain as a human shield and is wounded by police gunfire in the leg. *Nightwing*

#100 concludes the Tarantula storyline when she is imprisoned for Blockbuster's murder. However, Grayson does not follow up on her fate nor on her extensive knowledge of Nightwing's personal life for the rest of her run despite her extensive focus on the character in the previous 29 issues.

The final 11 issues of Devin Grayson's run, which began in #107 after Dixon and Beatty's six issue "Nightwing: Year One" flashback story, continue to present a darker Dick Grayson. Dick begins operating as a mob enforcer nicknamed "Crutches" (as he is still recovering from his gunshot wound), with no initial indication that this is undercover work. In fact, Grayson uses Dick's Romani heritage, which she had established earlier in her run, and circus past to justify Dick becoming a mob enforcer, having him narrate in #107:

> I know what you're thinking. I don't belong here, right? Well you're wrong. I belong here way more than I ever belonged in Bruce Wayne's mansion. I'm a Gypsy, after all. A circus boy. A carny. If not for Batman, is there any question that I would have ended up somewhere like this?[29]

In addition, in #110, Nightwing expresses shock and jealousy that Bruce Wayne offered to adopt the recently orphaned Tim Drake even though Wayne did not adopt Nightwing until well into his adulthood.[30] Though it could be chalked up to Nightwing's state of mind, it seems out of character for a character who had already long considered Drake as a younger brother (the Nightwing and Robin team-up story in 1994's *Robin* #0, written by Dixon, is even titled "Brothers in Arms.") However, the "Crutches" persona gives way to a villainous Nightwing persona called "Renegade" when Nightwing encounters his longtime nemesis Deathstroke in *Nightwing* #112. Deathstroke asks him to train his daughter Rose (known as Ravanger) to prove that he is no longer a hero after Nightwing insists, "I'm not undercover with the bad guys—I am the bad guys!"[31] At this point Grayson begins revealing that Nightwing was indeed working undercover (despite internal narration that indicated otherwise in previous issues) and tries to steer Ravager into becoming a hero. This revealed that despite outward appearances to the contrary, Nightwing was not betraying his heroic roots and remained, despite this storyline, an essentially "good guy." Nonetheless, he still refused to associate with his fellow heroes—including longtime Titans teammate Arsenal in *Nightwing* #114, whom Nightwing actually beats up to prove that he is a "bad guy." As a result, Grayson gave Nightwing a manipulative, dishonest "the end justifies the means" streak that previous writers did not feature in the character's personality.

In the 2004 interview with Comic Boards, Grayson expressed that she feared that the sheer length of this story arc turned off readers because it spent too much time depicting Nightwing as a darker character compared to his previous incarnations. She explained,

> We're finishing up a very dark, heavy storyline, and clearly Dick's responding with a lot of "Batmanish" moodiness. At his core, I think the character is more "Robinish," and although it will take him a while to get there, I think it will be a very satisfying point in the story when Dick finally re-emerges as a brighter, happier, more balanced individual. The nature of stories is to set up and resolve conflict. We're just not at the resolution stage with this story yet, and I apologize if it's taking too long. That may have been a miscalculation on my part, I was really hungry for a long, explorative, character-intensive story line and may have over-estimated the average reader's patience with drawn-out conflict.[32]

Despite her concerns of her storyline being too drawn out, Grayson's run ended in *Nightwing* #117 with each storyline thread being rushed to a conclusion, including Nightwing confessing to Batman his perceived role in Blockbuster's murder. Batman essentially calls Nightwing's involvement a mistake in judgment that he will need to come to terms with on his own, which serves as an unsatisfying conclusion to a narrative thread that had been built up by Grayson as potentially contentious for two years. In another example that demonstrates the rushed conclusion, the issue ends with Nightwing proposing to Barbara Gordon even though the characters had not interacted since the "War Crimes" crossover nearly two years prior.

Much of the criticism of Devin Grayson's portrayal of Nightwing can be blamed on the way her tenure on the series ended. In the lead-up to DC's *Infinite Crisis* mini-series—in which at one point DC Comics Editor-in-Chief Dan Didio planned to kill off Nightwing—the Nightwing character was in a narrative flux. Nightwing played a key role in *Infinite Crisis*, which required Grayson to return the character to his status quo before ending her run. Meanwhile, Judd Winick, the writer of *The Outsiders*, which was a book about a team that Nightwing led, depicted Nightwing and Starfire rekindling their sexual relationship despite the fact that Grayson planned on Nightwing reconciling with Barbara. *Infinite Crisis* also featured the destruction of Blüdhaven, a major storyline change that Grayson did not plan or anticipate but nevertheless had to address in her final two issues of *Nightwing*. In a 2005 interview with Comic Book Resources, Grayson expressed her frustration with the impact Nightwing's use in other titles had on her character, saying, "This is, without a doubt, the trickiest and least fun part of working with corporately-owned entities, but you know that when you sign up to do it. I do feel sad and frustrated that I won't get to tell the story I've been leading the readers up to for over a year, but hopefully the emergent story will be just as compelling."[33] More than anything else, these circumstances indicated that after more than two decades of Nightwing's personality being shaped by one primary writer at a time, Dick Grayson had returned to being an "editorially controlled" character.

In the May 2014 interview with The Batman Universe, Grayson continued to reflect on the editorial complications that altered her story. She recalls,

> I went from nearly ten years of rarely being asked to rewrite a single line to months of never receiving fewer than six complete rewrites on every script—not because the quality of the scripts had suddenly changed but because something in the fictional universe had shifted and needed to be accounted for. DC went from a model of group editors pre-approving story arcs to upper management micro-editing finished scripts.[34]

While Grayson was criticized for her portrayal of Nightwing, especially in the final two years of her run, she tried to do something that had not been done with the character before by separating Nightwing from his extensive allies and exploring the effect that would have on his easygoing personality. Indeed, Grayson's run on the character was arguably the most significant change for Nightwing's status quo since he took on the persona of Nightwing in 1984 because it significantly altered the established personality of the character for over two years. However, a combination of poor narrative choices and editorial interference robbed Grayson of the chance to have as lasting of an impact on Nightwing as Wolfman and Dixon had despite her lengthy tenure with the character. The editorial interference she faced in the latter half of her run signaled a return to the editorial control of the character that Wolfman and Pérez had to fight against over a quarter century before.

After Devin Grayson, Dick returned to his roots and was bounced from writer to writer. The *Nightwing* series concluded with April 2009's #153, and the series was written by four different writers over its final three years (even Wolfman, who returned to write his creation in *Nightwing* #125, only wrote the title for 13 issues). For a brief time afterward Nightwing became Batman in the aftermath of Grant Morrison's lengthy "Batman: RIP" story. The Nightwing title was relaunched in 2011 as part of DC Comics' line-wide reboot "The New 52," and a majority of its 30 issues were written by Kyle Higgins, though much of his run was comprised of crossovers with the other Batman titles.

After having just three main writers behind Nightwing for over two decades, since Devin Grayson there has yet to be a permanent voice behind the character since 2005. The last decade of more editorial-driven stories at DC Comics has required writers to approach writing long-running characters like Nightwing differently, and it is arguable that his narrative potential has suffered over the last decade without a long-term writer behind him. Regardless, for at least twenty years Nightwing was one of DC Comics' most developed heroes, something that seemed unlikely for a junior partner of the Dark Knight when he was introduced in 1940. That is a testament to the strength of the writers who ensured that Dick Grayson received the personality he deserved as one of the oldest characters in superhero comics.

Notes

1. For example, Bill Finger, Jack Kirby, and Roz Kirby, "The Green Arrows of the World," *Adventure Comics* #250 (New York: DC Comics, July 1958) was a rewrite of Edmond Hamilton, Sheldon Moldoff, and Charles Paris, "The Batmen of All Nations," *Detective Comics* #215 (New York: DC Comics, January 1955).

2. For a practical joke see France Herron, Sheldon Moldoff and Charles Paris, "The Second Boy Wonder," *Batman* #105 (New York: DC Comics, February 1957). For Jimmy Olsen see, Edmond Hamilton, Curt Swan, and George Klein "The Olsen-Robin Team vs. 'The Superman-Batman Team,'" *World's Finest Comics* #141 (New York: DC Comics, May 1964).

3. As an example of how Robin's age was depicted inconsistently during the 1940s and 1950s, Robin is depicted driving the Batmobile on the cover of *Batman* #20 (December 1943–January 1944) and in several stories in the 1940s, though he was often depicted as far younger than he would have to be in order to legally drive.

4. Jennifer M. Contino, "Marv Wolfman: From ROBIN to NIGHTWING: Chronicling the Adventures of Dick Grayson," mania.com, 19 Oct. 2006, http://www.mania.com/marv-wolfman-from-robin-to-nightwing-chronicling-adventures-dick-grayson_article_52561.html.

5. Ross Andru and Dick Giordano, *Batman* #330 (December 1980), Cover.

6. Michael F. Hopkins, "Subtlety and Power: The George Pérez Interview," *Amazing Heroes* #50 (1 July 1984), 21.

7. Gerry Conway, Gene Colan, and Klaus Janson, "Monster My Sweet!" *Batman* #344 (February 1982), 27.

8. Rob Gustaveson, "Gary Conway Talks Back to The Comics Journal," *The Comics Journal* No. 69 (December 1981), 37.

9. Hopkins, "Subtlety and Power: The George Pérez Interview," 20.

10. Matt Brady, "Marv Wolfman on Nightwing," *Newsarama*, 20 November 2006, http://www.titanstower.com/marv-wolfman-on-nightwing-2/.

11. Dennis O'Neil, Greg Land, and Mike Sellers, "The Resignation," *Nightwing* mini-series #1 (New York: DC Comics, September 1995), [10].

12. For an issue by Dixon displaying Nightwing's fun side, see Chuck Dixon, Scott McDaniel, and Karl Story, "The Boys," *Nightwing* #25 (New York: DC Comics, October 1998).

13. Chuck Dixon, Scott McDaniel, and Karl Story, "Warriors Two," *Nightwing* #15 (December 1997), [21].

14. Scott Brick, "Out of the Shadow of the Bat, Dick Grayson Flies on his Own as Nightwing," *Wizard* #72 (October 1997), 124.

15. Chuck Dixon, William Rosado, and Tom Palmer, "At the End of the Day," *Detective Comics* #725 (September 1998), [15].

16. Devin Grayson previously wrote 1997's *Nightwing* Annual #1, 1998's *Nightwing and*

Huntress mini-series, and Nightwing in *The Titans* from March 1999's issue #1 to October 2000's issue #20 (though she co-wrote 6 of those issues with other writers).Grayson also wrote all of the Bat-family characters, including Nightwing, in the *Batman: Gotham Knights* series, which she wrote from issue #1 (March 2000) through issue #32 (October 2002) with the exception of three issues.

17. "As a matter of fact, one of the reasons she got into comics was due to a fascination with the Dick Grayson character from 'Batman: The Animated Series.'" George A. Tramountanas, "Devin Grayson—The 'Nightwing' Crisis," *Comic Book Resources*, 10 November 2005, http://www.comicbookresources.com/?page=article&id=5934.

18. Devin Grayson, Greg Land, and Bill Sienkiewicz, "Cosa Nostra Part One: Familia," *Nightwing and Huntress* #1 (New York: DC Comics, May 1998), [20].

19. Devin Grayson, Greg Land, and Bill Sienkiewicz, "Cosa Nostra Part Three: Black Sheep," *Nightwing and Huntress* #3 (July 1998), [4].

20. Devin Grayson et al., "Fallout," *The Titans* (1) #13 (New York: DC Comics, March 2000).

21. Frank Miller and David Mazzucchelli, *Daredevil* #227–233 (New York: Marvel Comics, February–August 1986).

22. Devin Grayson, Patrick Zircher, and Andy Owens, "Snowball," *Nightwing* #87 (January 2004), [13–15].

23. Devin Grayson, Patrick Zircher, and Andy Owens, "Slow Burn," *Nightwing* #93 (July 2004), [11].

24. Grayson, Zircher, and Owens, *Nightwing* #93, [20].

25. Randy Burtis, "An Interview with Devin Grayson," *Comic Boards*, 9 August 2004, http://www.comicboards.com/devin.php.

26. Donovan Grant, "Devin Grayson on Her Batman Universe Work," *The Batman Universe*, 20 May 2014, http://thebatmanuniverse.net/tbu-exclusive-3/.

27. For example, after Starfire is forced to marry another man Dick Grayson becomes very withdrawn. See Marv Wolfman, Ed Barreto, and Romeo Tanghal, "Homecoming," *The New Teens Titans* (2) #18 (New York: DC Comics, March 1986).

28. Devin Grayson, Mike Lilly, and Andy Owens, "War Games: Act 1 Part 3: A Sort of Homecoming," *Nightwing* #96 (October 2004), [18].

29. Devin Grayson, Phil Hester, and Ande Parks, "Criminal," *Nightwing* #107 (June 2005), [7–8].

30. Grayson, Hester, and Parks, "Incorporation," *Nightwing* #110 (September 2005), [14–17].

31. Grayson, Hester, and Parks, "The Devil You Know," *Nightwing* #112 (November 2005), [4–5].

32. Randy Burtis, "An Interview with Devin Grayson," *Comic Boards*, 9 August 2004, http://www.comicboards.com/devin.php.

33. Tramountanas, "Devin Grayson—The 'Nightwing' Crisis," http://www.comicbookresources. com/?page=article&id=5934.

34. Grant, "Devin Grayson on Her Batman Universe Work," http://thebatmanuniverse.net/tbu-exclusive-3/.

The Heart and Soul

Dick Grayson as the Center of the DC Universe

MOLLIE HERLOCKER

Dick Grayson is one of the longest existing superheroes in the history of comics, surpassing even Wonder Woman and Captain America in years. Dick is unique among the older, original Golden Age heroes because he is one of the only child characters to remain prominent throughout the decades. His prominence goes beyond his sidekick connection to the Batman and has matured him into that of a solo hero and leader as a young man. Phil Jimenez noted during the Infinite Crisis storyline that Dick,

> has so many connections to other characters. In many ways, even more than Superman or Batman, Nightwing is the soul, the linchpin, of the DCU. He's well respected by everyone, known to the JLA, the Titans, the Outsiders, Birds of Prey—everyone looks to him for advice, for friendship, for his skills. He's the natural leader of the DCU.[1]

Dick Grayson formed these connections over the course of his lifetime, starting as the happy acrobatic sidekick in the dark heart of Gotham and moving forward through his growth as an independent man and hero in his work with the Batman Family, the Teen Titans, and the Justice League as Nightwing and Batman.

Overall, the city of Gotham, its residents, and its rogues are known for showcasing the darker side of the main DC Comics Universe, especially in a literal chromatic sense, with the main color scheme being black. This common perception overlooks the figure of Robin, whose red, green, and yellow uniform reflects the brighter demeanor of its originator. As a whole, however, where Batman, the Bat Family, and the Gotham City Police Department could be confined in the darkness of their surroundings, Dick Grayson as Robin frequently filled the role of someone who could save them from themselves through quips and optimism. Since his debut in

1940, Dick Grayson has provided a drop of sunshine in the dark nights of Gotham, most notably so in his original role as Robin, the Boy Wonder. Though his origin story nearly mirrors Bruce Wayne's, factors of both nature and nurture have consistently differentiated the paths the two men took. In every version, both witnessed the murders of their beloved parents, both were spared from that fate, and both left the event vowing to fight for justice. However, while Bruce began his mission by himself, leading him to suffer from a greater degree of survivor's guilt and an obsession with vengeance, Dick had Bruce to guide him away from that path, due to Bruce's own self-awareness. Another contributing factor to Dick's more positive approach to his fight for justice was his personal upbringing. In most versions of the Grayson murder, Dick is around ten years old, compared to Bruce's typical eight, and had a very close bond with his parents as both family and teammates. Working as a child acrobat inevitably leads to a greater level of instinctive trust in others than growing up in a huge manor with only your butler for company. Dick indirectly points this out to Bruce in Kevin Smith's Batman miniseries "The Widening Gyre" saying, "If you can't trust Superman, how can you trust ANYONE?"[2] Dick's comment here highlights Bruce's trust issues, while also highlighting both the value of Superman's presence in their lives and Dick's innate trust in others, especially because Superman is known for his honesty and trustworthiness.

Dick's ability to trust others and his childhood in the circus led him to be one of the most optimistic superheroes and certainly the most optimistic Bat. In the Golden Age of Comics, a lot of the optimism can be attributed to his youth and his secondary purpose as a narrative element intended to reflect how children in the audience should be reacting to the story. Similarly, his optimism in the Silver Age can be seen as reflective of the times and, probably more so, the pressure placed on comic book writers to be more positive, conservative, and in line with the status quo due to publications like Fredric Wertham's *Seduction of the Innocent* and the development of the Comics Code Authority.[3] As comics grew darker in tone in the Bronze Age and the Post-Crisis Dark Age, Dick's optimism had become an inherent part of writing his character, even though he was seen in much more serious roles as he aged. Since he "grew up" into a teenager and young adult, Dick has shown that optimism is more than childish nature. Alfred emphasizes this fact to Dick when he appears to lose hope in himself and the cause after the debacle with Blockbuster and Tarantula. For Alfred to see Dick lose the "luminosity of spirit" he had as a child which allowed him to "survive and thrive" where others, such as Bruce, did not, was heartbreaking and made him fear for Bruce and Dick's lives.[4] Dick, confused, denies the value of optimism because of Bruce's lack of it, but is rebuked by Alfred stating, "But of course he has had optimism! He has had you."[5] With the reinforcement of his value to Bruce's fight, Dick regains his footing as the member of the Bat Family who has the easiest time speaking up to Bruce to reassess the situation, especially when Bruce is trying to avoid thinking of the consequences of working in the dark.

Dick's other main role in the Bat Family as Robin, especially in the early years of the comics, was simply to provide Batman with someone to talk to. While many people today see Batman as a solitary figure, he only existed without Robin for eleven months. Creator Bill Finger felt Batman needed a partner and was inspired by Sherlock Holmes and Dr. John Watson.[6] Like Watson, Robin represented the reader by providing an outlet for the detective to discuss the solution to the crime without talking to himself. On a "personal" level, it helped Batman to have someone to talk to who could relate to his experiences. Having someone like that can help with the healing process and that is often seen in the development of the relationship between Bruce Wayne and Dick Grayson, as well as between Bruce and the future Robins.

No matter which version of the separation, be it a personal choice or a firing, Dick's graduation from the role of sidekick to a solo hero had a massive impact both on him and the Bat Family. The original, and most true-to-character, version of this transition, written by Marv Wolfman and George Pérez in *Tales of the Teen Titans* in 1984, portrayed Dick as a 20 year old ready to stretch his wings and leave the nest—or, rather, cave—and become his own man. He struggled for a few issues trying to create his new identity, as this was a transition, not a retirement. Choosing the name Nightwing, along with his original disco-esque costume, symbolized how he is a hero who is the sum of his parts, learning through working with others, not just assuming that he knows the way to do things. He chose the name Nightwing from a Kryptonian legend Superman told him; his original Nightwing costume was based on his dad's costume as a solo acrobatic act; his detective skills and training came from his time with Batman; and his confidence in his own abilities and himself as a hero came from his time with the Teen Titans, especially through his relationship with Starfire.[7]

In addition to building a base for his transition to Nightwing, Dick's involvement with the Teen Titans also connected him to an even bigger network than he had been in as Robin the Boy Wonder, sidekick to Batman. While his connection to Batman did link him with the heroes of the Justice

League, the Justice Society, and the Outsiders, the Teen Titans gave him a stronger connection to the heroes whose partners or relatives were involved in the Titans. The original Teen Titans from the 1960s consisted of Robin, Kid Flash, Aqualad, Wonder Girl, and Speedy; the strongest bonds he formed over all incarnations with the Titans were with Wally West and Donna Troy, also known as Kid Flash and Wonder Girl, the sidekick to the Flash and the younger sister of Wonder Woman, respectively. In the 1980s the lineup was changed, adding Starfire, Raven, Cyborg, and Beast Boy, and shifting Aqualad and Speedy to more independent roles outside of the team, though occasionally they would go to the Titans for help with their own missions. Because the stories of the Teen Titans focused on teen characters, a new opportunity was provided for writers to create a greater number of teen heroes outside of the realm of sidekicks and the known heroes. Some of the better-known results of this freedom during the first run of the Teen Titans in the 1970s series included Karen Beecher (Bumblebee; DC's first female African-American superhero), Mal Duncan (the Guardian), Hank and Don Hall (Hawk and Dove; brothers who embody aggression and pacifism), and Lilith Clay (Omen; demigoddess with psychic abilities). In the 1980s' New Teen Titans, additional new teen characters were added to the DCU, including Tara Markov (Terra; one of the villains of the 1984 story arc "The Judas Contract") and Joey Wilson (Jericho; son of Deathstroke the Terminator and new member of the Titans during "The Judas Contract")

After his graduation to Nightwing, Dick remained relatively close with his successors to the role of Robin. Due to his commitments with the Teen Titans, his main contribution to Jason Todd's time as Robin was through his "passing of the shorts," which symbolized his acceptance of his successor.[8] However, Jason and Dick did not have the time to establish firm connections because of the Titans' responsibilities and Jason's death. Dick compensated for this with the next Robin, Tim Drake, developing an extremely fraternal relationship with him. Because Dick and Tim were so close, Dick's network expanded into a third generation of heroes. While his time as Robin had integrated him with the sidekicks and heroes of his age and the heroes of Batman's, his time as Nightwing and mentor to Robin introduced him to the heroes and sidekicks of Tim's age. As the original sidekick, his reputation often preceded him, as noted by Superboy during *Infinite Crisis*. As they reflected on the past Titans and Dick encouraged Conner that "the future [was] up to [them]" and not for the others in their lives to decide for them; this advice prompted Conner to respond, "Everyone's right about you. You totally rule."[9] While Dick was embarrassed by the sentiment, it emphasized that he was able to be a mentor not just for his "siblings" in the Bat Family, but also the new members of the team he founded. Dick also bridged the gap between the Teen Titans and the Justice League when they nearly destroyed each other over the involvement of the new Wonder Girl, Cassie Sandsmark, in the Teen Titans.[10] It was Dick's skills as a mediator that got each of the heroes to discuss the situation rather than fight over it, notably reminding the Flash, Wally West, his best friend since they were both in the Titans, that they had always hated when the League kept tabs on the Titans.[11] Dick, because of his understanding of what it is like for the Titans to work in the shadows of the League and because of his closeness with the League members is able to reestablish the proper boundaries between the two teams in a way that Superman, another noted mediator, would never have been able to accomplish.

Because Dick Grayson spent his childhood under the watch of the Justice League, he easily earned their trust when needed. His biggest ally and mentor within the League, outside of Batman, is Superman. Superman has often provided a supportive role for Dick on matters for which Batman would be ill suited, such as what to do about wanting to transition from sidekick to hero.[12] Dick has also collaborated with Superman on missions, such as during his story arc "Freefall."[13] During "Freefall," graves of superheroes and villains from Metropolis and Gotham were being robbed for unknown purposes, drawing the attention of both Nightwing and Superman. The two met up in Central Park to "compare notes" about the exhumations one night. In a scene that showed their mutual respect for each other, Nightwing and Superman discussed the case and Superman promised Nightwing that we would be at Nightwing's "disposal whenever possible."[14] This scene is followed by a fun moment with a security guard that shows just how similar Nightwing and Superman are to each other: neither is put off by the guard's request for Nightwing to take a photo of him with Superman and neither acts as if they are more important to the fight against crime than the guard.[15] The issue also expands more on Dick's personality outside of Nightwing and shows him in his new job as curator of the Cloisters museum in New York, going on a date to a baseball game with a historian, and buying an apartment.[16] The significance of his placing roots in this new community is furthered by his repairs to the Cloisters, done with "a little help from [his] friends," emphasizing the trust and respect heroes like Wildcat, Hawkman, Power Girl, Green Lantern (John Stewart), Mr. Terrific, and Starman have for him, even though he typically works more with the Justice League than the Justice Society.[17] To continue the theme of showing how deep the connections Dick has made throughout his career and life go, he is visited one evening by his best friend and former teammate, Wally West aka The Flash, and the two men catch up on each other's lives over beer and cups of noodles.[18] Such a human moment is often rare in superhero comics because so often superheroes do not create many friendships that go beyond their work, but Dick is consistently an exception to this idea because his appeal, personality, and foundation are all built upon connections he has made with others. And, of course, his most important connection in his life comes into play in this issue as well when he realizes that quickly getting from one end of Manhattan to the other will be difficult without a dedicated shortcut; so he sends Bruce Wayne a fax asking him to buy six strategically placed buildings to create one.[19] Bruce's approval of the strategy demonstrates both his trust and pride in Dick's abilities and the results of Dick's lifetime of training and learning with Bruce.

In addition to teaming up with Superman and other prominent Leaguers, Nightwing has been sought out by other heroes for assistance on missions. In one instance, he was sought as an alternative to Batman by Deadman on the assumption that "he'd be as good as Batman, if not *better* at rallying the super-heroes" against Anttura, an evil mystic force that was causing problems in Tibet.[20] Here Dick proved that not only does he have his own ability to work with people, plus Bruce's logical mind, he also surpasses most other superheroes as "the one guy alive that every other crime-fighter trusts," next to Superman.[21] On this mission, Nightwing and Deadman team up with Hawkman to prevent a catastrophe and save Green Arrow, all while operating under the radar of the League. Dick is able to send the League on a bogus mission to protect them from potential possession by mystic forces. Because Deadman can only communicate with the living by possessing a human host, it is essentially just the trustworthiness of Nightwing that quickly convinces Hawkman to lend his expertise of ancient history and artifacts to their fight, rather than refusing on a basis of possession-aided coercion. This oddball trio works together using Deadman and Nightwing's shared acrobatic pasts and Hawkman's knowledge to quickly and successfully execute their mission. Even Green Arrow is impressed that "Batman's short-pants sidekick grows up to successfully bluff the entire Justice League" and jokingly bans Dick from Justice League Poker Night.[22] This issue is a fun standalone that showcases Dick's ability to participate in group settings and to inspire trust in others.

However, the most significant instance of Dick's former mentors trusting him as his own person was during "Obsidian Age." During this storyline, the Justice League of America, consisting of Batman, Wonder Woman, Superman, The Flash (Wally West), Green Lantern (Kyle Rayner), Plastic

Man, and Martian Manhunter were transported into Atlantis' past, abandoning the present to the unexplained forces causing mayhem. Just before the transport, Batman activated a safety measure, which called upon Green Arrow, Hawkgirl, Faith, The Atom, Jason Blood, Firestorm, and Major Disaster to join a new Justice League, led by Nightwing.[23] The story of the Obsidian Age, even when the story is not focused on Nightwing and his Justice League, demonstrates the significance of Dick's abilities to lead and to network. Batman chose Nightwing for the position because "he is the best" and can be trusted to lead the team with respect and honor.[24] Green Arrow, as sarcastic as he is accurate with archery, even is able to quickly get over his initial scorn about being led by "Robin" because of Dick's "fancy rhetorical skills."[25] The missing Justice League also acknowledges Dick's leadership skills: they are able to focus on the situation at hand and feel assured a solution is forthcoming because Dick Grayson (with whom Batman, Flash, Green Lantern, and Superman have all worked closely before) is leading the efforts. Dick understands how to balance the skills of his team, even though he barely knew some of his teammates, like Faith, before Batman called them to the new League, which reflects both his own interpersonal skills and his innate trust in others. While the true hero of the Obsidian Age storyline would most likely be Green Lantern, the sacrifice Kyle made in the past to set the plan in the present in motion would not have succeeded without Dick's leadership and trust in his teammates past and present.

As the original Robin, Dick Grayson was the natural successor to Bruce Wayne after the latter's presumed death left the role of Batman vacated. The so-called "Battle for the Cowl" was a massive crossover event for the characters with the most ties to Batman. The biggest focus was on the struggle between the first three Robins: a reluctant Dick Grayson, a resurrected Jason Todd, and an angry Tim Drake, along with the fifth and current Robin, ten year old Damian Wayne, also insisting that he should become Batman. However, in addition to the Robins and other direct members of the Bat Family looking to fill Bruce's cape, fringe members of the Gotham and Bat mythos entertained the idea as well. One of the more interesting cases of this was seen in issue #9 of Gail Simone's *Secret Six* ongoing book, in which Bane and Catman, along with Ragdoll dressed as Burt Ward—Robin, work their way through Gotham, violently stopping a terrorist group from kidnapping the children of wealthy and influential families. As they work, Catman and Bane discuss who is going to take over the role of Batman, which Catman has a notion of doing. The most interesting part of their discussion is Bane's understanding of how Batman is supposed to behave, conceding that, while it would be nice to have such a role, Bane would be a terrible Batman. Bane's comprehension of the symbolism and importance of Batman is furthered when Nightwing confronts them. Catman is infuriated by the presumption that Nightwing can tell them what to do, saying, "He's not Batman, for Christ's sake!" Bane, however, has them leave, asking, "Who else will be?"[26] Even though stories involving Bane and Gotham typically focus more on the relationship between Bane and Batman, Bane is able to see that Dick is the true successor to the cowl, not because he wants it or because he is the strongest or scariest, but because he skillfully walks the tightrope of compassion and intimidation, something that killers like Bane and Catman would never be able to do well.

As Batman, Dick filled in Bruce's roles as leader of the Bat Family, asset to the Justice League, and ally to the Gotham City Police Department (GCPD), while also adding his own touch and personality to all of those roles. In the Bat Family, Dick continued his role as a mentor for the current Robin, Damian Wayne, which provided a reversal of the typical personalities of Batman and Robin (Damian's personality is more sullen and dark like his father). This reversal of the roles not only freshened the story of Batman and Robin for the readers, but it also provided a great opportunity for growth for Dick Grayson and Damian Wayne, who both needed to learn how to work in their new roles and with each other. Through their work together, Dick adapted himself to his expanded role in the crime-fighting world and Damian learned that Batman and Robin do more than "beat down bad guys"—they also fight to prevent "any other innocent people from being hurt."[27] During his tenure as Batman, Dick led the Justice League through various missions. During one such mission, both he and Hal Jordan remarked to themselves that it was "Weird giving an order to Hal," and "Weird taking an order from Dick," which reflects how both men strongly remember Dick's time as Robin, but for neither man is such a recollection problematic for their work.[28] His best friend and former Titans teammate, Donna Troy, also compared Dick's leadership with the League to his leadership with the Teen Titans. Donna remarks on the scope of the missions having changed from their youth, but through all that, she "would follow [Dick] through Hell if [she] had to."[29] This ability to inspire such strong loyalty in others is a primary aspect of what sets Dick apart from the Bat Family, as well as other heroes (other than perhaps Superman), and is what places him in a central and unquestioned leadership position throughout his networks. This quality, when combined with his naturally easygoing and respectful personality, was also noticed by Commissioner Gordon and his officers in the GCPD on various occasions while Dick was Batman. During an incident with the Joker, after Gordon had established that this new Batman was formerly Robin, he lets Dick know that not only does he (Gordon) understand the pressure Dick is under in these "big black boots [Dick] probably thought would never fit" but that "most of [his] cops prefer [Dick] to [Bruce]."[30] This aspect of Dick's time as Batman not only further emphasizes Dick's interpersonal skills but also emphasizes the paternal connection Dick and Gordon had built over the course of their careers; it would be rare for Gordon to act paternally toward Bruce if for no other reason than Bruce seems unreceptive to that sort of interaction.

Dick Grayson has proven time and time again over the past seventy-five years that "a true hero is measured not by his strength, but by the strength of his heart."[31] It is Dick's heart that made his connections and networks so valuable for the criminal justice system of the DCU, not his powers, his wealth, or his technology. The fact that Dick's networks are formed on the trust in his personality and reputation over anything else demonstrates that Dick Grayson forms the heart and soul of his universe.

Notes

1. Geoff Johns et al., "Infinite Discussions," in *Infinite Crisis* (New York: DC Comics, 2006), [261].
2. Kevin Smith, Walter Flanagan, and Art Thibert, "Part Two: The Falconer," *Batman: The Widening Gyre* #2 (New York: DC Comics, November 2009), [10].
3. For more on Batman, Robin, and the Comics Code (and the Duo's possible subversion of the Code), see Will Brooker, *Batman Unmasked: Analyzing a Cultural Icon* (New York: Continuum, 2005), 143–158.
4. Devin Grayson, Zach Howard, and Andy Owens, "Back to the Life," *Nightwing* #99 (New York: DC Comics, January 2005), [14–15].
5. Grayson, Howard, and Owens, *Nightwing* #99, [15].
6. Dwight Finger, "Bill Finger," *Fingar and Finger Family Genealogy*, http://www.fingerfamily.com/html/bio-finger-bill-12367.html.
7. Marv Wolfman et al., "The Judas Contract Book 3—There Shall Come a Titan," *Tales of the Teen Titans* #44 (New York: DC Comics, July 1984), 21.
8. See *Batman* #368 (Pre-*Crisis*) and *Batman* #416 (post–*Crisis*).
9. Geoff Johns et al., "The Brave and the Bold," *Teen Titans* (3) #33 (New York: DC Comics, April 2006), [21].
10. Geoff Johns, Mike McKone, and Marlo Alquiza, "War and Peace," *Teen Titans* (3) #6 (February 2004).
11. Johns, McKone, and Alquiza, *Teen Titans* (3) #6, [14].
12. Chuck Dixon et al., "Year One, Chapter Two: Friends in High Places," *Nightwing* #102 (late March 2005).
13. Peter J. Tomasi, Rags Morales, and Michael Bair, "Nightwing: Freefall Chapter Two," *Nightwing* #141 (April 2008).
14. Tomasi, Morales, and Bair, *Nightwing* #141, [2].

15. Tomasi, Morales, and Bair, *Nightwing* #141, [3–4].
16. Tomasi, Morales, and Bair, *Nightwing* #141, [5–6], [10–11], and [12].
17. Tomasi, Morales, and Bair, *Nightwing* #141, [9].
18. Tomasi, Morales, and Bair, *Nightwing* #141, [16–19].
19. Tomasi, Morales, and Bair, *Nightwing* #141, [13–14], [20–21].
20. Mark Waid and Scott Kolins, "Wings and Arrows," *The Brave and the Bold* (3) #15 (New York: DC Comics, September 2008), [5].
21. Waid and Kolins, *The Brave and the Bold* (3) #15, [2].
22. Waid and Kolins, *The Brave and the Bold* (3) #15, [22].
23. The "Obsidian Age" storyline takes place in *JLA* #66–76 (July 2002–February 2003).
24. Joe Kelly, Yvel Guichet, and Mark Propst, "New Blood," *JLA* #69 (Early October 2002), 22.
25. Kelly, Guichet, and Propst, "Transition," *JLA* #71 (Early November 2002), 7.
26. Gail Simone, Nicola Scott, and Doug Hazelwood, "A Debt of Significant Blood," *Secret Six* (3) #9 (New York: DC Comics, July 2009), [22].
27. Fabian Nicieza et al., "In Storybook Endings," *Batman* #713 (New York: DC Comics, August 2011), [18].
28. James Robinson, Mark Bagley, and Rob Hunter, "Team History," *Justice League of America* (2) #42 (New York: DC Comics, April 2010), [5].
29. Robinson et al., "JLA: Omega Part 1—Worlds Collide," *Justice League of America* (2) #50 (December 2010), [9].
30. Grant Morrison and Frazer Irving, "Batman and Robin Must Die, Part 1: The Garden of Death," *Batman and Robin* (1) #13 (New York: DC Comics, August 2010), [14].
31. *Disney's Hercules*, performed by Rip Torn, Tate Donovan, Susan Egan, James Woods, Danny DeVito (United States: Walt Disney Pictures, 1997), DVD.

The New 52 (2011–present)

Jordan Hass *and* Star Schneider

Richard "Dick" Grayson has drawn in a lot of different fans over the years; whether they are attracted to his personality, his decision-making, or something as frivolous as his looks, fans love Grayson. The most essential—and the most important—part that makes Grayson "Dick" is his compassion and his sense of humor. He is somebody you'd love to have standing by your side in a fight or on a Friday night, or even in a fight on a Friday night. He doesn't have any superpowers—much like Batman—but unlike Batman, he is able to smile and retain a childlike innocence. Dick Grayson is a character everyone can relate to, but everybody has a different take on the character, and every decade shows a different side of Dick Grayson. In this section, we'll look at the New 52 Dick Grayson. Though some might argue that this new Dick Grayson is a departure from previous incarnations in major ways, the integral parts of his character remain the same up until the switch from *Nightwing* to *Grayson*, in which he begins to undergo fundamental challenges to his previously-defined character, and begins to make a departure from the Dick Grayson that most know.

DC Comics' New 52 is a change to the world that audiences have known for generations. It's a change in terms of tone, and even scenery, and some audiences are hesitant towards these changes, both cosmetic and thematic. But Dick Grayson is the character that embodies change and welcomes it, whenever possible. He can still tell jokes, he can still do acrobatic moves, he can still look for the good inside of people. He is capable of understanding the qualities that make every person complex and unique, and recognizes the contrariness about himself. He isn't as extroverted as he was in former decades, but he remains just as sociable as ever. Grayson is a character that knows his past, and no matter what, never lets it bother him, because he knows his future is going to be brighter. And even now, through a reinvention of the character in the New 52, we see a still-evolving Grayson.

In the wake of the Flashpoint arc in DC Comics, DC overhauled every character within the DC Universe. Characters like "The Flash" were rebooted with Barry Allen returning as the character, and Wally West absent. Major Events in other comic book timelines, such as the ones from *Infinite Crisis*, *Final Crisis*, and *Crisis on Infinite Earths* were removed and a revisionist history was created.

Dick Grayson, in this continuity, was never the admired Blüdhaven police officer. He was never even a member of the Teen Titans, and many relationships were altered (his close friend Donna Troy is, as of now, absent from the New 52). Still, some things have remained the same.

Born to Haly's Circus acrobats John and Mary Grayson, Dick Grayson spent his childhood learning his family trade and making friends with other circus children. Much like his characteristics in early comics, he was seen as a bit of an adrenaline junkie. On the day of his parents' deaths, he saved a guard by putting himself in danger from a moving train entering Gotham City. Though he saved the guard's life (who would have otherwise been crushed by the train), he was grounded for his actions. True to his character as an adult, he felt contrite for his wrongdoings, and apologized; in response, he gifted his mother with a wooden bracelet with a picture of her favorite bird: a Robin.[1] Like in previous origins, Dick's parents died that night in a trapeze accident due to the actions of mobster Tony Zucco, and Bruce Wayne first expresses interest in Dick Grayson as a potential ward. Grayson eventually impresses Wayne enough that he brings him into the Batcave, and presents young Dick Grayson with his first costume. But here's where there's some deviation: in the New 52, there are two different origins for the Robin suit.

In one origin, written by Kyle Higgins, Dick built the first suit using leftover pieces of Batman's costume. And it was called "Robin" as a sign of "Rebirth."[2] But in the origin story used later on by Tom King and Tim Seely, the vibrant red and green suit was designed by Bruce Wayne with the intention of distracting enemies from a lurking, shadowed Batman.[3]

But the New 52 Grayson is—out of flashbacks—exclusively Nightwing and Grayson the spy, and his Nightwing has a different costume than older versions. His 52 costume doesn't even have any blue. The suit is more of a tight black suit, with a V of sharp red going down from the shoulders. Higgins did fight for the blue, but lost the battle, to keep the thematic that all "Robins" had the color red. Red Hood, Red Robin, and Damian Wayne all had a Red aesthetic as well. While red might not be true to a long-standing tradition of the blue Nightwing, the bold red style does stand out, and overall isn't a poor change. When it comes to Dick Grayson, the aesthetic changes are the most noticeable, but that's all they are: aesthetic. Nightwing as he appears in *Nightwing* still retains many of the characteristics that make him the same old boy in the blue and black, even if now he is wearing red.

Kyle Higgins' *Nightwing* is written in a mix of action, mystery and comedy, almost if it's a television series that bounces back and forth between Dick's past as an acrobat and Robin and his present-day as a vigilante protecting Gotham alongside Batman and his family. The first arc sees Dick Grayson rediscover his love of the circus, as Haly's Circus comes to town along with a mysterious psycho (named "Saiko") who is hell-bent on destroying who he deems to be the most dangerous person in Gotham City: Dick Grayson himself.[4] It turns out Saiko is none other than Raymond, Dick's old friend in the circus. Higgins starts setting the foundation for a future Batman arc, the Court of Owls, as Raymond was snatched away on the night Dick Grayson left the circus by the Court of Owls (though they're not known as such yet).

This first arc of the New 52 Nightwing is important because it delves into Dick's psyche in a big way. In what would become a major location in Chicago-native Higgins' run, Dick visits Chicago in an effort to find another childhood friend from the circus, Zane. Upon being found, an antagonistic Zane uses radio waves on Grayson that shows what Dick Grayson's biggest fear is: letting down those around him. Dick hears words like "incompetent," "failure," "worthless," and "loser,"[5] and is reminded of all the people he couldn't save—including his own parents. This is the character we know: someone who will try desperately, no matter what, to not let people down. And if you are the one being let down, he will be the one to try to lift you back up. Though this trait was present in pre–New 52 Dick Grayson, the fact that this was so early solidified as part of the rebooted Grayson's character speaks strongly to Grayson's compassion and selflessness becoming a core trait of his character.

Dick eventually does defeat Saiko, and the arc is resolved, but this leads to the Court of Owls event, as Saiko (or Raymond) was trained by the Court of Owls. As Dick returns to the Batcave after his final confrontation with Saiko, he notices Bruce has a strange sickly person strapped inside a monitor; the man's name was William Cobb, and he was Dick's great-grandfather. This upsets Dick, and he vocally complains to Bruce that Bruce had never told him about his family being linked to the Court of Owls, and that he had been keeping secrets from Dick. But then Bruce punches Dick in the jaw, breaking a tooth.

What was really great about this moment was that Bruce punching Dick was seen from two different angles: one in Batman Issue 7 and the other in Nightwing Issue 7. This allows us as readers to see the moment from a perspective more linked to Nightwing, as well as one more linked to Batman. The context of each alters our understanding of it, as Batman has dealt extensively with the Court of Owls, facing rigorous tests of his own mettle in facing this new foe. So in punching Dick, the stress Bruce has been under makes it seem like he has reached a breaking point, providing more sympathy for him. However, when viewing this from the *Nightwing* issue, as Dick Grayson has not had any official introduction to the Court of Owls, and has not been privy to the recent stress Bruce has been under, the punch comes as an incredible shock with very little lead-in. It is a completely unjustified act of violence with no perceivable cause from the *Nightwing* issue and generates sympathy for Dick Grayson. As Bruce picks up the tooth, he shows it to Dick: the tooth contains an emblem of the Court of Owls—one that matches Cobb's. Bruce tells Dick that the Court of Owls had planned for Dick to originally be a Talon (a powerful foot soldier in the Court), but he managed to escape that fate. Dick then explains to Bruce what he feels is the truth:

> You might be seeing sides already, all of us birds on one and you, the bat, on the other. Hell, you're probably throwing up walls right and left. But the fact is, I don't care who my ancestor was. Or what the Court of Owls wanted me to be. I don't. We are who we choose to be, Bruce. Not the role the past says we should play.[6]

This is something that also comes back to the stories brought in the New-52 Nightwing, as it's something that recurs in Grayson's character. Unlike Bruce, whose entire life was defined by the past, Dick's past was just as troublesome, but being defined by that past isn't what he ultimately wants in life.

Dick Grayson is somebody who always looks forward and never looks back; he is somebody who is always about "what's next" instead of "what just happened," which might be his setback, but also one of his few coping mechanisms besides his sense of humor. This is a major characteristic for Dick Grayson, and one that has definitely carried over from previous incarnations of the character. Ultimately, Dick Grayson is adaptable. He can change, and though like everyone he sometimes feels stress and strife at having to, he is able to move on and move forward for himself and others.

This is why the Court of Owls story arc is such a good read. We can all relate to Grayson; we always change, and we're always modifying and adapting our self-identity. These moments of discovery and identity-modifying present themselves as challenges to Grayson in every story. As in the Saiko arc, Grayson solidifies himself as someone who deeply cares about being able to help others; this arc forces Grayson to really examine and accept that his past will alter his future, but not determine it. The sudden information that, at one point, Dick Grayson could have been a mercenary for the Court of Owls was actually a shocking revelation, and it had a serious impact on his sense of self-identity, though he still maintains his core values.

Dick Grayson must juggle between aiding the two communities who contributed to his development as a person. His childhood circus is left in ruins in the wake of Saiko, while his current loved ones face annihilation at the hands of the Court of Owls. As he fights his grandfather Cobb and learns about his family history, he first envisions how to help Gotham and save the circus: he decides to use life insurance money and all of his inheritance and to buy up Amusement Mile—his favorite place in Gotham—and make it also a permanent home for Haly's Circus. Gotham residents would finally have something more positive in their lives. As he is short on capital, his quest for funds eventually leads him to the only person willing to lend him money: Sonia Branch, repentant daughter of the murderer of Grayson's parents, Tony Zucco.[7] Though the relationship between the two is initially rocky, he eventually forms a short-lived romance with Sonia, despite his continued misgivings. But let's turn from the villains. The true measure of Dick's character isn't in the villains he fights—though they are what people usually focus on—but in the development he goes through as these stories progress.

The relationship with Dick and Sonia Zucco is crucial to the story; it's a character test for Dick. Can Dick trust Sonia, despite being the daughter of the very mobster who killed his parents? People love Dick Grayson, sometimes based on looks, sometimes based on his own charm. And the question remains: does Grayson understand this, and use it to his own advantage, or is he just naive and blindly following others' leads? This plot with Sonia seeks to explore and maybe answer some of these questions.

While the circus is being constructed, Barbara Gordon enters the scene.[8] Though she had previously guested on an issue of Nightwing, she now returns in a more crucial role. She is a messenger: everyone's favorite clown prince of crime, The Joker, has returned to Gotham.

The Joker has decided to raise hell on the entire Batman family, including Dick Grayson. Joker systematically kills some of Grayson's' friends, and forces Grayson to fight others by poisoning them with his Joker toxin. He leaves messages for Nightwing. On the corpse of Grayson's childhood friend Jimmy, Joker leaves a sign saying, "Nobody likes a knock-off," suggesting that all Nightwing will ever be is a pale imitation of Batman.[9] Joker "invites" Grayson to a "party" at Amusement Mile, telling Nightwing when he gets there that he's noticed that Nightwing has been in the same town as the circus in the past year, and it makes sense to Joker because "It's the place where bad kids run when they're running away from home," suggesting that all Nightwing has done is "run away" like an immature kid from a parent Batman.[10]

Joker has made it seem as if he has killed all of the Haly's Circus workers, despite Dick's best efforts to shuttle the remaining members to safety. This is Nightwing's breaking point: he begins to pummel Joker, almost to the point of death, but as he is almost ready to deliver a final blow, Joker stabs Grayson with a blade, and gets up, reminding him about his character. "You see, Nightwing, more than any of the others, you put your faith in relationships. You insist on surrounding yourself with people. But people will always let you down."[11] This is crucial to Dick's character, as even the Joker has recognized a pivotal aspect of both New 52-Grayson and previous incarnations. To put it simply, Dick Grayson has always been the "Relationship Robin"; he's the member of the Batfamily most known for cultivating relationships, and deeply trusting those who he cares for. In attempting to attack this part of Grayson's character, Joker aims to get at Grayson's very core. Joker attempts to demonstrate this in his normal style: he doses every member of Haly's Circus with Joker gas, and they attack Nightwing. Nightwing is brutalized and knocked unconscious, leading to the cross–Batfamily arc "Death of the Family," in which Batman, Red Robin, Batgirl, Red Hood, Robin, and Nightwing are pitted against each other as a result of Joker's illusions and Joker gas. Unlike most people, they survive the toxin, and persevere, though now they must all deal with the damage the Joker has wrought. For Dick Grayson, this takes the form of a destroyed Haly's Circus, bereft of all performers and staff.

This annihilation of Haly's Circus—something Grayson has put massive time and effort into revitalizing—disturbs Dick for a while, because The Joker finally got to him. Damian Wayne attempts to help Dick out (itself a major instance that demonstrates how far their personal relationship has grown) by explaining to him who he is: the person who trusts people.[12] And a week later, Damian Wayne passes away. But the words linger, as do Dick's memories of Damian. In one of his final moments,

Damian tries to reaffirm to Dick how vital his ability to trust and care is. Not only does it shape Dick's character, but it has grown to play a role in Damian's as well. Damian was initially known for his brusque personality and lack of care and trust in others. But this part of Dick's personality is so potent, it has even reached Damian—enough even to make Damian want to preserve this characteristic in Dick.

After all the stress he is put through, Dick starts to feel it might not be the worst thing in the world to be by himself. Depressed, Dick recedes, desiring to feel nothing except perhaps anger at himself. Batman soon sends him on a quest to retrieve one last memory of his family: a Flying Graysons' costume. But Dick soon faces a dilemma: he must choose between saving the costume and four people trapped inside the location. Even though these people were Nightwing's enemies, he realizes then that, given the choice, he would always pick saving people over memories.[13] Once again, Dick's compassion and faith in humanity is affirmed, this time in a dramatic way befitting Damian's memory.

It is at this point that Dick relocates to Chicago upon receiving news that Tony Zucco—his parents' murderer—is still alive and located in Chicago. The transition occurs in *Nightwing Annual* #1 (the only Nightwing Annual issue currently). What made this comic really controversial was the B-story, in which Grayson readies himself to move out to Chicago, and Barbara Gordon helps. As they pack up everything, Dick remembers a photo from early on, featuring a young Batgirl and Robin taking a selfie in which Batgirl kisses Robin on the cheek, as a "first date," belying a relationship on the verge of failing. One fight later, Barbara proposes that Dick show up in the morning to talk about it. But instead of talking about it, he calls Barbara, who is at an empty loft apartment that used to house Dick. He tells her that he couldn't wait, and already packed the truck and drove off to Chicago. "Look, we do this 'will they or won't they?' dance every time we're together. And every time, there's a reason not to. Every time."[14] Dick lets her know that he always cared about her, before they both hang up. This issue is somewhat of a departure from the New-52 Grayson we've grown accustomed to, and marks the beginning of further changes that redefine the character further away from his former characterizations.

Upon moving to Chicago, Grayson does something unusual: he decides to room with two others. Grayson's new room is not secure, but it does feature access to the Chicago train line that Nightwing decides to use as a means of getting around the city quickly. After dealing with shady characters, Dick finally finds information on Zucco. Though before much can be done to make Zucco repent, Nightwing finds himself a dangerous adversary in the form of one of the shady characters he used to find Zucco in the first place: The Prankster, a villain determined to destroy Chicago.

Zucco—now living under the guise of "family man" Billy Lester—realizes due to a conversation with his wife and child that he has not taken the responsibility he should have for murdering Dick Grayson's family. Upon confronting him, he tells Dick, "Look, what I did to the Graysons ... there's no excuse I can make. When all this is done, I gotta finally face up to it."[15] Like Dick's relationship with Zucco's daughter Sonia, Dick now must re-evaluate his relationship with a perceived enemy in favor of accomplishing his goals. The compromise with Sonia now becomes relevant as a foreshadowing event: just as Dick allied with Sonia to bring happiness to Gotham in the form of Haly's Circus, Dick allies now with Zucco in an effort to save the people of Chicago. Just as Dick chose to save four enemies over a memory of his family, Dick solidifies himself here as a character willing to sacrifice his own desires and wants to aid those around him. He is selfless, and strongly-principled, though it does also mean in this case compromising his own vigilante determination to see Zucco repent for his crimes.

It is Tony Zucco who ends up stopping the Prankster, not Nightwing. As order returns to Chicago, so do police, who promptly arrest Zucco. Yet Zucco does not take credit for saving anyone, only asking that a message be passed on to his son: he wants someone to tell his son that he loves him.[16] Though Grayson's story with Zucco is resolved, it is a very sobering end, and a good example of Higgins' nuanced writing.

The final part of Nightwing revolves around what happens now that Zucco is in prison and the aftermath of the events from The Prankster. A little girl named Jen begins regularly visiting the apartment, bonding with Dick and his two roommates. During one of these visits, as Joey (one of the roommates) and Dick have an argument, Jen drops shoes on a wooden floorboard, and opens the floorboard up to discover a Nightwing costume with escrima sticks. Dick initially panics and begins looking for another place to stay, but changes his mind and decides to remain living in his shared apartment.[17]

Jen's parents are eventually murdered, and the trio of roommates decides to keep Jen while the tragedy is sorted out. Though Joey and Michael question police about the crime, Dick is struck by the parallels to his own parent's murders, and remains solely focused on Jen (again demonstrating a willingness to suppress his vigilante role in favor of a more caring and nurturing persona. As Dick attempts to console her, she tells him that she knows that he's Nightwing. She didn't tell the police, because she wants to work together, the same way he did with Batman. As Grayson gets up to grab some water, he returns to see Jen has gone missing, and she's going after her parent's murderer: Mr. Zsasz.[18]

The following issue, 29, best summarizes Dick Grayson's life and character up to his point, and reminds people of every obstacle he has endured. Dick has lost his parents. He has fought criminals with Batman. He has fought Saiko and gained control of Haly's Circus. He has discovered his potential to be a Talon. He has lost it all at the hands of the Joker. And now, he is determined to track down Jen and prevent her from harm at the hands of Zsasz.

Following this confrontation, Dick attempts to console Jen, and explains to her his own philosophy on grieving and dealing with death.[19] He tries his best to comfort Jen, and in doing so symbolically gives her a defining part of his character, and a valuable memory of his own. He gives to her the same Robin bracelet that he had given to his mother before she died. After holding onto it for years, he decides to pass it on, because he sees it as a reminder that "no matter how dark things get ... remember they won't always be that way, they will get better."[20] Jen and Dick Grayson share a hug, and Jen moves to her aunt's house the following morning. It is at this time that Grayson decides to reconnect with Sonia Zucco.

The entire issue also had a huge narration from Dick Grayson about life:

> To focus on the positive. To keep looking forward. To really give someone a chance. Because when you get down to it, my life isn't about the costumes or the bad guys. It's not about cities or symbols. It's way simpler than that. I mean, I grew up in a circus. It's always been about catching people when they fall.[21]

This is a culmination of everything we have grown to know about this new Dick Grayson. This Dick acknowledges the stresses and problems his past has caused for him, but makes the active choice to attempt to keep living his life and move forward in the world. He is a man who is constantly evaluating and re-evaluating his identity: he is contemplative about who he is and action-oriented about who he wants to be. He feels that he has failed others sometimes, and that others have failed him, and he feels this deeply. But Dick Grayson—this Dick Grayson, and other incarnations before him—does not let this permanently destroy his overall faith in and concern for humanity. He is willing to catch people when they fall, and will always try his hardest to do so, even if it means sacrificing those symbols he has come to identify with in favor of affirming that deeper identity of compassion.

This was the last issue of Higgins' Nightwing and it felt like Higgins had a couple more stories he wanted to write, but DC Editorial decided to cut it short in favor of its series *Forever Evil*.

Forever Evil, written by Geoff Johns, was a big step in the story of Dick Grayson. It was hinted at for months prior to the publication that Dick Grayson would die in this story. But who dies in comics? Not Dick Grayson. *Forever Evil* begins with Nightwing getting a message from Batgirl. But as he was waiting, he is abducted by Superwoman and Owlman. The Crime Syndicate broadcasts to the entire world that the Justice League is dead, with Superman's Cape, Aquaman's Trident, and Wonder Woman's Lasso being shown to the world. The broadcast concludes with a tied up Nightwing, beaten-up and a bloody mess, revealed to the entire public as Richard Grayson. His personal information is spread as well, including his driver's license, the Flying Graysons incident, and being adopted by Bruce Wayne.[22] This, of course, is a critical blow for Dick Grayson, and will come to have lasting repercussions on how he navigates his world. Long story short, Dick Grayson is saved, but his secret identity cannot be salvaged, and his character's role is—for now—irreparably altered.

Nightwing #30—*Nightwing*'s last issue—was a strange issue. Released on May 28th, 2014, it was the only issue of Nightwing in New 52 that was not written by Kyle Higgins, but instead by upcoming *Grayson* writers Tim Seely and Tom King. The original script of Nightwing #30 was by James T. Tynion IV, with art by Meghan Hetrick-Murante. Her inks of the story included the funeral planned for Dick Grayson.[23] Major characters in Dick Grayson's life, including Barbara Gordon, Jason Todd, and Roy Harper, appear to be standing around his body grieving. It even included something that would have been a moment in *Red Hood and the Outlaws*, with Starfire actually remembering who Dick Grayson was. While in Wayne Manor, Bruce—dressed as Batman—tells Dick Grayson who is still in a bed about his plan to get info on Spyral. It concludes with the Batfamily, including Alfred, upset that Bruce missed the funeral of Dick Grayson. As well, Tim Drake examines the corpse and determines that it was a fake, and that Grayson may still be alive. It concludes with Grayson at an airport giving comfort to a child who is possibly afraid of his first flight on an airplane.

But that was just based on images. Instead what we got in Nightwing #30, by Seely and King was more of a "Grayson Issue 0." It had Dick Grayson recuperating in the Batcave accompanied by Bruce. Actually, it would be more accurate to say that it had Dick Grayson getting the crap beaten out of him by Bruce Wayne in the Batcave. The elevator to the Batcave is busted, and Alfred is crying over these events, because to Alfred Dick is "just a boy"; in response Bruce yells that Dick is not "a boy."[24]

It was a complete clash in terms of tone and character from the earlier 29 issues. This one had two people fighting shirtless and getting bloody, because to Bruce, he wanted to make sure that Dick was prepared to go out again, considering what happened to him in *Forever Evil*. Batman then tells Dick why he can't go out as Dick Grayson anymore, and why he can't be in contact with the family anymore. They even referenced the Nolan Batman films with the famous "Why do we fall?" line, but instead Dick Grayson counters with "We fall because we were pushed, and we get up and push back."[25] It's different from the response in the films, but true enough to Dick Grayson's character at this point, though it would have been more congruous if the phrase was more focused on sentiment rather than confrontation. Midway through this issue is when readers receive their first introduction to Spyral in the *Nightwing* comics.

Dick goes on his first mission, where we first controversially see this character with a gun (the Batfamily, Bruce and Dick Grayson most definitively, are known for their opposition to guns). It is also our first introduction to an updated Helena Bertinelli, who at this point is not yet revealed to be the Huntress. The series concludes with one final look into Dick's understanding of his own identity. As he and Helena fly away on a helicopter, he attempts to explain his identity, and comes up with a concluding answer that highlights the varied and layered psyche the character has: "Who am I? My name is Dick Grayson, I am who you want me to be."[26]

The *Nightwing* comic book series is now over, and we begin with a new series, *Grayson*. If *Nightwing* was written like a television series with mystery and action and slight comedy, the way Tom King and Tim Seely write *Grayson* is more of a spy thriller. Every page has either a twist in the mission, a piece of information that might be used ahead of time, or new knowledge of the character. This is Tom King's first foray into writing comic books; it's important to note he used to be an actual spy, working in counter-terrorism, and part of what he brings to the table is an understanding of how this type of job can present unique emotional challenges.

Grayson isn't a challenge of Dick Grayson's physicality or detective skills, but rather his characteristics, and it is perhaps mostly notable for challenging fans' perceptions of the character. The series generated some controversy because, as with the New 52 *Nightwing* before it, staple parts of Dick Grayson's character and image were reimagined. Whereas *Nightwing* reimagined mainly aesthetic parts of the character: notably the red suit instead of the classic blue, and the move from Blüdhaven to Gotham and Chicago, the new series challenges parts of Dick Grayson's character: his commitment to abstaining from using guns and his desire to avoid killing. Batman fans were a little upset when the front cover was revealed to be of Dick Grayson holding a gun into the camera. But this was a perfect first test and challenge for the character. Here is someone who was raised to not use guns, because they killed his adopter's parents. And he has a gun. Does he use it? You'll have to read the comics to find out. Or remind yourself, that before New–52, Grayson had a gun in his possession when he was a cop in Blüdhaven.

In Issue 2, we learn more about this new Dick Grayson, Helena, and the spy organization as well. As Dick Grayson goes after his first target, Dick goes on the chase and not only uses his trademark escrimas, but also fires the gun for the first time. It does not end up being lethal, and instead the criminal—a cannibal—is offered a position at Spyral by Helena. This upsets Grayson because of all the horrific things she did and the injustice of the murders she's committed, but it is also an insight into Helena's character, and a good predictor of the dynamic of Dick and Helena's future interactions. Helena is willing to reach a gray area that Dick isn't comfortable with, and this segues into a future major arc.[27]

Because DC has a habit of making sure there are "Zero Issues" and "Villains Month" and other gimmick issues every year, this year's gimmick was called "Futures End," in which they pose a question to all the writers: "What happens to your characters in the next five years?" Tom King had a pretty good answer, but he decided to make it a puzzle for people to solve. When you read it normally, the issue presents itself as a series of flashbacks that slowly move towards the beginning of the story. Reading it this way, the first impression of the story seems to be that it is a story about Helena hanging Dick Grayson by a noose and letting him die, with the flashbacks telling the story of how he killed KGBeast—the new leader of Russia. As well, there are flashbacks of memories of Grayson's life that act as background information for Grayson, all of them appearing to be formative for Dick Grayson's character, ending with Tony Zucco's murder of the Flying Graysons.

In reverse order, you get a different story, a story of his evolution, starting with the lyrics from "The Man on the Flying Trapeze." It is revealed that Zucco murdered the Flying Graysons with an undetectable acid that Dick would later hide for his own use (and later helps save his life in this issue). It is confirmed that the Robin suit was meant as a decoy to distract from Batman's own presence (Bruce tells Grayson he must "earn the night").[28] The relationship with Helena and Dick is shown as a growing romantic relationship: they were partners who also smooched on helicopters and rooftops. It even shows Dick getting his first tattoo: the Spyral logo on his bicep (it is revealed that Spyral makes their members get one as an incentive to avoid capture).

The Grayson in *Future's End* does kill. He ends up killing KGBeast after receiving a medal of honor with Helena. He feels remorse soon after, and begs for forgiveness, but instead of accepting, Helena decides to hang him. The peril is resolved in the comic, and marks a show of loyalty for Helena, as she saves Dick with the acid he had told her about in a previous flashback. It's an enjoyable series, but Helena's relationship with Dick is either she punches him or kisses him; it's jarring to say the least. Especially to audiences who just want him to keep his sense of humor, which only pops up a little bit at a time. But time will tell.

Ultimately, the future of Grayson appears to be changing. While the start of the New 52 gave us a Dick Grayson only superficially changed, and fairly true to his prior character, the character seems to be moving into a more morally gray area. With *Future's End*, though Dick does affirm that he does not wish to kill, it does not change the fact that this is a Dick Grayson who has killed. It is an alternate universe—taking place five years in the future—but it is one written by the writers of the current *Grayson* series, and a potential path of development for the character. It will be interesting to see how Dick Grayson continues to evolve, when he will take up the mantle of Nightwing again (as nothing in comics is ever permanent, even death), and what the future really holds for this beloved character.

Notes

1. Tom DeFalco et al., "Perpetual Motion," *Nightwing* #0 (New York: DC Comics, November 2012), 5.
2. DeFalco et al., *Nightwing* #0, 17.
3. Tom King and Stephen Mooney, "Only a Place for Dying," *Grayson: Future's End* #1 (November 2014), 19.
4. Kyle Higgins, Eddy Barrows, and J.P. Mayer, "Welcome to Gotham," *Nightwing* #1 (November 2011), 19.
5. Higgins, Barrows, and Eduardo Pansica, "Past and Present," *Nightwing* #3 (January 2012), 11.
6. Higgins et al., "Turning Points," *Nightwing* #7 (May 2012), 18.
7. Higgins et al., "The Tomorrow People," *Nightwing* #10 (August 2012), 6.
8. The New 52 has kept her continuity with her spinal injury at the hands of the Joker, but currently she's able to walk. Her relationship with Dick has become more antagonistic; they crack jokes at each other's expense, and even at one point dated, but the mystery of what happened between them was never carefully explained, only hinted at in *Nightwing Annual* #1.

9. Higgins, Barrows, and Eber Ferreira, "Cleaning House," *Nightwing* #15 (February 2013), 6.
10. Higgins, Barrows, and Ferreira, "Curtain Call," *Nightwing* #16 (March 2013), 5.
11. Higgins, Barrows, and Ferreira, *Nightwing* #16, 16.
12. Higgins et al., "Slow Burn," *Nightwing* #18 (May 2013), 1.
13. Higgins et al., *Nightwing* 18, 16.
14. Higgins et al., "Embers," *Nightwing Annual* #1 (Dec 2013), 14.
15. Higgins and Will Conrad, "Buyer's Remorse," *Nightwing* #24 (Dec 2013), 4.
16. Higgins and Conrad, *Nightwing* #24, 17.
17. Higgins, Conrad, and Cliff Richards, "Curiouser and Curiouser," *Nightwing* #27 (March 2014), 12–3.
18. Higgins and Russell Dauterman, "Butterfly Effects," *Nightwing* #28 (April 2014), 18–20.
19. Higgins and Dauterman, "Safety Net," *Nightwing* #29 (May 2014), 17.
20. Higgins and Dauterman, *Nightwing* #29, 18.
21. Higgins and Dauterman, *Nightwing* #29, 20–21.
22. Geoff Johns, David Finch, and Richard Friend, "Nightfall," *Forever Evil* #1 (Nov 2013), 30.
23. Rich Johnston, "The Entire Meghan Hetrick Art From Nightwing #30—Before It Was Binned," *Bleeding Cool* (2 June 2014), http://www.bleedingcool.com/2014/06/02/the-entire-art-from-nightwing-20-by-before-it-was-binned/.
24. Tim Seeley, Tom King et al., "Setting Son," *Nightwing* #30 (July 2014), 10.
25. Seeley, King et al., *Nightwing* #30, 20.
26. Seeley, King et al., *Nightwing* #30, 30.
27. Seeley, King et al., "Gut Feelings," *Grayson* #2 (October 2014).
28. King and Mooney, *Grayson: Future's End* #1, 19.

Grayson, Sex and Feminism

Tini Howard

Those of us that call ourselves "wing-nuts" are no strangers to danger. Whether it's editorial threats or dark portents of the future, we've seen a lot of our favorite characters getting killed off. So when DC Comics teased the death of Nightwing and the wrap-up of the character's long-running series, fans met it with a mixture of consternation and expectation. Is anything good meant to last?

At what felt like the eleventh hour, DC announced *Grayson*, a new project that would send the character off on an entirely different arc of self-discovery. *Nightwing* closed with a grim order from Batman: with Dick's identity exposed and the world at large convinced of his death, he was uniquely poised to infiltrate the mysterious agency known as Spyral.

Thus begins *Grayson*. *Grayson* is, among other praises, a sexy book. It's a really sexy book as the creative team, (Tim Seeley and Tom King writing, and Mikel Janin on art) promised it would be, and they have delivered. The series so far has given us Bond-level sexual liaisons, plenty of half-clothed secret agent beefcake, and even Midnighter, the DCU's resident leather-daddy, swearing a longing vengeance against our flexible young hero.[1]

What's sort of brilliant is how the series itself functions as both an homage to the secret agent genre *and* a crucifixion of a lot of male power fantasies, detailing how a character like Dick Grayson is made miserable by what many comics and media *insist* would be any young guy's dream come true. In a way, one of the story's underlying themes is that of "men need feminism because…"—*why* it is that a world of gun-toting power fantasies has been bad for men, women, and comics as a medium. Interestingly, the series has managed to do its job so far while playing into another tone oft-neglected in comic book land: the *female gaze*. And while all this is going on? It stays true to the character's appeal, laying out a lot of his emotional honesty, childlike ideals, and humor—arguably why he appeals en masse to male *and* female fans.

We'll approach the notion of the female gaze, first. It's primarily visual, and as such, is likely the simplest aspect of this whole thing to latch onto. It's simple, even to people who oppose ideas like feminism, *because* it relies on some basic, agreed-upon philosophical notions. They're not too complicated, so even if you're not a philosophy person, hang on—we're about to jump off the trapeze platform. Dick's got you.

In philosophy, there's something called the *subject-object problem*. It can get pretty complex, but the basic premise is such: we perceive ourselves as the *subject*, the protagonist, the focus of our own lives, and everything else as *objects*, outside, *not-us*. Kant and Schrodinger both wrote extensively on the topic, but I learned about it from Alison Bechdel, so there you have it.[2] The way fiction portrays that, the protagonist vs. their objects, so to speak, is at the core of a lot of perception and perspective. There's a problem in storytelling where men and male protagonists are typically approached as *subjects*, as doers of things, whereas women are portrayed as *objects*. Not always sexually, but often. They are the-thing-to-which-things-are-done.

A lot of famous literature about female protagonists has given a voice to the "object perspective." Memoirs of awful marriages and Regency novels about the misery of women's lives do a great job of this. And thankfully, we've started to enjoy works in which fictional women are portrayed as doers, heroes, and protagonists. We relate to protagonists because we're our own protagonists.

But there's a strange gap when it gets to men from an "object perspective." Narratives about male heroes who also find themselves the victims of others' control and desire aren't terribly common. Perhaps in literary circles, but in comics? This bright, colorful, web of a world where our male protagonists often fall into Bat-men, Super-men, or Men Without Capes?

We don't leave a lot of room for narratives in which a man is vulnerable. Showing men as vulnerable is a key aspect of the female gaze.

This is the place of honor Dick Grayson holds for many comics' fans, and we all need that. Men need to feel like they too have a hero who gets served the hard stuff from time to time. Men who have lost their loved ones, felt passed over, fallen in and out of love, experienced trauma and even rape—these are all a part of the story of Dick Grayson. For female readers, it's an even bigger triumph—the idea that these narratives about feeling like a victim, feeling powerless, and feeling beaten down aren't exclusively tied to womanhood and passivity—they are qualities that can be held by heroes.

Showing male characters suffering from feeling like the object is just as important as showing female characters prevail at being the subject.

So let's come back to that, to gender and sex, since I promised you sex in this essay, and I shall deliver: *Grayson* has it, Dick gets laid plenty in these pages, but he's not James Bond about it. Not even in his fantasies. To the contrary, there's a wonderfully sad thread through the whole thing, something terribly melancholy that Dick is suffering, something we don't see happen to male heroes all that often: **The sense that we're supposed to settle for sex, when what we often want is intimacy.**

This is an important concept for a comic like *Grayson* to skewer.

I mean, guys are sold this non-stop. And women, we're just sold that guys are better at things than us, hence the whole outdated Second-Wave Feminism idea that the Male Ideal is somehow superior to the Female Ideal. This isn't me whispering insidious feminism into your ear—this is accepted as academic fact in most circles. These are concepts you would learn in an entry-level Women's Studies course, so if you don't "buy in" to things like the idea that "male" is default and favored in Western pop culture and society, there are way better essays written by far smarter women to address that.

So, first issue, right off the Bat, we've got Dick using his powers to befriend his target for a moment of happy … comrade-ery. (I won't pun again.)[3]

We see him set up his secret clock radio contact with "Mr. Malone" and he seems like himself for a brief moment when he speaks to Batman back home, and then bam—Helena Bertinelli knocks on the door.[4] This isn't the first or last time this happens in *Grayson*, and it's notable. The female gaze at work again, in a strong visual reversal wherein fully clothed women barge into Dick's space while he's half-naked and treat him like an object. They kiss him, they screw him, they remind him that they're in control.

Now, this isn't a criticism. It's a bad thing for Dick, but it's not a bad thing for the comic. It's *key* to remember that this character has traditionally had a massive female readership.

I wondered at first if this was just played for kicks. While it is refreshing to see women in army pants and boots push around a pretty, half-naked Nightwing, I've had to give this series so much credit because I think it's doing a lot more than fanservice with these scenes rife with the female gaze.

And here's why.

1. Nobody Here Really Likes Dick.

Yes, in the *Future's End* issue, Helena tells Dick via the Cluemaster's code that she is in love with him. That issue takes place five years later, and is intended as a reflection of the darkest timeline possible. Dick, even the hardened, willing-to-kill Dick of the future, just falls apart at even a coded indication of affection.[5] It lends the idea that for five years he's been fighting for his life alongside these people, and the closest they get to *real intimacy* are highly coded deathbed confessions.

Additionally, Helena's kind of a jerk to Dick, at least in the present (and a bit in the gloomy Soviet future, as well.) So is Alia. So is The Tiger, who rescues him while calling him an idiot.[6] They all constantly remind Dick what a stupid kid he is.

While at the best of times, Batman and Robin were the best of chums, it wasn't always the case. Working with a bunch of emotionally-constipated jerks isn't *exactly* new to Dick Grayson, and it's something he has a contingency for. In *Grayson*, we see him seek out intimacy with the guys he's sent to kill. He attempts to relate to them, because he also feels kind of lost, kind of angry, and *he* isn't murderous about it, so why should you be? "It Gets Better." Classic Grayson.

It's key to remember that when I say intimacy, that isn't sex. Dick gets plenty of sex. Intimacy isn't necessarily sex, it isn't a chain of hot Bond girls throwing themselves in your bed, or your co-workers getting along with you when you're naked. Intimacy is when you trust someone, and it doesn't solely come with sex partners. Ideally, you experience intimacy during a good phone call with family back home, a late night chat with your best friend, or a clandestine, clock-radio sponsored report in to your former teacher, partner, and friend.

Spyral seems pretty standoffish, like maybe intimacy isn't a big part of what they do. And while there has been a lot said about losing aspects of Dick Grayson's character in the New 52, there's a big acknowledgement of the character's cuddly, emotional nature right there—without his close friendships, the kid kinda falls apart.

2. So He Trades on His Sexuality to Get By

This isn't to say that Dick doesn't like getting laid, or that the character doesn't have a long, healthy tradition of falling into bed with pretty girls. He does. But he also has a tradition of falling into bed with girls *he really doesn't get along with*. He ends up alternately fighting with and smooching Huntress in air vents in the pre–New 52 DC Universe, despite Dick's insistence that she's a little crazy.[7]

This also somewhat famously happens during the Tarantula arc of *Nightwing*. Dick ends up emotionally wounded and is coerced into bed with someone who he would ordinarily resist—because he's sad and wants company. He feels as though he's failed the people he truly cares about, and is not worthwhile to them any longer. Tarantula preys on his weak state and takes advantage of Dick. Beyond the bedroom, she continues to take advantage of him, attempting to force him into a long-term relationship and marriage.[8]

This is heavy, heavy, stuff. Typically, I'd avoid a discussion on the consent of fictional characters, but author Devin Grayson has confirmed it as an act of rape. While I don't expect DC Comics to have Dick coping with his sexual assault any time soon, and the portrayal of rape in superhero comics is something I could do without for a good long time, it's there. Which is bizarrely reflective of how we ought to handle sexual assault victims in real life: *even if they're not ready to talk about it, it's still a part of who they are.*

This isn't a parable, or a neatly wrapped up arc. It is, much like in the real world, a complicated and unfortunate act that takes a very long time to process. And it is, much like in the real world, a problem that continues to compound itself. Some people who don't seem to really like Dick Grayson when he opens his mouth to speak his mind seem to like him just fine when he's half-dressed and under them.

Talk about things that resonate with your female readership, right?

This isn't to say that Helena and Alia are villains. They're just as much a casualty of the power-fantasy world of secret agenting as Dick. Realistically, as women, they were probably socialized to be slightly more open with their emotions in their youth. And then they grew up. And wanted to be secret agents. And that's a "man's world," so put away your tears and your hugs. Grab your gun. You want to be a Spyral agent? There's no crying in Spyral. Women can be top agents, but only if they play by boy rules. The continued valuing of logos over pathos. There's a really obvious, *Zardoz*-esque metaphor here about embrace versus rejection of The Gun, which I don't think is intentional, but it *is* interesting.

3. It's Really Important to Tell Feminist Stories About All Characters

"Important" is a frustrating word in literary criticism, but bear with me.

There are some people, (mostly jerks,) who have the idea that inclusion in comics is going to turn the landscape into *Degrassi*. You know what I mean about *Degrassi*—an easily parodied after-school special of clunky, awkwardly-handled diversity parables. *Grayson* is a pretty effective death-blow to a lot of those concerns. It is, at its core, a story about a guy who has a lot of values and experiences that are coded as "feminine." From a boyhood spent in tiny shorts (rebooting a comic storyline doesn't change our cultural consciousness of a character, which is a whole different essay), to a menagerie of dramatic love affairs, to his physical objectification in canon, to the meta factor of his massive female fanbase—this is a guy who reads as feminine to a lot of people.

And yet, despite a lot of the disparaging things fans have to say about Robin, everyone pretty much likes Nightwing.

So what *Grayson* achieves, pretty spectacularly, is telling a feminist story, to a massive, multi-gendered fanbase, from a publishing company that gets a lot of hate for not telling diverse stories.

So, is it problematic to tell a feminist story about a straight white[9] male character?

Some will argue that including men in these conversations and "making it about them" is damaging, but this isn't a real person that we are using to distract from existing women. This is an existing, fictional character, a marketable name and face that we can put on a book and know people will buy it. The team could have told another sexy secret agent story, but they didn't. They used *existing* media that people are already *buying* to tell a subversive story with a real message. Feminism is for everybody. Comics are for everybody. A world that devalues women and traits that are coded as feminine is bad for *everyone*—even straight white guys—and you can be a hero and still feel feelings.

And isn't that story so often coded to women and sold as "romance"? Aren't we taught that it's not a *real* story? We're told that the narrative of a person *wanting* intimacy but *settling* for sex is a purely female desire, that that's a story only sold in romance novels and misty movies, but that's not the case here. For once, we have a high-action, high-tension super-spy story, and it still functions as an explicitly pro-feminism narrative.

Maybe the future isn't so dark and gritty, after all.

Notes

1. Tim Seeley et al., "Gut Feelings," *Grayson* #2 (New York: DC Comics, October 2014), [6].
2. Alison Bechdel, *Are You My Mother?* Boston: Houghton Mifflin, 2012.
3. Tim Seeley, Tom King, and Mikel Janin, "Grayson," *Grayson* #1 (September 2014), [10].
4. Seeley, King, and Janin, *Grayson* #1, [18–19].
5. Tom King and Stephen Mooney, "Only a Place for Dying," *Grayson: Future's End* #1 (November 2014), [9].

6. Seeley et al., "The Gun Goes Off," *Grayson* #3 (December 2014), [11–12].
7. Chuck Dixon, Scott McDaniel, and Karl Story, "Back to Back to Back," *Nightwing* #29 (New York: DC Comics, March 1999), 7.
8. See *Nightwing* #93–95 (July–September 2004).
9. In the reboot, we haven't had much discussion of Dick's racial identity. His Romani heritage is briefly mentioned in *Secret Origins* #8 (February 2015), but that is the full extent of it. A casual reader of Grayson who had no previous knowledge of the character would assumedly parse him as white. Rather than an attempt to erase, this could be seen as a call for more explicit portrayal of this heritage.

Part IV

Ties That Bind: Relationships with Family and Friends

Mother Alfred
The Influence of Dick Grayson's "Other Parent"

Bethany F. Brengan

Officer Gannon: Oh, and some old guy called for you. Said to tell you to "ring home" when you "had a moment." That your grandpa or something?
Dick: More like my mom...[1]

Much is made, both in the comics and among comic readers, of Dick Grayson being "raised by Batman." It's hard to overstate the influence of Bruce on Dick's life (and vice versa), but sometimes these conversations overlook the fact that Bruce wasn't the only person to take in the young acrobat, or to have an impact on his life.

Both Dick's and Alfred's roles in the comics have changed significantly over time and in conjunction with each other. As Bruce's relationship with Dick became more fraught with tension, Alfred's position in the Bat-family metamorphosed from comical servant to secondary parental figure. Frequently, Alfred's parenting of Dick is presented as a contrast to Bruce's: an authoritative style to Bruce's more authoritarian style of parenting, a nurturing figure to Bruce's protective figure, "Mom" to Bruce's "Dad."

Ultimately, it is Alfred's influence, as well as Bruce's, that has shaped Dick, as both a vigilante and a civilian.

In the early days of comics, Batman and Robin were the inseparable "Dynamic Duo," and Alfred was the interloper. Alfred first appeared on the Wayne Manor doorstep in 1943, three years after Dick's debut as Robin.[2] Instead of being Batman's earliest confidant, Alfred stumbled onto the secret of Batman and Robin through a combination of luck and poor Batcave security.

In the 1980s, the story started to change. Comics began exploring the psychological toll that losing his parents must have had on Bruce. Alfred became the long-time servant of Bruce Wayne, present before his parents' deaths and responsible for raising the grieving child.[3] At the same time, Dick Grayson was growing up, no longer the "laughing young daredevil," but the serious leader of the Teen Titans.

It's no coincidence that Alfred's involvement in the Bat-family increased at the same time that comic books were entering the "Dark Age."[4] On the one hand, who could be more easily written to fit the sensibilities of the times than DC's Dark Knight—a man already lurking in the shadows with a grim backstory at the ready? On the other hand, fans knew that Batman had raised Dick Grayson who is generally viewed as a healthy, stable hero. If Batman's new portrayal as an unhappy loner was to be believed, how could Dick Grayson be explained? And given everything that had happened to him, why wasn't Bruce *more* unstable in his crusade to avenge his parents' deaths?

The answer to both of these questions lies in Alfred. Alfred became, and continues to be, a stabilizing influence in both Bruce and Dick's lives, and he balances out Bruce's parenting methods—complementing Bruce's better qualities and making up for his omissions. This essay will examine Dick's relationship with Alfred from the mid-eighties through the early issues of the New 52.

Dick Grayson's Early Influences

Ten-year-old Richard Grayson didn't arrive at Wayne Manor as a blank slate.[5] Before delving into Alfred's influence, it would be wise to examine the influence of Dick's biological parents: John and Mary Grayson.

Developmental psychologist Mary Polce-Lynch notes that between the ages of four and seven "adults can do a lot to shape boys' emotional responses and behaviors *regardless of the boys' temperaments*. Whether boys are 'easygoing,' 'slow-to-warm up,' or 'difficult,' they all need practice naming and expressing their emotions."[6] Similarly, popular author and family counselor Michael Gurian states, "If we called the infant years the age of attachment, the toddler years the age of order and play, and the early school years the age of education, we would do well to think of our seven- to ten-year-olds as living in the age of relationship."[7]

In the comics, the Graysons are almost universally portrayed as open and encouraging parents—praising Dick when he tries new things, giving him physical and verbal proof of affection:

MARY GRAYSON: I've got you
 (as she catches YOUNG DICK's hands)
 —Mommy's *here*, little Robin.
 (gently releases DICK onto a platform)
 You did *great*! You're learning *so* fast.[8]

When Dick complains about Damian's attitude, Alfred reminds him that he started with an advantage Damian never had: "Yours were *loving* parents. Your *role models* were of the highest caliber."[9]

Dick seems to lean toward emotional openness due both to his natural temperament and his early influences. His experiences with authority figures have been largely positive, and he already has the building blocks in place to start healthy relationships.

Alfred as Mom

Although the experiences of the early years are formative, they are not complete, nor even entirely irreversible. Social psychology expert Shelley Taylor admits, "The trajectories of mental and physical health are not written in stone at the end of the first few years."[10] This sentiment is echoed in *Parenting from the Inside Out*:

> Some people worry that the findings of attachment research indicate that our early years create our destiny. In fact, the research shows that relationships with parents can change and as they do the child's attachment changes. This means that it's never too late to create positive change in a child's life. Studies also demonstrate that a nurturing relationship with someone other than with a parent in which the child feels understood and safe provides an important source of resilience, a seed in the child's mind that can be developed later on as the child grows.[11]

The sort of guidance and nurturing Dick receives after the abrupt and traumatic loss of both of his primary caregivers will be essential to his view of the world and his ability to connect with others. In many ways, Bruce is the ideal person to take Dick in: he can relate to the boy's grief and anger on a deep, personal level; he can help the boy direct his anger away from revenge and towards justice; and he is more than able to provide for the boy's physical needs. But Bruce (particularly Post-*Crisis* Bruce) struggles with emotions, his own and other people's. In *Batman: Dark Victory*, he doubts his ability to fill the emotional void in Dick's life, telling his parents' graves: "I don't see myself as any sort of father figure. But ... I think I can make a difference in his life."[12] Bruce successfully fulfills many of the obligations of a father—to the point that Dick, even when his relationship with Bruce is fractured, is able to say, "You were the best father you could be. Given the circumstances."[13]

However, Dick didn't just lose a father. He also lost a mother.

It's a running joke among the Bat-boys, and the readers, that Alfred is "the mom."[14] The Batcave is very much a "man-cave": its life revolves around the relationships between fathers and sons (and father figures and sons); women who occupy the Bat-family tend to either have their own spaces (e.g., Barbara Gordon and Kate Kane), or to get written out of the comics (e.g., Stephanie Brown and Cassandra Cain). Within this feminine void, Alfred is still a father figure, but he is also the "mom," the nurturer to Bruce's protector.

When describing general differences between mothers' and fathers' parenting methods, Gurian lists nine "mothers tend to" statements. The statements may not be universal, but six of the nine apply to Alfred. (The statements that didn't apply to Alfred either involved the care of infants and toddlers or physical touch, which Alfred doesn't seem to employ any more or less than Bruce does.)

A mother, writes Gurian, tends to "work constantly and intimately toward helping a child express his or her emotions in *words*."[15] Oddly, it is the reserved, "stiff upper lip" British butler who encourages Dick to talk about his emotions, asking questions of young Robin like "Master Richard ... are you happy?"[16]

Likewise, Alfred's conversations with adult Dick are more open than his conversations with Bruce. Alfred tells Dick, "You're not like *Bruce* where my attempts at conversation at any level above *sarcasm* would be met by various *emotional brick walls*."[17] This spoken expression of emotions may be particularly necessary for Dick, who describes himself as "unique in this family, a talker among writers."[18]

It's not that Bruce never has heart-to-heart conversations with Dick, but these tend to be awkward for both of them. For example, while tracking criminals, Batman and Nightwing engage in a rooftop conversation about their differences—with Bruce admitting that the role of Batman has become a hiding place for him. Dick is shocked and moved by this confession. But when he attempts to physically reach out to his mentor, Batman holds up his hands, rebuffing the gesture and the sympathy.

BATMAN: No regrets. I'd make the sacrifice all over again. In a heartbeat.
  [Silent panel.]
BATMAN: Gunfire. Automatic.
NIGHTWING: Thank God.[19]

Gurian notes that a mother also tends to "teach *direct empathy* when someone is hurt, even at the expense of other goals, games, tasks, or work."[20] According to Martin Hoffman, a professor of psychology who specializes in empathy, altruism, and the development of moral principles, even psychologists with very different theoretical perspectives agree that empathy may be "the most significant factor in altruistic behavior"[21]—and few things require more altruism than unpaid nightly crime-fighting. Without empathy, the work of the Bat-family could easily become about violence and cheap thrills rather than protecting people.

Alfred frequently encourages his charges to consider other people's feelings. When Dick is frustrated with Damian, Alfred says, "There's no denying he can be *difficult*, but underneath all the defensive *bluster*, young Master *Damian* is the inheritor of his father's *courage*, his *determination*, his desire to do what is *right*. If anyone can bring out the *best* in the boy, it *will* be you, I have no doubt."[22] Alfred wants Dick to notice that the boy's anger is a defensive posture, hiding fear and uncertainty. He makes a similar point to Bruce after Damian disappears and Alfred finds a journal full of violent drawings.

> BRUCE: ...Look at *all* of them ... Damian's been drawing these—
> (throws journal into the fire)
> *since he got here!* I *haven't* been listening ... I've let my own son slip away...
> ALFRED: Poor boy, to have kept this level of rage in check for so long.
> BRUCE: We're getting him back, Alfred. I *won't* let him down again.[23]

Bruce is focused on his supposed failure and his goal to get Damian back, but Alfred wants him to also consider how his son must have felt when he drew the pictures and the effort the boy made to hold that rage inside.

Along with tending to emotional needs, a mother tends to "*relinquish personal, daily independence* in order to care for children's various needs. (Moms multitask in complex ways, which include altering their schedules and diverting minute-by-minute concentration in order to address the child's immediate needs.)"[24] Alfred goes above and beyond what could be expected of any butler, valet, or housekeeper, no matter how well paid. He seems to be constantly on call: cleaning up after other members of the family, serving food, caring for costumes and crime-fighting equipment, nursing the injured, and providing telecommunications. As Alfred would say, "A multi-tasker's day is never done."[25]

It is not just Alfred's willingness to relinquish personal independence that makes him seem like a "mom"; it's also the sort of tasks that he performs—tasks that in modern Western culture generally fall to women. Half the time Alfred enters the Batcave, he bears some kind of food or drink. When Dick is depressed, Alfred cooks his favorite food.[26] Taylor notes that concern about sustenance seems to be a particularly female trait:

> Women seem to have a special relationship with food. It's not just that women are the ones who buy it, although they are, by a large margin, the food shoppers of the world. And it's not just that women prepare it, although this task, too, is more commonly a woman's province than a man's. Food seems to have a special meaning for women. When women want to celebrate a special occasion, they think of food. When they get together, eating is commonly the activity. "Having lunch" means something special to women that it doesn't necessarily to men. When women want to send a message of caring or affection to someone, they often cook for them.[27]

In a similar vein, mothers still perform more housekeeping and childcare tasks than fathers do.[28] Alfred is responsible not just for basic childcare but for teaching various social niceties. "Young gentlemen chew with mouths *closed*, Master Richard,"[29] he reminds Dick. And when Nightwing inadvertently threatens Alfred (disguised as Two-Face), the butler murmurs, "I thought I raised you to display better manners, Master Richard."[30]

A mother tends to "see the child as an *emotional extension of herself*, and thus is unlikely to distance herself emotionally from the child when the child does wrong."[31] Although Alfred never states that he views his charges as emotional extensions of himself, he is much less likely than Bruce to emotionally distance himself from them when they are in trouble. Few things upset either Alfred or Bruce more than Dick getting hurt, particularly if it's through Dick's own recklessness, but they respond differently to these situations.

In *Robin: Year One*, after Dick disobeys orders and is beaten by Two-Face, Bruce tells Dick that he cannot be Robin anymore; then he turns away and stares out the window. Bruce was terrified for Dick's life, and it hurts him to say Robin is finished. But when Dick pleads with him, Bruce snaps, blaming the boy for what happened.[32] Afterwards, Bruce and Dick avoid each other, and Alfred describes Dick as "quite withdrawn and receding more and more each day,"[33] but Bruce does not make any attempt to reconnect with the boy (perhaps as much because of guilt as anger).

Alfred is certainly capable of becoming angry with and shouting at Dick, but he does not express the same level of emotional withdraw afterwards. When a grown Dick ends up at the manor after being shot, Alfred is distressed. He repeatedly tells Dick to stay in bed, only to have Dick repeatedly attempt to leave. Alfred urges Dick not to try his patience, and when Dick ignores him, he finally explodes.

ALFRED: *Richard John Grayson!* GET BACK INTO BED THIS INSTANT! This is the second bullet you've taken in a matter of several months, and I will not allow you to compromise your care!
DICK: Look, you can't keep me here against my—
ALFRED: The hell I can't!
[Silent panel. ALFRED turns away and faces the window.][34]

This outburst startles Dick and leads him to ask the older man about what's troubling him. Alfred then expresses concern about Dick's recent change in spirits. In both examples, Bruce and Alfred turn away and face the window, and both of them attempt to show less than they feel. The difference is that, even though Alfred is upset with Dick, he does not shut himself off emotionally.

Part of Alfred's emotional availability involves praise (another one of Gurian's traits of motherhood), to "promote the child's development of skills and talents through an emphasis on *verbal encouragement.*"[35] This is perhaps one of the most immediately obvious differences between Bruce and Alfred. Alfred frequently offers verbal encouragement such as "That was very *well* done. The public displays of heroics are always the *most* challenging"[36] or "*Remarkable* work, young sir, if I may say so."[37]

Bruce is usually sparing with praise. This may be partially because Bruce is better at communicating through action. At the end of *Nightwing: Year One*, Jason delivers a case to Dick from "Him," meaning Batman. But the note with the costume is from Alfred:

Because the costume I last saw you wearing was tattered and torn.
The robin's egg blue was inspired.
But how can one take flight without new wings?
If the feathering is familiar it is because you once wore this color to great distinction in your youth.
And I've no doubt you will again.
—A.[38]

Bruce sending the costume is his way of acknowledging that Nightwing is his own man now. But it is Alfred who manages to put that into words.

Alfred often praises his charges in Bruce's stead, saying things like "Master Bruce was always proud of you, sir. I know he'd be *especially* proud of you now."[39] Alfred also pushes Bruce to say these things himself. When Bruce comments that Damian has started showing more restraint on patrol, Alfred asks if he managed to tell Damian that he was proud of him. When Bruce insists that he did, Alfred is suspicious, knowing how much Bruce struggles with verbalizing his emotions, and with a raised eyebrow, asks exactly what Bruce said:

BRUCE: I said his actions were commendable.
ALFRED: The words "great job" or "I'm proud of you" never crossed your mind?
BRUCE: What's wrong with *"commendable"*? It means even more than proud—it means admirable, praiseworthy.
ALFRED: *Hnnn.* I'm afraid it *means* you have a lot of work to do.[40]

Finally, Gurian writes that a mother tends to "try to help the child quickly resolve inner and emotional conflicts and stresses so that the whole bonding system can *feel better.*"[41] After Bruce ignores him, a young Dick asks Alfred, "What did *I* do?" and Alfred replies, "Do not take it personally. Master Bruce has these … moods."[42] When Dick is banned from being Robin, Alfred tries to assure him that life is not over: "You will rest. You will recover. You will go on with your life."[43] And when the stress of trying to be Batman builds up so much that Dick is shouting and throwing his hands up over minor details of the Bat-costume, Alfred breaks the tension by starting to laugh, causing Dick to relax and admit that he's being "a handful."[44]

Alfred is a mother in the sense that he provides the reliable, nurturing support that people tend to associate with good mothers. He is not just a prop to the other family members' heroics. Taylor might say that his "mothering" is in itself an act of heroism:

> When we think of heroism, we usually envision a young, fit man putting himself at risk to save others. So potent is this image that it shapes our very definition of heroism, restricting and constraining it to dramatic events such as these. While it is true that women less often hurl themselves in harm's way to protect people other than their own children, their heroism is as legitimate, if not as celebrated, as men's. It is a quieter kind, but in important ways just as risky as men's, involving sacrifice and risks to health and well-being.[45]

These are the acts of heroism Alfred has been performing ever since that fatal night in Crime Alley.

A Parent, Twice Over

If Alfred raised both Bruce and Dick, why are they so different? Dick eventually employs many of Alfred's techniques when dealing with Damian. So why hasn't Bruce picked up more of Alfred's parenting style? Is this just a difference in personalities?

Certainly Dick has a different personality than Bruce. Alfred notes that "He's never the brooder his mentor was as a child."[46] But is this difference actually the result of personality? Or a reflection of the fact that, unlike Dick, young Bruce never saw his parents' killer brought to justice? Did this injustice turn Bruce into a brooding, emotionally distant adult? Or did Bruce's more withdrawn personality push him to deal with his childhood tragedy in a different way?

These questions may never be completely settled—in Bruce, nature and nurture are inextricably intertwined—but psychologist and superherologist, Travis Langley, offers several possible explanations for why Bruce seems to rely so little on Alfred's model of parenting and instead pulls more from his parents' example:

- The Waynes' early lessons lay his basic psychological foundations.
- Bruce grows distant from others during the years after the murders, hence the more dismissing-avoidant of his traits.
- Driven by his parents' demise, Bruce fixates on them.
- Alfred, whose approach seems more permissive than the Waynes', goes along with Bruce's intentions of raising himself.
- With Martha and Thomas gone, Alfred in his domestic role becomes Bruce's mother figure as Bruce endeavors to father himself through his adolescence.
- The Waynes aren't around when he gets old enough for any adolescent rebellion to kick in.
- Bruce leaves home at 14, after only six years in Alfred's care.[47]
- Why try to parent the Robins the same way Alfred parented him when Alfred's right there to do that himself?[48]

Jeph Loeb's interpretation of Bruce's upbringing in *Dark Victory* sheds some light on the differences between Bruce and Dick's childhoods. Alfred promises a grief-stricken young Bruce: "I will endeavor in every way I can to see to it you are brought up in the same manner your parents would."[49] But in the world of *Dark Victory*, Thomas Wayne is distant, both literally and emotionally. Bruce's memories of Thanksgiving involve waiting for his father to come home from the hospital while the turkey gets cold.[50] And when a young Bruce is frightened by a storm, instead of comforting his son, Thomas holds him "at arm's length" and says, "'You will be stronger if you learn to stand on your own.'"[51] In attempting to raise Bruce as his parents would have, Alfred may have, unintentionally, also held young Bruce "at arm's length."

Or perhaps the suddenness of Alfred's new burdens combined with the odd balancing act of being both servant and authority figure left Alfred uncertain about the appropriateness of closing the distance between himself and his young master.

Alfred seems to blame himself for grown Bruce's unhappiness. In *Batman: The Long Halloween,* as Bruce is disappearing down the hall, wondering if Gotham would be better off if his father hadn't saved a mobster's life years ago, Alfred murmurs that those kind of what-ifs are "as fruitless as *my* wondering ... had *I* been a different sort of father to you, how much better *your* life might be."[52] In *Dark Victory*, a flashback shows young Bruce in his parents' bedroom, declaring, "I'm all alone now, Alfred." Alfred appears to be at a loss for what to say, and he lets the boy leave the room in silence. When Dick appears, Alfred seems determined not to repeat this mistake. A young Dick echoes Bruce's statement about being alone now. But Alfred puts his hands on the boy's shoulders and says, "I can only tell you, Dick, something I wish I had said a long time ago to someone else. You are *not* alone. I imagine you never will be again...."[53]

Alfred and Bruce's relationship is a close one (at various points they speak of each other as "father" and "son," although they rarely say this *to* each other), arguably even closer than Alfred and Dick's relationship. But Bruce and Alfred's relationship is also more complicated. Alfred may be the man who raised Batman, and he may have license to say things to Batman that no one else would dare to, but he is still in Bruce Wayne's employ. Bruce has little difficulty using this position of power when he is in an argument with Dick, telling Alfred, "Stay out of this,"[54] or "*Don't* take his side."[55] (Of course, Bruce tends to be this commanding with *everyone*, employee or not.) Dick, although less formal (often calling Alfred "Alfie"), tends to treat Alfred with more deference, perhaps in part because he spent his early years without servants or wealth. Also, Alfred, as part of Bruce's less romanticized memories of the day-to-day reality of schoolwork and domestic duties, has a hard time competing with the model presented by the enshrined Thomas Wayne.

Authoritarian vs. Authoritative: The Batman Growl vs. the Alfred Eyebrow

Langley writes:

> Alfred's *parenting style* (his general approach to child rearing) is mostly *authoritative* (*not* authoritarian), encouraging his surrogate son's independence with warmth, nurturance, and verbal give-and-take, while also exerting authority, enforcing rules, and making *maturity demands* (expectations for age-appropriate conduct). Difficult as it may be to imagine Alfred telling Bruce at 10 or 11, "No, you may not," Bruce's social competence and self-control suggest that Alfred found ways to place limits and exert discipline.[56]

This is somewhat in contrast to Thomas Wayne, who, in later comics, tends to be presented as *authoritarian*, i.e., not uncaring, but stern and inflexible, more interested in obedience than communication. For example, when a young Bruce comes home with a black eye, Thomas demands that Bruce tell him who he has been fighting with, and Bruce, reluctantly, refuses:

> THOMAS (as ALFRED cleans a cut on BRUCE's face): But you might have been badly *hurt*! Are you *afraid* to tell me, is that what it is?
> BRUCE: No, sir.
> THOMAS: I *insist* you tell me!
> BRUCE: N-no, sir!
> THOMAS: Then you leave me no option ... up to your room! *Now!* And *no supper* for you tonight![57]

Thomas is drawn on this page as though from Bruce's perspective: tall, looming, and mostly in shadow. Thomas often takes on mythic proportions in young Bruce's mind—to the point that Bruce is shocked when his friend, Tommy Elliot, causally responds, "You got it, Doc" to a command from Dr. Wayne.[58]

When demands for honesty fail, Thomas resorts to punishment (although later he is seen carrying food up to Bruce's room). Alfred, on the other hand, sneaks some food into the boy's room, and by getting him to talk about shared interests, eventually manages to learn something about what is troubling Bruce and to offer him some advice. This fits Langley's description of the authoritative parent, who "communicates well, listens receptively to the child's questions and requests, and teaches though explanation."[59]

Of course, most parenting doesn't fall completely into one category but is a mixture of permissive, authoritative, and authoritarian styles. Langley notes, "The fact that Bruce is so accustomed to getting his own way might suggest that Alfred and Bruce's birth parents before him preferred to risk erring a little on the side of permissiveness."[60] Langley concludes that "Bruce shows too much self-discipline to have been completely spoiled. Alfred likely applied authoritative guidance based on logic, ethics, and Bruce's inherent guilt."[61]

If, on the sliding scale of *permissive* to *authoritative* to *authoritarian*, Alfred tends to fall in authoritative territory, then Bruce takes after his father, and depending on the writer, runs from authoritative to utterly authoritarian. Ultimately, the difference between authoritative and authoritarian parenting is in the amount of control the parent tries to exert over the child. Channeling Thomas Wayne's more authoritarian moments is probably not a deliberate choice on Bruce's part, but he may feel that by acting like Thomas he is giving Dick what was denied him after that night in Crime Alley. Meanwhile, Alfred's less authoritarian, more emotionally open parenting may remind Dick of his biological parents, so he may be more predisposed to internalize and replicate Alfred's parenting model.

In *Unconditional Parenting*, Alfie Kohn notes that

> On an unconscious level, some people fear that once the thin veneer of adulthood is shattered, time will rush backward and they will revert to being powerless. They deal with that fear by pretending they're *in*vulnerable as adults. Because it's terrifying to be out of control, they need to believe they're always in control.
>
> Alas, that can easily turn into a need to have control over others, to come out on top and feel triumphant, to regard disagreements even with their children as battles that they must win. They fear that to yield an inch, to change their minds, to admit they're wrong, to fail to put their foot down, will be to lose everything.[62]

Bruce has a particular reason to fear being powerless since his most poignant moment of childhood powerlessness resulted in the loss of those he loved the most. Any subsequent loss tends to bring Bruce's need for control to the forefront as he both pushes Dick away and demands that he follow orders without question. After the second Robin, Jason Todd, dies, Batman asks Nightwing for help on a case. When Nightwing suggests a change to Batman's plan, Batman refuses to listen, saying, "You're *not* with the Titans now. If you want to be with me, you follow *my* orders. Now do as I say."[63]

When it seems like Nightwing hasn't obeyed, Batman thinks, "Why isn't he following my orders? I can't protect him unless—"[64] Batman's thought is interrupted, but it's obvious he felt he couldn't protect (the grown) Nightwing unless Dick did exactly what he told him.

Gurian suggests that "fathers tend to employ more authoritarian parenting styles than mothers and retain that authority well into the child's adulthood, waiting for the child to prove himself (this generally applies more to sons) worthy of being respected as an adult."[65] The problem is that Bruce, unlike Alfred, does not know how to acknowledge Dick as an adult. Langley notes that "Batman relates better to the Robins when they're children. Because he doesn't grow into relating to his mother and father as fellow adults, he doesn't know how to relate to his sons as adults either."[66] He has a tendency to view pushes for independence as personal rejections. In the *Nightwing: Year One* version of Dick's transition from Robin to Nightwing, Bruce fires Dick because he spends too much time with the Teen Titans, a group Dick leads. In the *New Titans* issue quoted in the previous paragraph, even the smallest attempts to change Batman's plans are treated as rejections.

"Authoritarian parents," Kohn notes, "...are more likely to see conflict—especially between themselves and their children—as something to be eliminated. They fail to distinguish between different kinds of conflict or between better and worse ways of handling the conflicts that will inevitably arise."[67]

Alfred, as shown earlier, is willing to discuss and listen—chastising and advising, but not controlling, his boys and encouraging them to be themselves, even if he frequently wishes this did not involve their running into danger.

Leaving the Nest

Alfred's parenting style manifests itself in numerous ways in Dick as an adult, but the two main effects are the way Dick views his civilian identity and how he treats those under his mentorship.

Alfred often wishes that Dick would lead a more normal, less dangerous life. He attempts to remind a young Dick that Bruce's battles do not have to be his own:

> ALFRED: The decision is yours alone, Master Richard. You could very well walk away from this crusade and spend your life in happier pursuits.
> DICK: Or I could do some good. Somebody's got to help him ... might as well be me.[68]

Eventually, Alfred reluctantly accepts that Dick and the other members of the Bat-family are too dedicated to justice to throw in the towel for those "happier pursuits." He even tells Bruce, "You've given all the boys a moral and ethical road to follow. You've been their compass. And if there's one thing I've always been sure of, it's that Batman will need a Robin, and Robin will need a Batman."[69] However, Alfred never stops encouraging "his boys" to take time to embrace their civilian identities.

One of the ways that Dick does this is his career on the Blüdhaven police force. A career that worries Batman.

> BATMAN: You'll be *blurring* your two personas.
> NIGHTWING: *What* personas? Dick Grayson *isn't* a masquerade. Not like Bruce Wayne is.[70]

Perhaps it is not a coincidence that the person who most encourages Dick to embrace his civilian identity also wishes Bruce had joined law enforcement:

ALFRED: Master Bruce attended the *F.B.I.* Academy as you are aware. I only regret that he did not *continue* in that ambition rather than this *darker* path.
DICK: You sound like a *parent*, Alfred.
ALFRED (deadpan): *Never.*[71]

Alfred is the only member of the Bat-family without an alter ego. (Somewhat ironic given that he is also the only member of the Bat-clan with professional theater experience.) He is a grounding force, continually reminding the family of the importance of their identities beyond the masks. This balance of civilian and vigilante is one that Bruce constantly struggles with, but Dick embraces both sides of his identity, just as he embraces the values of both Bruce and Alfred, bringing his passion for helping people to legitimate law enforcement as well as to Batman's "darker path."

When he has to take on the mantle of Batman, Dick is afraid the cowl will overwhelm him, will turn him into Bruce, brooding and fractured. Alfred reassures Dick that he can be Batman without becoming Bruce— and that he can mentor Damian without having to channel Bruce.

Dick leans toward a more Alfred-esque form of caring in his relationships with his younger "Bat siblings." He gives Jason, the second Robin, his phone number, offering what Bruce has difficulty giving: a sympathetic ear.[72] Although he reaches out to Jason, Dick is cut off from the Bat-family at this time (due to both his involvement with the Titans and his estrangement from Bruce). After Jason's death, Dick makes an effort to be more involved in the life of the next Robin. He helps train Tim Drake and makes time for the new Robin, even when he is living in Blüdhaven. In these cases, however, Dick acts as an older brother. It's not until Damian comes on the scene and Bruce vanishes that a more parental bent develops in Dick's relationship with Robin.

At first, Dick attempts to behave like Bruce, which leads to Damian tearing the Robin symbol off his chest and stalking out of an argument about following orders. A despondent Dick tells Alfred: "I sounded so *fake*, like a kid trying to do *Batman's* voice."[73] Alfred reminds him that he doesn't have to do things exactly as Bruce would have, saying, "Attempting to take his *father's* place won't work, Master Richard...."[74]

Dick is eventually able to earn Damian's respect, not by pretending to be Bruce, but by playing to his own strengths, both as Batman and as a mentor. He gives Damian space to talk, and he offers frequent verbal encouragement, acknowledging the good he sees in the boy. When a villain targets people based on their familial connections, Damian is disturbed (although he tries to hide it), and he asks Dick whether he's on the side of nature or nurture. Dick places his hand on Damian's shoulder and assures him that he is on neither side—and that Damian "made a choice to *help*, to make a difference, which is *always harder*." Alfred is quick to add, "We go to someone's aid because we want to, because we need to, and *that* is what defines us—that is what defines *you*, Master Damian.... In the end, *you make you*. No one else."[75]

While parenting between Bruce and Alfred had the air of a balancing act, Alfred and Dick take more a tag-team approach to raising Damian with both of them using a more authoritative and nurturing style to get the new Robin to open up and trust them.

Conclusion

When Dick begins his career as Nightwing, he records a message to Bruce. His description of seeing Alfred in the cave before Bruce fired him is telling: "At least the *other* parent was glad to see me. Me, not just Robin, the *late partner*. And that's where master and servant differ. Alfred always went out of his way to make sure I felt at home. That I belonged in this place, above in the manor, or down in the secret grotto where we wear masks and talk in code...."[76]

There's no question that Dick and Bruce love each other, but during times when their relationship is fraught with misunderstandings and hurt, it is Alfred who can be relied on—to smooth things over, or to help Batman and Robin interpret each other, or simply to be there for Dick in ways Bruce can't always be. Alfred, by taking on a more nurturing role, helped Dick feel at home in both his identities and to grow into a man who could make *all* his parents proud.

Notes

1. Devin Grayson, Rick Leonardi, and Jesse Delperdang, "Venn Diagram, Part 1: Close Encounters," *Nightwing* #80 (New York: DC Comics, June 2003), 11.
2. Don Cameron, Jack Burnley, and Jerry Robinson with George Roussos, "Here Comes Alfred," *Batman* #16 (New York: DC Comics, April–May 1943).
3. The earliest mention of Alfred raising Batman is probably a 1985 episode of *The Super Powers Team* titled "The Fear." This idea was first incorporated into the comics in Frank Miller's *The Dark Knight Returns* (1986).
4. While "dark" comics existed prior to this, the Dark Age of Comic Books is widely thought of as starting in 1986—the year Alan Moore's *Watchmen* and Frank Miller's *The Dark Knight Returns* hit the shelves. The general tone of comics, even mainstream comics, became grimmer and grittier than before. The Dark Age coincides with the beginning of DC's post–*Crisis* timeline.

5. Some writers have Dick lose his parents at a slightly younger age; some, older—but the average age is ten.

6. Mary Polce-Lynch, *Boy Talk: How You Can Help Your Son Express His Emotions* (Oakland, CA: New Harbringer, 2002), 69.

7. Michael Gurian, *Nurture the Nature: Understanding and Supporting Your Child's Unique Core Personality* (San Francisco: Jossey-Bass, 2007), 171.

8. Chuck Dixon, Scott McDaniel, and Karl Story, *Nightwing: A Knight in Blüdhaven* (New York: DC Comics, 1998), 144.

9. Grant Morrison and Frank Quitely, "Batman Reborn, Part Two: The Circus of Strange," *Batman and Robin* (1) #2 (New York: DC Comics, September 2009), [18].

10. Shelley Taylor, *The Tending Instinct: How Nurturing is Essential to Who We are and How We Live* (New York: Times Books, 2002), 69.

11. Daniel J. Siegel and Mary Hartzell, *Parenting from the Inside Out: How a Deeper Self-Understanding Can Help You Raise Children Who Thrive* (New York: Jeremy P. Tarcher/Penguin, 2004), 102–3.

12. Jeph Loeb and Tim Sale, *Batman: Dark Victory* (New York: DC Comics, 2001), 259.

13. Dixon et al., *Nightwing: Year One* (New York: DC Comics, 2005), [134].

14. See *Batman #312*, *Nightwing #80*, *Detective Comics #698*, and *Batman: Gotham Knights #1*.

15. Gurian, *Nurture the Nature*, 97.

16. Chuck Dixon et al., *Robin: Year One* (New York: DC Comics, 2002), 13–14.

17. Judd Winick, Ed Benes, and Rob Hunter, "A Battle Within," *Batman* #687 (August 2009), [21].

18. Dixon et al., *Nightwing: Year One*, [10].

19. Chuck Dixon, William Rosado, and Tom Palmer, "At the End of the Day," *Detective Comics* #725 (New York: DC Comics, September 1998), 19.

20. Gurian, *Nurture the Nature*, 97.

21. Quoted in Myriam Miedzian, *Boys will be Boys: Breaking the Link Between Masculinity and Violence* (New York: Lantern Books, [1991] 2002), 92. References the author's interviews with Hoffman, 1988, 1990.

22. Morrison and Quitely, "Batman Reborn, Part One: Domino Effect," *Batman and Robin* (1) #1 (August 2009), [11].

23. Peter Tomasi, Patrick Gleason, and Mick Gray, *Batman and Robin, Vol. 1: Born to Kill* (New York: DC Comics, 2012), [96–7].

24. Gurian, *Nurture the Nature*, 97.

25. Peter Tomasi et al., *Batman and Robin, Vol. 2: Pearl* (New York: DC Comics, 2013), [75].

26. Dixon et al., *Robin: Year One*, 129.

27. Taylor, *The Tending Instinct*, 97.

28. Kim Parker and Wendy Wang, "Modern Parenthood: Roles of Moms and Dads Converge as They Balance Work and Family," Pew Research Center (March 13, 2013), http://www.pewsocialtrends.org/2013/03/14/modern-parenthood-roles-of-moms-and-dads-converge-as-they-balance-work-and-family/.

29. Dixon et al., *Robin: Year One*, 30.

30. Dixon et al., *Nightwing: Year One*, [124].

31. Gurian, *Nurture the Nature*, 97.

32. Dixon et al., *Robin: Year One*, 114.

33. Dixon et al., *Robin: Year One*, 117.

34. Devin Grayson, Zach Howard, and Andy Owens, "Back to the Life!" *Nightwing* #99 (January 2005), [12], [15].

35. Gurian, *Nurture the Nature*, 97.
36. Winick, Benes, and Hunter, *Batman* #687, [11].
37. Morrison and Quitely, *Batman and Robin* (1) #1, [14].
38. Dixon et al., *Nightwing: Year One*, [135].
39. Morrison and Quitely, *Batman and Robin* (1) #1, [12]. Of course, in this example Bruce is literally unable to offer verbal encouragement, having "died."
40. Tomasi et al., *Batman and Robin, Vol. 1: Born to Kill*, [41–2].
41. Gurian, *Nurture the Nature*, 97.
42. Loeb and Sale, *Batman: Dark Victory*, 353.
43. Dixon et al., *Robin: Year One*, 115–16.
44. Judd Winick, Mark Bagley, and Rob Hunter, "Long Shadows, Part One: Old Sins Cast Long Shadows," *Batman* #688 (September 2009), [13–14].
45. Taylor, *The Tending Instinct*, 150.
46. Dixon et al., *Robin: Year One*, 65.
47. In some versions; in many other stories, Bruce waits until he is older.
48. Travis Langley, *Batman and Psychology: A Dark and Stormy Knight* (Hoboken, NJ: Wiley, 2012), 250.
49. Loeb and Sale, *Batman: Dark Victory*, 253.
50. Loeb and Sale, *Batman: Dark Victory*, 83.
51. Loeb and Sale, *Batman: Dark Victory*, 15.
52. Jeph Loeb and Tim Sale, *Batman: The Long Halloween* (New York: DC Comics, 2011), 248.
53. Loeb and Sale, *Batman: Dark Victory*, 254.
54. Dixon et al., *Robin: Year One*, 114.
55. Marv Wolfman et al., *Nightwing: The Lost Year* (New York: DC Comics, 2008), 67.
56. Langley, *Batman and Psychology: A Dark and Stormy Knight*, 246–47. Referencing Diana Baumrind, "The Influence of Parenting Style on Adolescent Competence and Substance Use," *Journal of Early Adolescence*, 11 (1991): 56–95; and E. E. Maccoby and J.A. Martin, "Socialization in the Context of the Family: Parent–Child Interaction," *Handbook of Child Psychology: Vol. 4 Socialization, Personality, and Social Development* (4th ed.), ed. by P.H. Mussen and E.M. Hetherington (vol. ed.) (New York: Wiley, 1983): 1–101.
57. Alan Grant, Scott McDaniel, and Ray McCarthy, "Of Mice and Men" in *The Batman Chronicles* #5 (New York: DC Comics, 1996), 30.
58. Jeph Loeb, Jim Lee, and Scott Williams, *Batman: Hush, Vol. 1* (New York: DC Comics, 2003), [77].
59. Langley, *Batman and Psychology*, 247, referencing Baumrind, "The Influence of Parenting Style on Adolescent Competence and Substance Use": 56–95; and Maccoby and Martin, "Socialization in the Context of the Family: Parent–Child Interaction," in *Handbook of Child Psychology: Vol. 4 Socialization, Personality, and Social Development*: 1–101.
60. Langley, *Batman and Psychology*, 247, referencing Baumrind, "The Influence of Parenting Style on Adolescent Competence and Substance Use": 56–95. And Maccoby and Martin, "Socialization in the Context of the Family: Parent–Child Interaction," in *Handbook of Child Psychology: Vol. 4 Socialization, Personality, and Social Development*: 1–101.
61. Langley, *Batman and Psychology*, 247.
62. Alfie Kohn, *Unconditional Parenting: Moving from Rewards and Punishments to Love and Reason* (New York: Atria Books, 2005), 109.
63. George Pérez et al., "A Lonely Place of Dying, Part 4: Going Home," *The New Titans* #61 (New York: DC Comics, 1989), 16.

64. Pérez et al., *The New Titans* #61, 19.
65. Gurian, *Nurture the Nature*, 99. Interpreting Paul D. Hastings and Joan E. Grusec, "Parenting Goals as Organizers of Responses to Parent-Child Disagreement," *Developmental Psychology* 34 (1998): 465–79. Note: Along with his nine "mothers tend to" statements, Gurian lists nine "fathers tend to" statements. All of these fit Bruce except for the one involving pushing children to be independent.
66. Langley, *Batman and Psychology*, 250.
67. Alfie Kohn, *Unconditional Parenting*, 240.
68. Dixon et al., *Robin: Year One*, 196–7.
69. Tomasi et al., *Batman and Robin, Vol. 1: Born to Kill*, [32].
70. Dixon et al., "At the End of the Day," *Detective Comics* #725, [15–16].
71. Dixon et al., "Bruce Wayne, Fugitive: Time & Motion," *Nightwing* #68 (June 2002), 5.
72. Jim Starlin, Jim Aparo, and Mike DeCarlo, "White Gold and Truth," *Batman* #416 (February 1988), 20.
73. Morrison and Quitely, *Batman and Robin* (1) #2, [18].
74. Morrison and Quitely, *Batman and Robin* (1) #2, [18].
75. Peter J. Tomasi et al., "Dark Knight vs White Knight: Tree of Blood, Conclusion," *Batman and Robin* (1) #22 (June 2011), [7].
76. Dixon et al., *Nightwing: Year One*, [22–23].

Big Brother Dick
Yasmin Lysaker

Despite being the only child of John and Mary Grayson, Dick Grayson is one of comic's best-known big brothers. In addition to his close relationship with his Teen Titans family, Dick as a sibling is best known for his relationships with his brothers and sisters in the name of Robin and in the name of Wayne. This essay explores two of Dick's brotherly relationships: that with Jason Todd, which made Dick into a big brother and that with Tim Drake, probably Dick's closest sibling. Although Dick and Jason see each other as family, Dick was a more involved older brother and mentor to Tim Drake. Yet both bonds have withstood disagreements, indicating these brotherly connections run deep despite their differences.

Jason Todd

Dick first became a big brother with the introduction of Jason Todd, and this is easily Dick's most complicated brotherly relationship. Initially Dick and Jason were amicable, despite not being particularly close due to Dick living in New York and working nearly exclusively with the Teen Titans. After Jason returned from the dead, his relationship with Dick was more antagonistic. Still, the two seem to consider each other brothers, even if largely estranged, given how often they bail one another out and provide second chances.

The First Jason

In Jason's pre–*Crisis*, circus origin, the two bonded quickly over their shared heritage as childhood trapeze artists. So similar were Dick and Jason's origins that Dick initially offered to adopt the newly-orphaned Jason because he knew what it was like.[1] Jason, of course, is taken in by Bruce instead, but Dick shows how much he cares for Jason when he gives him the greatest gift he can—the Robin mantle.[2]

Over in *The New Teen Titans*, Dick and Jason appear brotherly together. As Jason is about to head back to Gotham after assisting the Titans on a case, he comments that he neglected to tell Batman where he was and hopes Batman didn't see him in action on television. Dick immediately offers Jason support, praising his efforts and telling Jason to have "the old man" call him if Jason gets into trouble. Dick promises to tell Bruce how well Jason did and thereby get the Bat off Jason's "case real fast."[3] In referring to Bruce as "the old man," Dick gestures towards a brotherly relationship: he and Jason have the same old man. Furthermore, Dick performs the role of the protective older sibling, vouching for the younger sibling and redirecting possible parental anger.

The New Jason

In June 1987, the month after Jason finished his case with the Teen Titans, the second Robin received a new origin. Instead of being a carbon-copy of Dick, Jason was now a street kid caught stealing the tires from the Batmobile.[4] Since Dick has already left the nest, the first and second Robins don't meet until sometime later, when Dick first reads about the new Robin in a newspaper.[5] Dick is furious, but his anger is directed at Bruce, who replaced him without having the courtesy to tell him, rather than at Jason.[6] Despite their rocky start (Dick bails Jason out after Jason attempted to bust a drug ring before the drugs were delivered), Dick gives Jason his old Robin uniform, letting Jason know that Dick supports him as Robin. Of even greater importance, though, is the card Dick gives Jason with his phone number, encouraging the younger man to call him whenever he needs to talk. Dick offers his unconditional support, telling Jason, "There's going to be times when you're going to want to talk to someone. ... I've been where you're at and I'm a good listener."[7] In addition, Dick advises Jason not to bottle his feelings up as Bruce does; combined with Dick's earlier offer, it's clear Dick hopes to serve as a sympathetic ear and even a big-brother mentor.

Unfortunately, Dick and Jason didn't have much time to develop this relationship. In the 1980s, once Dick became Nightwing, he rarely appeared in Batman-group comics. In relationship terms, Dick's bond with Jason was weakened by Dick's poor relationship with Bruce (who had fired Dick) and his work with the Teen Titans. It was never that Dick didn't like Jason (Dick thought Jason had skill and might even be a better Robin than him),[8] it was that other circumstances kept the first two Robin brothers from being as close as they might have been.

Jason's Death

When Jason died in *A Death in the Family*, his death cast a long shadow over the Batman family. In *New Titans* #55 (June 1989), Dick is utterly distraught to learn of Jason's death and reacts violently (although the news was broken to him in a cavalier way). Later he blames himself: "I gave Jason my old Robin costume. *I* should have been there, Kory."[9] For Dick, giving Jason the Robin costume was a defining act that indicated trust, acceptance, and a relationship. Although Dick logically recognizes that Jason's death is not his fault, he feels that he has failed someone very close to him.

Although Dick processes his grief and moves on with his life, he still feels connected to and protective of Jason. In *Nightwing: Secret Files and Origins*, Dick is knocked unconscious and hallucinates Robin, who is revealed to be Jason at the end of the story. When Dick momentarily suggests that he might have preferred to live a "normal" life, Jason is skeptical and says, "It's me you're talking to, remember?"[10] This indicates a profound level of trust that Dick has in Jason: he can admit to him that he would not, in fact, trade his hero life to have his parents back (something Dick doesn't share with Bruce, who he thinks would immediately cast aside the Batman gig for a chance to have his parents alive).[11] This might also reflect another common bond between the two Robins, in that both prefer their superhero lives to what came before. Dick's willingness to share this secret with Jason (albeit a Jason of his own creation) suggests a brotherly bond between the two as they maintain confidences from their "father," as siblings are wont to do.

Even years after Jason's death, Dick is still protective of his memory. During *Joker: Last Laugh*, Dick believes Robin (Tim Drake) dead. When Nightwing confronts Joker, the clown uses it as an opportunity to commit suicide by vigilante (he had originally intended to have Batman do the honors but decides it would hurt Batman more if "one of his litter did the dirty deed.")[12] Despite Nightwing's anger, he doesn't allow himself to lose control, even permitting Joker to get in some hits of his own. It's only after Joker taunts him about Jason, noting that "I hit Jason a lot harder than that" that Dick beats the Joker to death.[13] The reference to Jason's death is what drove Dick over the edge, as Dick's protective instincts went into overdrive, and he made the Joker pay for adding insult (the crass joke about Jason's death) to injury (Jason's murder by the Joker). Later, as Dick deals with his guilt, he gazes at an old photograph of him and Jason against a backdrop of snowy mountains, suggesting the two were on vacation together.¹⁴ Dick's extreme reaction and the added insight into their relationship further supports the idea that Dick sees Jason as a younger brother, albeit a somewhat distant one.

THE RETURN OF JASON

It is after Jason returns from the dead that their relationship turns antagonistic. Jason has a chip on his shoulder over how the Bat Family behaved after his death and now fundamentally disagrees with their method of crimefighting. Jason, in his new vigilante identity as the Red Hood, kills criminals without remorse in order to prevent them from engaging in future criminal acts. Dick disagrees profoundly with this philosophy and comes to regard Jason with suspicion since he is now on the other side of the law, as it were. In addition, Jason occasionally tries to harm members of the Bat Family, such as when he attacks Nightwing and Batman with a super-powered android.¹⁵ Jason might be family, but Dick has reason to distrust him.

Despite Dick's distrust and caution around Jason, he still comes when Jason calls. In *Outsiders* #44, Jason asks Dick to meet him in Gotham City, where the two promptly start fighting because Jason has a gun on Dick and Dick initially doesn't trust him not to use it. When Jason complains the two have had a bad start to the night, Dick retorts, "I don't think *tonight's* what tipped the boat over!"¹⁶ In other words, Dick has plenty of reasons not to trust Jason but he came anyway. Dick's post-resurrection relationship with Jason seems based on that tension—a willingness to do right by Jason tempered with a heavy dose of skepticism.

Aside from their trust issues, Jason's willingness to kill upsets Dick deeply. When Dick moves to New York City after spending the past year on a trip with Bruce and Tim (in the *One Year Later* event), he is dismayed to find Jason has coopted his Nightwing identity and is murdering criminals. Dick even goes so far as to ponder, "God, I wish he [Jason] *had* died that night with Batman and Joker...."¹⁷ Callous as that initially sounds, Dick does not actively wish Jason dead, given how deeply the younger man's death affected him. More likely this encapsulates Dick's grief at seeing Jason blithely murder his way through New York City: as a hero, Dick is compelled to bring murderers to justice but it's hard to do that to a family member. Consequently, Dick might wish to himself that Jason were dead, if only to spare himself the pain of watching Jason become someone he has sworn to fight against. Throughout the story arc, Dick (as Nightwing) periodically checks in with Dr. Bridget Clancy, his former Blüdhaven landlady now turned psychiatrist, who suggests that Nightwing might be deliberately letting Jason get away. Dick hotly denies it, but his reaction veers slightly into protesting too much.[18] Later Nightwing seeks out Clancy to discuss Jason and whether he, as a murdering vigilante, deserves to be saved from his kidnappers. Dick decides he should do what he thinks is ethically correct—and goes to save Jason.[19] Given his Bat-training, Dick probably would have saved the murderer in question anyway, but Dick makes no effort to track Jason down after the incident, allowing his familial ties to override his devotion to jailing criminals. Interestingly, Jason sends Dick a telegram in which he calls Dick "brother" and states "I just wanted to believe we could be family again," indicating that Jason also feels the ties of brotherhood, perhaps even to a greater degree than Dick.[20]

Dick also still cares for Jason, even if it is tempered by a heavy dose of distrust. In *Battle for the Cowl*, Dick twice offers to get Jason help (based on the circumstances Dick is likely referring to psychiatric help), but also reaches out his hand to keep Jason from falling off a moving train into a river below immediately after Jason attempts to kill him.[21] Later, even after Jason has attempted to expose the identities of Batman (Dick) and Robin (Damian) and take their place as Gotham's protector, Dick still reaches out to Jason to request that he allow "us" (presumably Dick, Damian, and Alfred) to help him.[22] Even though Jason has recently murdered numerous people, Dick still feels that familial connection and wants to reform Jason. While Jason is not pleased to go to Arkham Asylum, Dick hopes Jason can be rehabilitated once he is off the streets.

As for Jason, his relationship with Dick is equally complex. Prior to Jason's death, their relationship was amicable on both sides. Once Jason returned, though, things changed—but not entirely. Despite repeated violent outbursts, Jason maintains some regard for Dick. For instance, Jason took up Dick's Nightwing identity for a time, which Clancy suggests is flattery and possible evidence that a younger Jason hero worshipped Dick.[23] Jason also offers tips to Dick, such as the one about Black Lightning being innocent of manslaughter.[24] And for every time Jason attempts to harm Dick, there's another time when he doesn't do as much harm as he could. For instance, Jason ties up Dick and Damian and threatens to expose their identities; if the Red Hood was able to tie up the Dynamic Duo, he could have easily killed them.[25] In the end, Jason's hostility towards Dick likely springs from Jason's general rejection of the Bat Family's method of operations and unresolved issues with Bruce's parenting. Jason comments to Dick, "I guess that's why 'Dad' always loved you best," which (while more of a snarky comment than a confession) indicates that Jason might have some resentment towards Dick as a result of Bruce's perceived favoritism.[26]

Tim Drake

After Jason's death, the *Batman* authors decided that Batman needed a new Robin both to lighten the mood of the dark comics and to save Batman from himself. Having learned from their mistakes by creating a Robin who was not initially approved by Dick,[27] the writers had Dick involved in Tim's hero life from the get-go. Timothy Jackson Drake, most commonly known as Tim Drake, would carry the mantle of Robin from 1991–2009, surpassed only by Dick in number of years in the red Robin tunic. During those years, Dick was a mentor to Tim. Not only does Dick coach him as Robin, but he also teaches the much younger boy how to do tasks around the house and conduct business for Wayne Enterprises in Bruce's absence. In part, Dick's mentor role takes the form of a surrogate parent when Tim's biological parents are out of reach and Bruce is absent. To Tim, especially as leader of Young Justice, Dick is a model for how to lead a group of young superheroes. Tim also seeks Dick's counsel in hard times and for advice on living the hero life.[28]

BIG-BROTHER MENTOR

Tim enters Dick's life forcefully, tracking the elder vigilante down and trying to convince him to become Robin again. When Dick refuses to revert back to childhood, Tim takes up the Robin mantle in order to keep that symbol alive. Dick's role as mentor begins shortly thereafter when Tim shows up unannounced at his apartment, Bruce having sent Tim to New York for training. Batman could teach Tim all he needs to become a better athlete, better detective and so on, but only Dick can teach him to be Batman's partner.[29] This establishes a powerful mentor-student dynamic between Dick and Tim, as there are things Tim needs to learn that only Dick can teach him. But Tim also has Bruce as his primary mentor, which means Dick can serve as a chummy, fun mentor—in essence, a cool older brother—because Bruce is already providing the sterner, more regimented vigilante conditioning. Dick is someone Tim can turn to when other adults in his life have failed him, and Dick will take Tim's concerns seriously. Early on in their relationship, when Jean-Paul Valley (the vigilante Azrael) is disastrously serving as Batman, Tim seeks out Dick for help. Dick strikes an agreement with Tim: he will promise not to treat Tim like a child as long as Tim remembers he still is one. Tim agrees, happy that he has Dick to partner up with and that he is treated like an equal.[30]

While Bruce recovers from his broken back in *Knightfall*, Dick takes over as Batman for a while,[31] Tim at his side as Robin. With Dick, Tim does not (as he did with Azrael) have to worry about the damage Batman will cause or how self-destructive he will be. Dick and Tim's relationship strengthens and their trust and reliance on the other for backup deepens. *Batman: Prodigal* is full of good-natured jesting and banter, but we also see a very young Tim struggling with guilt and remorse over believing he has failed Batman when he wasn't able to prevent Azrael's destructive forces from being unleashed. We also see Dick being too preoccupied with self-doubt and traumatic memories, tormenting himself about his worthiness as Batman and not able to lead Tim at first. We get a glimpse into Dick and Tim's everyday life at Wayne Manor: Dick is the adult who has to teach Tim things like doing laundry and sweeping floors.[32] From this point on, Dick and Tim are now not only brothers in the crime-fighting world, but also as civilians and this further establishes their mentor-student relationship, which continues until the end of the DCU.

During these early years, Dick's affection for Tim also grows. For instance, during the storyline *Contagion*, Tim is infected with a deadly virus and Dick is there by his side, worrying, catching him when he falls, and desperately hurrying Tim to the Batcave.[33] Scared for Tim's health, Dick stays underfoot working with Batman and others to find the cure. When Dick learns that Batman has beaten him to Tim with the cure, he is so relieved that Alfred has to have him sit down in fear of him fainting from the shock of seeing Tim on the mend.[34] In the sequel *Legacy*, Dick worries for Tim when it is discovered that the virus that almost killed him lays dormant and reassures him that he will be there with him every step of the way as they search for the real cure.[35]

This closeness enhances Dick's friendly, brotherly mentorship. Shortly after Dick moves to Blüdhaven, Tim comes to visit him. As Dick reflects that Tim is the "closest thing to a brother I'll ever have," Tim seeks reassurance in Dick that his abilities are up to par.[36] Like a good mentor and sibling, Dick boosts Tim's confidence while also discussing areas for improvement: Tim is the cerebral one while Dick, in addition to years more experience, has the street smarts. They do not agree on who is the better detective, but Tim has more computer literacy than Dick.[37] Each of them clearly think very highly of the other and the ease with which they discuss sensitive topics suggests brotherly closeness and a desire to improve.

Dick maintains his brother-mentor role through fun training and lending an ear to conversations Tim would rather not have with his father(s). Tim trusts him implicitly, allowing Dick to guide him in balance exercises while blindfolded atop a moving train. As they train on the train, Tim looks to Dick for a wide variety of advice including working with

Batman and dealing with a pregnant girlfriend.[38] An entire issue is devoted to this conversation, and the care and trust the two have in each other shines off of every single page. Tim trusts Dick to not only have his safety in mind as they balance one-footed on the moving train, but also that he has good advice when Tim reveals his heart to him. Dick, on his part, trusts Tim to listen to what he teaches. This dynamic continues as the two age; for instance, Dick teaches Tim how to use money and influence positively when they are in Monte Carlo during their one year away from Gotham,[39] showing that Dick can also mentor his little brother in the business world that they are a part of thanks to being Bruce's family.

The Many Faces of Brotherly Affection and Support

There are many examples of Dick and Tim's deep brotherly affection for each other throughout both their eponymous series and the other Batman books. When a horrid earthquake largely destroys Gotham Dick and Tim work together to assist the residents. Thanks to their various exploits, such as—in part—crawling through sewers, both Dick and Tim become ill.[40] During their recovery, Tim calls Dick for advice on how to handle his father who is very worried for him, thinking Tim is trapped in Gotham. A recurring theme with Tim is his constant lying to the people around him—Batman included. This holds particularly true regarding his father, who only finds out that his son is Robin after several years. Lying to his own father naturally causes Tim a great deal of stress. Dick, his biological parents dead and Bruce knowing about his career in crime fighting from the start, cannot really relate to Tim's plight but he supports him the best he can—with lighthearted banter that reinforces that Tim also has a family in Dick and the other members of the Batfamily.[41] When Tim is forced to go to an all-boys private school, in part because of his exploits after the earthquake, Dick takes him crime-fighting, having a last night out with the boys. As they talk about Tim's upcoming challenges, Dick reminisces about his own home-schooling from when he was a boy, giving Tim some insight into his life while avoiding empty platitudes.[42] Dick's actions talk for him, and he makes sure that Tim takes lead on the case they are solving, boosting his confidence with actions instead of words.

Throughout most of their history together, Dick is generally the one who looks out for Tim.[43] When a war amongst the gangs breaks out in Gotham, Tim is trapped at his high school, doing his best to help out without giving away his identity as Robin. Dick sneaks in and hands him a bagful of smoke grenades and various other gadgets they normally use in their war against crime.[44] This early problem is a premonition of the further troubles the Bat-Family experiences during the extended *War Games* arc. In a fight with Firefly, Dick takes a bullet in his right thigh, which leaves him laid up for weeks and hinders his being Nightwing for months. At the same time, Tim leaves Gotham for reasons of his own. Bruce is less than informative about Tim's whereabouts and, delirious with fever and heartsick,[45] Dick believes Tim is dead because *someone* important to the Bat-family is believed to be dead.[46] Not knowing what is going on causes the injured vigilante great stress.

Dick also wants to protect Tim from some of the darker realities of life—especially his own failings. After *War Games*, Dick does not want Tim to see him barely able to walk, clinging to a crutch. When Tim finally catches up with Dick in Blüdhaven, it is Dick's turn to become taciturn. Despite his few words, Dick thinks deeply and fondly about Tim both as a person and as Robin as he watches him fly across the rooftops and take down the criminals; "God, I love this kid. Too much to let him see me like this."[47] Dick trusts Tim with his life, but he does not want to show him how weak he feels and how he came to be working undercover. When they meet on the rooftop, their conversation is stilted and they go their separate ways after a short interaction that leaves both of them wanting, Tim not quite understanding why Dick isn't willing to put on his Nightwing costume and join him. He offers several suggestions, but Dick is not willing to talk about why, partially in fear of Bruce learning about it via Tim. This underlines that Dick and Tim are still close, and that they want to understand each other and be there for each other. Tim wants to help Dick if he can, but Dick decides it is not the best time for him to do so.

The brothers' trust in each other is later put to the test in *The Resurrection of Ra's al Ghul,* an arc where the topics of family, life and death, choice, and sacrifice come to the fore. Damian's grandfather, the evil Ra's al Ghul, wants to download his consciousness into the young boy in order to preserve his life longer than what the soul-stealing but bodily rejuvenating Lazarus Pits would provide. He sends a large amount of ninjas to ward off the Bat-Family so he can snatch Damian. While Batman himself is in Asia fighting with Ra's, it is up to Dick, Tim, and Alfred to fight off the ninjas swarming Wayne Manor. Simultaneously, Damian is fighting Tim for his role as Robin, claiming he has inherent right to it, being Batman's biological child.

When Dick arrives on the scene, his respect and affection for Tim are foremost in his mind. "My first thought is—all of this for *Damian*? (…)

And, then I think ... no ... It's for *Tim*. For him a thousand ninjas is just the start of what I would do."[48] Dick's supportive presence lets Tim focus on the task at hand instead of Damian's antics. While they fight the ninjas, Dick struggles visibly between his need to protect Damian, a boy whom he does not yet know very well, and his desire to help Tim. Dick trusts Tim to hold his own, as he has seen numerous times that he can, but he also knows that Tim is worn out from fighting Damian and needs Dick's assistance. When Tim and Damian are taken, Dick's thoughts turn promptly to Tim: "I'm coming Tim…. I'm going to *save* you."[49]

When Tim stands before Ra's, Ra's does his best to poison Tim's mind, trying to make him believe that Batman cares less for him now than he did before Damian came to them. Ra's offers Tim the chance to rejuvenate his parents, his best friend Superboy, and his girlfriend Stephanie by using the Lazarus Pit. Tim is willing to sacrifice his own life for theirs but Dick arrives in the nick of time, it appears, and is more than willing to stop Tim from entering the Lazarus Pit in a sort of baptism to join Ra's side. It pains Dick to realize that Tim might have joined the darker side.[50] To Dick there is no price he is not willing to pay in order to help Tim see the futility of aligning with Ra's. Dick's almost uncanny ability to read people he cares about comes greatly into play here. Because of his losses, Tim has become paralyzed and sees only death, not life. But Dick does not want to undermine Tim, contemplating, "No win. If I stop him, I don't trust him. If I don't stop him it shows that I shouldn't have trusted him."[51] Ultimately Dick puts his faith in Tim, telling him, "I let you make that choice for yourself because I knew you would make the *right one*."[52] Dick knows he can rely on Tim, while Tim resigns himself to Dick's care and takes comfort in the embrace of his brother's arms, realizing at last that it is impossible to bring back the dead and that he still has a family that cares very deeply for him.

Another Robin

For years Tim and Dick had an easy, affectionate relationship. In the immediate wake of Bruce's apparent death, their relationship became strained. With Batman gone, Dick reluctantly steps up to take the cowl and appoints Damian Wayne as his Robin in order to keep watch over the child-assassin and mold him into a hero. Tim, already grief-riddled after having just lost his father, best friend, and girlfriend, naturally is not too keen on the idea of giving up the Robin mantle as he sees himself more as a Robin than a potential Batman.

Dick was in a difficult situation when he gave Robin to Damian. Tim was no longer Batman's partner and Dick had to struggle with being a brother, a parent, and the change from Nightwing to Batman on top of tackling his grief over losing Bruce. Giving Robin to Damian was a lesser of two evils kind of choice for Dick. He needed something to hold over Damian in order to effectively mentor him; the Robin identity was the best Dick could do. In addition, Damian was young and volatile while Tim was someone Dick could trust; as Dick told Tim, "You are not my protégé, Tim…. You're my *equal*. My closest ally. You'll be okay."[53]

The problem is that Tim very much does not feel he will be okay; in a reversal of stereotypes, Dick meets the situation with logic while Tim reacts from emotion. Tim feels lost without Bruce to guide him and Dick's words only manage to alienate instead of anchor him.[54] In all the despair, Dick telling Tim that he sees him as an equal and that he cannot be Dick's Robin is a *compliment*, an olive branch Tim does not take, forgetting in his emotional turmoil that it is there for him to cling to. Dick later tries to make amends, but at that moment Tim is not ready to listen to him. Damian does not make things easier for the three of them, antagonizing Tim to the point of blows. Angry and hurt beyond measure, Tim stomps off and starts his search for Bruce, taking the name Red Robin.

Dick, however, does not give up on reconciling with Tim. In *Red Robin* #4, Tim remembers a conversation he had with Dick before he left Gotham. Dick wants to help, but Tim refuses his help and Dick's conviction that Bruce really is dead.[55] This stubbornness makes it possible for Tim to find Bruce and bring him home, but it prevents him from truly understanding that Dick and his friends only worry for him. Dick, on his part, wants the people he cares about close by and his need to protect his loved ones initially makes him resistant to letting Tim actually go on his search for Bruce.[56] When it comes down to it, Dick does trust Tim to know what to do; in the process Dick goes against his principles and inclinations.[57]

It takes Tim a long time to accept Damian as Robin, but he eventually gets there and recognizes that Dick's decision had merit, difficult as it was to accept at the time. Tim later notes,

> …It feels *great*. More than that. It feels *right*. Yes, even Damian as *Robin*. Dick has done *exactly* what I expected he would—put on *Batman's* cowl without getting lost in its shadows. And with everyone believing *Bruce Wayne* is alive and working to help find him—I don't feel *alone* anymore."[58]

Painful as this short estrangement was for fans of Dick and Tim's close brotherly relationship, it injected some nuance and realism into their relationship. Siblings do not always get along perfectly, although Dick and

Tim had been blessed with a long run of relative brotherly harmony. Their disagreement and reconciliation in the wake of Bruce's ostensible death showcased their indelible bonds by testing them. Their connection emerged stronger than before because they had proven their deep affection and close brotherly status was not simply rooted in their ability to get along. They truly cared, prioritizing those ties even when the going got tough. As Tim aptly summed up to Dick, in the opening salvo of their reconciliation, "You're my brother, Dick. You'll always be there for me."[59]

Conclusion

For Tim, Dick is that brother he never had. To Dick, Tim and Jason, along with Bruce and others, provide a family to substitute for the one he lost. While Dick and Jason's relationship was never as affectionate as Dick and Tim's, both have withstood major fractures. Although Dick disagrees with Jason's policy on killing criminals, the two still care deeply about one another. For a long time, Dick and Tim's relationship was smooth sailing, making it easy for readers to recognize their closeness and brotherly connection, but their estrangement after Bruce's death tested their bond. What emerged was an even stronger connection in which both could completely trust the other (Tim even to the extreme length of trusting Dick to catch him when he was pushed out a window) because they knew their relationship was based on more than their uncanny ability to get along.[60] Dick's relationships with his two younger brothers thus reflect two very different types of sibling relationships, ranging from the caring but distant to one based on the deepest levels of mutual trust.

Unfortunately, the New 52 has not done much with these brotherly ties. Compared to the long and vast history Dick and Tim have together in the pre–2011 comics, the direct interaction between them in the rebooted DC Universe is practically non-existent. With Dick currently believed dead by everyone but Bruce, readers are left wondering just how these sibling bonds will be used in the new universe.

Notes

1. Gerry Conway, Bob Kane, and Don Newton, "All My Enemies Against Me," *Detective Comics* #526 (New York: DC Comics, May 1983), 55.

2. Doug Moench, Don Newton, and Alfredo Alcala, "A Revenge of Rainbows," *Batman* #368 (New York: DC Comics, February 1984).

3. Marv Wolfman et al., "Resolution," *The New Teen Titans* #31 (New York: DC Comics, May 1987), 22.

4. Max Allan Collins, Chris Warner, and Mike DeCarlo, "Did Robin Die Tonight?" *Batman* #408 (June 1987).

5. Jim Starlin, Jim Aparo, and Mike DeCarlo, "White Gold and Truth," *Batman* #416 (February 1988), 14.

6. This is true in *Nightwing: Year One* as well, in which Dick and Jason begin working together very quickly.

7. Starlin, Aparo, and DeCarlo, *Batman* #416, 20.

8. For instance, see Judd Winick, Guillem March, and Andrei Bresson, "The Streets Run Red: Ins and Outs," *Batman and Robin* (1) #23 (New York: DC Comics, July 2011), [1–2].

9. Marv Wolfman, George Pérez, and Romeo Tanghal, "Transitions," *The New Titans* #55 (New York: DC Comics, June 1989), [9].

10. Chuck Dixon and Scott McDaniel, "Taking Wing," in *Nightwing: Secret Files and Origins* (New York: DC Comics, October 1999), 6.

11. See Devin Grayson, Roger Robinson, and John Floyd, "Sibling Rivalry," *Batman: Gotham Knights* #14 (New York: DC Comics, April 2001), especially page 21–22.

12. Chuck Dixon et al., *Joker: Last Laugh* #6 (New York: DC Comics, January 2002), 14.

13. Dixon et al., *Joker: Last Laugh* #6, 21 (quote), 23 (death). Joker is revived by Batman on page 24.

14. Chuck Dixon, Trevor McCarthy, and Karl Kesel, "Red, Fright and Blue," *Nightwing* #63 (New York: DC Comics, January 2002), 15.

15. Judd Winick, Doug Mahnke, and Tom Nguyen, "Under the Hood Part 3: Overnight Deliveries," *Batman* #637 (April 2005).

16. Judd Winick, Carlo Barberi, and Art Thibert, "Pay as You Go Part One: The Skeleton Crew," *Outsiders* (3) #44 (New York: DC Comics, March 2007), [16].

17. Bruce Jones, Joe Dodd, and Bit, "Pleased to Meet You—Hope You Guess My Name!" *Nightwing* #119 (June 2006), [8]. The death Dick references is from *Batman* #650 (April 2006) when Jason, Batman, and Joker are nearly killed in a building explosion.

18. Bruce Jones, Paco Diaz, and Bit, "Yours, Mine, and Ours," *Nightwing* #120 (July 2006), [9]. Dick also lets Jason go in *Batman and Robin* (1) #25 (September 2011). Although Jason has placed bombs around Gotham, Dick concedes the chase quickly.

19. Bruce Jones, Paco Diaz, and Bit, "Sorry I Brought That Up," *Nightwing* #121 (August 2006), [13].

20. Bruce Jones, Paco Diaz, and Bit, "Odd Couples," *Nightwing* #122 (September 2006), [23].

21. Tony S. Daniel and Sandu Florea, "Last Man Standing," *Batman: Battle for the Cowl* #3 (New York: DC Comics, July 2009), [14], [28].

22. Grant Morrison, Philip Tan, and Jonathan Glapion, "Revenge of the Red Hood Part Three: Flamingo is Here," *Batman and Robin* (1) #6 (New York: DC Comics, January 2010), [17].

23. Jones, Diaz, and Bit, *Nightwing* #120 (July 2006), [8].

24. Winick, Barberi, and Thibert, *Outsiders* (3) #44 (March 2007), [21].

25. See Morrison, Tan, and Glampion, *Batman and Robin* (1) #6 (January 2010).

26. Winick, Barberi, and Thibert, *Outsiders* (3) #44 (March 2007), [19].

27. Marv Wolfman et al., *Batman: A Lonely Place of Dying* (New York: DC Comics, 1990), *Introduction* by Dennis O'Neil, [1]–[3].

28. For example, Adam Beechen and Freddie E. Williams II, "The High Dive," *Robin* #156 (New York: DC Comics, January 2007).

29. Marv Wolfman, Tom Grummett, and Al Vey, "Dejavu," *The New Titans* #65 (New York: DC Comics, April 1990), 1.

30. Doug Moench and Bob McLeod, "Robin and Nightwing: Partners," *Showcase '93* #12 (New York: DC Comics, December 1993), 8.
31. Doug Moench, Mike Gustovich, and Romeo Tanghal, "Prodigal, Part 1: Robin and Batman," *Batman* #512 (November 1994), [1].
32. For example: Alan Grant and Brett Blevins, "Prodigal Part Two," *Batman: Shadow of the Bat* #32 (New York: DC Comics, November 1994), 4.
33. Alan Grant, Vince Giarrano, and Ray McCarthy, "Contagion, Part 7: Angel of Death," *Batman: Shadow of the Bat* #49 (April 1996), 15 and Chuck Dixon, Graham Nolan, and Scott Hanna, "Contagion, Part 8: Babylon Falls," *Detective Comics* #696 (April 1996), [1].
34. Chuck Dixon, Mike Wieringo, and Stan Woch, "Contagion, Part 11: Bitter Dregs," *Robin* #28 (April 1996), 3.
35. Alan Grant, Dave Taylor, and Stan Woch, "Hobson's Choice," *Batman: Shadow of the Bat* #53 (August 1996), 8.
36. Chuck Dixon, Scott McDaniel, and Karl Story, "The Visitor," *Nightwing* #6 (March 1997), 19.
37. Dixon, McDaniel, and Story, *Nightwing* #6, 11–13.
38. Dixon, McDaniel, and Story, "The Boys," *Nightwing* #25 (October 1998).
39. Fabian Nicieza, Joe Bennett, and Jack Jadson, "Scattered Pieces," *Robin* #175 (August 2008), [18].
40. Chuck Dixon, Staz Johnson, and Wayne Faucher, "The Lizard King," *Robin* #71 (December 1999), 10–11.
41. One example of this is in: Dixon, Johnson, and Faucher, *Robin* #71 (December 1999), 10.
42. Chuck Dixon, Pete Woods, and Jesse Delperdang, "The Worst is Yet to Come," *Robin* #74 (March 2000), 6.
43. Tim looks out for Dick as well, of course. One particular instance where Tim's resourcefulness and resilience comes to the fore in a way that belies his young age and experience: when Bruce is thought to have died during an explosion at Wayne Enterprises, Dick is so overcome with grief and shock that he becomes entirely numb. Tim takes him home to the Batcave and summons Alfred's help. See Devin Grayson, Roger Robinson, and John Floyd, "Transference, Parts 2 and 3," in *Batman: Gotham Knights* #9–10 (November–December, 2010).
44. Bill Willingham, Kinsun Loh, and Aaron Sowd, "Last stand at Alamo High," *Batman* #631 (October 2004), [11].
45. Devin Grayson, Zach Howard, and Andy Owens, "Back to the Life," *Nightwing* #99 (January 2005).
46. It is actually Stephanie Brown, the Spoiler, who is later revealed to have not died.
47. Devin Grayson, Phil Hester, and Ande Parks, "Incorporation," *Nightwing* #110 (September 2005), [12].
48. Fabian Nicieza, Don Kramer, and Wayne Faucher, "The Resurrection of Ra's al Ghul, Part 2: The Lesser of Two Evils," *Nightwing* #138 (January 2008), [8].
49. Nicieza, Kramer, and Faucher, *Nightwing* #138, [23].
50. Nicieza, Kramer, and Faucher, "The Resurrection of Ra's al Ghul, Part 6: Living Proof," *Nightwing* #139 (February 2008).
51. Nicieza, Kramer, and Faucher, *Nightwing* #139, [15].
52. Nicieza, Kramer, and Faucher, *Nightwing* #139, [16].
53. Chris Yost and Ramon Bachs, "The Grail, Part 1," *Red Robin* #1 (New York: DC Comics, August 2009), [10].
54. As the scenes are written, they stand out as one of Dick's worst moments because

so much of the context is up to the reader to interpret. It is frustrating for readers that so much is left unsaid, especially in the main *Batman* titles.

55. Yost and Bachs, "The Grail, Part 4," *Red Robin* #4 (November 2009), [13].

56. Yost and Bachs, *Red Robin* #4, [20].

57. Chris Yost, Marcus To, and Ray McCarthy, "Collision, Part 3," *Red Robin* #11 (June 2010), [17].

58. Nicieza, To, and McCarthy, "The Hit List, Part 1: The Domino Effect," *Red Robin* #13 (August 2010), [2]–[4].

59. Yost, To, and McCarthy, "Collision, Part 4," *Red Robin* #12 (July 2010), [17].

60. See *Red Robin* #12.

Dick and Damian
The Second Batman and His Robin

Kalina Keester

In 2009, a new Batman and Robin took the stage. Dick Grayson, the first Robin, donned his adoptive father's cowl and became Batman. He then gave the mantle of Robin to Bruce Wayne's son, Damian Wayne. Damian was a very angry and arrogant boy strongly influenced by his assassin upbringing when he first became Robin.

The two become the new Dynamic Duo of Batman and Robin and move from a relationship based on obligation (Dick) and necessity (Damian, if he wants to eventually inherit the cowl) to one based on mutual respect and affection. Dick helps Damian grow into a hero worthy of the Bat Family, while Damian helps Dick mature as he develops his parental side. Dick makes Damian a Bat, but Damian makes Dick a Batman.

The Beginnings of Batman and Robin (2.0)

Damian meets his father's family some time before he comes to live in Gotham.[1] While Damian possesses some esteem for his father, the rest of his father's family is shown a complete lack of respect.[2] He's spoiled, entitled, and has no sense of moral right and wrong.[3] Damian is portrayed as an unruly villain-in-the-making. His own mother, Talia al Ghul who is the daughter of super villain Ra's al Ghul, says that he lacks discipline.[4] Despite all of this, it is incredibly clear that Damian craves approval from both of his parents. After a short stay in Gotham with his father, Damian returns to his mother's care.

Dick doesn't meet Damian until later when Damian runs to Wayne Manor in an attempt to get away from Ra's al Ghul, who wants to use

Damian's body to resurrect himself.⁵ When Dick finds Tim Drake, the current Robin, and Damian in the Batcave fighting ninjas, he sees that Damian is wearing a makeshift Robin costume. He thinks to himself, "Notice Damian's costume. Note to self: smack a clue into this kid."⁶ Damian refuses to work with Tim and Dick, flat out ignoring what Dick tells him to do during the fight. Dick isn't happy with him about that, and Damian's actions ultimately mean his own and Tim's capture by Ra's al Ghul's ninjas.

In the end, they all survive this event and Talia takes Damian with her. Prior to the start of *Batman R.I.P,* Damian senses that someone is out to get his father and returns to Gotham with his mother. He is later left in the care of Alfred Pennyworth to be trained by Dick. At this time, Batman, Bruce Wayne, is believed to have been killed by Darkseid during the events of *Final Crisis*.⁷

A Duo Built of Obligation and Convenience

When Damian is left with Dick, he hasn't changed much. He's still spoiled, entitled, and not really a hero. He recognizes that Dick does have at least some authority over him. Dick, for his part, doesn't like Damian very much (because Damian's a brat) but he feels responsible for Damian's wellbeing and safety. Despite their mutual antipathy, when their lives are put in danger, even before they are Batman and Robin, they are shown caring about each other's safety. During the *Battle for the Cowl* mini-series, Gotham is in chaos and several villains find Damian when he has snuck out alone and attack him. Dick locates Damian and rescues him, but then they are attacked by Jason Todd. Dick and Damian both show *some* concern for each other during this attack.⁸

Later on, when their relationship improves, they have become very protective of each other. At one point, Dick jumps to protect Damian, along with a civilian, from an explosion while investigating Una Nemo.⁹ In addition, both of them are very loyal to the other. This is easily seen when Una Nemo places the two of them in a seemingly deadly trap. If one of them pushed back, that one would survive while the other would die. Neither one pushed back.¹⁰

Part of Dick's concern for his new charge comes out in the role he allows Damian to take. After becoming Batman, Dick makes Damian his Robin. Dick justifies his decision to the former Robin, Tim Drake, by saying, "But him…. Tim, you know better than anyone that left on his own, he's going to kill someone. *Again*. You have to understand—."¹¹

This seems to be a recurring thought to him as Dick later says to Alfred, "It's that know-it-all super-villain sneer, that snide, aristocratic.... Gahh. Who's going to save him if we don't?"[12] This implies a concern not just for Damian's physical safety but also his emotional and moral wellbeing. It also shows that Dick doesn't seem to care much for Damian's personality at this time.

Their relationship definitely starts out as one of obligation and duty on Dick's part. He's incredibly loyal to Bruce and it makes sense that with Bruce gone, Dick would want to do whatever he could for Bruce's legacy and, in this case, Bruce's son. Dick is also a hero; he can't help himself when it comes to saving people. In Dick's eyes, Damian needs to be saved, both from himself and from his mother's side of the family.[13]

For Damian, his alliance with Dick is one of necessity and he offers the older man little to no respect. Damian has made it abundantly clear that he intends to inherit the cowl and carry on his father's legacy; he is working with Dick only as a means to further that goal. If Dick is Batman, Damian will be his Robin so that he can be on hand to claim the mantle of the Bat should (or in Damian's opinion, *when*) Dick fails to adequately uphold his father's legacy.[14] Damian certainly doesn't think he has anything to learn from Dick and has no qualms about letting him know just that. Early on in their partnership, Damian tells Dick, "I was bred for the job, and trained in the arts of war by the masters of my Mother's League of Assassins. I could just as easily continue my father's work on my own."[15]

As they first begin to fight together as Batman and Robin, Damian doesn't have much true respect for Dick as Batman and as a mentor. Damian says, "...You can have my respect if you earn it, that's **all** I'm saying. You're *not* my father."[16] He isn't willing to give Dick his respect, even though Dick has by all rights proven to be worth his respect. Dick has been a superhero for longer than Damian has been alive. Dick has lead multiple superhero teams and earned the respect of some of the greatest heroes in the DC universe. Dick has rescued Damian from a few dangerous situations before this. The fact that Damian doesn't give Dick his respect is very telling of Damian's character and attitude towards their current situation.

After a fight with a group of villains goes poorly, Damian even says to Dick in a fit of anger, "*Look* at you! This pathetic *impersonation* of my father makes a *mockery* of his memory! Keep your *clues* and your 'detective skills' and your *limits*."[17]

This is their first big argument. Damian is completely self-assured in his own skills and abilities and fails to consider that Dick could have anything of value to offer him.

In the same way that Damian is struggling with his new situation, Dick is struggling to find his footing as Batman and as Damian's mentor. "As long as I was *Nightwing* I could pretend I'd never *have* to take over as *Batman*. I could act as if he'd *always* be around. And as for *Damian* ... what am I letting myself *in* for, Alfred?"[18] Dick's worries reflect that he still does not yet understand Damian or know him well. Dick simply knows that he must be there for Damian, just as Bruce was there for him all those years ago when Dick was alone after his parents' deaths.

They fight and disagree with each other often during these early days. It reaches the point that Damian runs away from Dick and Alfred, even ripping the Robin symbol off of his chest, and seeks out Professor Pyg, who is a dangerous villain that Batman and Robin were investigating. Damian's life is endangered from Professor Pyg, but Dick comes for him and saves him just in time. Damian asks Dick why he came to Pyg's hide out and Dick replies with, "Partners, remember? Batman and Robin."[19]

Damian is genuinely surprised that Dick would come to save him after they fought and he ran away, which reveals a lot about Damian's early childhood. It seems likely that Dick is one of the first people in Damian's life to stand by him even after Damian pushed him away. Maybe no one had shown Damian through their actions that they cared about him before. Whatever the reason, Damian is surprised by Dick's actions. This is definitely a turning point in Damian's mind about their relationship. After this, their interactions take on a more familial quality and Dick seems to view his relationship with Damian as more than just an obligation.

Keeping the Peace

Dick often acts as something of a peacekeeper between Damian and the rest of the Bat-family. For example, when Damian found that he was included in Tim Drake's list of individuals that Tim felt could be a threat one day, he was very upset. Damian attacked Tim and Tim decided to fight back as harshly as he could. Dick finds them fighting, breaks it up, and brings them back to the cave to sort it all out. Dick understands where both of them are coming from so he does his best to get them to reach a truce.[20] Dick recognizes that Damian has changed from the murderous kid who Tim first met. Damian has earned Dick's trust. However, Dick also understands why Tim felt the need to create that list and to place Damian on it. This incident showcases Dick's place in the family as someone who helps keep everyone together. Later on, Dick also tries to break up an argument between Tim and Damian while the family is attempting to have a portrait painted.[21]

Similarly, when faced with insecurity over his place as Robin, Damian challenges all of the former Robins to one-on-one battles.[22] Damian announces his plan to the group of former Robins; Jason Todd, Tim, and Dick. While the other two are merely incredulous, Dick is visibly hurt at the threat of attack from Damian. After Damian has fought both Jason Todd and Tim Drake, having taken trophies from them after each battle, Dick gives him one of his escrima sticks as a trophy in order to prevent Damian from challenging him. "No need for us to tangle. Here, hang this on your wall. You don't need to try so hard, Damian. If you haven't noticed, kid, you're already wearing the 'R' on your chest."[23] Dick is concerned for how Damian is acting, so he tries to reassure Damian that none of the former Robins are trying to replace him and take the "R" on his chest away. It's a touching level of brotherly support for Damian when he experiences, as we all do, self-doubts.

A Duo Becoming Brothers

After the initial bumps and bruises, Dick and Damian get well settled into their relationship and partnership. They are often teasing and picking on one another, much like brothers.[24] Such as this exchange in which Damian says, "…So, we're agreed. It's **Robin and Batman** from now on." Dick replies with, "That'll catch on."[25]

They show through their actions that they have come to truly care for each other.[26] They still have issues with each other, such as Damian not listening well on occasion and Dick being short with Damian sometimes,[27] but it isn't anything that they aren't able to overcome.

Dick and Damian know each other well by this point and have become familiar with each other's quirks and habits. Dick shares little tidbits of information with Damian, like why Gotham isn't infested with pigeons. (Because there are EPA protected falcons around Gotham that like to hunt pigeons). Damian isn't terribly interested by that and snipes at Dick over it, which eventually leads to this exchange:

> Dick says, "You know your sense of humor kinda sucks, right?"
> "I was leaning more towards esoteric." Damian replies.
> "Well I was leaning more towards stupid." Dick answers.[28]

Dick is capable of giving Damian back what he gets. They both will often pick on each other throughout their series. Despite this, Dick makes it clear that he respects Damian and the sacrifices that Damian has made to be Robin. When Damian is affected by comments made about what the White Knight, a villain who is killing the family members of criminals in order to cut off their bloodline, believes about nature vs nurture, Dick reassures him. He tells Damian, "You turned away from *evil*—You didn't embrace the *Al Ghul* playbook even though it was easier—even though it was in your blood. You made a choice to *help*, Damian, to make a difference, which is *always harder*."[29]

Damian has come to highly value his position as Robin. When his mother attempted to convince Damian to leave Gotham and Dick, he tells her, "Being Robin is the best thing I've ever done, Mother. And even if my father does return, this is the life I've chosen to lead. I don't need you to save me."[30] It's worth noting that at this time, Damian believed that his father might not accept him as Robin and that he would force Damian to stop being Robin. Despite that worry, Damian still chooses the possibility of being a hero over his mother's wishes.

The respect Dick has for Damian isn't one-sided either. Damian tells the story of Batman and Robin to three children and when he reaches the part with him as Robin and Dick as Batman, he has this to say, "And the new Robin, who had been too focused—unrelenting, so ... unforgiving ... slowly found himself ... learning ... from his new mentor—his new ... friend. And being his friend was ... an honor. Robin would never tell him that, but it was how he felt."[31]

This shows a significant change in Damian's feelings about Dick. A lot of the progress Damian has made can be attributed to Dick's influence in his life. Similarly, Dick isn't unaffected by his relationship with Damian. It's difficult to figure out which changes are a result of being Batman and which are a result of being responsible for Damian. However, after their time together, Dick has grown to be a more serious and a bit darker person. He was never a completely carefree and light character, but after this period, there are many darker tones to him. Dick also has developed more of an appreciation for Bruce due to his relationship with Damian, as most adults do once they have children. He is more mature, having to become so because he was responsible for Damian.

The New 52

Their relationship changes again when Bruce returns. Bruce Wayne was not dead, as was believed for a time by his allies, but sent through time.

His close allies, such as Tim Drake, Dick Grayson, Alfred Pennyworth, and Damian Wayne had figured this out a short time before his return but were unable to help him. Bruce returns to his family during a fight between the 99 fiends and in the midst of a plot by the Joker.[32] They defeat all the villains together and then comes the hard part—figuring out how everyone fits in the family now. Damian is very concerned over what will happen to Batman and Robin now that Bruce is back. Bruce does try, in his own way, to bond with Damian but it doesn't go well at this time. Bruce is too reserved and still distrusts Damian, while Damian is incredibly wary of his father. So it doesn't seem too surprising that Bruce ultimately decides to leave Gotham in Dick and Damian's hands while he travels the world building Batman Incorporated.[33]

Eventually, Dick does turn over Gotham City and the Bat mantle to Bruce. He steps aside and lets Bruce resume his place in Gotham and gives Bruce a chance to build a real relationship with Damian. He leaves Gotham and things naturally shift between him and Damian. They seem to drift apart during this time, perhaps due to Damian's difficult adjustment to living and working with his father[34] and Dick's attempts to distance himself from the family. Once Bruce and Damian begin to get along better, Dick and Damian are able to start redefining their relationship.

After the Joker attacks Dick's first home, Haly's Circus, Dick goes through a really difficult time. He struggles to cope with the destruction wreaked on the circus and the surviving circus members, his first family, deciding that they don't want to see him anymore.[35] Damian watches Dick during this time and eventually confronts him when it becomes clear that Grayson is not handling this tragedy well. In a reverse of what their original roles were, it's Damian who stops Dick when he becomes overly violent while dealing with some criminals. Damian and Dick jump across the roof tops together and talk. After Dick voices what's been troubling him since the circus was burnt down and people left him, Damian says, "You got burnt by people you leaned on. Guess what? It's going to happen again, that doesn't mean that you should stop. You trust people. It's what makes you who you are."[36]

Those aren't things that one would expect to hear from either Talia al Ghul, Damian's mother, or Bruce Wayne. Neither of them trust people easily or typically suggest that trusting might be a good thing. Dick, however, does usually believe that trusting people is a good thing. It stands to reason that Damian is simply reminding Dick of something that Damian learned from him.

After their talk, Damian suggests that they should hang out together more, which implies that they haven't seen each other much lately. Dick has been out of town with Haly's Circus for some time, while Damian has been stuck in Gotham with Bruce. Damian is probably experiencing something similar to what younger siblings feel when their older siblings go off to college. Like any good older brother who's been away, Dick agrees, in a roundabout way, to hang out more.[37]

Not long after this, a crime organization run by Talia al Ghul called Leviathan launches an attack against Batman. Despite being grounded and ordered to stay in the Batcave, Damian sneaks out and joins the battle in hopes of trying to reason with his mother. Dick sees Damian heading towards Talia al Ghul's location and follows him there in order to provide him with back up. In typical fashion, Dick gets there just in time to save Damian from an attack. They banter back and forth with each other as they prepare to fight back.[38]

Right before they jump into the fight, Damian tells Dick, "We were the best, Richard. No matter what anyone says." Dick replies with, "Hey, we can't help being awesome."[39]

During the fight against Leviathan, Damian and Dick come across The Fatherless. Once Dick realizes how hard it will be to defeat this enemy, he tries to draw The Fatherless away from Damian and to handle the fight himself. Unfortunately, The Fatherless brutally attacks Dick, grabbing him by the neck and tossing him around. Damian, seeing the danger that Dick is in, attacks The Fatherless himself. Once the enemy is distracted from Dick, who is now unconscious, Damian does his best to keep the Fatherless's attention. He fights the enemy very heroically, while also trying to get his mother to call off the attack.

Unfortunately, Damian was overpowered by the Fatherless. He died trying to stop his mother's plan of destroying Gotham and Batman. He died a hero.[40]

When Dick regained consciousness; he was shocked by what had happened. Once he saw Damian's body, he cried, "No, no, no. This isn't happening. He was okay, just a minute ago. What just happened?"[41]

Dick takes Damian's death very hard initially. He doesn't bother with shaving, even when he's out as Nightwing. The remains of multiple take-out containers and soda cans litter his apartment. When Batman comes to speak to him, Dick is very hostile and rude to him. He admits to distancing himself from others. As he fights with some criminals, he becomes very brutal and almost cruel. He begins to think that darkness might be easier than continuing to be hurt by people.[42]

After choosing to save some lowlifes from a fire rather than his father's circus costume, he remembers what Damian said to him a few weeks ago about trusting and relying on people being a part of who he is. Dick visits Damian's grave after that and confronts his very mixed feelings about Damian's death. He's angry that Damian ran into danger like he did. He's upset with himself that he couldn't save Damian. He's grieving over losing his little brother. As he leaves a video game that they were supposed to play together at the grave, he says to Damian, "You were my brother. In every sense of the word. I loved you."[43]

Dick later tells a friend that it's going to take time to heal from Damian's death but he looks much better and it seems clear that he's reached some level of acceptance over Damian's death. When he visits Bruce not too long later, in an attempt by Alfred to help Bruce stop reliving Damian's death, Dick does what he can to help Bruce accept that he couldn't have saved Damian. He consoles Bruce by telling him that Damian did leave something tangible behind, his family.[44]

Final Thoughts

Dick and Damian took the traditional roles of Batman and Robin and flipped them on their head. Batman, rather than being grim and utterly serious, became happy and known to make the occasional joke. Robin, instead of being the jokester and almost the comic relief, became very focused and dark. That reversal of roles is part of what makes this dynamic duo so intriguing for some comic fans. Certainly, another part of the appeal is the story of redemption that plays out over all of the comics that Damian had a lead role in. Here is a boy who seems set on the dark path of life. Here is a boy who has been raised to murder and attack with no regard. It looks as if this will simply be another tragic tale of fate. Then, Damian's story changes. He comes to Gotham and he makes an honest effort to be *good*. He has no idea how to be good and is rather bad at heroics. Dick sees the dark path that Damian seems almost destined for and Dick decides to try to save this boy. He wants to give this boy a real chance to be a good hero. Under the tutelage of Dick, Damian does come to understand what it means to be a real hero and a good person. Damian comes to value the friendship of a man that he would otherwise likely have dismissed as beneath him. Damian turns away from the path of violence and domination that his mother had chosen for him and chose a path for himself. When looked at from a wide view, *Batman & Robin (2009–2011)* is about Damian's redemption.

Dick's story doesn't draw attention the way that Damian's does. Damian changed so much over the course of their relationship that it is easy to overlook the subtler ways that Dick changed. Dick matured and became more responsible over their time together. When Damian died, Dick was deeply impacted by that. He had mentored Damian, had been Damian's guardian for quite some time, and remained close to Damian even when he left Gotham. Dick was probably one of the people most affected by Damian's death.

Dick and Damian will never be as well-known as Dick and Bruce were as Batman and Robin, but that doesn't lessen their significance as the dynamic duo. Their differences are what makes them stand out from all the other combinations of Batman and Robin that have followed the first duo. Their relationship redefined the traditional roles of their names and continued on after Dick put down the Batman suit and Damian became Bruce's Robin. Had Damian lived, and after he returns, their relationship would likely continue to be perpetually one of mutual respect and admiration, similar to that of Bruce Wayne and Dick Grayson. This is comics after all; Dick and Damian may one day be able to fight crime together again.

Notes

1. Judd Winick, Ed Benes, and Rob Hunter, "A Battle Within," *Batman* #687 (New York: DC Comics, August 2009), [6].
2. Grant Morrison, Andy Kubert, and Jesse Delperdang, "Batman & Son, Part 3: Wonderboys," *Batman* #657 (November 2006), [7].
3. Morrison, Kubert, and Delperdang, *Batman* #657, [10].
4. Morrison, Kubert, and Delperdang, "Batman & Son, Part 2: Man-Bats of London," Batman #656 (October 2006), [21].
5. Fabian Nicieza, Don Kramer, and Wayne Faucher, "The Resurrection of Ra's Al Ghul, Part 2," *Nightwing* #138 (New York: DC Comics, January 2008), [6].
6. Nicieza, Kramer, and Faucher, *Nightwing* #138, [16].
7. Grant Morrison, et al., "How to Murder the Earth," *Final Crisis* #6 (January 2009).
8. Tony Daniel and Sandu Florea, "Hostile Takeover," *Batman: Battle for the Cowl* #1 (May 2009), [29].
9. Paul Cornell, Scott McDaniel, and Rob Hunter, "The Sum of Her Parts," *Batman and Robin* (1) #17 (New York: DC Comics, January 2011).
10. Cornell, McDaniel, and Hunter, "The Sum of Her Parts" *Batman and Robin* (1) #19 (March 2011).
11. Chris Yost and Ramon Bachs, "The Grail, Part 1," *Red Robin* #1 (New York: DC Comics, August 2009), [10].
12. Grant Morrison and Frank Quitely, "Batman Reborn, Part Two: The Circus of Strange," *Batman and Robin* (1) #2 (September 2009), [18].
13. Daniel and Florea, "Army of One," *Batman: Battle for the Cowl* #2 (June 2009), [17].
14. Winick, Benes, and Hunter, *Batman* #687, [12]; Morrison and Quitely, "Batman Reborn, Part One: Domino Effect," *Batman and Robin* (1) #1 (August 2009), [14].

15. Morrison and Quitely, "Batman Reborn," *Batman and Robin* (1) #1, [19].
16. Morrison and Quitely, "Batman Reborn," *Batman and Robin* (1) #1, [21].
17. Morrison and Quitely, "Batman Reborn," *Batman and Robin* (1) #2, [17].
18. Morrison and Quitely, "Batman Reborn," *Batman and Robin* (1) #1, [12].
19. Morrison and Quitely, "Batman Reborn, Part 3: Mommy Made of Nails," *Batman and Robin* (1) #3 (October 2009), [16].
20. Fabian Nicieza, Marcus To, and Ray McCarthy, "The Hit List," *Red Robin* #14 (New York, DC Comics, August 2010), [20].
21. Peter J. Tomasi, Patrick Gleason, and Mick Gray, "Terminus, Scar of the Bat," *Batman and Robin* (2) #10 (New York: DC Comics, August 2012), [5].
22. Tomasi, Gleason, and Gray, *Batman and Robin* (2) #10, [11].
23. Tomasi, Gleason, and Gray, "Terminus Last Gasp," *Batman and Robin* (2) #12 (October 2012), [17].
24. Grant, Morrison, Philip Tan, and Jonathan Glapion, "Revenge of the Red Hood Part Three: Flamingo is Here," *Batman and Robin* (1) #6 (January 2010), [3]; Tomasi, Gleason, and Gray, *Batman and Robin* (2) #10 [12]; Fabian Nicieza and Cliff Richard, "The Great Escape," *Batman* #703 (November 2010), [21].
25. Morrison and Quitely, "Batman Reborn," *Batman and Robin* (1) #3, [26].
26. Morrison and Frazer Irving, "Batman and Robin Must Die, Part 3," *Batman and Robin* (1) #15 (December 2010), [17]; Nicieza and Richard, *Batman* #703, [21].
27. Morrison and Irving, "Batman and Robin Must Die, Part 1: The Garden of Death," *Batman and Robin* (1) #13 (August 2010), [10], [19]; Morrison and Irving, "Must Die," *Batman and Robin* (1) #15, [17].
28. Peter J. Tomasi, Patrick Gleason, and Mick Gray, "Dark Knight vs White Knight, Part 1 of 3: Tree of Blood," *Batman and Robin* (1) #20 (April 2011).
29. Peter J. Tomasi, Patrick Gleason, and Mick Gray, "Dark Knight vs White Knight: Tree of Blood, Conclusion," *Batman and Robin* (1) #22 (June 2011).
30. Grant Morrison and Andy Clarke, "Batman vs Robin, Part 3: Mexican Train," *Batman and Robin* (1) #12 (July 2010), [15].
31. Fabian Nicieza et al., "In Storybook Endings" *Batman* #713 (August 2011), [15].
32. Grant Morrison, Cameron Stewart, and Frazer Irving, "Black Mass," *Batman & Robin* (1) #16 (Early January 2011), [10].
33. Grant Morrison et al., "Planet Gotham," *Batman: The Return* (January 2011).
34. Tomasi, Gleason, and Gray, "Born to Kill," *Batman and Robin* (2) #1 (November 2011), [12].
35. Kyle Higgins, Juan Jose Ryp, and Roger Bonet, "The Long Week," *Nightwing* #17 (New York, DC Comics April 2013), [7].
36. Higgins, Ryp, and Bonet, "Long Week," *Nightwing* #17, [18].
37. Higgins, Ryp, and Bonet, *Nightwing* #17, [19].
38. Grant Morrison, Chris Burnham, and Jason Masters, "The Boy Wonder Returns," *Batman Incorporated* (2) #8 (April 2013), [12].
39. Morrison, Burnham, and Masters, *Batman Incorporated* (2) #8, [12].
40. Morrison, Burnham, and Masters, *Batman Incorporated* (2) #8, [20].
41. Morrison, Burnham, and Masters, "Fallen Son," *Batman Incorporated* (2) #9 (May 2013), [5].
42. Higgins et al., "Slow Burn," *Nightwing* #18 (May 2013), [15].
43. Higgins et al., *Nightwing* #18, [18].
44. Peter J. Tomasi et al., "Acceptance," *Batman and Robin* (2) #23 (October 2013), [15].

Titans Together

Shelly Sposato *and* Pamela Shah

Dick Grayson is a character known for his relationships with other heroes. This piece examines some of Dick's most important connections outside the Bat Family.

Dick and Donna: Platonic Soul Mates

By Shelly Sposato

Created in 1965, Donna Troy is Dick's oldest intimate female friend who remains strictly platonic well into their adult life. The two met at the age of thirteen and became two founders of the Teen Titans, making her one of Dick's first longtime friends. They grew as close as siblings, supporting each other through hardships and difficulties, while Donna also takes on a maternal role in Dick's life, offering him sympathy and guidance. So important is Donna in Dick's life that Dick started down a dark path when Donna died.

Dick and Donna grew up together, resulting in Donna blending into a sisterly and motherly role in Dick's life. When they were young, they stayed up late on the phone to offer each other love advice and help each other through break-ups.[1] "I'd known Donna for almost eight years, since before we formed that first group of Teen Titans. I'd risk my life if it meant helping her."[2] Being raised by Bruce and Alfred, Dick didn't have many female figures in his life, and over time, Donna fulfilled that maternal and sisterly void for him. "I could have fallen easily in love with her then. Now, years later, I knew I did love her, more than I ever could if I were only her lover."[3] They act as anchors to one another, with Donna being one of the few people Dick will open up around, admitting when he has insecurities or doubts and going to her for advice. After acting tough toward a group of children, Dick tells

Donna, "I hated being the 'bad cop.' Was I too harsh? Were they scared?" Donna answers, "A little, maybe. But you've got nothing to worry about. You did what needed to be done."[4] She reassures Dick, which is the reaction he seeks out when he's worried about acting like Bruce. Barring his intimate relationships, Donna is one of the few people Dick is comfortable being himself and dropping his walls around. He admits his thoughts around her while he might keep that barrier up around his other friends. Donna is easy-going and natural, connecting to Dick in a familial capacity that lures him out. She plays the strongest maternal role in his life, asking about his love life and making comments like, "Had any heart-to-hearts with your mentor lately?" and "What about sleep? Are you getting enough sleep?"[5]

Both Dick and Donna will do anything for each other and openly express their mutual love and affection. When Donna married, Dick gave her away at her request. "I'm so glad that you're giving me away, Dick. I wouldn't dream of anyone else." Love is a recurring theme between them, unparalleled among their friends in the way they consistently reaffirm it to each other. "Donna, we've gone through so much together, and in not all that many years. Yet, I feel as if I've known and loved you all my life."[6] Terry Long, Donna's husband, comments on this, saying, "Hmmm. Kory, shouldn't we be jealous over these two?"[7] Dick and Donna are so close that Donna can tell Dick's longtime girlfriend, "I know Dick maybe *better* than you."[8] Dick and Kory have been intimately involved for over four years, but Donna has a window into Dick's soul that not many people can see. They're comfortable holding each other in their arms during a camping trip with their friends while dating other people.[9] They're prone to intimate gestures, such as Dick kissing Donna's forehead,[10] while remaining platonic in every sense of the word. On Donna's wedding day, she and Dick reflect over how well they know each other, contrasted pages later when Dick and Bruce address a subject they have trouble being expressive over: Dick's place in Bruce's life. "Bruce, understand I don't begrudge your wanting to adopt Jay, but something keeps nagging at me…. Why didn't you ever try to adopt me?"[11] Where Bruce falls short, Donna compensates, addressing the familial stability and support Dick's seeking out. She provides warmth and emotional affirmation to counteract the stagnant atmosphere of Wayne Manor. In return, Dick does the same for her.

Dick and Donna offer each other emotional stability. While Donna was trying to uncover her past to discover who she was, Dick accompanied her every step of the way.[12] He refused to give up even when she did and acted as an anchor throughout the emotional whiplash Donna went through. Later, when Dick was upset and falling apart over a falling out with Kory, Donna was a similar anchor. She came to his apartment and forced Dick to talk about it, knowing that he'd cage up his emotions otherwise. "Whether you like it or not we're going to sit here and talk.... No matter how long it takes."[13] Dick shut his friends out from his life once again when Bruce died. "This, *this* is why Batman keeps ... kept everyone at a distance. Better to be removed than to get hurt over and over and over again!"[14] Donna forcefully puts an end to this line of thinking, telling Dick that they will always be there for each other, him included. Dick reflects to Donna, "Hey, this is me you're talking to. The guy you've looked out for and worried about and comforted for years and years now."[15] Dick has the same intuition to Donna's needs. When a group of friends were hanging out in Dick's apartment, Dick noticed Donna slipping away and immediately followed her into the kitchen, asking her what was wrong.[16] They have a fluid back-and-forth trust to their relationship, supporting the other when they're struggling.

After a clone of Superman shot a laser through Donna's chest, Dick cradles her lifeless body in his arms.[17] Donna's death had an abrupt and lasting impact on Dick, arguably the biggest hit to him since his parents died. As a result, he quit the Titans directly after Donna's funeral. Dick has lost a number of teammates and allies over time in the line of fire (Raven, Joey Wilson, and Jason Todd to name a few), but Donna's death tipped him over the edge. "What do you want to do? Just strap on our guns and wait for the *next* thing?! Wait for the next madman, or alien, or psychopath to come along so I can shove people I love into harm's way?! How many should we kill before it seems like a bad idea?! It was *Donna*, Roy. *Donna.*"[18] Dick isolates himself from human contact to grieve, ignoring Roy's phone calls to sit on his sofa with a picture of Donna.[19] Dick rejects every offer of comfort, but at Roy's insistence, joins the Outsiders.[20] The following months are riddled with tension. Dick accuses Roy of not caring about Donna and distances himself from his new teammates, treating them as chess pieces rather than people. Dick is under the impression that detachment is the key to avoid being hurt again. "I don't need a team. I can do this alone."[21] This mentality backfires on him, breeding more problems than solutions in his interactions with others. Dick has come close to turning down a dark path multiple times during his life, but a combination of his resolve, positive outlook, and his friends have prevented this from becoming a reality. The loss of Donna struck so deeply, Dick's defensive reaction was to close himself off and become a copy of Bruce.[22] Raven's empathic powers detect the change. "Richard seems distant, Roy. I sense no love for us. Only something else ... longing, perhaps?"[23]

Months later, the Titans realize Donna can return to life, and Dick flashes a rare smile. "Roy, do you know what this means—?" Roy responds, "Yeah. Once we find her, you're gonna have to rethink your whole 'distant leader—I quit' shtick, boss."[24]

Dick does. With Donna's return, he heals, and his personality shifts back to normal. Donna's impact on Dick is profound, existing on a level few can compete with. Their friendship has thrived since they were kids and flourished into adulthood. Donna's place in Dick's life is invaluable, giving him stable familial comfort with none of the complications that come with romance. They love each other without restriction and affirm it to each other unabashedly. Donna is a friend Dick is comfortable around, where he can be himself and seek out sympathy and guidance without being judged.

Tough Love: Dick Grayson and Roy Harper

By Pamela Shah

Unlike Donna Troy or Wally West, Dick had not established a deep and personal relationship with Roy Harper until his twenties. After Roy had gotten back on his feet from his drug addiction, he re-established a connection with his friends, family, and reality due to the sobering experience of fatherhood. Dick and Roy have been known to engage in physical fights often with one another, but it should not be mistaken for hatred— quite the contrary. Dick is someone whom Roy confides in while Dick looks to Roy for a voice of reason. In hoping that Dick will inform Roy of his mistakes, Roy does the same for Dick, not because he wishes to alienate him, but because he cares about him and wants him to do the right thing. Through Dick's guidance, Roy grows into someone capable of organizing and co-leading a team of hunters called the Outsiders. In addition to routine banter, Dick displays fondness, protectiveness, and even possessiveness when Roy is in danger or is being interrogated. Roy functions as a voice of reason and an emotional anchor at times when Dick is unbalanced and lost. Since Roy is someone who understands Dick in a unique way, he is as capable of discussing Dick's flaws as he is of helping him overcome them, even if it means igniting conflict.

While Roy had not been an original member of the Teen Titans, he was a valued member of the team for many years as Speedy, which was the start of his friendship with Dick.[25] They've grown and matured together, both under the wing of rich and distant vigilantes. From day one, Roy has admired Dick for his skills as both an acrobat and as Batman's sidekick. Dick has been nothing short of everything Roy could ask for in a friend, a brother, or a part of his family. Dick has helped him through the difficult teenage years and assisted in his reunion with his daughter, Lian. Dick was one of the people that Roy had to thank for his successful transition into adulthood.

"Why can't we ever save them, *Dinah? How come there's never a chance to give back?"*—Arsenal #1[26]

Roy not only feels a moral obligation to give back to the people that have helped him, but he is very eager to do so as well. This mentality will explain why Roy has gone to such great lengths to try to help Dick as much as he did—to help save his life in return. This an essay that will focus on later parts of their relationship, primarily in comics that were written after *The New Teen Titans* because it is the most dynamic and controversial stage in their relationship. It's a time in their lives when their closeness is the strongest because it is when it was tested the most. Roy is one person among many who has admired Dick Grayson for the genuine, kind, intelligent, and charismatic person that he is.[27] He considers Dick his family just as Dick considers him the same in return. Their devotion and deeply imbedded trust that they've built because of their life-long friendship has persevered through the troubles of their teenage years and adulthood.

It was because of Dick that Roy hadn't died when they hunted down Cheshire in order to obtain Lian. Living a relatively lonely and meaningless life after he had been fired by Oliver Queen, Roy found a purpose once he reached his early twenties, which revolved around his daughter Lian.[28] Observing Roy taking care of the toddler, Dick had come to the conclusion that fatherhood suited him.[29] Lian provides an extremely important anchor to reality for Roy, from which he can find the courage to help others, to be fair, and to be the best possible person he can be. In living for Lian, Roy is therefore able to become an anchor for everyone he cares about, which is something that he actively strives to do. Given the admiration and closeness that Roy shares with Dick Grayson, especially after he had helped him recover his daughter from Cheshire, Roy proves his loyalty and kinship to Dick time and time again.

While physical fights are not uncommon between them, there are many layers that embody their relationship. Dick and Roy have a relationship that is just as unorthodox as it is dynamic. Over the decades, they built a foundation of perpetual trust, to the point where they can discuss insecurities and doubts openly, such as Dick commenting on Roy's confidence in a dire situation being "…a new kind of denial for him," to which Roy responds, "Thanks. How's the nervous breakdown coming along?"[30] In *Outsiders,* when Roy feels as if an argument is inevitable, he informs Dick that he's not "…up for their usual banter,"[31] which makes it clear that banter is not an uncommon occurrence between them. However, despite the two of them having a tendency to be explosive when they fight, when it comes time for them to spar, both of them can be found smiling.[32] There is an undeniable closeness between them, so much that they are open to express it verbally as well as physically.

Throughout the years, Roy has demonstrated an unrelenting trust in Dick and his decisions, so much that he does so instinctually. As long as Dick was leading the Titans, Roy follows his instructions without a second of hesitation. When Damage had turned to Roy asking if he should trust Nightwing's decisions, Roy immediately barked at him to do what Dick told him to do.[33] When Roy had suspected that one of the Outsiders had been a spy who was conspiring against them, Roy put the bunker in complete lockdown and brought each of the team members under interrogation while hooked up to a lie detector. The first person he questioned was Dick, not because he suspected him, but because he trusted him the most. Once they were alone, Roy admitted that he was just putting on a show, that he knew it wasn't him.[34] Roy considers the idea of Dick ever backstabbing or betraying him completely absurd, so much that he does not even give the matter a serious thought. This instinct to trust Dick can also be seen when Dick began working undercover along-side Deathstroke. Dick asked Roy to do him a favor and stay down, then proceeded to kick and punch him until he was thrown off balance.[35] Far from incapable of fighting back after only a couple of hits, Roy stayed down, remained immobile, and waited until Dick left the room before standing up. He trusted that there was a reason for it and that Dick had a plan like he always did.

During the *Graduation Day* book, there is a contrast between Roy's level-headed nature and Dick's emotional responses. When proposed with an offer from wealthy corporations to fund and have surveillance on the Titans, Dick let his skepticism and bitter attitude towards being funded drive him to stomp out of the room. Roy, having past experience working for the government, immediately follows and urges him to have an open mind about the idea.[36] Roy is reasonable without being unrealistic and, given that Dick prefers to function with his head rather than his heart, it is a quality that makes communicating with Roy much easier for him. Roy tried to act as a crutch for Dick while they were grieving Donna's death and even managed to stay shockingly calm while Dick shouted and screamed his anguish an inch away from Roy's face.[37] Furthermore, Roy tried in vain for several weeks to console Dick. The messages left on Dick's machine had Roy begging him to pick up the phone while confessing that he wanted to "...get through this *together* ... if you'd let me,"[38] and even when he kept failing to get an answer, Roy promised Dick that he would be there for him whenever he was ready.[14] It is a bit of a stretch to assume that Dick purposefully alienated Roy during this time and much easier to assume that sorrow and guilt heavily influenced his reactions. While it might seem to most people that Roy is ignoring the past and forgetting about Donna Troy, it is quite the contrary: he accepts that it has happened. Unlike Dick, Roy has a responsibility to his daughter and it is just the emotional motivation that he needs to remain strong and persistent. Roy knows that no matter how much he grieves, his life must go on. This is exactly the emotional stability that makes Roy capable of being an anchor to everyone he loves. Roy's emotional adaptation is something that helps to keep Dick in the present rather than the past, however heartbreaking or frustrating the situation might be.

When the two had been on an island with their friends (courtesy of Donna wishing for the original five Titans to rekindle and ease tensions between them), they fell victim to Gargoyle's powers, putting them in a dream-like limbo. In order to get out, the Titans concluded that solving their tensions and trying to put their minds at ease would be the solution. Roy quickly grew irritated of the compliments and praise, saying that he did not wish to have his friends telling him that he's "...effing perfect."[39] From this quote alone, one can conclude that friendship means something a little different to Roy in comparison to everyone else. He counts on his friends to point out his flaws, his mistakes, and his downfalls for the simple reason of not wanting to repeat them and furthermore, to become a better person.[40] In return, Roy gives his friends the same gesture, Dick especially. The one thing that worked to break Gargoyle's limbo had been when Roy shouted to Dick that they loved him, but he needed to "...cut the Bat-trash already,"[41] and then proceeded to grab his collar and punch him in the face. This is symbolic of how Dick and Roy's relationship works—by vocally and physically demonstrating his point, Roy was able to knock some sense into him and therefore bring them back to reality.

In the transition between the *Titans* and *Outsiders*, we see Roy manifesting his natural ability to adapt. In *Outsiders*, Roy takes on a new responsibility: he steps up as a leader. While his trust and loyalty to Dick remained untarnished, at this point Roy no longer takes a passive role in the team dynamic. Upon visiting Dick in Gotham, he does not ask Dick to start a team, instead he asks him to join one.[42] For the first time, Roy takes the initiative and creates something new without Dick's guidance. This is, without a doubt, a significant change to the structure of their relationship. Prior to this point, Roy relied on Dick exclusively and followed his orders without question. He begins to raise his voice and even sometimes argues against Dick's orders, such as when the Outsiders were heading towards their first mission as a team and Dick critiqued his flight pattern. In the discussion that followed, Roy was firm, in control, and confident about his choices.[43] Roy not only proves that he is capable of leadership, but also that he had grown into someone that Dick can rely on and follow in return.

Roy shows his love by giving both praise and criticism when either of them are deserved. It is a method that is not only helpful, but it is also extremely effective in getting through to Dick when he needs to be reigned back to reality. At a point where Dick had alienated, angered, and irritated the Titans so much that even Donna Troy would not speak to him, Roy had smiled and reminded Dick of his strengths: the reasons why the Titans love him.[44] This was a situation where Dick felt guilty for his strictness and Roy was able to convince him that it was not necessarily a bad thing. He implied that being in control is what makes him capable rather than hated. Something similar occurs in the *Outsiders*, where Roy uses his brutal honesty to talk some sense in to him, such as "Get your head out of your ass and act like the leader I know you are."[45] When Dick persists in acting like an unsuitable leader to the Outsiders, Roy tells him this:

"Your greatest fear in life, the thing that eats at you—is that you're terrified of being Batman!! A cold, detached, emotionless *loner*. I've got news for you, that's *exactly* what you are."[46]

Roy understands Dick much better than Dick understands himself at times.

Now, it is critical to not misunderstand Roy's knowledge of Dick's less favorable traits as a barrier between them. Roy understands that there are flaws about Dick, but he also understands that they don't negate the good qualities that Dick possesses either. One lesson that Roy had taught to Lian was that people need to "…strive to overlook our friends' shortcomings,"[47] which is advice that he both practices and preaches. To many people, Dick seems like the shadow of Batman: dark, calculative, emotionless, and determined. Grace Choi (one of the most prominent and consistent members of the Outsiders) had once told Roy that whether Dick likes it or not, he's "...got the ice water in his veins." Knowing better, Roy effortlessly responds with "...you couldn't be more wrong."[48] It is obvious that Roy is well aware of Dick's shortcomings but he doesn't reinforce them when someone else comments on them. Instead Roy argues against them because he knows that Dick does not, in fact, have ice water flowing through his veins. Dick demonstrates this loyal behavior towards Roy as well. When the Outsiders started to scrutinize Roy for setting them up with amateur villains that the team was over qualified to take down, Dick defended Roy's decisions and then threatened to fire anyone who had issues with them.[49] In the very next panel, when it was just the two of them having a private conversation, Dick then admits that the team had a valid point. Besides the obvious fact that Dick has a deeper relationship with Roy than he does the other members of the team, Dick proves that his initial reaction to people attacking Roy—even if he agrees with their argument—is to defend him.

Dick Grayson is as kind as he is passionate and his driven spirit is something that is an inspiration to many people, Roy included. However, how does Dick feel about Roy in return? Happier than Roy has ever been in his life to have his daughter in his custody, he thanks Dick for helping get Lian into his care, telling him how much he envies him and how inferior he feels standing next to him. Dick was quick to reassure Roy that he thought he was a caring man and not a failure.[50] Dick later tells Kory that he had been shocked by Roy's admiration because Dick envied Roy for his ability to be open and carefree.[51]

"...but if you're asking me if I think you've lost your edge. Or if I think you shouldn't be on this team, or ... if I wouldn't put my own life in your hands—man, there is no one ... no one I'd rather have fighting by my side than you."—Outsiders, *v3, #11*[52]

After Roy got shot in the chest several times during the early issues of Outsiders, unsure of whether or not Roy would survive, Dick did not hesitate to go after Brother Blood immediately, but he attacked him with the intention of beating him to death, screaming at him *"Murder!!"* and then said that this time he was "...not coming back."[53] Dick's passionately angry outburst demonstrates just how deeply affected he was by the possibility of Roy dying in the hospital. The operation to attack Brother Blood was abrupt, quick, and brutal; hardly calculated like most of Dick's plans, so it becomes apparent that this plan was more driven by anger and revenge than anything else. Roy had nearly been killed and Dick lashed out in a fit of rage against the perpetrator, to the point where he fully intended on killing him. He unleashed the same reaction against the Joker when he thought Tim had died. Dick loves people passionately and just how strongly becomes evident when his emotions get the better of him. However, the most memorable example of this can be seen when Roy returns to the Outsiders after being bedridden for over a month. He tells Roy that there is not a single person that he would rather have fighting by his side than Roy.[54] This is a very bold declaration, one that Dick does not often admit to even his closest of family. It's a statement that is genuine, meaningful, and a prime example of how Dick shows devotion to the people he cherishes.

After listing the actions that Roy has taken to help Dick through difficult times in his life, is it possible to say that Dick has done the same for Roy? Absolutely. In the aftermath of Prometheus' attack on Star City, Roy had lost both his right arm and Lian. He lost his anchor to reality and in turn, lost more and more of his sanity until he was taking heroin once again. He became extremely violent and the one person that came to find him was Dick. He was persistent and tried to be understanding even after Roy began attacking him, explaining he was his friend, not his enemy.[55] Here we see an interesting parallel that defines the tough love nature of their relationship. Dick is doing exactly what Roy had done when they had fallen into a limbo: used physical violence while shouting out feelings of love and appreciation.

There is even a parallel of persistence. After promising Roy that everything was going to be okay, Dick took him to a drug rehabilitation prison where he had a chance to get clean.[56] Even after Roy had broken free from that institution and joined forces with Cheshire and Deathstroke, Dick kept insisting to Roy that "…no matter what choices you've made, it's not too late to change sides."[57] It is obvious that Dick uses these methods of getting through to Roy specifically because it was what Roy used to get through to him. As stated previously, Roy is the type of person who will act a certain way to his friends because he wishes to be treated that way in return, which is exactly what Dick does. During a time when Roy has lost his connection to the world and his purpose in life, Dick tried to bring him back to reality, just as Roy had done for Dick many times before.

Unlike Dick—someone who sometimes has troubles expressing his own emotions—Roy is the contrary: he knows exactly how his emotions function and the opportune and inopportune moments to express all of them. It makes him level-headed, understanding, and patient, which are traits that come in handy when Dick is being anything but reasonable. However, Roy also possesses a flaw that he is not very aware of: he gives people the benefit of the doubt to the point where it backfires. When he reconstructed Indigo to be beneficial to the team, she still betrayed the team in the long run. Grace told him that if he were to have the opportunity to go back in time and kill a murderer while they were a child, he would try to reform them instead.[58] Roy is aware of the corruption that lies within everyone, but he chooses to give people another chance regardless. He has faith in the goodness of people and that with the right conditioning, it will shine through their flaws. Having this belief is what motivates Roy to bring Jade into Lian's life as much as possible, even though Cheshire struggled being in and out of captivity because of her crimes against humanity. This is not a surprise when we take Roy's past experiences of being abandoned into consideration. He does not wish for anyone he cares about to feel unloved and neglected like he did. For someone like Dick, who has pushed people away because his emotions clouded his logical judgment, Roy's loyalty and patience goes a very long way.

The Chemistry of Dick and Koriand'r

By Shelly Sposato

Dick and Koriand'r have had an instantaneous attraction since Kory debuted in 1980. They started dating when Dick was still Robin and continued after he had become Nightwing; their relationship lasted for over ten real-time years, making it one of the longest comic-book relationships in history. Even after Dick and Kory stopped officially dating, they fell in and out of love for the following twenty years. Kory's is an essential role in Dick's life—rather than an ex-lover, she's a lifelong friend. Kory was present while Dick was maturing, figuring himself out, and transitioning from Batman's partner to a hero in his own right. She continues to be one of his strongest emotional attachments and one of a handful of people who know him on an intimate level. Their relationship endured for years despite personal trials and stress-ridden situations. Dick and Kory put in tremendous effort to make their relationship work, including the acceptance of each other's flaws and overcoming external stresses related to their dangerous lifestyles. Kory's vibrancy and forceful nature served to relax and draw Dick out, while her attentive and caring personality fostered the emotional needs that Bruce had neglected while Dick was growing up.

When Kory makes her first appearance, she and Dick rub each other the wrong way. The story starts with Kory escaping her enslavement and crash landing on Earth, bringing her Gordanian enemies with her.[59] She and the Titans team up to fight off the invaders, but Dick quickly grows frustrated with Kory for incinerating all of their clues in battle.[60] Dick's first impression of Koriand'r is that of a violent, blood-lusting alien, in part because Kory can only speak her native tongue, Tamaranean, creating an aggravating language barrier between them. Dick tells Wally that Kory seems to "relish violence" and that she's "too dangerous to be left free." Without the ability to understand her, Dick thinks Kory is a dangerous enemy they will have to physically restrain for the safety of others. Kory, however, isn't preoccupied with any lingering tension between them, and on sensing Dick's frustration, kisses him, catching him off-guard.[61]

When the kiss ends, Kory speaks English for the first time, telling Dick that he's "really cute." Tamaraneans have the ability to absorb language by touch, but Kory explains that she doesn't need to kiss in order for this ability to work—she just finds it more enjoyable that way.[62] In this way Kory's attraction to Dick is obvious from the start. Dick's attitude towards her shifts once she can speak English. Dick was frustrated because he perceived Kory as an unknown variable out of his control. Once she's able to talk, he realizes that she isn't hostile or on Earth to wreak havoc. In fact, Kory is level-headed, light-hearted and conversational—a direct contrast to how she acts in battle. Dick warms up to Kory quickly in response, reflecting the mutual allure they have toward each other despite the unorthodox beginning to their relationship.

Although Dick and Kory share this immediate attraction, there are a number of barriers, mostly on Dick's side, preventing them from being together. Dick has a history of channeling Bruce Wayne's traits, both the good and the bad. He's devoted to his own war on crime, is a workaholic, and takes most aspects of his life too seriously. Because of Bruce's influence, Dick puts his vigilante work first and his relationships second. After knowing each other for a month, Dick pulls Kory aside and says, "Kory, we can't keep seeing each other like this. It's bad for our teamwork."[63] At this point, Kory and Dick have no intimate history. Dick is serious enough about his work that he outright refuses to partake in any sort of seemingly romantic connection. In his Robin days, he was worried dating would sabotage the team dynamics or distract him from crime fighting. Dick is prone to sacrifice his personal life for work, but Kory is so open and expressive that Dick develops romantic interest in her anyway, spurring him to end their "relationship" before it can even start. After Dick turns down her interest, Kory moves on and starts dating a new man named Franklin Crandall. Dick admits to his friends that he's jealous of the guy as soon as he hears. Despite this, he refuses to act on his feelings and doesn't interfere in their relationship.

Dick's resistance in large part revolves around paranoia about not living up to Bruce's expectations. He devotes his time and energy to proving that he can handle being a hero without staying at Batman's side, causing him to be hard on himself or self-deprecating. He holds himself to higher standards than his friends, and when Donna calls him out on this, Dick tells her that he feels like a kid repeating fifth grade for the third time after recently partnering up with Batman again.[64]

In recent continuities, Dick's upbringing with Bruce is as detrimental as it is positive for him. When Dick was growing up with his parents, he lived in a happy circus environment that was carefree and lighthearted with few rules and regulations. He had dozens of people that he could go to for support or comfort. While there was the burden of always traveling from place to place, Dick was too young at the time to be stymied by these stresses. After his parents died, his primary support structure crumbled away, causing Bruce Wayne to step into his life in their stead. As positive as Bruce's intentions were, he was an emotionally distant guardian at the best of times and cold and borderline abusive at the worst.[65] Alfred played a relevant and crucial role in raising Dick, but it still wasn't enough to fill that void his parents left behind. Dick went from a warm, emotionally fostering atmosphere to a cold, stifling one. It was a disorientating contrast to his initial upbringing that had permanent consequences. Although Dick lit up the manor with laughter and found new meaning in his life during his first year as Robin, he quickly learned the gravity and repercussions of his vigilante lifestyle. He adopted a grimmer outlook in response, even carrying the personal guilt of a man's death.[66] From then on, Dick fell into a habit of making personal sacrifices for their endless mission.

Because of Bruce's obsession with vigilantism, Dick approaches fighting crime with equal fervor, striving to live up to his mentor's impossible expectations without disappointing him. Kory was the first person to separate Dick from these looming ideals and to help him embrace himself for who he is. Dick remarks, "Kory realized something was wrong with me. Bless her she did try to help."[67] Over time, Kory teaches Dick how to relax. She symbolizes freedom, flight and passion, all things Dick is inherently attracted to. She's emotionally brimming, supportive, and attentive when he's been deprived of that type of attention for several years. Although

Dick has many close friends, Kory pays acute attention to his emotional needs at a time when no one else is. She fills a void that hasn't been filled since his parents were alive. "I should find Dick. He probably needs to be comforted.... Always being in charge isn't easy for him."[68] Kory understands the pressure Dick is under. He feels responsible for his friend's lives, and this causes him to be uptight and serious about the job. Kory recognizes this and is there for Dick when Dick himself is unaware that he needs that level of comfort and reassurance. Kory is brazen with her affection, one time lifting Dick into her arms bridal style to tell him he needs "some tender loving care."[69] When Dick is hurt in a fight and tries to continue fighting anyway, she flies him atop a roof and disregards his heated protests saying that he will take orders from her for his own safety.[70] Because of Dick's stubborn nature, his friends typically leave him alone after a certain point, especially when he's brooding or moody. Kory is not intimidated or put off by Dick's attempts to brush his friends off. Throughout their relationship, Kory urges Dick to unwind and express himself, taking charge when he lapses into dark, brooding moods. Dick has a stubborn personality and needs people to be forceful with him in turn in order for him to open up or take time off. Dick has friends like Donna who are sympathetic, but Dick knows how to brush their concern aside while Kory will stubbornly put her foot down. Dick and Kory are well-matched in this respect, and Dick is better for it. "Somehow, whenever I'm depressed, thinking of Kory makes me feel better."[71]

It's only after Kory's relationship with Franklin falls through that she and Dick start dating, creating fresh problems. Throughout their relationship, Kory's ferocity alarms Dick. Tamaraneans are a race of warriors who slay their enemies ruthlessly, a concept that goes directly against the "no killing" philosophy Dick was raised under. During *The New Teen Titans* run, Dick warns Kory to hold back and rein in her power continuously. For someone to have so much power and be willing to kill scared him. He goes to Donna for advice, asking, "But what if she kills on Earth? How can I settle down with someone like that?"[72] Dick constantly questions their relationship. Emotionally, he's attracted to Kory, but logically, he doesn't understand why he's with someone like her. It isn't just that Kory is *willing* to kill, but that she's so passionate and unrestrained with her emotions, Dick is worried she'll cross the line unintentionally. She doesn't see killing as morally wrong in the way Dick does. Kory describes her nature by saying her people "loved their friends with an unrestrained heart and hated their enemies with equal fervor."[73] Dick has difficulty comprehending that someone can live like this, flying off the handle with their emotions at the simplest provocation, yet still remaining in control. Due to this, Dick exerts a lot of effort in controlling Kory himself. He wants to be with her romantically, but he also wants her to fit a mold that he feels comfortable with, resulting in him trying to change her. This is the unhealthiest aspect of their relationship and isn't an easy concept for either of them. Dick reminds Kory to hold back so often that she'll let out her frustration with him after it builds up into a bad mood. Kory's an inborn warrior and Dick's attempts at restraining her went against her natural temperament and her training. She puts in a valiant effort to change her ways in order to make their relationship work, but it results in frequent tension.

Dick has good reason for worrying about Kory's restraint. In one of their first fights against Deathstroke, Kory shoots a blast from her hands unaware of Deathstroke's healing factor. When he stands up, she says, "You still live? Impossible!"[74] Kory doesn't succeed, but her intent to kill is clear. Years later, Kory actually does kill, though the situation is morally grey. Deathstroke's wife, Adeline Kane, is abducted to be used as a hostage to control Deathstroke. During the fray, her throat is slit. While the Titans fight, Adeline's life drains away past the point where she can be saved due to too many minutes of oxygen deprivation. Kory shoots a blast to kill and ends the woman's misery.[75] Dick reprimands Kory immediately, both heated with each other over what the right call should have been. They're both driven by compassion in this situation, though Dick's is for a life, black and white, while Kory's compassion is centered on ending another woman's suffering. This concept is a constant tug-of-war for them, neither Dick nor Kory willing to budge on their moral stance.

The effort Dick puts into making their relationship work stands out. He could have easily walked away and chosen not to deal with the extra complications Kory brought upon them. Dick is paranoid that Kory will break the one cardinal rule Bruce raised him on, yet he fervently tries to keep their relationship alive, in large part by drilling the no killing concept into her. He doesn't want to be involved with someone who will willingly take a life, but Dick is also worried that she'll be arrested under U.S. law and taken from him. There are few people that Dick will go to these extensive lengths for. He has little tolerance for a person who doesn't treat life as sacred.

Ignoring fights caused by this natural tension, their relationship is smooth sailing. When they did have their first major fight, it spurs Dick to go to Donna to ask if she and her husband fight as well.[76] It's rare for Dick and Kory to fight to the point where Dick questions if it's a natural part of being in a relationship. Unsurprisingly, their first major fight revolves around

Dick reigning in Kory's power, indicating that this issue never dissolves. They have minor arguments frequently with Kory lamenting that Dick is always telling her what to do. Kory defends her confusion about Earth's culture early on by saying, "From what I've seen, you Earthlings are suspicious of your friends and show compassion for those who hate you."[77] Kory sees nothing wrong with being merciless with enemies who show intent to harm and thinks that Dick is the strange one in their relationship.

Kory's cultural differences are as much a hindrance as they are a strength in their relationship. Although she is relentless against their enemies, she's equally caring with her friends. Kory teaches Dick to be accepting of himself, flaws included: "Once you're comfortable with what you are, you can be at ease with what you look like." Dick responds saying that's easier said than done.[78] A couple years later when Dick is Nightwing, he admits to the Titans that he's uncomfortable with how little they know about each other. "This is hard to say because the Batman taught me to keep my feelings inside … to not trust anyone other than myself. But the Batman's intense and frantically private and I can't be like him … and it bothers me that we don't always talk to each other."[79] As Dick matures, he realizes he can't live like his mentor. He mimics Bruce in many ways but comes to realize he needs social ties and interaction. Kory is the driving force to push Dick toward opening up more, and he finally does around the age of twenty as Nightwing. As Dick comments later, he fell in love with Kory's freedom to "feel at home with even her strongest emotions … the one kind of freedom that Batman wouldn't allow! That's what I was longing for—and that's what Kory slowly taught me to embrace!"[80]

Further into their relationship, a small group of the Titans travel to Tamaran to address the civil war tearing the planet apart. In order to bring peace to her planet, Kory agrees to participate in a state marriage with another royal Tamaranean named Karras.[81] This ends up being a roadblock in their relationship. Dick has a history of gentlemanly conduct in his relationships, once telling Roy Harper he can only have sex with someone if he truly loves them[82] and telling Garfield Logan that he felt uncomfortable living with a woman he wasn't married to.[83] Although Kory married Karras for political reasons, Dick took it personally and ended their relationship on the grounds that she was married to another man she had consummated with. He can't be part of an adulterous relationship.[84] Dick leaves the relationship on his terms, but it has a profound impact on his psyche. After returning to Earth, he shut himself inside his apartment and cut himself off from social contact. When Donna visits Dick, she finds him with overgrown stubble, wearing a bathrobe with his apartment in disarray. Dick tells her to leave, and when Donna refuses, they get into a heated argument that turns physical.[85] Donna throws Dick through a wall, and Dick verbally lashes out at her in return, later remarking in his inner monologue that he knew what to say to hurt her and did just that.[86] Dick has an attitude with Alfred as well, telling him to "mind his own damn business."[87] The pause in Dick's relationship with Kory ends up being a dark period for him. Over time, Dick heals, becoming more in control of himself, though still refusing to be with Kory due to her marriage. Kory is upset as well and attempts to placate Dick by saying the marriage means nothing and is merely a formality.[88] She and Karras had respectfully split ways shortly after their marriage and neither of them actually loved each other.[89] Dick refuses Kory anyway, admitting that he still loves her but that he feels morally compromised and unable to continue their intimacy because of it. Although it took a while, Dick eventually softens his stance, telling Kory, "I know when we're together I feel right."[90] Dick comes to realize that not being together is hurting both of them, and her state marriage is more of a superficial barrier than anything. Dick's slip into depression stops once he allows himself to be open with Kory again. This speed bump shows that although Dick is rigid with his morals, Kory is important enough to make exceptions for.

As time goes on, Dick and Kory's relationship grows strained again. Mirage, a woman from an alternate timeline, tricks Dick into bed under false pretenses by impersonating Kory.[91] Dick and Kory are both upset by this, and Dick heavily berates himself over it after. In an attempt to fix their relationship and prove his love to her, Dick proposes to Kory, feeling it would seal their relationship once and for all.[92] Dick wastes no time in making the wedding happen, and although Kory goes along with it, she holds deep reservations. Kory asks Donna if she's doing the right thing, saying, "Maybe it's just nerves, but I'm not sure Dick and I should be getting married just now. I mean, I love him completely. I really do. I want to be with him, but am I imagining things or has Dick been on edge lately?"[93] They love each other, but Dick is marrying her for the wrong reasons and it shows. Throughout their wedding day, Dick is moody and snapping at people.[94] Dick has the idea that marrying Kory will make everything else in his life fall into place, in large part because that was the effect he perceived from Donna's marriage to Terry Long. Kory decides that even if the wedding isn't everything she hopes it will be, at least she'll be with the man she loves. Dick and Kory came close to saying their vows, but the wedding ended in death. Raven, a fellow Titan possessed by her evil father, Trigon, crashes the wedding, killing the priest.[95] After the chaos of their failed wedding, Dick and Kory share an unspoken agreement that it isn't meant to be and drift apart. Dick and Kory had been fighting against the current for most of their relationship. After the disappointment of their failed wedding, they're disenchanted and decide that despite loving each other, they're exerting too much effort in an aspect of their life that should be natural.

From here, Dick and Kory start a pattern of falling in and out love without officially establishing a relationship again. Because they already know each other intimately, it's difficult for them to be together without that spark cropping up. This trend continues for the next two real-time decades. While Kory is heading out into space, she and Dick speak over a connection that's faulty and nearly out of range. They both confess their love to each other, but due to the bad connection, neither of them hear the other's admission and nothing came of it in response.[96] Later, Dick and Kory are influenced by Lust, one of the sons of Trigon with the power of a deadly sin. They're spurred into intimacy and have sex, though neither of them consciously decides to do it.[97] Later, Dick and Kory discuss the incident, debating whether they should attempt their relationship again. Although Kory is still in love with Dick, she tells him they can't continue being wishy-washy about their relationship: "We became a couple when we were very young, and that connection has never gone away.... But we cannot keep doing this. Start. Stop. Lovers. Friends. Then back again. We have to stop."[98] Dick and Kory have trouble figuring out where to draw the line. Kory wants to be with Dick, but only if it will be a real, devoted relationship. She asks Dick if he loves her as more than a friend, in which Dick answers, "No," finally ending their back and forth relationship.[99] Although Kory played a vital role in fostering Dick's emotional needs while he was maturing, he didn't need to be closely attended to once he was an adult. After years of being Nightwing and then Batman, Dick carried confidence and security about who he was. He still loves Kory as a close friend, but he no longer needs her to fill the dark void he grew up with. She taught him to balance his life in a healthy manner, and he was able to carry that away from their relationship independently.

Dick and Kory remain strong, passionate friends, both of them understanding the other on deep levels and continuing to be there for each other. Kory remarks to Dick when he's Batman that she knows his heart no matter which mask he wears.[100] Dick remarks that his other friends have difficulty talking to him with the cowl on, but Kory doesn't have this issue. She sees him as more than the symbol he wears and can look past his masks with ease.

Kory made a dramatic difference in Dick's life, and she's the reason he lightened up by the time he became Nightwing. As Robin, Dick was predominantly serious and held himself to strict standards. He refused to date his teammates despite being eighteen years old because it was unprofessional. Kory drew him out, teaching him to be expressive and free while emotionally fostering him. Although Dick remains a workaholic, Kory's a stepping stone that taught him how to balance it among other aspects of his life. Similarly, Dick was a stable force in Kory's life, often keeping her grounded. She rekindled a part of his personality that had been subdued after years of living with Bruce. In his early Nightwing days, Dick grew to trust and open up to his friends more. By the time he had been Nightwing for a couple of years, Dick was fully mature and emotionally balanced considering the many traumas he's faced. Dick has frequently gone down a path where he acts like Bruce, which is one of his greatest fears.[101] His friends are a large reason that he doesn't lose himself down this darker path.

Notes

1. Marv Wolfman et al., "With Every Little Step We Take," *The New Titans* #89 (New York: DC Comics, August 1992), 8.
2. Marv Wolfman, George Pérez, and Romeo Tanghal, "Who Is Donna Troy?" *The New Teen Titans* (1) #38 (New York: DC Comics, January 1984), 1.
3. Wolfman, Pérez, and Tanghal, *The New Teen Titans* (1) #38, 9.
4. Jay Faerber, Paul Pelletier, and Bud LaRosa, "Kid Stuff," *The Titans* (1) #29 (New York: DC Comics, July 2001), 6.
5. Devin Grayson and Rodolfo Damaggio, "Like Riding A Bike," in *The Batman Chronicles* #7 (New York: DC Comics, December 1997), 10.
6. Marv Wolfman et al., "We are Gathered Here Today..." *Tales of the Teen Titans* #50 (New York: DC Comics, February 1985), 14.
7. Marv Wolfman, George Pérez, and Dick Giordano, "The Judas Contact Book One: The Eyes of Tara Markov!" *Tales of the Teen Titans* #42 (May 1984), 4.
8. Marv Wolfman, Tom Grummett, and Al Vey, "The Darkening Chapter Four: Something Old, Something New, Something Borrowed, Something ... DEAD," *The New Titans* #100 (August 1993), 14.
9. Marv Wolfman, George Pérez, and Gene Day, "The Changeling," *Tales of the New Teen Titans* #3 (New York: DC Comics, August 1982), 7.
10. Jay Faerber, Paul Pelletier, and Bud LaRosa, "The All-Nighter," *The Titans* (1) #28 (June 2001), 20.
11. Wolfman et al., *Tales of Teen Titans* #50 (February 1985), 28.
12. Wolfman, Pérez, and Tanghal, *The New Teen Titans* (1) #38 (January 1984), 4.
13. Marv Wolfman, Eduardo Barreto, and Romeo Tanghal, "Homecoming," *The New Teen Titans* (2) #18 (New York: DC Comics, March 1986), 24.
14. Eddie Berganza et al., "The Way Things Were," *Titans* (2) #23 (New York: DC Comics, May 2010), 20.
15. Grayson and Damaggio, "Like Riding A Bike," 2.
16. Jay Faerber, Paul Pelletier, and Bud LaRosa, "Interludes," in *The Titans Secret Files and Origins* (1) #2 (New York: DC Comics, October 2000), 9.
17. Judd Winick et al., "Part Three: Recessional," *Titans/Young Justice: Graduation Day* #3 (New York: DC Comics, August 2003), 16.
18. Winick et al., *Titans/Young Justice: Graduation Day* #3, 20.

19. Judd Winick et al., "A Day After," in *Teen Titans/Outsiders Secret Files and Origins* (1) #1 (New York: DC Comics, December 2003), 2.
20. Judd Winick, Tom Raney, and Scott Hanna, "Role Call, Part One: Opening Offers," *Outsiders* (3) #1 (New York: DC Comics, August 2003), 8.
21. Winick, Raney, and Hanna, *Outsiders* (3) #1, 6.
22. Judd Winick, Dan Jurgens, and Nelson, "A Change of Plans," *Outsiders* (3) #16 (November 2004), 15.
23. Adam Beechen, Darryl Banks, and Sean Parsons, "I am Donna Troy," in *Teen Titans/Outsiders Secret Files and Origins* (1) #2 (New York: DC Comics, October 2005), 17.
24. Phil Jimenez, José Luis García-López, and George Pérez, "The Return of Donna Troy, Chapter 2: Stark Contrast," in *DC Special: Return of Donna Troy Vol. 1* #2 (New York: DC Comics, September 2005), 11.
25. Roy was later granted status as a founding member of the Teen Titans in the final issue, *Teen Titans* #53 (February 1978).
26. Devin Grayson et al., "Six Degrees, Part 1—Next of Kin," *Arsenal* #1 (New York: DC Comics, October 1998), 19.
27. Roy admiring Dick's combat skills in action; see Devin Grayson, Phil Hester, and Andre Parks, "Cowboys and Indians," *Nightwing* #114 (New York: DC Comics, January 2006), [19].
28. Marv Wolfman, Chuck Patton, and Tom Poston, "The Cheshire Contract: Conclusion," in *Nightwing: Old Friends, New Enemies*, (New York: DC Comics, 2013), 80.
29. Cherie Wilkerson, Marv Wolfman, "Rock and Hard Places," in *Nightwing: Old Friends, New Enemies*, 83.
30. Tom Peyer, Barry Kitson, and Rich Faber, "Chemical World Part One," *The Titans* Vol. 1 #42 (August 2002), [13].
31. Judd Winick, Tom Raney, and Sean Parsons, "Devil's Work, Part 1: Sacrifice," *Outsiders* (3) #8 (March 2004), [9].
32. Winick, Will Conrad, and Parsons "Scream Without Raising Your Voice," *Outsiders* (3) #11 (June 2004), [26].
33. Grayson, Mark Buckingham, Wade Von Grawbadger, "That Strange Buzzing Sound," *The Titans* (1) #1(March 1999), [3].
34. Winick, Sean Moll, and Kevin Conrad, "Lockdown," *Outsiders* (3) #23 (June 2005), [10].
35. Grayson, Hester, Parks, *Nightwing* #114, [20–21].
36. Jimenez et al., "Graduation Day," *Teen Titans/Outsiders: The Death and Return of Donna Troy* (New York: DC Comics, 2006), 13.
37. Jimenez et al., "Graduation Day," 69.
38. Judd Winick et al., "A Day After," *Teen Titans/Outsiders: Secret Files and Origins* #1 (December 2003), [5].
39. Grayson, Buckingham, and Marlo Alquiza, "Gargoyle's Revenge," *The Titans* (1) #16 (June 2000), [20].
40. Roy explains that having his friends calling him a junkie was just the "kick in the pants" he needed to grow up. See Grayson, Buckingham, Alquiza, *The Titans* (1) #16, [21].
41. Grayson, Buckingham, Alquiza, *The Titans* (1) #16, [21].
42. Winick, Raney, and Scott Hanna "Roll Call, Part One: Opening Offers," *Outsiders* (3) #1 (August 2003), [9].
43. Dick had said that Roy was flying too low, that they needed to come in from above so that they could survey the area. Roy had argued back that flying too high would make them a target. Winick, Raney, and Hanna, "Roll Call, Part Two: Lawyers, Guns and Monkeys," *Outsiders* (3) #2 (September 2003), [5].

44. Roy reminds Dick that he has a history of having control over himself, over the circumstances, and over his team since they'd first met him—that it was just the kind of person he was—and that it was a reason why his friends love him. Peyer, Kitson, Faber, *The Titans* (1) #42, [14–15].

45. Winick, Raney, Parsons, *Outsiders* (3) #8, [11].

46. Winick, Dan Jurgens, and Nelson "A Change of Plans," *Outsiders* (3) #16 (Nov 2004), [13].

47. Winick and Carlos D'Anda, "Most Wanted, Part 1," *Outsiders* (3) #17 (Dec 2004), [13].

48. Winick, Matthew Clark, and Art Thibert, "Out-of-Town Work," *Outsiders* (3) #31 (Feb 2006), [8].

49. Winick, ChrissCross, and Parsons, "Brothers in Blood, Part One: Small Potatoes," *Outsiders* (3) #4 (Nov, 2003), [11].

50. Wolfman, Poston, and Roy "The Cheshire Contract: Conclusion," *Nightwing: Old Friends, New Enemies,* 75.

51. Wolfman, Poston, and Roy "The Cheshire Contract: Conclusion," 80.

52. Winick, Conrad, and Parsons, *Outsiders* (3) #11 [21].

53. Winick, ChrissCross, and Parsons, "Brothers in Blood, Part 3: Pandora's Box," *Outsiders* (3) #6 (January 2004), [15].

54. Winick, Conrad, and Parsons, *Outsiders* (3) #11, [21].

55. J.T. Krul et al., "Domestic Disturbance," *Justice League: The Rise of Arsenal* #3 (July 2010), [24].

56. Krul et al., *Justice League: The Rise of Arsenal* #3, [28].

57. Eric Wallace, Fabrizio Fiorentino, and Cliff Richards, "Family Reunions, Part 3: The Future's So Dark…" *Titans* (2) #30 (February 2011), [14].

58. Winick, Clark, Thibert, *Outsiders* (3) #31, [8].

59. Wolfman, Pérez, and Tanghal, "The New Teen Titans," *The New Teen Titans* (1) #1 (November 1980), 13.

60. Wolfman, Pérez, and Tanghal, "The Terminator," *The New Teen Titans* (1) #2 (December 1980), 7.

61. Wolfman, Pérez, and Tanghal, *The New Teen Titans* (1) #2, 8.

62. Wolfman, Pérez, and Tanghal, *The New Teen Titans* (1) #2, 9.

63. Wolfman, Pérez, and Tanghal, "Starfire Unleashed!" *The New Teen Titans* (1) #16 (February 1982), 2.

64. Wolfman, Pérez, and Tanghal, "Dear Mom and Dad," *The New Teen Titans* (1) #20 (June 1982), 7.

65. Wolfman, Pérez, and Tanghal, "Transition," *The New Titans* #55 (June 1989), 16.

66. Chuck Dixon et al., "Book Three," *Robin: Year One* #3 (New York: DC Comics, December 2000), 11.

67. Wolfman, Pérez, and Bob McLeod, "Study in Steel," *The New Titans* #57 (August 1989), 10.

68. Wolfman, Pérez, and McLeod, "Who Is Wonder Girl? (Part III of V)—Trackdown," *The New Titans* #52 (January 1989), 19.

69. Marv Wolfman et al., "Resolution," *The New Teen Titans* (2) #31 (May 1987), 29.

70. Marv Wolfman, Chuck Patton, and Mike DeCarlo, "Fearsome Five Minus One!" *Tales of the Teen Titans* #56 (August 1985), 16.

71. Wolfman, Pérez, and Tanghal, *The New Teen Titans* (1) #38, 12.

72. Wolfman, Eduardo Barreto, and Tanghal, "Crisis," *The New Teen Titans* (2) #13 (October 1985), 10.

73. Wolfman, Pérez, and Frank Chiaramonte, "The Fearsome Five!" *The New Teen Titans* (1) #3 (January 1981), 5.

74. Wolfman, Pérez, and Tanghal, "Promethium: Unbound!" *The New Teen Titans* (1) #10 (August 1981), 12.
75. Devin Grayson, Mark Buckingham, and Wade Von Grawbadger, "The Immortal Coil, Part 3," *The Titans* (1) #12 (February 2000), 17.
76. Wolfman, Barreto, and Tanghal, *The New Teen Titans* (2) #13, 9.
77. Wolfman, Pérez, and Chiaramonte, *The New Teen Titans* (1) #3, 6.
78. Wolfman, Grummett, and Al Vey, "Beginnings ... Endings ... and (we promise) New Beginnings!" *The New Titans* #71 (November 1990), 5.
79. Wolfman et al., "Titansmania," *The New Teen Titans* (2) #6 (March 1985), 22.
80. Dan Mishkin, Erik Larsen, and Mike DeCarlo, "The Secret Origin of Nightwing," in *Secret Origins* #13 (New York: DC Comics, April 1987), 17.
81. Wolfman, Chuck Patton, and Tanghal, "The Night Before," *The New Teen Titans* (2) #16 (January 1986), 9.
82. Wolfman, Patton, and Tom Poston, "First Blood" in *Action Comics Weekly* #614 (New York: DC Comics, August 23, 1988), 6.
83. Wolfman, Barreto, and Tanghal, "Crimes and Punishment!" *The New Teen Titans* (2) #48 (October 1988), 10.
84. Paul Levitz, Eduardo Barreto, and Pablo Marcos, "Trivial Pursuits," *The New Teen Titans* (2) #32 (June 1987), 10.
85. Wolfman, Barreto, and Tanghal, "Breaking Up is Hard to Do," *The New Teen Titans* (2) #19 (April 1986), 9.
86. Wolfman, Barreto, and Tanghal, *The New Teen Titans* (2) #19, 17.
87. Wolfman, Barreto, and Tanghal, "Homecoming," *The New Teen Titans* (2) #18, 26.
88. Wolfman et al., "Resolution," *The New Teen Titans* (2) #31, 25.
89. Wolfman, Barreto, and Tanghal, "Loser Take All!" *The New Teen Titans* (2) #23 (August 1986), 27.
90. Wolfman, Barreto, and Tanghal, "Non Compos Mento: Epilogue," *The New Teen Titans* (2) #34 (August 1987), 26.
91. Wolfman, Grummett, and Vey, "The Darkening Part One: An Unholy Pact," *The New Titans* #97 (May 1993), 11.
92. Wolfman, Grummett, and Vey, "The Darkening Part Three: The Brotherhood," *The New Titans* #99 (July 1993), 23.
93. Wolfman, Grummett, and Vey, "The Darkening Chapter Four: Something Old, Something New, Something Borrowed, Something ... DEAD," *The New Titans* #100 (August 1993), 14.
94. Wolfman, Grummett, and Vey, *The New Titans* #100, 15.
95. Wolfman, Grummett, and Vey, *The New Titans* #100, 19.
96. Devin Grayson et al., "The Price of Victory," *The Titans* (1) #19 (September 2000), 21.
97. Judd Winick et al., "Family Affair (Part II)—Sins of the Father," *Titans* (2) #3 (August 2008), 12.
98. Judd Winick et al., "I Know Your Heart Because I Know Mine," *Titans* (2) #5 (October 2008), 11.
99. Winick et al., *Titans* (2) #5, 12.
100. J.T. Krul, Angel Unzueta, and Wayne Faucher, "Fractured, Part 1," *Titans* (2) #21 (March 2010), 13.
101. Judd Winick, Dan Jurgens, and Nelson, "A Change of Plans," *Outsiders* (3) #16 (November 2004), 15.

Darkly Deconstructing the Dynamic Duo

Dick Grayson in Frank Miller

ALEXANDRA SCHULZ

In the spirit of honesty, and with all due respect to the excellent pedigree that this book possesses: *All-Star Batman and Robin, The Boy Wonder* (ASBAR) is one hell of a mess. Since it came out in 2005, it has become a thing of notoriety, launching an entire fleet of memes and inside jokes due to its lurid writing, relentless over-the-top grittiness, and equally over-the-top, radical interpretations of beloved DC characters.

It is the home of "I'm the goddamn Batman." Multiple copies of an issue had to be recalled in order to keep Barbara Gordon from announcing herself as "the fucking Batgirl."[1] It has Wonder Woman calling men "sperm banks," then falling in lust with Superman some pages later because he's strong enough to knock her off her feet. And a few pages after declaring himself "the goddamn Batman," the goddamn Batman exclaims "Nuts? You want nuts, kid? I'll show you nuts!" before running down a couple of police officers while Dick Grayson ("age twelve") screams in the passenger's seat. And we haven't even gotten to the part where Batman abandons a traumatized Dick in the Batcave, suggesting that food "will present itself," at which point a rat comes scuttering out.

ASBAR contains all of that and more, which makes it ripe for parody and has earned it a reputation as a sometimes reviled, often inexplicable Batman book. It says something when people argue to this day whether the work is meant to be taken seriously, or meant to be read as an author's vicious parody of a style that he himself helped popularize.[2]

So why, then, do I love this book so damn much?

The easy answer is that all of the above also makes this title endlessly entertaining. In a world where entertainment is focus-tested and carefully calibrated for our enjoyment, it is really fun to discover something that makes you stare at every page in sheer disbelief. And it helps that those pages are gorgeous. While Frank Miller's story goes off the rails, Jim Lee's artwork never falters, delivering beautiful, sharply rendered scenes to the last panel. With its idiosyncratic, eccentric tone and splashy, luxurious artwork, ASBAR appears to be nothing short of a deranged miracle. I'd call it a gem, if gems could also be certifiably insane.

But that's not why I'm writing this essay, for this book.

For someone interested in the relationship between Dick Grayson's Robin and Bruce Wayne's Batman, ASBAR presents a stark, unique re-imagining that is deeply fascinating. Frank Miller uses all of the familiar beats of Dick Grayson's origin story and then turns them on their head, which results in a dark funhouse mirror image of the Dynamic Duo. Amidst all the chaos that ASBAR unleashes, Bruce's encounter with Dick is the emotionally fraught (and occasionally psychologically plausible) thread that keeps it together. It's also the only arc that reaches a remotely satisfying momentary end point in an otherwise unfinished series.

Seeing Bruce Wayne's and especially Dick Grayson's portrayal in ASBAR becomes even more intriguing considering that it's officially part of Miller's "Dark Knight Universe" (Earth–31 in DC multiverse terms)—where their partnership was revealed to have ended bitterly off-panel in *The Dark Knight Returns* (TDKR), and their relationship is *permanently* ended by Bruce dropping Dick down an active volcano on-panel in *The Dark Knight Strikes Again* (DK2). Both TDKR, and more importantly DK2, were written before ASBAR (in 1986 and 2001, respectively), so it is interesting to see Frank Miller re-visit an earlier point in time for his rendition of Batman, and a relationship and character—Dick Grayson—that came to a sardonic end in the finale of his saga.

Much has been written about Frank Miller's interpretation of Batman and Bruce Wayne, and with good reason. For all the macho posturing, he outfits the hero with a psychology and pathology that remains fascinating to explore to this day, even if the gritty comic anti-hero archetype of the 1980's may have run its course.

However, his take on Dick Grayson is quite interesting, since the Dark Knight Saga presents a trajectory that's incredibly unusual for this character, who is known for his optimism, be it as Robin, Nightwing or Batman, and who is often associated with being the "light" to Bruce Wayne's "darkness." Dick only appears in two of Miller's four main Batman works (incidentally, it's the two that are notorious for being insane), and both books offer a radically different view on him that contradict in parts and correspond in others.

On the following pages, I would like to track Dick Grayson's role throughout the Dark Knight Saga, with a special focus given to his star turn in ASBAR, which contains hope and horror in equal measures, and might or might not lead him down the homicidal path he finds himself on in DK2.

A Short History of Dick Grayson in Miller

Dick Grayson, the first Robin, is merely a faint memory in Frank Miller's highly influential *The Dark Knight Returns*, which came out in 1986. It's two other characters that shape the Robin legacy in TDKR—Jason Todd, the second Robin, whose death prompted Bruce Wayne to hang up the cowl,[3] and Carrie Kelley, the idealistic teenager who claims the Robin name for herself and provides Bruce with the shot to the spine that he needs once he swings back into action as Batman.

Dick is almost wholly absent from TDKR's narrative, except for an interesting moment where Batman, out of retirement, goes to confront a gang of Mutants, simultaneously thrilled and terrified about facing a new, upgraded kind of foe. Out of nowhere, Bruce—lonely and profoundly isolated from all former allies except for a retired Gordon and his butler Alfred, who implores him to turn back—starts to narrate his upcoming adventure to Dick Grayson in his mind.[4]

In this tense, decisive moment, Batman's thoughts go back to the partner that he lost, as if for comfort. This becomes even more pronounced some pages later, as Batman is losing his fight against the Mutant leader, and is moments from passing out from his injuries: "…Dick … Where are you … Dick … You were always … my little monkey wrench…." This is the cue for Carrie to arrive and make her debut as Batman's helper, while a delirious Bruce mistakes her for his former partner: "…Got yourself in deep again, Dick … Always … in over your head…."[5]

Of course, in the context of TDKR, this entire scene marks Bruce's realization that he needs help in his crusade, and lays the groundwork for his future relationship with Carrie. But it also implies that, no matter what might have transpired between Bruce and Dick to end their partnership, Bruce remembers him with some fondness and a sense of bittersweet nostalgia.

However, this notion gets turned on its head in *The Dark Knight Strikes Again*, the direct sequel to TDKR that came out 15 years later. Here, Bruce and Dick's shared past re-emerges with a vengeance, and the reader is presented with a radically different picture.

DK2 is a garish book, both in its grim content and frenetic, often distorted artwork. In terms of Miller's Batman output, it represents a departure from the ambitious, but tight plotting in TDKR (and *Batman: Year One*), hinting at the unchecked chaos that will reign in Miller's final Batman book. DK2 has even more going on than ASBAR, with Batman leading a revolution against Superman and a corrupt U.S. government puppeteered by Lex Luthor and Brainiac.

Dick Grayson's return to the fray is a stealthy one. Throughout the pages of DK2 and mostly untethered to the main storyline, a grotesque, seemingly immortal Joker lookalike is shown stalking and killing super heroes (among his victims are Martian Manhunter and the Creeper). Since the original Joker has killed himself by snapping his own neck in TDKR, his identity remains a mystery for most of the book.

It soon becomes clear that, much like the old Joker, he has a specific obsession with Batman, but even more so a seething hatred for Carrie Kelley, former Robin, now Catgirl. At the end of the book, the killer finally commits a vicious assault on Carrie, one that is clearly motivated by jealousy of her relationship with the Batman: "He loves you. The daughter he never had. So pretty. Sweet Sixteen. I'm going to skin you alive."[6]

Batman, who has successfully orchestrated his revolution at this point, is forced to return to the Batcave in order to save Carrie's life, and, in a twist that surely comes as startling to first time readers, the mysterious killer is revealed to be Bruce's discarded first Robin, Dick Grayson. What follows is the true showdown of DK2—a bitter, deeply personal confrontation between the two former partners who have nothing but contempt for each other.

It's a scene that will inevitably lead readers to believe that Frank Miller, to put it lightly, does not care for Dick Grayson very much. In a book that's full of character renderings that border on caricature, Dick's portrayal seems flat-out mean-spirited, his appearance and demeanor grotesque. Dick has not been idle during those years apart, as it turns out. Instead, he's allowed some unseen nefarious force ("your bosses," as Batman refers to them, and that is all we learn[7]) to turn him into a genetic experiment, making him ostensibly indestructible. With his hairy, adult body squeezed into the boyish, classic Robin uniform, he looks bizarre, emphasizing the stark contrast between the smooth, wholesome image of Robin and the bleak reality of an aged and deranged Dick unwilling to let go of his past (as Batman puts it, he's "pathetic" and "plain weird-looking"[8]). It's apparent that he's undergone this procedure in order to get back at Batman. Disappointed love looms large over the entire confrontation, as Dick repeatedly screams "I loved you!"[9] while Bruce cruelly mocks him by calling him pet names like "Peach," "Button," and "Plum."[10]

(This scene can, of course, be read as a confrontation between an abandoned son and his distant father; reviewer Peter Sanderson calls it an "Oedipal nightmare."[11] But there is a strong undercurrent of both homoeroticism and homophobia to the exchange that suggests other readings, as well. Frank Miller has called the Joker a "homophobic nightmare"[12] and gave him effeminate mannerisms in TDKR; now Dick first assumes the identity of the Joker for a while, and is then acting like a jilted lover towards Batman. There is also an unmistakable triangle going on between Bruce, Carrie, and Dick[13]; Dick's hatred of Carrie can be interpreted as sibling rivalry, but it also has shades of something else, with Dick calling Carrie Bruce's "daughter he never had," but then also his "little piece of jailbait."[14]

There's a disturbing notion here almost as if Dick's—possibly romantic or sexual—infatuation with Bruce and his effeminate demeanor are supposed to make him even more repugnant and deserving of Bruce's contempt. However, the treatment of homoeroticism in Miller's work goes so deep that exploring it would go beyond the scope of this essay. It is hard to ignore the subtext of this scene, however.)

We also now finally get privy to more details about the falling out of Bruce and Dick's working relationship, when Batman says that he fired him "For incompetence. For cowardice,"[15] which are obviously not the first things that come to mind if you think of Dick Grayson as he is usually portrayed. It also seems to contradict the earlier characterization in TDKR, where Batman does mention that Dick was called "the Boy Hostage" by Two-Face, but also fondly remembers him as his little "monkey wrench" who'd "get in over his head," but apparently provided essential support. In DK2, he tells him, "You were pathetic. You were always pathetic. You're still pathetic."[16]

The Dick Grayson of this universe has turned into an insane murderer, and it's therefore not surprising to see Batman take a stand against him (even though Batman abandons his no-killing rule in this very comic, applauding the killing of Lex Luthor and musing that it's "a whole new ballgame"[17] now). But the vitriol on display seems to transcend the character level, crossing the line into author's point of view. This impression grows even stronger considering that this scene comes out of nowhere and has no relation to the main storyline; it appears to stand for itself, speak for itself.

At the end of the encounter Bruce, after having unsuccessfully tried to decapitate Dick with an axe (he simply puts his head back on), throws himself at him in a deadly embrace—another mockery of spurned affection—and hurls them both into the mouth of the volcano that somehow resides underneath the Batcave. But he wouldn't be Batman if he didn't have an exit strategy. A now compliant Superman saves him, while Dick falls to his death.

There is some significance to this scene that does tie into the larger themes of DK2. A big motif in the book is the clash between Silver Age style comic book heroics, and the moral complexities of the Modern Age. Instead of fighting muggers or showy supervillains, Batman overthrows governments, because that's where his crusade against crime takes him in a corrupted world. Dick Grayson's Robin, as he is known to most readers, represents the idealism of a bygone era—a brightly colored, wide-eyed boy whose best friend is a man dressed as a Bat. In DK2, this image gets perverted into a shrill nightmare, since such innocence can't exist in the pages of this book.[18]

When Bruce finds Dick in the Batcave, his reaction is to activate its self-destruction sequence. He does it with the words, "ZAP. BIFF. POW.," a callback to the 1960's Batman TV show, which had Batman at his most playful and whimsical—the complete opposite to Miller's Dark Knight.[19] The Batcave is a relic from a different time, and it self-destructs while the resurrected "Robin" takes his last stand.

As Batman watches Dick plummet to his death, he utters a line that could be laconic but might also be nostalgic: "So long, Boy Wonder."[20] There simply is no place for Boy Wonders where he is going.[21]

On a meta level, this offers some explanation for the state of Bruce and Dick's relationship at this point in the Dark Knight Saga; but on a story level, the reader is left wondering exactly what happened. Due to the nature of the scene, both Bruce and Dick are unreliable narrators of the past they've shared. Driven mad, Dick is stuck in a loop of rejected love: "I loved you! I would've done anything for you!"[22] he screams, even as Batman lobs his head off. Bruce, ever the ruthless cynic as written by Miller, purposely riles him up by repeating said rejection: "So what? You were useless. You didn't have the chops. You couldn't cut the mustard[,]"[23] and recounts with glee how Dick "bawled like a baby" when he fired him.[24]

Since one is a deranged killer and one the titular hero of the book, the implication is that the scene is supposed to play out in the Dark Knight's favor. But from Dick's needy insanity to Bruce's incessant taunting, Miller seems to suggest something ugly and abusive about the original Dynamic Duo that remains unexamined. In the end, whatever those issues were, they get buried along with Dick. However, only three years later, they rose again when Miller took on writing duties for *All Star Batman and Robin, the Boy Wonder*, re-telling Dick Grayson's origin and his encounter with Bruce Wayne's Batman as arguably only he could.

It's ironic, since the title was supposed to turn a fresh page for these characters. DC's *All Star* imprint was intended as a place to tell timeless, classic stories that weren't bogged down by current comics' continuity, providing easy access for first-time readers, or people who hadn't been following recent events but wanted to pick up a Batman or Superman book anyway. For this purpose, *All Star Batman* was outfitted with a stellar cast of creators with Miller on writing, the highly accomplished Jim Lee on art, and long-time Lee collaborators Scott Williams and Alex Sinclair on ink and colors respectively. Launched with great fanfare in 2005, the comic did definitely not turn out as advertised. As Batman traumatizes a newly orphaned Dick Grayson on the page, the comic traumatized readers and critics alike.[25]

In his foreword to the 2008 trade edition, DC editor Bob Schreck restates his trust in the creative team behind ASBAR, assuring readers that "they know exactly what they are doing."[26] However, in 2010, DC announced that the still unfinished title would be re-branded as "Dark Knight, Boy Wonder,"[27] therefore moving it from the "timeless" *All Star* brand and incorporating it into Frank Miller's Dark Knight universe—which is where it belongs. As a "classic" re-telling of Dick's origin, ASBAR will make your head explode—as a dark companion piece to DK2, it not only makes some sense, but also enriches a character who formerly appeared as a mean-spirited gag.

Analysis: Dark Knight, Boy Wonder

Dick Grayson's appearance in the first volume of ASBAR couldn't start out further away from his mean-spirited rendering in DK2. On the very first page, we see a young Dick as the epitome of carefree innocence, bright-eyed and laughing as he soars through the air in the circus tent. ("We love him from the moment we first see him," Frank Miller writes in his script.)[28]

"This should get me killed. But it won't," Dick thinks. "They're always there for me. They always catch me. Mom and Dad. They always catch me. They're always there for me. They're always there for me. I fly."[29] Much fun has been poked at the repetitive writing in ASBAR, but it can make certain moments land, as it does here. Rather than an ongoing train of thought, this illustrates Dick's state of being, as a child secure in his parents' love and protection, like any child should be. He's filled with confidence and optimism and most importantly, trust, and that is what enables him to fly. But flying is, by design, a state of in-betweenness. Dick is depicted suspended in mid-air, frozen in a moment of happiness that can't possibly last, primed for either a landing, or a fall. It's not subtle, but it builds the tension towards the moment we know is coming, the moment where all of this will be taken from him.

In his script, Miller emphasizes Dick's "trusting, sweet smile"—and the shattering of trust and any feeling of safety will be a repeating motive for Dick's arc in this book.[30] Over the course of the first issue, Dick's trust in his parents always being there will be destroyed by the bullets ending their lives. His trust in the authorities will be destroyed when the police ostensibly take him in for questioning, but then drive him out to a solitary gulch to silence him permanently, since they apparently have a stake in the Graysons' murder.[31]

And by the end of the first issue, Dick will be grabbed (literally) by the shadowy figure of the Batman, who informs him that he's been "drafted" into a "war."[32] He throws him into his car, and they go on a nightmarish ride that marks the beginning of an unstable relationship. Dick Grayson is saved by Batman; but it becomes clear throughout the book that he isn't *safe* with Batman.

In order to fully examine Miller's deconstructive take on Dick's origin story, it might be prudent to acknowledge a certain fact—the way Bruce Wayne and Dick Grayson's relationship is established in the Batman universe is a little weird to begin with, especially for modern readers. As it goes, Bruce Wayne is in the audience the night that Dick's parents get murdered; he's deeply moved by the boy's tragic loss, not in the least because it mirrors his own, so he "takes him in," and Dick becomes his ward.

Written in the 1940s, where it wasn't uncommon to pair an adult hero with an adoring boy sidekick in order to draw in young readers, there is a wholesome story in there, the story of two kindred spirits finding each other and forming a surrogate family. However, in a certain sense, it is *also* the story of a rich man taking an orphaned boy that he has no affiliation with, simply because he can. This in itself might raise a few questions; and that's even before they both embark on a double life together that prompts them to assume secret identities and lie to everyone.

This inherent weirdness is threaded into the relationship, and has been the cause for speculation and nervous laughter for ages,[33] from Fredric Wertham's gay panic in *Seduction Of The Innocent*,[34] to the mocking reaction of a panel of DC comic writers to an audience member's suggestion that Bruce and Dick's is a "father and son"-relationship in 2013.[35]

The other aspect that raises eyebrows with Dick's inception is his age when he assumes the identity of Robin. An 8 to 12 year old boy fighting crime alongside the Caped Crusader is perfectly acceptable as an escapist fantasy, but as comics became grittier and Gotham City's violence more realistic, it now potentially invites the unfortunate implication of a grown man building a traumatized orphan into a child soldier. (Especially since Bruce Wayne later repeats that pattern with no less than four other children/teens that cross his path, at least two of which die).[36]

This issue can be sidestepped by sensible writing; in several re-tellings of Dick's origin, he's so consumed by a desire for vengeance that he begins hunting his parents' killer on his own, and Bruce only intervenes in order to keep him from endangering himself or others. He reveals himself to be Batman and involves Dick in his crime fighting with the expressed intention to save him from treading on a darker, lonelier path, and he properly trains him, so he will be prepared for the things he will be facing.[37] While Bruce's decision to let Dick take part in his crusade will probably never look entirely reasonable through a modern lens, it turns into something a little more empathic and benevolent this way.

In ASBAR, Frank Miller takes the already existent, discomforting implications of Dick's origin and toys with them throughout, painting an unsettling picture. In the noir-ish world of ASBAR, Bruce's "taking" of Dick becomes a literal kidnapping, stripped of any attempts to make it socially acceptable.[38] Even the repeated mentions of Dick's age throughout ASBAR (he is referred to as being "age twelve" no less than 10 times over 10 issues, by my count), which border on the ridiculous, serve to hammer home the twistedness of the situation.

Bruce Wayne is present at the circus when Dick's parents die in this version, as well, but he's there for a reason. "I've had my eyes on him for a while," he tells his date Vicki Vale about young Dick, without making her privy to the reason, of course.[39] Bruce has been secretly scouting the promising acrobat for a possible role in his crime fighting crusade and contemplates recruiting him, though by his own admission not "until he's old enough to shave."[40] This calculated approach already sets ASBAR apart from many other versions of Dick's origin, where Bruce being at the circus is painted as more of a chance—or even fated—encounter. Right from the start, there's a creepy predatory element to a grown man stalking a young boy for his own purposes, an element that's consistently present in ASBAR, such as when Batman later remarks that Dick "just might *do*,"[41] and that he needs him "good and scared."[42]

But whatever Bruce's plans may be—and his later actions suggest that he hasn't gotten *too* far in mapping those out—they all go to hell once Dick's parents get shot, and suddenly, Bruce gets stuck with a traumatized child. And Dick Grayson, age twelve, gets stuck with a strange man in a costume whose car is a rocket and who sets people on fire for fun.

It's a small detail, but the demise of Dick's parents differs from the classic versions as well. Instead of falling to their deaths, they both get shot by a sniper, a moment that is rendered in deliberately brutal detail, with blood shooting out of their heads as the bullets pierce their skulls; blood that splatters all over their twelve year old son, who looks on, dumbstruck. It's a crass and cruel image that immediately establishes the violent world that Dick will be dragged into. It also makes for a stronger parallel to the death of the Waynes, which is very important to the way Bruce and Dick's relationship unfurls in ASBAR.

Bruce, watching from the bleachers, witnesses the scene and immediately starts identifying with Dick. "He doesn't understand. He can't possibly understand. I couldn't, when it happened to me."[43]

Like in any other version, Dick's trauma evokes empathy in Bruce, but instead of making him openly compassionate, it leads to him lashing out against the boy. Because this Bruce Wayne hasn't even begun to heal. He's unstable, driven by rage. From the very first moment, Batman's main priority is to keep Dick from grieving—when the boy breaks down over his parents' death, Batman hits him. He immediately regrets it, and his inherent empathy resurfaces ("I'm *torturing* this boy. *Torturing* him. Just *look* at him. He's a *baby*. And I'm *torturing* him. It's a *terrible* thing to do."[44]). But then his thoughts circle back to his refusal to acknowledge his own grief, which cuts to the very heart of every interaction that takes place between Bruce and Dick: "It's the only *way*. If I don't keep the *pressure* up, he might find time to *grieve*. I can't let him *grieve*. *Grief* is the *enemy*. […] *Grief* turns into *acceptance. Forgiveness. Grief* forgives what can *never* be forgiven."[45]

Whenever Batman starts getting affected by Dick's pain, he clings harder to the crutch that he's built for himself—"the *mission*."[46] The very thing that makes Bruce Wayne and Dick Grayson's connection so strong—the shared trauma of watching their parents die—turns into something volatile and dangerous.

On the other end of this interaction, Dick Grayson (age twelve) finds himself in the company of a masked stranger who kidnaps him, attempts to dose him with drugs, hits him when he nearly begins to cry, and tells him never to talk to cops, a series of actions with implications so grim it almost crosses over into pitch-black comedy (because all of these things make sense in Batman's overheated mind, yet they come across horribly). Considering his circumstances, Dick conducts himself admirably. Contrasting Batman's statement from DK2 about Robin's "cowardice and incompetence," this early iteration of Dick displays neither. Despite the terror he understandably feels,[47] he resists Batman's attempts to intimidate him. He is astute enough to realize that Batman is a put-on persona, and to notice the cracks in the façade.[48] He's also able to pick up on the fact that there's something about him that affects Batman on a personal level. ("I guess I get a *reaction* out of him."[49]) Dick Grayson has always been a character known for his empathy and adeptness, and both are on display here.

But beneath that, something darker is happening with Dick. He is terrified of dealing with his parents' death—he reminds himself twice to "not go there"—a behavior that is amplified by Batman, who actively tries to push him away from pain and into anger. When he tells him to "Be brave, Dick Grayson,"[50] it sounds almost encouraging and compassionate compared to the rest of his behavior, but Batman's idea of bravery is one that represses all vulnerability.

He delivers Dick to the Batcave, a subterranean playground outfitted with weapons and cars, robots and dinosaurs.[51] The cave, like Bruce's Batmobile (the name of which gets mocked twice, once by Dick and once by Black Canary), is a testament to his arrested development. Like a spoiled child, he vies for Dick's approval of his cave of toys ("Whatta you *say*, junior? Is this cool, or *what*?"[52]), and is displeased when Dick downplays how impressed he is in front of his kidnapper. ("I guess this is okay."[53])

"I don't think I like this kid," Bruce determines. "Not one bit."[54] It's another characteristic of ASBAR that Bruce, who is emotionally stunted, and Dick, who is a very perceptive boy, approach each other on a similar level of maturity.[55] "Cool," thinks Batman as he's out hunting criminals during a thunderstorm. "Cool," thinks Dick as he finds a battle axe in the Batcave and decides to wield it.[56] But of course, Bruce holds all the power and Dick none, which makes it extremely disturbing. It's notable that Bruce's influence leads to Dick committing his first act of violence, when he uses said axe to kill a rat—not for eating, but because it won't stop hissing at him. ("I've never killed *anything* before," he states, "Maybe I've gone as *crazy* as *he* is."[57])

On a certain level, Bruce is aware that he is not prepared to handle Dick.[58] His only response is to keep forcing the boy into the patterns that he went through in order to push his pain as far down as possible. His suggestion that Dick eat rats is shocking, but we later find out through Alfred that this is something that Bruce inflicted on himself as well, spending "time below" in order to steel himself.[59]

His next move is to apprehend the man who shot Dick's parents and deliver him to the boy, offering him the choice to kill him. He judges that Dick "passes muster" when he chooses to interrogate the man instead.[60] Bruce wears a proud grin as he watches Dick kicking the living daylights out of the tied-up assassin, and admires his athletic capabilities. "I'm starting to *like* this little *snot*."[61] Moments later, he refers to himself as a possible "father" to Dick for the first time.[62] The thirst for vengeance is the common ground on which they start to build a less hostile relationship. (In a sense, this common ground is not a far cry from the classic depiction of Bruce and Dick, but in a much more straightforward way.)

Dick has no choice but to adapt to this, and does so swiftly, again demonstrating his quick wit and adeptness. On Batman's orders, he builds a vigilante identity for himself, a hooded archer called "Hood" (he *is* twelve years old), based on an old movie that his father used to watch with him— Robin Hood. He's again mirroring Bruce, who took inspiration from Zorro, also in reference to his father. Batman dismisses his chosen name and costume immediately, pointing out how a hood can be used against him in a fight, and chooses his identity *for* him: "Lose the hood. You're *Robin*."[63] Dick is left thinking, "I can't do *anything* right around this guy."[64] Isolated from the rest of the world, Batman's approval is the one thing he has left to gain.

In order to get the police and the media off his trail, Batman stages a press conference in which Dick resurfaces to the public eye. He makes Dick perform for the cameras, assuring everyone that he's fine, and that Batman is "about ten feet tall" and "hairy all over," but that he's "nice."[65] Bruce therefore makes him complicit in his own kidnapping. Dick officially gets admitted to a trauma clinic, but in reality stays tucked away in Bruce's cave. It's unclear whether Miller had planned to rectify this and give Dick some sort of official legal status later on—but as it stands, this vanishing act amplifies his isolation and the sense of him being a captive of Batman.

However, for a while, Bruce's approach to Dick appears to work; the boy adopts his new role and seems to cope. He makes his debut as Robin in a confrontation with Green Lantern (as it turns out, the Justice League has taken note of Batman's activities in Gotham—including the kidnapping of a young boy—and they don't approve). Here, Batman and Robin appear as a unit, a functional double act, striking poses, trading quips and taking turns to mock and provoke Hal Jordan.[66] Their unity is further emphasized by the slightly bizarre fact that they're both painted yellow, since Batman has made Robin paint their entire hideout in the color that's Green Lantern's one weakness. As Robin, Dick seems to have perfectly internalized Batman's antagonistic attitude toward the outside world, and he proves it by stealing Hal Jordan's Lantern ring in a power play. A fight breaks out, and that is the moment where it all comes crashing down, and the effect of Batman's tutelage *really* comes to fruition. Unleashed for the first time after he's been taken, Dick assaults Green Lantern and crushes his trachea, nearly killing him. Under the influence of Batman, he has become so separated from his empathy and so tuned into his anger that he does it without blinking. "I almost *killed* a man tonight. A man who never did me any *harm*. And I *enjoyed* every *second* of it," he reflects later, "More than I've ever enjoyed *anything*. I *wanted* to *kill* him."[67] The bright-eyed kid that used to take so much joy in soaring freely through the air at the circus seems a long way away. He has become as vicious and vindictive as his mentor/captor; or, trapped in an unsafe environment, he might have become something worse. And Bruce, who has been using scare tactics on Dick ever since they've met, is terrified.

It's a turning point, and not only because Dick finds out in this scene that Batman is Bruce Wayne (he pulls off his cowl as he works on Hal Jordan, therefore showing Dick more of himself than he ever has before.) After narrowly saving Green Lantern's life, Batman and Robin flee the scene, which is when Dick finally breaks down and cries, and Bruce lets him. "I'm *crying* and *gulping* like the little *snot* he *said* I was," Dick thinks, already counting this justified emotional breakdown as a failure.[68]

Meanwhile, Bruce has no choice but to confront the true extent of his actions. "I've taught him how to *fight*. I've taught him how to *kill*. And that's *all* I've taught him. […] I *blew* it." In a direct reversal of his thought process in the night of the Grayson's murder, Bruce realizes that he's been lying to himself: "I had *years*—to *grieve*. To *grieve*. That's where it started…."[69]

Humbled for the first time in the pages of ASBAR, Batman takes Robin to the Graysons' grave so he can say goodbye. In this moment, Bruce fully accepts responsibility for Dick. ("Me, I pray for a *second chance*. A fresh start."[70]) Batman and Robin, two orphans, share an embrace at the grave of Dick's parents. After their emotionally fraught start, this embrace seems comforting (or deeply terrifying, depending on how you view their relationship). But even more important is the fact that they are *both* crying. Over the course of the series, interacting with Dick has brought Batman near tears twice. Once when Dick calls him out on "wasting" the police officers chasing them, which causes Bruce to have to withdraw and collect himself before he can speak again. This also leads to the first moment of human connection between them, as Dick notes that Batman's voice goes "kind of soft" when he warns him about the Gotham cops, and then asks him to "be brave."[71] The second time occurs when Dick asks for new clothes, because his clothes from the circus have his parents' "blood and stuff" on them, which prompts Bruce to flash back to the night of his own parents' murder. It's the other moment where the veneer breaks and Bruce softens up toward Dick: "His *hand* lands on my *shoulder*, weightless as a falling *leaf.* Those bigass *fingers* of his *squeeze* like a gentle *caress.* His *voice* is a *croak.* Like he's about to *cry* or something."[72]

At the gravesite, Batman stops cutting both Dick and himself off from experiencing loss and pain, therefore allowing for a truly human moment. However, it's left open whether this change of heart will last, and if the "fresh start" that Bruce hopes for can really occur, since they have both been irreversibly damaged—Dick in no small part through Bruce's involvement. "We mourn lives lost," is Bruce's closing thought. "Including our own."[73]

Conclusion

After the cathartic scene at the Grayson's grave, we only see the Batman and Robin of ASBAR one last time, as the following issue is the last one that has ever been published. It's the only time we see them fully go into action (with no yellow paint and no attempted murder this time) as they save Catwoman, who has been brutally beaten by the Joker. The Boy Wonder seems to be in a better place than we've seen him before, as he clearly enjoys being on the prowl with Batman, stalking the night and "hitching a ride" on a subway train. But the issue isn't focused on him. What we do get is some inner monologue by Bruce, who makes more of an effort with Dick than before, but is still torn between being impressed by him, and feeling conflicted about him. In the previous issue, he already suspects that Dick "might just be a *genius*. A *genius*—or something *worse*...."[74] In the last issue, he describes Dick as a *"dynamo"* who "dances like a *pixie* across a filthy *room* and makes a *bullet* of his fist," in a clear reference to the way both their parents have been slain, hinting that Dick might have already internalized the violence that made him an orphan.[75]

Since the series ends at this point, it remains unclear whether or not Dick's new life will take a turn for the better or worse. Miller lays the groundwork for both. We have gotten to know Dick in ASBAR as a brave, empathic boy, and the embrace at the gravesite hints at the possibility that he might ultimately bring out the humanity in Batman, so they may help each other to heal. On the other hand, we have seen Batman fan the flames of his anger, we've seen him disconnect from his emotions and learn to use violence as a way to cope with his fear and pain. In a sense, Dick ends ASBAR in the same position that he started out in: in suspension.

The key to whether he crashes or makes a landing is, of course, whether you consider ASBAR and DK2 as part of the same continuity.

I have always liked the fact that both readings are possible. Officially, they both belong into Frank Miller's Dark Knight universe. However, there are enough contradictions to give room for interpretation. When Batman berates Dick in DK2 for being useless and a coward, he doesn't seem to talk about the boy we get to know in ASBAR. Then again, Batman's recollection in DK2 might be false, since his goal in the scene is clearly to upset him. ASBAR has Dick growing reckless and violent, as well as dependent on Batman's approval. With these issues left unchecked by an equally reckless mentor, he might become a character who allows himself to be turned into a human weapon like in DK2. He might return to seek reparations for abuse and abandonment. Personally, I tend to view DK2 as one possible outcome of what ASBAR lays out. In that sense, I like that ASBAR fills in some of the gaps that DK2 has left open, and I especially like how ASBAR deals with Bruce's involvement in Dick's potential descent into madness, after Dick has been painted as purely a villain in DK2.

In DK2's predecessor, TDKR, Batman has the following recollection as he rides into battle against the Mutants: "The *Batmobile*—that's what you called it, Dick. The kind of name a *kid* would come up with...."[76]

In ASBAR, however, the following exchange takes places between Bruce and Dick.

DICK: So what do you call this thing, anyway?
BRUCE: The Batmobile.
DICK: That is totally queer.
BRUCE: Shut up.[77]

These two comic books were written nearly twenty years apart, and in fact, people are debating if even TDKR and its sequel DK2 take place in the same universe. However, I like the contrast of these scenes; in TDKR, Bruce muses that the "Batmobile" is a childish name for a car; in ASBAR, *Bruce* is the grown-up child giving it that name, not Dick (age twelve). This, to me, is exemplary for the shift in perspective that takes place in ASBAR. In DK2, Bruce is the brutally "sane" man vanquishing a Dick

Grayson who's been driven mad. In ASBAR, it becomes clear that *Bruce* is the psychotic, and might as well have been the one setting Dick on that path. Dick's unsympathetic treatment in DK2 turns into a sympathetic one in ASBAR, elevating him from a mean-spirited caricature into a tragic character within the Dark Knight universe. Whether one chooses to view these two books as directly connected or not, they are both enriched by existing alongside each other.

Notes

1. Rich Johnston, "Wash Your Mouth Out With Batsoap," *Lying in the Gutters*, 9 September 2008, http://www.comicbookresources.com/?page=article&id=17985.
2. Jon Morris, "The Year In Tights: the Best (and Worst) Superhero Comics of 2006," *Potlatch,* 2006, http://www.thehighhat.com/Potlatch/007/top10_morris.html.
3. TDKR also provides the first instance of a Robin actually having died in action. The death of Jason Todd as mentioned in TDKR pre-dates the "A Death in the Family" storyline from 1988, where Jason actually meets his cruel fate at the hands of the Joker.
4. Frank Miller, Klaus Janson, and Lynn Varley, *The Dark Knight Returns*, Tenth Anniversary Edition (New York: DC Comics, 1996), 77.
5. Miller, "Book Two," *TDKR*, 82.
6. Frank Miller and Lynn Varley, *The Dark Knight Strikes Again* (New York: DC Comics, 2002), 239.
7. Miller, "Volume Three," *DK2*, 241.
8. Miller, "Book Three," *DK2*, 241.
9. Miller, "Book Three," *DK2*, 243.
10. Miller, "Book Three," *DK2*, 241–242.
11. Peter Sanderson, "Comics in Context #34—Knight Makes Right," 16 April 2004, http://www.ign.com/articles/2004/04/17/comics-in-context-34-knight-makes-right.
12. Christopher Sharrett, "Batman and the Twilight of the Idols: An Interview with Frank Miller," in *The Many Lives Of The Batman,* edited by Roberta E. Pearson and William Uricchio (New York: Routledge, Chapman and Hall, 1991), 36.
13. When asked in an interview if his introduction of Carrie served to defuse and simultaneously acknowledge the inherent homosexual tension in the Batman and Robin relationship, Miller called the notion "preposterous," and defines Bruce and Carrie as a "father/child relationship." However, said homosexual tension is very present in this scene in DK2. Sharrett, "Batman and the Twilight of the Idols," 37–38.
14. Miller, "Book Three," *DK2*, 241.
15. Miller, "Book Three," *DK2*, 241.
16. Miller, "Book Three," *DK2*, 241.
17. Miller, "Book Three," *DK2*, 233.
18. It's of course reductive to see Dick Grayson simply as a representation of the more light-hearted Batman era, as he's a character who has undergone considerable character development, and has successfully been updated for the Modern Age, especially as Nightwing. However, in DK2 he clearly fills that role, since he hasn't psychologically grown since he was Batman's partner. He merely went insane.
19. Miller, "Book Three," *DK2*, 239.
20. Miller, "Book Three," *DK2*, 244.
21. It's interesting to note that Miller has no trouble incorporating *Carrie Kelley's*

Robin into his Batman mythos, at least in TDKR, which is set in a marginally less shattered world than DK2. In his intro to TDKR's Tenth anniversary edition, he talks about how he didn't even consider having Robin in the book until he conceived of Carrie as a character: "I'd never intended to use Robin. But then, one day, I pictured a little bundle of bright colors leaping over buildings, dwarfed by a gray-and-black giant ... and there she was. Robin." (Miller, TDKR, 7.)

As Peter Sanderson speculates: "Maybe Miller just really dislikes the kid sidekick characters of past decades, and created Carrie as an improved version." Sanderson, "Knight Makes Right," 5 (http://www.ign.com/articles/2004/04/17/comics-in-context-34-knight-makes-right?page=5).

This may very well be the case, though the vitriol in DK2 still suggests that his dislike is aimed at Dick Grayson as Robin—or at what he represents—specifically.

22. Miller, "Book Three," *DK2*, 243.
23. Miller, "Book Three," *DK2*, 243.
24. Miller, "Book Three," *DK2*, 241.
25. An exemplary reaction by reviewer Iann Robinson: "I was unable to deal with what I saw on those pages when I first gazed upon this horrible tragedy that claimed to be a comic book." Iann Robinson, "All Star Batman and Robin the Boy Wonder," 17 December 2007, http://www.craveonline.com/comics/articles/154736-all-star-batman-and-robin.
26. Bob Schreck, "Trust. It's all about trust" in Frank Miller and Jim Lee, *Absolute All Star Batman and Robin, the Boy Wonder* (New York: DC Comics, 2014), 8.
27. DC Editorial, "What's Next for Frank Miller and Jim Lee?" 2 April 2010, http://www.dccomics.com/blog/2010/04/02/whats-next-for-frank-miller-and-jim-lee.
28. Frank Miller, "The Complete Script and Penciled Art for All-Star Batman and Robin, the Boy Wonder" in Miller, *Absolute ASBAR*, 245.
29. Miller, "Episode One," *Absolute ASBAR*, 9–10.
30. Miller, "The Complete Script," *Absolute ASBAR*, 245.
31. Miller, "Episode One," *Absolute ASBAR*, 27.
32. Miller, "Episode One," *Absolute ASBAR*, 30.
33. On episode #22 of his podcast, "Fat Man On Batman," filmmaker and writer Kevin Smith applauds the decision to retcon Dick as having not lived with Bruce anymore for the DC reboot "New 52," commenting that this aspect made it look like "Some billionaire just bought a little child who lost his parents." (This retcon has since then been retconned, though Dick's actual living circumstances during his Robin years were never quite cleared up.) Kevin Smith, "Episode #22–#23: Kyle Higgins," Fat Man On Batman Podcast (2012), http://smodcast.com/ channels/fatman-on-batman/ and http://smodcast.com/episodes/kyle-higgins-master-of-dick/.
34. Fredric Wertham, *The Seduction of the Innocent* (New York: Rinehart & Company, 1954).
35. Commenter Scott Mateo at the bleedingcool.com forums recounts: "I asked [Mike] Marts why Dick was no longer Bruce's ward during a panel and he just kinda scoffed and remarked, 'Yeah, some guy and a kid living together,' and rolled his eyes. I quickly threw in '...but I always thought of them as father and son.' To where one of the other panelists chimed in, "Yeah, an adolescent, an adult and their butler all living together," in a mocking tone to where they all, including [Scott] Snyder, broke down giggling like a bunch of school boys. It felt like there was some kind of super secret gay joke or something and they were all making fun of me for it because I just didn't get it." See http://www.bleedingcool.com/forums/front-page-comic-news/74150-fate-nightwing-forever-evil-1-its-implications-spoilers-obviously-20.html#post659753.
36. Jason Todd, Tim Drake, Stephanie Brown and Damian Wayne. Both Jason and

Damian get killed. Stephanie gets presumably killed, but her death was later written as her having gone into hiding.

37. Jeph Loeb and Tim Sale's *Batman: Dark Victory* (New York: DC Comics, 1999, 2000) contains a fairly straight iteration of this.

38. It might be worth noting that Batman repeats a line from TDKR in ASBAR, telling Green Lantern that vigilantes "have to be criminals." By extension, it makes perfect sense that his handling of Dick is criminal.

39. Miller, "Episode One," *Absolute ASBAR*, 20.
40. Miller, "Episode Four," *Absolute ASBAR*, 83.
41. Miller, "Episode Two," *Absolute ASBAR*, 34.
42. Miller, "Episode Two," *Absolute ASBAR*, 44.
43. Miller, "Episode One," *Absolute ASBAR*, 22.
44. Miller, "Episode Two," *Absolute ASBAR*, 51.
45. Miller, "Episode Two," *Absolute ASBAR*, 51.
46. Miller, "Episode Two," *Absolute ASBAR*, 51.
47. Miller, "Episode Two," *Absolute ASBAR*, 45.
48. Miller, "Episode Two," *Absolute ASBAR*, 40, 52.
49. Miller, "Episode Two," *Absolute ASBAR*, 53.
50. Miller, "Episode Two," *Absolute ASBAR*, 53.
51. Miller, "Episode Four," *Absolute ASBAR*, 85–87.
52. Miller, "Episode Four," *Absolute ASBAR*, 88.
53. Miller, "Episode Four," *Absolute ASBAR*, 88.
54. Miller, "Episode Four," *Absolute ASBAR*, 88.
55. You could even argue that Dick is more mature than Bruce, who spends big portions of ASBAR cackling madly, incinerating criminals, and then having sex with Black Canary while said criminals burn to death in the background.
56. Miller, "Episode Five," *Absolute ASBAR*, 116, 120.
57. Miller, "Episode Seven," *Absolute ASBAR*, 161.
58. Miller, "Episode Eight," *Absolute ASBAR*, 179.
59. Miller, "Episode Four," *Absolute ASBAR*, 97.
60. Miller, "Episode Eight," *Absolute ASBAR*, 178.
61. Miller, "Episode Eight," *Absolute ASBAR*, 178.
62. Miller, "Episode Eight," *Absolute ASBAR*, 179.
63. Miller, "Episode Eight," *Absolute ASBAR*, 195.
64. Miller, "Episode Eight," *Absolute ASBAR*, 195.
65. Miller, "Episode Nine," *Absolute ASBAR*, 202.
66. Miller, "Episode Nine," *Absolute ASBAR*, 201–203.
67. Miller, "Episode Nine," *Absolute ASBAR*, 214.
68. Miller, "Episode Nine," *Absolute ASBAR*, 214.
69. Miller, "Episode Nine," *Absolute ASBAR*, 215.
70. Miller, "Episode Nine," *Absolute ASBAR*, 217.
71. Miller, "Episode Two," *Absolute ASBAR*, 53.
72. Miller, "Episode Four," *Absolute ASBAR*, 94.
73. Miller, "Episode Nine," *Absolute ASBAR*, 218.
74. Miller, "Episode Nine," *Absolute ASBAR*, 207.
75. Miller, "Episode Ten," *Absolute ASBAR*, 227.
76. Miller, "Book Two," *TDKR*, 74.
77. Miller, "Episode Three," *Absolute ASBAR*, 75.

Part V

Interviews

Interview with Dennis O'Neil

Kristen L. Geaman[1]

Dennis "Denny" O'Neil is a legendary comic-book writer and editor, having worked for Marvel, Charlton, and DC Comics. For DC fans, O'Neil is probably best remembered for his groundbreaking work on both Green Arrow and Batman; during the 1970s, both heroes were reimagined as darker, grittier, and more socially-conscious. O'Neil tackled the heroin problem in the most famous Green Arrow story to date, a cross-over in *Green Lantern* #85–86 (1971), in which Green Arrow's ward Speedy became addicted to the drug. O'Neil also revived Batman's role as a detective and returned characters such as the Joker to their darker, more homicidal roots. After a stint at Marvel, O'Neil became the editor of the Batman group from 1986–2000. As editor, he oversaw some major moments in the Batman comics, including the death of Jason Todd (the second Robin), the introduction of Tim Drake (the third Robin), and the development of new Bat-Family titles such as *Robin* and *Nightwing*. O'Neil has won several Shazam Awards in recognition of his innovative and compelling work in comics. He currently volunteers for The Hero Initiative charity.

What are your memories of Dick Grayson/Robin when you were a comics-reading kid in St. Louis? What did you think of the whole kid sidekick phenomenon then? (And later?)

I had no opinions—about anything?—at age six. Batman has a kid friend? Okay, Batman has a kid friend. Later, as comics storytelling matured, I thought Robin could be a liability, but by then the relationship was a firm part of the mythos and so the thing to do was work with it.

Your earliest work in superhero/action hero comics was at Marvel and Charlton, which eschewed the kid sidekick characters. And then you came to DC. How did you view its established teen characters, and Dick Grayson/Robin in particular?

Again, no strong feelings. I saw not much wrong with the sidekick concept and by then I may have been hip enough to see the story uses for such a person.

We've heard you are a big proponent of the idea that Batman needs a Robin. What does Robin add to the Batman mythos? What do you think Dick Grayson in particular added?
Well, Batman needs someone to be a stand-in for the reader, to provide exposition, to soften the edges of unavoidably violent plots. Robin, with an occasional assist from Alfred, served those purposes.

What does Robin, and the things he represents, add to superhero comics in general?
See above. He does for Bats what Watson did for Holmes, Archie Goodwin did for Nero Wolfe.

Has Batman outgrown the need for a Robin? If he hasn't yet, might he someday?
You could do Batman without Robin.

You started writing Batman stories when DC was trying hard to move the character away from his portrayal in the "New Look" stories of the mid–1960s and on TV. What do you recall of the decision to send Dick Grayson to Hudson University and give Robin solo stories?
We thought that Batman didn't really need an apprentice, but that having an adolescent in the continuity might come in handy.

How did you decide when to use the Dick Grayson/Robin character in your Batman stories of the 1970s? How did he fit (or not fit) into that period's Batman mythos? Was he more than a useful plot point, as in the "Daughter of the Demon" story? Were you ever asked to remove or add Dick to a story you had already planned?
I said that such a character might come in handy and in the Ra's al Ghul stories, he did. Later writers got some sibling rivalry mileage from him, all to the good. We were never asked to change anything about Robin, per se. I really don't think the execs were much involved in what we did except when it made the papers or maybe when it raised a fuss.

You and Neal Adams made major changes to Speedy's life in *Green Lantern/Green Arrow*; did you discuss using Dick Grayson/Robin's character the same way?
Nope.

You were editor of the Batman comics when *Crisis on Infinite Earths* offered the chance to rewrite Batman and Robin's original origin. How did you decide to leave them mostly unchanged?

I had the option to make changes, but when something isn't broken, why fix it? I didn't, and don't, think we could improve on what we inherited.

On the other hand, a large change was made concerning how Dick Grayson became Nightwing. Before *Crisis on Infinite Earths*, Dick had voluntarily given the Robin mantle to Jason. Post-Crisis (issues #408 and #416), Dick was shot by Joker and fired from the Dynamic Duo by Bruce. Why the change? Whose idea was it? What did it add to the Batman mythos?

I was working for another company at the time and so ... darned if I know. I do recall being told that some of the creative folk wanted to change Robin, but the writer, Gerry Conway, was told to simply clone Grayson and hand another name on him.

In your interview in 1991's *The Many Lives of the Batman*, you commented that many comic-book writing decisions, perhaps even the decision to make Dick Grayson Nightwing, "are seldom made with any long-range plans" (20). Would you agree that becoming Nightwing seems to have been a good move for the Dick Grayson character? Why or why not?

I stand by the interview. Comics guys are not notorious long-range planners. As for Nightwing ... I guess I could argue it either way. But if creative people made it work, they've given us answer. The criterion is, will it make a good story?

How did Dick Grayson return to the Batman desk in the early 1990s? (Or had he never fully left?) The "Knightfall" arc led to "Prodigal," Dick's first stint as Batman—was that always part of the story plan? How did you and your team imagine Dick to be a different Batman?

Once the readers gave Todd the thumbs down, we thought we had a year or so to come up with a substitute Robin. We didn't. I yelled for help and Marv Wolfman and Chuck Dixon answered the call.

Some fans argue that returning Dick to the Batman-fold (and away from the Titans) was not in the best interests of Dick's development as a character and has served to keep him in Batman's shadow. Is that a fair criticism? Are fans misunderstanding what it takes to keep characters entertaining in the world of serial storytelling?

Were they good stories? I realize that "good story" is a matter of opinion, but asking it is the only way I know to deal with the changes you note.

The mid–1990s brought the *Nightwing* miniseries and finally an ongoing series. What was the thinking behind that launch—did the character's popularity push you and your team into coming up with a storyline, or was there a type of story no one else was telling in the DC Universe?

I don't remember who decreed the Nightwing miniseries, or why I got the job of writing it. A possible guess: somebody thought the character needs establishing. So maybe 't'was thought that Nightwing was popular enough to warrant a series. Or it could have been a pilot for a monthly book.

One of the most important things to come out of that 1995 mini-series was Nightwing's new costume. Whose idea was that? How did you reach the decision that the previous costume had to go? Who had the idea for the fingerstripes?

O Lord ... the new suit was probably a ploy to give the character a more distinctive persona. As for the stripes ... I don't think they were my idea. But whose were they? Shrug. The artist's, maybe.

From 1986–2000 you were working with writers on multiple Batman books and some well-remembered crossovers. How did you see Dick Grayson, Nightwing, and his series fitting in with and standing out from the line?

Nightwing was a given, a character who had become part of our playpen. We did the best we could with him, and maybe that was pretty good.

We understand you prided yourself on being a hands-off editor, but are there times when you had to steer creators away from their ideas for Dick Grayson?

I was hands-off in that I tried not to micromanage; my job was to make my people look good and that could mean catching and correcting errors. But I did discuss virtually every plot with the appropriate writers and once or twice a year I tried to get everyone I could under one roof for a day or three of brainstorming/plotting.

When were you surprised by fan reactions to stories about Dick Grayson, either through complaint letters, online chatter, or changes in magazine sales?

Not much fuss reached my desk.

After a break, you returned in 2009 to write *Detective Comics* #852 and *Batman* #684, a two-part story which strongly hints that Dick Grayson/Nightwing will be the next Batman. Why was Dick a good choice for Batman after Bruce's "death"?

He was a logical choice. Good? It really depends on what stories were told about him.

In this story, the character Millicent Mayne narrates many complimentary things about Dick. Despite that, Dick also berates himself in-story for allowing his motorcycle to get stolen. In what ways did you intend for these different strands to work together in setting Nightwing up as the next Batman?

We showed that, admirable though he was, Nightwing was not the ultra-competent Batman. He was in a learning curve and maybe that helped make him interesting. And to the best of my recollection, I wasn't setting Nightwing up for a promotion.

By the way … Millicent Mayne left my computer as Morag Mayne, who was a character in the old Shadow series. Editor differed.

You also did a great job of capturing Dick's more light-hearted personality, especially with quotes such as "Just call me Mr. Snoopypants." Why do you think the original Robin has been able to maintain his fun, optimistic personality even as he ages?

I dunno. Genetics?

In 2010, you wrote *Detective Comics* #866, which featured Dick Grayson as Batman interspersed with flashbacks to his days as Robin. What was it like to write a former Robin as Batman?

It was a job. I'm not going to pretend that I have no emotional attachments to these characters, but when I'm doing a story I'm usually concentrating on the problems that story entails, not any kind of bigger picture.

Are there particular stories about Dick Grayson in any of his roles that you're particularly proud to have been part of, as a writer or editor?

Well, he's an important element in the first Ra's story and that gets him props.

* * *

You are considered a pioneer of the interpretation that Batman is the true identity and Bruce Wayne is the secret identity. This does not seem to hold true for the Robins. Why?

Different character. And it might not be effective storytelling to make one a carbon copy of the other. (Are you old enough to remember carbon copies?)

In your interview in *The Many Lives of the Batman*, you mentioned that historically Batman did not appeal to women (31). Do you think this is still true today? Do you think the Robins are more female-friendly characters?

I think they have evolved toward feminism. A natural and desirable progression. But the stuff is still action/adventure/fantasy melodrama, a genre not associated with women. But there are so many exceptions that the subject is difficult to discuss, especially in a limited format.

Dick Grayson in particular seems to have a large number of female fans. Any idea why? When you were at DC, did the company recognize this and play to female readers at all?

News to me. But I approve. I don't recall ever being told to tailor stuff for a particular audience, male or female.

In the *Many Lives* interview, you noted that you see your Batman and Frank Miller's Batman as the same person—although Miller pushed the concept further (19). Do you see your version of Robin as the same person?

I wonder how Frank would answer your question. Off the top of my (bare) head, I'd say no. But not very loudly. I just don't know.

What impact did Dick Grayson's history and popularity have on the stories of the next two Robins you were enmeshed with: the doomed Jason Todd and the new Tim Drake? Did Dick's character get adjusted to make more room for those characters?

No. Jason, as a character, had lost his way. I felt that we either had to somehow transform him or write him into limbo. Grayson's story had little to do with this. We set out to make a Robin in tune with the times, eliminating or softening some aspects of the Robin persona and amplifying others. And Robin, like Bats, was actually interpreted inconsistently, depending on who was doing what. We wanted to eliminate those inconsistencies.

What do you see as the benefits and drawbacks of the Batman comics having an increasing number of former Robins—Nightwing, Red Hood, and Red Robin?

My gut says no because each additional version detracts from the character's uniqueness and adds to new reader confusion, which may cause them to become ex-readers. But I don't know the particulars, so I can't really comment.

Although Jason's death was unpopular when it occurred, it gave him a prominent place in the Batman saga. How do you think that incident has benefitted the character?

It kept him going. Is that a benefit?

Was bringing Jason Todd back from the dead something you would ever have considered?

No.

As can be seen by earlier questions, you greatly enriched the DC universe with your creations. Of all the characters you created, who is your favorite? The one you are most proud of?

I guess The Question, though the original was a Steve Ditko creation.

In your years as a writer and editor of Batman comics, is there anything you wish you had done differently? Any stories you wanted to tell but were never able to?

I wish I'd handled Azrael differently, made him meaner. No stories I burned to tell, but couldn't. According to one source, I published at least 1,000 comics stories and the total may be higher. That is a lot of yarn and I think I pretty much used it up. But occasionally, I still get an idea...

Note

1. The questions asked herein were solicited from online fans. Geaman compiled and edited them, presenting them in a written format to the interviewee for their answers.

Interview with Marv Wolfman

Kristen L. Geaman[1]

Marv Wolfman is a legendary comic-book writer, probably best known to Dick-Grayson fans as the writer of *The New Teen Titans* and one-half of the Dynamic Duo of Wolfman and George Pérez. In addition to *NTT*, Wolfman also wrote 1985's *Crisis on Infinite Earths*, a watershed series that streamlined the DC universe; thirteen issues for Dick's solo *Nightwing* title (#125–137); and created Tim Drake (the third Robin). Over at Marvel, Wolfman worked on the horror series *The Tomb of Dracula*, for which he created (with artist Gene Colan) the character Blade. He also wrote *The Amazing Spider-Man* (and created *The Black Cat*), The Fantastic Four (Created Terrax), Daredevil (created Bullseye) and many, many others. Wolfman was Founding editor of Disney Adventures magazine. Beyond comics, Wolfman writes animation, videogames and novels.

What is it like to have been involved with so much comic book history?

It's nothing I think about; I just do what I love and have wanted to do since I was a kid. But when you collect all the different things I've worked on or created it's kind of surprising, even to me. And when fans come by my table at cons and tell me how this story or that meant so much to them, it's extremely gratifying because I remember what I felt like when reading comics as a kid.

What do you see as the overall impact of Dick's transition to Nightwing on both the DCU and comics as a whole, since he was the first sidekick and one of the very first to "grow up" and become his own hero?

When George Pérez and I started New Teen Titans one of my major goals was to take Dick Grayson, who back then was just an acrobat who told outrageous jokes and acted as Batman's boy hostage, into someone worthy of leading a group like the Titans. On George's side, he took this character who looked like a little kid and turned him into a very sexy adult. That meant aging him, making him serious and his own man. He was a teen growing up into becoming a man and I was interested in exploring that. I think George and I succeeded.

What would you say is the greatest legacy and/or impact of the Judas Contract story arc? What did you like most about writing this wonderful arc?

When I first told George my idea for the Judas Contract it was all about surprising the readers by making them assume we were going one way when in fact we went the other. We took known comic book clichés which all readers expected and anticipated (trouble kid is bad at first but is turned around and becomes a good guy) and turned them on their head. At the same time, we had Dick Grayson give up his Robin identity, become Nightwing, introduced Jericho and gave Deathstroke's origin, complete the mission that introduced him, as well as tell the entire Terra story, all in four issues. I'm not sure but I also think this was the first or one of the first times in a comic where a run of stories had their own title "The Judas Contract" as if it was a novel and each issue was a chapter. Today that's done all the time but not back then where it would just have been four issues of the comic.

You've mostly written Dick as Nightwing or as an independent Robin. How differently would you have written him as Batman or Robin, the sidekick? Would you want to write Dick in those roles?

Once I was a teenager I never much liked Robin as the kid partner. I never understood why Batman would put this pun-spouting 10 year old in constant danger. It would be fun to write once or twice but not more than that.

Dick has been Robin, Nightwing, Batman, and is now a "secret agent." What do you feel the future holds for Mr. Grayson? If given the chance to write Dick as something other than a costumed hero, what path might you have taken?

I have no idea. As the person who took Dick Grayson from being the little kid to the responsible adult, I certainly can't complain that someone else moves him into other directions. I just hope every creative team honors the character.

What do you think of the New 52 Dick Grayson? Any thoughts on DC's decision to have the current New 52 Teen Titans as the first incarnation of the group, basically erasing your New Teen Titans and the earlier Teen Titans from existence?

I do not ever read my characters once I leave them. Every new team needs to have the same freedom I had to take the characters and do with them what they believe best. So I have no idea how Dick is treated today. Sorry.

Note

1. The questions asked herein were solicited from online fans. Geaman compiled and edited them, presenting them in a written format to the interviewee for their answers.

Interview with Chuck Dixon

Kristen L. Geaman[1]

Chuck Dixon has a long and storied career in the world of comic books. He began at Comico Comics in 1984 before transitioning to Marvel the following year. Chuck was writing various Punisher titles when he was lured away to DC in 1991. Chuck flourished at DC, and is currently the third most prolific writer in DC's history.[2] Chuck is most noted for his work on Batman comics, including a lengthy run on *Detective Comics* in which he co-created the villain Bane, famous for breaking Batman's back. In addition, Chuck launched three beloved Bat-Family series: *Robin* (for which he wrote 106 issues), *Nightwing* (77), and *Birds of Prey* (46). If you enjoyed the comics about Batman and his allies in the 90s, you can thank Chuck. He left DC around 2008 and has since spent his time writing *GI Joe*, *The Simpsons*, and *Bad Times*, a series of science fiction novels.

When did you first encounter the character of Dick Grayson? What did you think of that version of Robin? Did you keep track of the character as he developed in the '70s and '80s? Were there any particular stories you found most memorable or important when you got the assignment to write him?

My earliest memories were of Dick Grayson as Robin. My favorites were Batman 80-page giants that reprinted Golden Age stories by Bill Finger, Dick Sprang, Jerry Robinson and others. Of them, my favorite was a story called The Strange Costumes of Batman reprinted from a 1950 issue of Detective Comics [issue #165]. It was ostensibly about Batman's all-purpose wardrobe but it's really an awesome Robin story. Batman is shot up by a gangster and the Dynamic Duo fear that Gotham will turn lawless during Batman's recovery. So Robin masquerades as Batman in a special exo-skeleton kind of costume created for just such an eventuality. Robin captures the thug who wounded Batman and protects Gotham and

Interview with Chuck Dixon (Geaman)

proves, to an eight-year-old me anyway, that he's a partner to Batman not a sidekick. I never looked at him the same way again. The story is so important to me that I used elements of it in my second Robin mini-series with Tim Drake. I've also satirized it twice in The Simpsons and SpongeBob Squarepants comic stories.

What was your role in getting the *Robin*, *Nightwing*, and *Birds of Prey* titles off the ground? Did you campaign for the creation of these titles? Was there resistance to creating titles for "sidekick" characters?

Denny O'Neil plucked me from the back benches to work on *Robin*. He told me that he was impressed with my work on Eclipse Comics' Airboy series. Denny says I showed I could write a convincing young character and hired me based on that. *Nightwing* was assigned me after the original writing team had to bail on it. I had three weeks' notice before the first script was due. *Birds of Prey* was the brainchild of editor Jordan B. Gorfinkel who worked hard to convince me that the concept was a winner. He stuck with me until I agreed to write the first special. And he was right, the characters had a great chemistry.

How did you get the assignment to write the *Nightwing* magazine? Was it sudden? How much of Dick Grayson's solo story had been determined for you? Did you plan from the start for him to join the Blüdhaven police force?

I had an inkling that I might want to give him a "day job." Being a cop seemed the right fit since the cops were so damned crooked in Blüdhaven. The biggest challenge on the book was the creation of a new town in the DCU that had never been seen before and to give it its own distinct personality. The other aspect was to make sure that Nightwing was an entity separate from his mentor and not "Batman Lite." My editor, Scott Peterson, gave me my marching orders. He wanted each issue to be a Jackie Chan movie. This was back when every Chan movie was jaw-droppingly wonderful.

Did you decide to give Nightwing escrima sticks, and what did they bring to the stories/action? Who decided to cut his hair?

I wanted that damn ponytail gone IMMEDIATELY! I think I inherited the sticks from an earlier one-shot by another writer. You know, I'm not clear on that one.

You had a few years of writing Tim Drake as Robin before starting *Nightwing*. What do you see as the most important differences and similarities of the two characters as teenagers? As sidekicks for Batman? What did their presence in each other's stories provide? Did you ever imagine

them in serious conflict? Did you pull back on any of Dick's established skills (e.g., computers in *New Teen Titans*) to make space for Tim?

They were the product of their backgrounds. Dick was always the greater risk-taker of the two and a natural athlete. I took my cue from Alan Grant and made Tim more cautious, more deliberate, in his actions. My self-imposed guideline was that Dick would jump in without thinking while Tim would observe and call for back-up. I consciously made Dick less technological, less intuitive about those things. He was more about the hardware than the software. Thus he builds his own ride from an existing car. I also made Dick less formal in his speech and actions. He used words like "gonna" and "wanna." He was Steve McQueen.

How would you characterize the relationship between Dick and Tim?

They had a big brother/little brother relationship that each was comfortable with. Tim knew that he had a lot to learn but Dick never made him feel like an inferior. In that way it was purely a fantasy version of brothers.

You've compared *Robin* to the early years of *Amazing Spider-Man*, with a teenager hustling to hide his masked heroics from his family. What models, if any, did you consider for *Nightwing*? What did you do to differentiate *Nightwing* from *Batman* and the recent *Daredevil*?

Dick was more a blue collar, hands-on kind of guy. He's also comfortable in his own skin and, unlike every other Batman character except Catwoman, he likes what he does. He likes being Nightwing. He's not a big brooder. Never a fool but never a total cynic either. And, as I said, he had a more informal style than Batman. Sure, he's a badass but he relies more on his reputation than his legend, if that makes any sense.

Were there any noticeable differences (age, gender, etc.) between the kind of fans reading *Robin* and the kind of fans reading *Nightwing*?

More females read Nightwing. I was conscious of that early on and made the storylines richer on that title with a touch more romantic tension. Guys like the romance stuff too though they won't admit it. But female readers, from my experience, don't like contrivance. The stories had to have more substance than simple conflict and resolution. From discussions with fans at the time, a lot of boys identified with Tim Drake. That was my aim with that title. Other than that mostly they shared the same readership with Nightwing having the edge in sale of additional female readers.

In the late 1990s, you wrote *Detective Comics*, *Robin*, and *Nightwing* each month. In the early 2000s, you wrote *Robin*, *Nightwing*, and *Birds of Prey*.

What were the benefits of having one writer on so many Bat-titles? What were the drawbacks for you?

No drawbacks!

I had the freedom to create my own consistent pocket universe within the DCU. I really love building worlds like that so having multiple titles sharing characters and locales and sometimes even storylines was comic book heaven for me.

What were the challenges of working with Dick Grayson when he was in two magazines from two desks (*Titans* and *Nightwing*), as well as a supporting character in *Batman* crossovers? What did Dick Grayson provide for *Batman* crossovers that no other character could?

Dick is the heir apparent. When the doo-doo hits the fan for Batman he has his oldest partner and friend to call on. As far as conflicts with the Titans, under Denny O'Neil I was told to treat his involvement in the Batman titles as a separate reality.

What do you see as Dick's major strength both personally and in terms of the wider DC universe?

The fans love him. He was comics' (and the world's) most famous sidekick. He has a legacy shared by few other characters. He was crime-fighting partner to Batman and got to hang out with Superman. He's kind of a wish fulfillment character; a kid picked from the crowd to be second to the coolest comic book character of all time.

What sets Dick Grayson apart from other heroes within the DC Universe? What is that character's unique significance or symbolic value within the sprawling DC Comics mythos? How has that changed over the years, or over media?

I'm not sure if other media gets Dick Grayson or Robin or Nightwing. The animated shows nailed it but the movies either get it all wrong or ignore it entirely. It's Batman AND Robin, people. Sure it may be goofy and strain credulity that comicdom's gloomiest vigilante hangs with an adolescent named for the first bird of Spring. But you have to embrace the silliness sometimes. Like I said, he's the kid who got to hang with Batman and BE Batman. The mythos is poorer without him. It's hollow without him. A guy who dresses as a bat and has no reality check other than his enabling butler. Sorry, that does not make for seventy-five years of continued popularity.

***Detective Comics* #725, which you wrote, is a beloved Bruce and Dick issue. How would you characterize the relationship between Bruce and Dick?**

I think of Dick as the child who has surpassed the parent. Sure, Batman is THE baddest comic book hero EVER. There's no question of that. But he's a broken man. Dick has almost the same past but, perhaps because of Bruce Wayne's negative example, has avoided the same pitfalls to become a more well-rounded personality. Seriously, who would you rather go on a long road trip with?

You were writing *Detective Comics* in the early 1990s when Dick was removed from *The New Titans*. According to a user on Comic Book Resources, Dick was supposed to marry Kory and become a sort of space cop. When that fell through, the Batman writers "took him back, which saved the character, but the price was to re-establish him within the Bat Shadow, and that's where he's been [f]or the last 20 years."[3] Do you agree that you and the other Bat writers saved Dick but at some cost?

There's a lot of Inside Baseball behind those decisions and I was not privy to all of it. I benefited from the results of whatever agreement the Powers That Be at DC came up with. Apparently there are Things That Must Not Be Spoken Of left over from deals made in the 1970s. Somehow it was all ironed out and as Denny put it, "We got Dick Grayson back." Looking back, I don't think Dick Grayson, Space Cop would have lasted very long.

***Nightwing* appeared after Dick Grayson had been paired with Koriand'r for over a decade, and it revived an affair with Barbara Gordon that had slight roots in a few stories from the late 1970s. Why did you decide to move Dick away from Kory and towards a relationship with Barbara? How did that storyline develop? What reactions did it produce in-house and among fans? After George Pérez showed Dick and Kory in bed together, Dick became DC's first hero with an undeniable sex life; how did that aspect of the character play into your stories?**

Kory was a poor fit for the more street-level direction we were taking in the Batbooks. Denny was boss and despised any SF elements or even super-science elements in the stories. He disliked villains like Mr. Freeze and Clayface because they were basically science fiction characters. So, I made a few oblique references to Kory but she never appeared in the titles I worked on. Because female readers liked Nightwing I wanted him to have some kind of romantic relationship but didn't want to mirror Tim Drake's tribulations or have a Mary Jane/Gwen situation as that felt so "been there." Barbara seemed like a character he would be attracted with because she would understand him better than perhaps any person on earth. Also, the relationship would cause tension between Dick and Bruce. I

LOVED the idea of them keeping a secret from Batman that he was clueless about because human relationships are his blindside.

As far as sex goes, I don't really like the idea of an openly sexual relationship between superhero characters. One consideration was their role model aspect and the other was the kind of creepy fetishistic nature of folks who wear masks and spandex getting it on. So, I kept it vague in an old movie kind of way. We KNOW that Jimmy Stewart and Grace Kelly are lovers in *Rear Window* but it is never shown. There's deniability. You can believe that these two are chaste and platonic or that they're going at it like minks. It was up to the reader how far it went. I like to think that keeps it more interesting.

Speaking of relationships: after Dick's brief encounter with Huntress/Helena Bertinelli in the *Nightwing and Huntress* mini-series, you distanced the two in *Nightwing*. What about that encounter specifically or the idea of a relationship between Dick and Helena doesn't work for you?

Helena is crazy. I firmly established that when I re-introduced her to DC continuity. She has real issues that make her dangerous both as a lover and a crime-fighting ally. She's not the right love interest for Dick even though there's heat between them. And I certainly showed there was heat.

You did a lot of world building for Dick in the *Nightwing* series. What are you most proud of?

The idea that Blüdhaven is a city with a half million residents but the major highway that passes through it has no off-ramps.

And the notion that the east-west streets are named for hard-boiled crime novelists and the north-south avenues are named for whaling terms.

Why did you decide to have Dick become a police officer?

When he realized that Blüdhaven's biggest, most dangerous gang was the police department, Dick's only option was to fight them from within.

Who is your favorite supporting character that you created for *Nightwing*?

Dudley Soames. I still love the idea of a bad guy who literally has his head on backwards.

Really good heroes require really good villains. Who do you believe are/have been Dick's major nemeses?

Soames and Lady Vic were perfect foils. One a dangerous psychopath with a high IQ and more self-control than the Joker. The other an aristocratic lady with absolutely no sense of right and wrong. Both were smart and offered real challenges.

How did you go about creating nemeses for Nightwing? Are there particular characters or stories you're most proud of?

They had to either be Dick's physical or intellectual equal. In Blockbuster's case he was both. You can't have Nightwing fighting chumps. Either that or female villains with a sexual angle that would throw him off. The Sylph and Double Dare fit that bill. I fondly recall the fight in the whale-themed mall in Nightwing ½. Man, Scott McDaniel could just draw the hell out of any crazy thing I came up with. Another was that three-parter with the Huntress. That got dark without being unrelentingly grim.

Why did you have Nightwing beat the Joker to death in *Last Laugh* (2001)?

To create some real tension between he and Batman. They've resolved so many of their issues that their relationship (which must always have some dissonance to it) was becoming flat. Also, to give the readers at least one instance where that grinning a-hole got what was coming to him. It's something I would NEVER have Batman do.

In writing the *Year One* stories with Scott Beatty, how did you collaborate and divide up the labor? How did you decide to rewrite certain episodes from DC Comics history, such as Dick's first meeting with Jason Todd?

Scott and I work in such an organic way that the work never seems divided. The separation line is that if there's some reference to an obscure event in continuity then that's Scott. It was his idea to bring in Boston Brand as part of Dick's origin. How brilliant was that? I wanted the meet between Dick and Jason Todd altered. I knew those two Robins would, and should, mix like gasoline and fire.

In *Nightwing: Year One* you have Bruce fire Dick in the harshest manner ever presented in the DCU. Why did you decide to write it that way?

To show that Bruce was wrong, wrong, wrong and never understood what Dick Grayson meant to him. I think I was unwittingly having Bruce stand-in for all those wrong-headed fans who think that Batman is better without Robin. And it's Dick's story. It's his pain. We wanted it to be palpable and real for the reader.

The Teen Titans also play a relatively small role in *Nightwing: Year One*. Why?

We had to nod to them but it was, essentially, a Bat-universe story. In 75 years of continuity the Titans' role in his history is still a minor phase.

In *Robin: Year One* and Detective #679 and #680 (*Prodigal* Parts 3 and 7), Dick's first big mistake involves Two-Face. Did you create that storyline? What inspired you? Why Two-Face and not some other villain?

For some reason I fixated on this notion that Robin was as much a nemesis for Two-Face as Batman was. I had a long and complex continuity in mind in which Dick Grayson is the one who foils Two-Face in his earliest encounter with the pair and it follows that Tim Drake would become the focus of Dent's loathing. After all, the guy is all about the duality and Robin makes his greatest enemy into a pair; a double threat. In the end, Two-Face, in my mind became a kind of rite-of-passage for any prospective Boy Wonder.

What is the relationship between Two-Face and Dick? Does Two-Face have a special interest in Dick in particular (whether as Robin or Nightwing) or just the Robins in general?

I don't think Two-Face is aware (or cares) that it's different kids behind the mask. He lives in his own reality. If he ever knew there was more than one Robin it would shake his tenuous grasp on what sanity he had left. I think I played with that in a story; having him deny, despite all the evidence, that there was more than one Robin.

What is your favorite issue or arc that you wrote for *Nightwing*? For *Robin*?

I liked that Huntress three-parter. And Tad Ryerstad holds a special place in my heart. One of the only bad guys who was Dick's inferior in every way but still dangerous. What a sad, pathetic wretch. For Robin, I like the one where he's trapped and slowly dying with Cluemaster in that buried armor car. And *Robin: Year One*.

What major changes did you see in Dick Grayson over the years you wrote him?

Well, he only gained in popularity which means I didn't screw him up.

Was there anything in the *Nightwing* series that, in retrospect, you wish you had done differently? Or not done at all? Anything you wanted to do that never happened? Any storylines you pitched for Dick Grayson that never got off the ground?

Nothing for Dick Grayson. I have no regrets over that run.

Was there anything you wrote that fans hated but you thought they would like? Anything you thought they would dislike and they loved?

No. Nightwing remained a favorite, as far as I know. It was, for all of my run, a bellwether book for DC. I was told many times that it was the book that the editors watched to indicate how the whole line was doing.

Do you see being Batman as part of Dick's ultimate destiny?

Hopefully, that day will never come. I do see Tim Drake as a guy who would retire the mask and cape.

Did any writers or stories (comics or otherwise) particularly influence how you wrote Dick?

All of them. Everyone who works in comics works in the shadow of those who came before. I was a steward not an auteur.

What was your favorite part about writing superhero comics? Your least favorite part?

Each time I typed the words "Batman and Robin" was like the first time. It NEVER got tired and I would never abbreviate their names. It was "Batman and Robin" every time. The eight-year-old in me lived again each time. I was making up stuff for my childhood heroes to do. The least favorite part was never about writing the superheroes. Let's just say that there are personalities in this business who are dedicated to making the work harder and it's NEVER to make the end product better.

On *Nightwing* you wrote for artists with a wide range of styles, from Scott McDaniel to Greg Land. How did you adapt your storytelling to their interests and talents?

With Scott it was "Katy, bar the door" every issue. I could just go wild. Greg's style is more deliberate and more strictly cinematic so I would play to those strengths.

In your comics writing career, you got to see the growth of previews and internet discussions. How has that environment changed the business? Does it affect the way stories and characters are written?

I don't pay attention to any of it. Some editors have encouraged me to go on the message boards dedicated to the titles I'm writing. That way lies madness. I write to make myself happy first and re-write to make my editors happy. I can only hope that by fully and earnestly investing myself in the characters that I write that I will also please the readers. But if I think of the readers first I will not create stories that surprise or challenge them. That way of creating results in the one-size-fits-all kind of entertainment that we see in far too many summer blockbusters.

What are you up to now? Any chance you might write Dick Grayson or another Bat-character again?

That looks highly unlikely. These days I do mostly creator-owned projects like Winterworld for IDW, Bad Times, my own series of SF action novels available on Amazon and the upcoming Joe Frankenstein with Bane co-creator Graham Nolan and Seven Deadly Sinners with cartooning legend Bob Hardin.

Notes

1. The questions asked herein were solicited from online fans. Geaman compiled and edited them, presenting them in a written format to the interviewee for their answers.
2. http://league.jmkprime.org/2011/07/31/list-top-100-most-prolific-dc-comics-writers/
3. By user Dzetoun http://forums.comicbookresources.com/showthread.php?377028-Nightwing-Appreciation-Thread&p=18019052&highlight=#post18019052 (post from 7 January 2014).

Grayson on Grayson

Kristen L. Geaman[1]

Devin Grayson[2] is an avid gamer, former acting student and voracious reader fortunate enough to have turned a lifelong obsession with fictional characters into a dynamic writing career. Not having read comics in her youth, Devin was introduced to the Batman mythos through *Batman: The Animated Series* (1992–1995) and immediately bonded with Dick Grayson. Showing the kind of gumption many of us wish we possessed, Devin decided she wanted to write comics and avidly pursued a career change. Her hard work was rewarded when her first story was published in *The Batman Chronicles* in late 1996. Devin is best known for her extensive body of work in the Batman (and Dick Grayson) Universe for DC Comics, including: a four year run on *Nightwing* (2002–2006), *Batman: Gotham Knights* (2000–2002), *The Titans* (1999–2000), and *Catwoman* (1998–1999). She has also written for Marvel, Vertigo, Marvel Knights, Random House/Del Rey, Dynamite Entertainment and Zenescope. Her published work includes comic books, graphic novels, licensed publication novels, short fiction, essays and scripting for casual games and MMOs. She lives in Northern California with her family and thoroughly enjoys the commute to Gotham whenever called upon to make it.

Let's start at the beginning. You were first introduced to the Batman mythos through the 1990s cartoons, right? Was there anything surprising you had to learn or "unlearn" to write about Dick Grayson and friends in the comics continuity?

That's a good question! I don't think there really was; *Batman: The Animated Series* was unusually good at distilling the Batman mythos into a pure, clean story world. To this day I still hear Kevin Conroy's voice when I think of Bruce. The first exposures we have to these legends are so powerful, aren't they? After the Animated Series, it was more a matter of taking those stories and then adding in decades worth of other material, including books like the *Teen Titans* (the first two iterations) where we really got to see a different side of Dick. I always kind of approached the material with the idea that everything that came before what I wrote was more or less true—was, at least, a legend about what was true in the superhero community or in Gotham. Like the really out there Batman tales from the sixties and early seventies—maybe those were stories that Ollie told at JLA parties. And the super early Batman material where he was carrying a gun—well, I'm sure someone in Gotham would swear that they saw just such a thing. So my job was to figure out, if all of that stuff had happened or was, at least, part of the characters' personal mythologies, who did that mean these people were?

After becoming a fan of Dick Grayson, how did you study his history? Did you focus on particular periods or try to read all stories? Did you find any stories especially inspirational? (For instance, did "How to Be the Batman," written in 1952 and reprinted in 1999, inspire the amnesia story in *Gotham Knights*, #8–11?)[3]

I did try to read everything, but not in order, which got very confusing but also kind of helped make their histories more three-dimensional and less linear—like the way you make friends with someone and over time start hearing stories about their past misdeeds. I think with *Teen Titans*, especially ... weren't there two separate print runs that ended up with similar numbering structures? I remember thinking I was reading them in order and then realizing—as the story made less and less sense ("wait, where did Kory go...?")—that I was accidentally mixing together two totally separate volumes. ;-p

I also submerged myself in fandom and learned a lot from an APA [Amateur Press Association] I started writing fanfic with—I think getting perspective from some of Dick's biggest fans was incredibly helpful, because it is in the passion of the people who are authentically drawn to the character that the character's true nature begins to emerge.

I don't remember "How to Be the Batman,"—it's possible that I missed that one. The amnesia story in *Batman: Gotham Knights* 8–11 was my way of examining what Dick might go through—initially, at least—upon losing Batman. Not Bruce, mind you, but Batman, who I've always sort of thought was the guy he had more of a relationship with anyway. Dick, of all people, knows that Batman is way more than a mask.

What sets Dick Grayson apart from other heroes within the DC Universe? What is that character's unique significance or symbolic value within the sprawling DC Comics mythos? How has that changed over the years or over media?

Well, I'm not a scholar; I can only give you my emotional response as a writer. For me, Robin represents the reader's desire to be accepted into Batman's world—he is a very relatable character for a young reader—and Dick Grayson represents loyalty. Part of what makes Batman so unique is that his heroic brilliance comes from the darkest part of his psyche; his dedication to good was kindled and continues to be fed by exposure to evil. Dick is a very different animal. Although he relates to Bruce in terms of having tragically lost his parents in his early childhood, his commitment to good is fueled by gratitude and hope and loyalty. Bruce is broken in a way that pretty much condemns him to a life of crime-fighting; his resounding competence aside, there's pretty much nothing else he could realistically do with his life. Dick could do *anything*. He is a much more complete person inside—thanks in large part to Bruce himself, of course—and also more naturally extroverted and emotionally resilient than Bruce. Which brings us to Nightwing who, in some small but spectacular way, represents choice.

Many of the heroes in the DCU have had their identities thrust on them … they often start in fairly ordinary lives and then something happens to them that propels them into heroism. Or, conversely, there is nothing ordinary about them; they're aliens or goddesses or multidimensional beings who are destined from day one to do great things on the mortal plane of Planet Earth. Dick is different—his life was *never* ordinary. He starts out in the remarkably self-reliant, well-traveled and transnational but also somewhat insular community of the circus, in which, at a very young age, he is expected to carry his own weight and work for a living. That falls apart in spectacular, tragic fashion and he's taken in by Batman who is *willing* to train him but would not for one minute force the life of a costumed vigilante on him. Though I believe that Batman was an extremely strict and demanding mentor, I also believe that he would have been more than happy to set Dick up with a comfortable civilian life if Dick had even hinted at ever wanting such a thing. But Dick is adamant about joining forces with him and more than endures the years of unforgiving training that follow; he thrives in them. And of course there are moments—especially in his teen years—when it chafes and Dick wants to walk away from one or many elements of that life, but over and over again he comes back, he recommits, he chooses to stay. And sure, part of it is the desire to avenge his parents' death, but secretly—and by secretly I mean that he barely even admits this to himself—secretly, that's a very small part of it. That wound heals much more quickly and completely for Dick than it does for Bruce. Dick is not motivated by anger or grief or revenge; he's motivated by awe and enthusiasm and, as I will continue circling back to, loyalty. That is terrifically unique; in the DC Comics universe and also in real life.

I think one of the reasons I was dismissed from *Nightwing* was because Dan Didio and I so fundamentally disagreed on the character. Didio saw no need for Nightwing—he referred to him as "Batman lite," and couldn't understand the role Dick played. In Didio's mind, Dick wanted to be Batman, and never would be (beyond a passing story line here or there), so what was the point? I don't think Dick wants to be Batman. Batman is not a position for Dick, Batman is a person. He would and will be Batman, of course, when needed, but Dick's goal is to *honor* Batman, which is an entirely different thing. That loyalty, that gratitude, that enthusiastic choice to continue the work is what sets Dick Grayson apart from every other hero in the DC Comics universe.

You came to comics writing out of fandom aided by the internet (TV cartoons, fan fiction). You worked when writers seemed to be responsible for publicizing upcoming magazines through online interviews yet also to maintain suspense about plot twists. How did your views and relationships with the online fan community change?

I feel like Otto from *A Fish Called Wanda*: what was that middle part? But let's try to unpack this. The order, for me, was actually exposure to the cartoon, then comics and then intentional submersion in fandom and fanfic. DC handles all of its own marketing and advertising—back in the day, they would occasionally send a creator to a convention to help promote a series and would sometimes arrange the really big publicity pieces—like an interview in a magazine or newspaper—but for the most part, then and now, they are not directly involved with creator interviews. Creators are independent contractors (also known as freelancers); when we do online interviews and such, it's to help promote our individual careers as much as any particular project we might be working on at the time. When giving interviews of any kind though, for sure, you want to encourage readers to be excited about what's coming next but you don't want to give major plot points away. I don't think anybody even needs to coach you on that, it's just common sense.

The fandom I was initially part of was not web-based—it was a little Amateur Press Association (APA) based mostly in Ohio. We would email or mail in our submissions, which would then be correlated and sent back out. When I started working for DC professionally, one of my editors strongly advised me to leave the APA ... the association ran the risk of creating legal complications for DC. So I did that and stayed close to some of the members and lost contact with others.

Now we get to the online fan community, which I was first exposed to via DC-editor hosted online chats and then, a little later, the comments section at the end of online interviews. I initially felt very close to the online fan community and received a lot of support from them, but then started to be followed by three specific posters—one of whom was from that APA I had been part of—who were very invasive and hostile. Still, three guys, right? I could handle that. But then as my exposure increased, so, too, did the negativity. I have always been open to criticism of my work, but online attacks get weirdly personal, especially the ones motivated by misogyny (and there are, unfortunately, still a crushing number of those). It became more and more unpleasant to interact with fans online, so I started to withdraw slightly—at which point one poster took it upon him or herself to "defend" me by impersonating me online. That really freaked me out—you can't, of course, control what other people say about you, but you're supposed to at least be able to control what you yourself say! I felt at that point that I had no choice but to announce that I would not be posting anymore and that any additional posts that were attributed to me were fakes. With the exception of classwork-related message boards, I've stuck to that.

I know that the vast majority of fans are kind, well-mannered people—I've met thousands of them at cons. But the haters—especially online—have, unfortunately, colored my take on online fandom. These days it feels politically and socially important to maintain an online presence as a female, if for no other reason than to support one's peers, but it hasn't been a joyful or inclusive-feeling experience for a long time.

There's some indication that *Young Justice* was cancelled because the studio execs did NOT want girls in the audience, they wanted boys.[4] You mentioned in an earlier communication that, although exact stats are unknown, Dick Grayson draws in a very large female audience for a male superhero. How do you think the "female issue" affects Nightwing?

First of all, how much do you love the statistic at the end of that io9 article indicating that doll sales are significantly higher than action figure sales? It's hard to know where to even start with the kind of corporate thinking Dini and Smith were lamenting in that piece. It would be one thing if it at least made sense on a financial level, but it patently does not. We see this with movies, cartoons, comic books, video games, toys, even literature. Somehow, corporate America has convinced itself that marketing to 51 percent of the population is verboten. It's insane. Did the cosmetics, yogurt and house-keeping industries win exclusive rights to market to females in some shady poker game we don't know about? Will Hollywood get in trouble if it takes money from girls? I am usually pretty good at identifying corporate logic, but this particular brand of financially-punitive misogyny we're dealing with now mystifies me.

As for *Nightwing* specifically, I don't have empirical statistics about who buys it but I do know who my readers are and there's no question in my mind that Dick is popular with the ladies. As of this writing, "Nightwing" has been stripped of his costume and super-heroic identity and is, I think (I refuse to read it), running around with a gun. To put it bluntly, I think the people who hired me to write Nightwing—none of whom are still with DC—completely understood and appreciated Nightwing's female audience and also believed, as I do, that good stories are usually accessible to all genders. The people currently in charge of the character—all of whom are taking detailed creative notes from a guy who has admitted to not liking or understanding him—are working in a much more heavily micromanaged environment with a strong emphasis on homogenized stories. It's not even about what boys like over there right now, it's about what one specific man likes. I guess it's working for them as a business model, but it's certainly not geared toward attracting a diverse audience and it's not creatively advantageous to all of the characters.

From your perspective(s) as a fan and creator, are there significant differences in what male and female superhero fans look for in a story? Do comics publishers perceive such differences? Do they perceive/design certain characters or magazines to be more appealing to certain groups of readers?

That first question—do males and females read differently—that's really hard and it's tortured me for most of my creative life. I want so badly to believe that we don't ... that a good story is a good story is a good story. But the truth is, when I'm reading superhero comics or watching superhero movies with my male friends, we are often looking at and responding to different things. It's a gross oversimplification, and of course there will always be members of both (all) genders with unique and gender-norm-defying interests, but to some extent (can I qualify this anymore?) males seem to be more engaged by action and females seem to be more engaged by relationships. Again, that's a huge generalization, but even if we take it at face value for a minute, doesn't it raise the question of why there aren't more comics (or movies or cartoons, etc.) that include both? Because those elements are not at all mutually exclusive. I do not write for any particular gender, but I do put effort into being at least somewhat inclusionary. Without qualification, I can say that people long to see themselves in stories. As story-tellers, we owe them those reflections.

As for the perceptions of comics publishers, I can't speak for them, of course, but my sense is that they don't even get that far. Perceiving the difference between male and female fans requires being aware of male and female fans, and as we were discussing earlier, females are total non-entities in so much of contemporary corporate thinking. Characters are designed to appeal to the people designing them and, even more significantly, to the people approving those designs. And many of the people doing that kind of work right now are not very good at thinking beyond their own knee-jerk reactions.

Have you faced difficulties/prejudice as an openly bisexual creator in the industry?

Not at all. Being out of the closet is such a gift, because it makes you visible to and puts you in touch with such a loving, supportive community. I've thought about this a lot, and looking over my whole life, my sexuality has never been anything but a positive. I know I'm very lucky in that respect and that many other people have tremendously different experiences, but I can't think of a single negative thing—in my personal or professional life—that has come from being bisexual. I think it helps my writing, it gives me political and social focus and it has allowed me to love a small group of very unique and diverse people.

Being female, on the other hand, that's hard. That's a whole different story.

You've stated in the past that you interpret Dick's character as bisexual—how does this inform how you see him as a person?[5] Is this something you would've liked to expand on (including possibly giving Dick a male love interest) in the comics had DC permitted it?

If DC had permitted it, I actually would have loved to explore that, but I do understand why they couldn't and won't. The two pieces of that I would have really loved to play with, though (and of course have played with in my personal fanfic) are: (1) how this might relate to his anxiety about his relationship with Bruce as he hits adolescence (more on that in a minute) and (2) how closeted he might have kept that part of himself for fear of disappointing or in any way alienating Bruce, and what it might finally look like if he decided to stop hiding it. I'm sure I've said this already, but I keep coming back to the idea of how physical Dick is as a person. I understand him as someone who reacts and relates and processes information through his body. I think that's one of the reasons I love writing him so much, really—because that is so markedly different from how I move through the world and it's just absolutely thrilling to imagine having that kind of connection to the corporeal plane.

I do think of his relationship with Bruce as being primarily filial, but I think there was anxiety around that as well, especially during adolescence when Dick starts to realize that a) he is not, technically, this man's son, and that b) he can't be Robin forever. Fueled by adolescent hormones (I think we all remember how awful those can be!), I imagine this anxiety growing into a full-blown panic, and in that panic Dick is desperately trying to figure out how to remain relevant and connected to Batman. And somewhere in that worry—which is also, of course, tinged with rebelliousness and the desire to become autonomous and a genuine maturation of self—Dick has to at least consider the prospect of becoming this man's lover. And, I mean, you've seen Batman … that's not a wholly distasteful scenario. But it is also a genuinely bad idea, because it does so blatantly dismiss the familial connection they've developed over the years. And I guess that's why it feels so powerful to me … because teenage-hood is full of *really bad ideas*. And if the actual goal—whether Dick the teenager understands it consciously or not—is to get a reaction out of Bruce, some reassurance that he sees him and he matters … well, holy shit he could not do better than suddenly demanding that the guy who raised and trained and shaped him acknowledge him as a sexual being. It is really, really, really hard to get a rise (no pun intended!) out of Bruce, but this would do it, and once Dick saw that, saw Bruce flinch… There are themes I'm going to keep coming back to again and again, and one of them is this idea of Dick as the irresistible force to Bruce's immovable object. And that aspect of their relationship is never better illustrated than in this dance of sexual tension. If Bruce were able to calmly counter it … to just kind of gently but firmly say, "that is not going to happen, we do not have that kind of relationship," it would diffuse Dick completely, and Dick would go on to the next thing. But if Bruce blows up or shuts down or in any way hesitates (not because he's considering it, mind you, but because it comes from *so* far out of left field for him) … Dick then becomes *relentless*. And eventually all of that thwarted tension has to express itself somewhere else, which is how I imagine Dick first exploring the possibility of bisexuality—almost defiantly, the way young women sometimes go after married men, feeling like being able to get sexual attention from someone who is already "taken" somehow validates their own desirability. But somewhere in that mess of defiance and experimentation and emotional desperation it could become real for him, especially, obviously, if he meets the right guy … a good guy, someone waaay calmer about such matters, someone very very *not* Bruce.

Anyway, you can see I've thought about all of this a lot. I think it's a great story, but it's not appropriate for a mainstream superhero comic.

In that same *Shameless* interview, you characterize Dick as a "contact junkie." Some fans have interpreted that discussion as you saying Dick has a "flight or fuck" response. Do you agree?

Ha ha! That's great. I don't see the flight option in him, though. I would say his response is *fight* or fuck. It's all about the tactile heat of contact. And of course he doesn't feel the same way about the people he's fighting as he does about the people he's fucking (most of the time, anyway—there are always exceptions), but using his body to express himself is utterly natural for him and is in many ways the purest expression of his particular being.

We all know the guy is smart—like, genius smart—and there's no question that he could explain almost anything to almost anybody, but the intellectual is more abstract for him, as a personal experience, than the physical. Part of the tension in his relationship with Bruce is that Bruce—or, more specifically, Batman—is very guarded about his personal space. He's not big on being touched. And as a kid, you pick up on those things quickly, so when he's talking to Bruce, Dick has to be deliberately physically restrained. It's not something he's even conscious of most of the time, but it's there. And Bruce is aware of it too, and fortunately very good at helping Dick channel all that somatic energy, but it can be exhausting for him, which is another place where you get that great irresistible force meeting immovable object dynamic of their relationship.

I'm probably way off topic now, but another way I like to visualize it is to think about the difference in Bruce and Dick's fighting styles. Bruce is a very solid, hard, mid-range fighter (mid-range not in terms of skill, but in terms of striking parameter). Fighting with Batman, if you're unfortunate enough to find yourself doing so, would be a little like trying to dodge a Mac truck. When you go to hit him, he has melted into the shadows, but when he finally hits you, he's right in front of you, dead center, fixed and solid. Dick, on the other hand, is totally fluid; acrobatic, of course, but also literally all over the place, coming in from high range and then suddenly sliding under your feet and then at mid-range and then—holy shit!—behind you! It would be breathtaking to watch and *maddening* to try to defend against; overwhelming in the same way he's romantically overwhelming. You can imagine both his opponents and his lovers throwing up their hands at some point to cry, "Jesus Christ, just be *still* for a second! I have to catch my breath!" So maybe instead of saying Dick's a contact junkie, I should say that his effect on people is to leave them breathless, no matter what kind of interaction they're having with him. The last thing I want to say on this subject is that part of Dick's attraction to touch leads directly back to his early work on the trapeze. In trapeze work, making contact with the catcher's wrists can be literally life-saving. So whereas many of us respond positively to touching and being touched, for an acrobat trained in aerial arts, physical connection is that much more powerful. Contact with other people is literally what keeps you from the abyss.

How was it different writing Dick in a team book than writing his solo book? Are there things you can do in a team book with the character that you can't do in a solo book? What are the major drawbacks of doing a team book rather than a solo book?

It's very different and very fun to be able to do both. With *Nightwing*, part of the way I expressed Dick's relentless energy was by having him narrate, so you got to hear his internal voice in his solo book. He talks to himself in part because he's a very social person, and when he's with his friends he's actually quieter, because that longing for community—established early in his life in the circus—is being met. You have a great many more opportunities for dialog in a team book, obviously, and you get to show how each individual responds to every other individual. None of us act exactly the same way alone as we do when we're with our dads, and that's different than how we act with our best friend or a former crush or someone we grew up with. Part of the humor in Batman is that Bats does act pretty much the same way with absolutely everybody, and that can be funny precisely because it's rare. Most of us are much more socially flexible. So you get to show a lot more sides of a character in a team book as you play him or her off the other members of the team. You also get to show how other people feel about each character and elucidate personal histories. For example, if Dick, in his solo book, tells somebody he was raised by Batman, there's probably a reason for it in the context of the story and our takeaway is that this other person now knows this salient fact. But if Dick in *The Titans* starts to mention that he was raised by Batman and is immediately interrupted by Roy, who finishes the sentence for him, we suddenly know that Dick brings up this being raised by Batman thing a lot, like maybe to the point of annoying his friends. And that, in turn, suggests that it's more than just a fact, or even a point of potential intimidation, it's a point of pride. We now know the fact *matters* to Dick and is a stable part of his personal mythology.

I actually really like writing team books because of all the amazing opportunities for interpersonal dynamics. I guess the drawback of a team book—at least a team book using characters that all have their own solo or "parent" books—is editorial coordination of characters and the reality that more than half of your stories are likely to get derailed by elements beyond your control. There's a lot of last minute story editing involved and sometimes it's difficult to accurately reflect the nuances of a fictional relationship … for example, I've always thought of Dick and Wally as being quite close, but I didn't get to use Wally much in my run of *Titans*. Characters that should spend time together sometimes can't for purely editorial reasons, and you still have to find a way to explain that in the context of your story.

How would you characterize Dick as a leader? During *The Titans*, Dick's leadership style seemed to be a bit more Batman-esque than it had been during *New Teen Titans*. Would you agree? If so, what was the reasoning behind this?

I don't think I'll surprise anyone by admitting that I find the relationship between Dick and Bruce to be probably the most interesting dynamic in either individual's life. That relationship was, in fact, what brought me to comics in the first place. So when I have the opportunity to explore it—either by having them together or by having them reflecting nuances of how they've influenced each other in their solo adventures—I'll usually do so.

Dick is actually a very different kind of leader than Batman. He's way more in tune with his teammates, more empathetic, and in many ways more hands-on. And he likes working with a team a whole lot more than Bruce does. Batman works best alone—that's his default. When he does have to work with other people, he'll fall into the leadership position out of pure impatience (Dick is more likely to lead out of enthusiasm). Bats is a brilliant tactician (as is Dick) and can think waaay more steps ahead than basically anyone else in the DCU. But the essential difference is that Batman deploys people. Dick inspires them.

And yet, as much as Dick sometimes resents being on the receiving end of Batman's authoritarian utilization, he absolutely recognizes its effectiveness and will fall back on similar tactics when he feels like he needs to reinforce his leadership. I think I felt like *The Titans* was happening in a less certain time period than *New Teen Titans*. Coming *back* together has a lot more tension in it than initial formation; relationships are more complicated, the stakes are sometimes higher (socially, that is—there are no higher stakes than "guys, I think my demon-father is coming to destroy this entire plane of existence,") and individual lives are less flexible. The Titans are really good friends—more than good friends, they're family—

but at the beginning of *The Titans* they had drifted apart a little and that was weighing on all of them. When you're trying to recreate something, you have to acknowledge that there was some reason the original incarnation fell apart in the first place. And if the first incarnation happened when you were a teenager, there's going to be a nagging concern that maybe it's not going to work as an extension of your adulthood. If you think of the Titans as a band, my run starts after everyone's gone off and done a bunch of solo projects and although it feels great, on one level, to be together again, it also brings up all those arguments about "creative differences" you started having at the end of the last tour. Plus there're new members joining … it's complicated. So Roy's defensive, Donna's worried, Garth is reserved, Kory's cautious, Wally's being cagey about committing and Dick has his figurative cowl down—at least in the beginning.

What were the challenges of planning stories for Dick Grayson when he was in multiple magazines from two editorial desks (*Titans, Gotham Knights, Nightwing, Outsiders*)? Did Dick have a standard role in Batman crossovers?

Nightwing was always included in the Batman crossover events—*The Titans* (and *The Outsiders* and the other team books) usually weren't. I was in a pretty good position in as much as that I came from the Bat-office—that was my editorial home base—and I was therefore basically trusted by the editors in charge of it. Really the hardest aspect of dealing with crossovers was the inability to tell longer story arcs; you always had to be prepared to tie up whatever you were doing in time to start the next connected continuity event. In many ways the more connected titles you're writing the easier it is, because you of course then know exactly what's going on in each book. But before big crossover events we'd always have "Bat-Summits" where the editors and writers would get together to outline the event and make sure everyone more or less knew what everyone else was doing. For something massive like *No Man's Land* we had a very detailed outline we were all working from—we'd put it together on a white board and then make digital copies for everyone once every book, character and story beat was in place. You can't wing a story like that. Though of course things would come up that would have to be addressed and at that point you do your best to think on your feet. Usually by then there's a story logic in place, though, so you're not reinventing the wheel, you're just trying to figure out where the cart's going to go.

How did you make the decision to retcon [retroactively change] Dick's ethnicity?[26] Did you need to get approval for the decision? In your opin-

ion, how could him being Romani be used to inform his characterization? Why is having a Romani superhero important? How much research did you do on Romani history/culture in order to write Dick?

Maybe I'm wrong, but I never thought of that as a retcon. As far as I know, there had never been any discussion of or verdict on Dick's race—that's not the kind of material comic writers normally walked up to in the forties. But if you look at his history and his coloring ... I didn't feel like I was changing anything so much as clarifying it. And then yes, I made some decisions about the specifics of his ethnicity (like that the Romani heritage came from his dad's side and that they were Kalderasha), but that was also based on what felt to me like fictional evidence. It just made sense, and it was interesting and it felt authentic to the character. In any case, I did a lot of research into both circus and Romani culture (which is how I came across that connection in the first place). And I don't know that I'd say having a Romani superhero is important as much as I'd say that not assuming that all superheroes are white Europeans is important ... I guess that's why I'm bristling at the term "retcon"; I didn't change his ethnicity from one thing to another, he had no ethnicity. The truth is, we never talk about that stuff, we just make assumptions, and in this case those assumptions are based on a really boring, banal and in many ways harmful representation of America.

So how does it inform his character? Well, it presents a narrative for his family's history that makes sense in light of their occupation. It reinforces his "otherness" where Bruce is concerned in what I think is a useful, interesting way (economically, for instance), and in my mind it enhances his early childhood adventures. If his family was initially connected to a *kumpania*, it means that Dick didn't necessarily spend the circus off-seasons in Gibtown—he could have been traveling the world, which seems likely given the poise and self-possession he showed as an eight-year-old. It also presents the opportunity for there to be a slight chip on his shoulder, which maybe speaks to his scrappiness. It also maybe gives him a slightly deeper way to relate to someone like Helena—someone who is white but other—and gives the people who love (or lust after) him a potential cultural excuse for feeling as bewitched as they sometimes do. I also just love the idea of Bruce occasionally calling him "hot blooded," just to mess with him, because Dick would of course deny being so in an extremely hot-blooded manner.

Also, you know, when you talk about decisions ... I'm a writer. Characters present themselves to me and tell me who they are. Obviously I'm responsible for those interpretations on some deep, unconscious level, but the experience isn't an intellectual one, it's one of discovery.

Oh, and no, I don't remember needing or getting special permission, because I think my editors agreed with me that it wasn't a change so much as a clarification or enhancement.

You were also responsible for Bruce finally officially adopting Dick[7]—how did you decide to write this scene? What does it mean to you? If you'd had your way, would Bruce have adopted Dick long before this? How does having him be adopted as an adult change things?

That *was* a conscious change and it was about language. Being someone's "ward" totally makes sense in 1939, but it doesn't work in 2001 or whenever that issue came out. I think if the story were told today as a brand new mythology, Bruce would have adopted Dick right away—making him his ward was kind of an accident of historical language; it had no significant meaning at the time, but sixty years later it becomes kind of loaded ... suddenly there's a connotation of familial detachment in it like, "I'm responsible for you, but you're not family." I could have just retconned it, but I felt like that implied detachment resonated in their relationship and needed to be addressed. It makes very little legal difference for Bruce to adopt Dick as an adult, but I think—if that truly had not been done up to that point—it would make a pretty huge emotional difference, especially if Bruce had in fact adopted other people, like Jason Todd, in the interim. It basically meant, as Dick correctly experienced it, "I love you." And I think that was an important acknowledgement for them to make.

One of the elements of Dick's personality that I have the most trouble explaining is his sociological framework, because he stayed basically the same age for five decades. We are all very influenced by the politics, fads, technological developments and socioeconomics of the eras that we grow up in, and this is impossible to pinpoint for Dick; in my mind he was somehow a child in the early forties, a teenager in the eighties and a young adult in the two thousands ... but other people's experiences of him are going to be different depending on which material they read and when. In some ways the extraordinariness of his life is very helpful in this regard, because it somewhat removes him from any social norms he might otherwise have been experiencing; you kind of need for him to have been raised in a cave at that point, because nothing else will adequately divorce him from the influences of society as dictated by time.

But back to the adoption ... I strongly feel like it was the right thing to do both in terms of contemporary language and in terms of the evolving relationship between the two characters.

Do see Dick and Bruce's relationship as an essentially unhealthy one? Your portrayal of their relationship has sometimes been called particularly dysfunctional, yet you also emphasize the love between them consistently. Can a relationship be unhealthy in some ways and healthy in others?

Ah, can a relationship NOT be unhealthy in some ways and healthy in others? Isn't that kind of the *definition* of a relationship? Some of it works and some of it doesn't. I've always put my bias on the table about this: I was raised by a therapist and a sociologist. I don't for one second believe in idyllic families or happy childhoods. Growing up is really hard, and raising kids is even harder. And when you add adoption (or a weird lack of it) and orphanhood—not to mention nightly life-or-death encounters—it's going to get even more complicated.

So some of it is perspective, some of it depends on who you ask. I think Dick's friends think Batman was way too strict and overbearing and they worry that Dick didn't get the kind of nurturing he deserved. If you ask someone who actually witnessed it, like Alfred, he'll admit that there were more good times than bad, but that there were a lot of challenges and personality clashes. Bruce wouldn't answer you, but he's very aware that Dick saved him from himself. And Dick ... Dick would defend Bruce with his last breath. Dick chafes against Bruce, he sometimes struggles under his shadow, he aches for more frequent and expressive praise and reassurance, but he wouldn't trade his childhood with Bruce for anything. He feels saved by him, actualized. John and Mary Grayson brought him into the world, but Batman helped him find his place in it. He can't imagine being anything other than a hero and can't imagine how he would have become one without Bruce.

So no, I don't think Dick and Bruce's relationship is fundamentally unhealthy, but I do think it's really, really challenging, especially later. You have, on the one hand, someone who's very shut off and guarded, and he's suddenly put in charge (or, more accurately, he suddenly puts himself in charge) of the care and well-being of someone who's naturally effusive and social and demonstrative. The relationship is based on a shared experience—which is healthy and helpful—and it is in many ways good and necessary for both parties ... I never got the chance to write much about this period, but I think in Dick's early years it was actually really great for both of them for a really long time ... Dick was already trained to follow orders and take responsibility for his own safety, and until Dick's arrival into his life, Bruce was deeply lonely in a way that he was incapable of acknowledging, much less addressing. I think Bruce probably threw a lot at Dick but I also think Dick always rose to the occasion, generating a lot of mutual trust and respect. I mean, again: if you asked Dick the question you just asked me, he would look at you like you were crazy. He gets frustrated and he gets fed up and he gets discouraged, but he *worships* Bruce—it has honestly never occurred to him that the relationship is responsible for anything other than his complete and total salvation. Dick can't imagine his life without Batman; in my mind, his most deeply held, shameful secret is that at some point during his childhood with Bruce he fell so in love with the thrill of being Robin that he stopped wanting his parents back—his life with Batman was *better* than what he'd had before. He could never admit that to Bruce, of course—Bruce who mourns his parents the way the rest of us breathe; habitually and persistently. And although he's much quieter about it, Bruce has the same basic feeling about the relationship—he knows Dick saved him from himself. Where the relationship gets messy is when you have to start untangling that, when it becomes time to move on and redefine the bond. Dick devoted his childhood to being Batman's partner ... can you imagine how uncomfortable it must have felt to realize that all of that was coming to an end? We all come to a point in our lives when we have to renegotiate our relationship with our guardians. I think *that* part went really badly for Dick and Bruce, and the repercussions of it echoed through their relationship for a long time after that.

Also, as a writer I of course admit to dragging my own material into the stories I write—I don't do it consciously, but that element has to be there. I occasionally look back at how I've framed a fictional relationship and suddenly see a real one in a whole new light. That can be a very shocking, surreal experience. It always made me nervous when my parents read my Batman work.

Your novel *Inheritance* went about as far as any DC publication has in acknowledging the homoerotic subtext some fans like to see in that couple (albeit that acknowledgment coming from the unreliable mouth of Oliver Queen). How did editorial attitudes change?

So, this is interesting.

My intention there was to have Ollie acknowledge that reading without suggesting that it was necessarily accurate. He basically just says, "I can understand why people would jump to that conclusion." Again, this circles back to my idea of trying to acknowledge, and trying to have the characters acknowledge, the entirety of their legends. They're not dumb. They know what people say about them. And not all people say the same things. So let's walk up to as much of that as possible.

I was also contrasting Batman and Green Arrow's partnering styles. There's a chapter in the book where Green Arrow is partnered with Nightwing and basically teasing him about being sexually ambiguous, and this material is arguably more offensive than Ollie's line acknowledging the gay subtext. It's got a lot of bad homoerotic innuendo and it's poorly written and I don't remember but I have to assume that I was hugely over-caffeinated and desperately trying to make deadline when I wrote it. It goes too far and there's no reason for it in terms of the plot or even the characters. It is one of those hugely embarrassing learning-in-print experiences. I so wish I could rewrite that chapter—it's undisciplined and fanfic-y in the worst sense of that designation—but I assumed that had it been truly egregious, harmful in any serious way to the characters or the company, somebody would have said something.

The whole time I worked in comics the understanding was that writers were supposed to push the envelope and that, because these characters are such icons, editorial would, whenever necessary, push back. Sometimes you would really click with an editor and they would become a genuine creative partner and sometimes you weren't quite as much on the same wavelength, but either way, they were always very involved. If you ever wrote something unacceptable the editor would hopefully call you and give you a chance to rewrite it or sometimes they'd just get in there and fix it and you wouldn't even know it had been changed until the issue came out, but there was no rubber-stamping. These characters were guarded. And although that may sound stifling, it's actually hugely reassuring, because you're never alone with the responsibility of safeguarding a legend's reputation. As a creator working with licensed characters, you anticipate and accept and even to some extent rely on that editorial pushback. When you go too far with a mainstream superhero story, someone is always there to reel you in.

So I was delighted when I didn't get any pushback for that line or those scenes. The licensed publication novel department is a wholly separate entity from the comics: different editors, different corporate culture, different floor of the building (at least at the time I was writing *Inheritance*) ... so I figured that maybe they were a little less dogmatic than the guys downstairs. The edits I did get were about another issue entirely, a structural problem I had to address, so apparently the handful of cringe-worthy lines spread throughout this 336 page book that was written in three months weren't as bad as I had feared. The novel also contained, I thought, some strong writing, and overall it accomplished what they had asked me to do. All of the material made it through editorial into publication within a company that does not hesitate to ask for rewrites, so although I would have happily rewritten the material in question, there was never a request or an opportunity to do so. And with no one giving me any feedback about it one way or another, I assumed we were okay.

In fact, I assumed we were okay for *years*—literally nearly a decade. I assumed we were okay until less than a month ago, when a friend in the industry let me know that there was, in fact, a huge uproar over that line of Ollie's (or possibly the material surrounding it)—a couple of people very high up were apparently apoplectic. Again, I had *no clue*, but looking back now at the timing of my dismissal from *Nightwing* and *Batwoman* it's actually quite possible that this played a major role in my being suddenly and thoroughly blacklisted at DC. And if that is the case, it's almost worse than if those firings had in fact been arbitrary. Because although it's a personal and professional low point and I take full responsibility for how awful that writing is, it also isn't anywhere close to the worst of what DC has put out. I have never seen a male colleague cast out as quickly or as thoroughly as I was. And more to the point, I would have absolutely rewritten any or all of that without a second thought had I been asked to. I wasn't the least bit wedded to the material, it was just manic silliness. And I wish I could say that it somehow forwarded the cause of gay rights or something, but it really doesn't, it's just dumb, coy banter. But it's *just* dumb, coy banter. It's hard to imagine that it was worth tanking someone's career over.

It's puzzling to me because I had always gone out of my way to be an extremely cooperative freelancer. There's a saying that freelancers can be brilliant, fast, or easy to work with, and that the really good ones are at least two out of three. There's not much you can do to guarantee that you're brilliant, so you make damn sure that you're fast and easy to work with. I was very aware of being in somebody else's sandbox with these characters and although, as you can see from my answers to other questions in this interview, I have very strong and sometimes off-the-wall ideas about them, I honestly never made any attempt to push any kind of personal agenda or stray too far from the company line in my professional work. The mistakes I made came from rushing, and there was no reason anyone at the company would have been afraid to approach me and ask me to pull back. It's kind of horrifying now to think that there were people that offended by it and that disgusted with me and that no one said anything. The turn-around in publishing—especially serialized publishing—is so fast that there are inevitably times when something makes it into print that never should have. I don't know what the institutional policy on how to deal with that is, but I hope it's not to just reflexively dismiss the creator, because they stand to lose a lot of good people that way.

In any case, I love working in long form prose and I loved working for that department and I'm very sad to learn, so many years later, that there was so much going on behind the scenes that I was not aware of. I guess the real answer to your question is that editorial attitudes have not changed very much at all. There have always been, and still are, people around who are so comfortable with gay references and humor that they hardly even notice it, and there have always been, and still are, people around who have absolutely no tolerance for it.

Other than Bruce, who do you see as the most important people in Dick's life? Are there any relationships of his you particularly enjoyed writing?

Oh, Alfred, hands down. In my understanding of their relationship, Dick sends Alfred Mother's Day cards every year. So much ties those two characters together; their devotion to Bruce, their essential sanity and their willingness to forgo it in an effort to make a difference in the world, their understanding of and commitment to improvised family ... I imagine them playing chess together in the Wayne Manor kitchen or having long, rambling phone conversations while tidying up their respective domains ... Bruce's influences on Dick are more obvious in Dick's heroing life, of course, but if you go to Dick's apartment and visit him in his civilian mode, signs of Alfred are all over the place, from the kitchen spice rack to the bedroom sock drawer. Alfred believes that there are *proper ways to do things*, and Dick just does them that way now, out of casual habit. And Alfred is one of the very few pacifists in the DCU, which is such an important influence to have around Dick and Bruce, even if they ignore it most of the time.

I also think Dick's relationship with Barbara is hugely significant, as are his relationships with Donna and Wally and, to a slightly lesser extent only by virtue of proximity, Garth, Roy, Raven and all the other Titans.

And then there's Tim. I *loved* writing Dick and Tim together, there's such genuine respect and compassion in their interactions. Tim acknowledges all of Dick's heir apparent rights to the same extent that Bruce tends to ignore them, creating a lovely, healing balance. And Dick—who does absolutely feel responsible for Batman but knows how impossible a burden that is to commit one's self to—whole heartedly takes responsibility for Tim in a way that Tim—provided he's given his autonomy—appreciates and allows. I don't think they actually spend much time together, but that doesn't affect the underlying intimacy. When they are together they're both better off for it. The affection and veneration between them is palpable.

Are there any characters you would've enjoyed the chance to write Dick interacting with but never got the chance to?

Hmm ... if there were it was my fault, because I was given a lot of free range. There were many I wish I could have done more with ... I did so much in fanfic and background writing, too, I'm honestly having a hard time remembering what went where. Like Superman—I have at least two stories about Dick and Clark but I can't remember if they were published or not. And I have a lot more background in my head about Dick and Wally's friendship than I ever got to put on the page because of a scheduling conflict with Wally while I was writing the Titans.

Actually, I wish I could redo the *Nightwing/Huntress* miniseries, because my understanding of Helena deepened greatly a few years after I wrote that. Most of the same things would have happened, but they would have played out differently. And I had background business between Dick and Selina that I don't think ever actually made print. There's a lot more I wish I could do, but I'm also very grateful to have had the time and access I had.

Let's talk about Nightwing #93.[8] That issue has been quite controversial, partially because of an interview you did in 2004 before the arc was finished. In an interview, you replied "For the record, I've never used the word "rape," I just said it was nonconsensual (I know, aren't writers frustrating? *smiles*)."[9] Were you being coy because the arc wasn't finished? Now that it's ten years later, could you tell us exactly what happened in issue 93 and that arc as a whole?

I really appreciate the opportunity to talk about this, because I screwed up and do owe *Nightwing*'s readers an apology. So, where to start ... let's tackle the interview first. I was being coy because I didn't know what the hell I was talking about. I was uncomfortable with the intensity of the reaction readers were having and annoyed that no one seemed to understand the scene the way I'd intended it. That annoyance pretty quickly turned to self-recrimination, of course, but that interview happened during a beat when I had not yet realized how big a mistake I'd made or how little time I was ultimately going to have to correct it. So, that was a dumb, defensive thing to say, and I regret it.

So, here's what I had intended with the scene, more or less (with the caveat that it is now ten years later and I can no more say exactly what I was thinking at the time than any of us can ever explain anything from our past): the arc had been leading up to the murder of Blockbuster. I had played with the idea of having Dick actually do it, but decided there was pretty much nothing you could do to him that would allow him to justify something like that to himself, to take that kind of action. But what he could do, and could feel just as horrible about, is fail to stop someone else from taking that action. And I think we all suspect, and he firmly believes, that he could have stopped Catalina had he committed to doing so (which in the normal course of events would have been his default, automatic response). That's what I wanted to explore; someone pushed so far out of their own comfort zone that they can't even access their inherent, authentic self. Ideally, that eventually leads that character to have to reassess, recommit to and reclaim their own power, but that didn't happen because of the interruption of the story arc. But back to that moment: here's a guy who's been taught his whole life that killing is categorically unjustifiable, but he's facing someone he basically wants dead, someone who has taken an enormous amount from him and is in that very second making it as clear as he possibly can that he will continue to do so with the entirety of his resources and being as long as he draws breath. It is, as Dick begins to realize to the exclusion of all other thoughts, never going to stop. Blockbuster is going to keep coming after the people he loves. And Dick is at the end of his emotional rope here, he's out of resilience, he needs it to stop.

The other piece is that Dick is traumatized by everything that's come before this moment and his response to that trauma is to fall back into old survival habits. And in Dick's case, despite all the years of competent solo work and leadership, the emotionally wounded survival mode involves falling into step behind the most dynamic, effective being he can find. The pattern he's accessing here is of course about Batman, but Batman isn't there, Tarantula is, and Dick has surrendered a great deal of his will to her as he's sunk further and further into despair. And unlike Batman, Tarantula is not a safe person to abdicate one's will to; she does not genuinely have Dick's best interest at heart and she is not personally capable of carrying him through this challenge. And I think this element of the story really intrigued me, but clearly I wasn't precise enough with it, because I don't think it was communicated to the readers. I got asked a lot of questions about why Catalina was following Dick around, which seemed odd to me—it was pretty obvious what she was getting out of the deal; here's a guy in a totally different league and she feels elevated by proximity. The more interesting question—in my mind, anyway—was why was Dick following Catalina around? What the hell was he getting out if it? And I think, if I had presented it properly, the answer is actually pretty interesting; he's getting a chance to sidekick again. And if he thought about it lucidly, he would of course immediately realize that Catalina and Bruce have almost nothing in common and that Tarantula is in no way an appropriate person to be partnering with—she is morally, physically, psychologically, socially and experientially miles behind him. But she's dynamic and driven and of course none of this is a conscious decision on his part, it's a survival instinct, automated.

So these two things come together. He's desperate to stop Blockbuster and he's in sidekick mode when he really should be in leader mode and he fails to stop Catalina from murdering Blockbuster. And the second that gun goes off, the second it becomes too late to change what's happening, Dick starts to come out of the numb trance he's been in and starts to feel just the tiniest flicker of his authentic self again. And it is *unbearable*. It is unbearable to be who he is and not to have stopped that murder. He's literally vomiting off the top of the building, in a moral tailspin, when Catalina—flushed with triumph and completely oblivious to his distress (in her mind she's just done the world, and Dick, a huge service)—taps into that weird sex/death impulse and assumes he's right there with her (even though he's very clearly saying "no" and "don't touch me.")

But for me—and here's where the biggest misstep came in—that gesture was basically metaphorical. It was a physical demonstration of the power she had over him in that moment, the degree to which she'd co-opted him, the extent to which he'd subjugated his will to hers. It's a picture of their disconnect. The rape was an afterthought, it wasn't even in my original outline, so that that, rather than Blockbuster's murder, became the focal point of the issue was really confusing for me. I didn't understand at the time that you can't use rape metaphorically; the reality of rape and sexual assault has too much immediate meaning for too many people. And ironically, I think it was my own experience with sexual abuse that numbed me to that. Somewhere in the back of my mind, rape had become an emotional portrait of distress ... a piece of depression and all of its attendant miseries ... rather than an actual, immediate, resonant event.

I feel terrible about it now, and especially about the fact that I didn't have time to follow up on it, to at least let Dick and the readers process it. Rape is used so casually in comics as a gesture of "something really bad happening to someone," ... I am deeply sorry to have contributed to that trope.

Do you see rape and non-consensual sex as two different things? Many fans felt the interview implied that, and they were upset. Thoughts?

No, no, no. Non-consensual sex is the *definition* of rape. As a woman in my early forties with two kids and a shockingly recent education in gender studies, it's difficult to fathom, much less explain, how I could have ever been so uneducated and disconnected from that reality. The fans had every right to be upset. And for the record, when someone who is normally fairly articulate and intelligent says something that egregious, you can pretty much bet that there are huge, unresolved personal issues behind it, in addition to a lack of education on the subject. That script and interview exposed so much of my own baggage and this weird, ongoing resistance I had to associating myself with and learning about the social reality of being female in this culture. The only solace I can take from it now is that even someone who said something that ill-informed can be taught.

Could you talk about the aftermath of issue #93? How did Dick deal with his sexual assault? Do you think he fully dealt with it? Did you get to show the aftermath to your satisfaction or were you hampered by War Games, editorial, or comic code constraints?

No, he didn't deal with it all. I don't think it even came up again, right? I was just starting to come to terms with the mistake I'd made there when we hurled into War Games, which also marked the beginning of the end of my career at DC. I never truly had control of the Nightwing series from that point on and, to take responsibility for my part in it, it took me much longer than it should have to stop feeling defensive and misunderstood and start realizing that I'd screwed up and needed to fix it. I'm not sure I could have fixed it, but absolutely he should have addressed it. I think I would have had him tell Barbara, who would have made him tell Bruce, who would have sent him to Leslie Thompkins. And Leslie could have helped Dick and the readers process and put some context around it. As it is, it exists in a void, which is just the worst thing that could have happened there.

If you had to write the Nightwing-Tarantula arc over again, would you change anything? What worked with this arc? What didn't?

I'd change that scene in a heartbeat. I think her impulse might still have been to try to initiate sex. Dick would still have had a second vomiting on the roof, but then he would have gotten up and realized that the consequences of not being in control of his own life were disastrous. He should have come back into himself, his power, sooner. I think I'd actually have him arrange for her arrest right then and there. The whole arc was paced wrong, really—I would have sped a lot of things up.

I stand by Catalina, though. Not her actions, of course, which were reprehensible, but her integrity as a character. The high concept behind her was to show what could happen if you took someone with the same impulses as the Bat-gang but with a very different socioeconomic background—a different experience of the world and how to move through it effectively. I think there was an internal consistency in her, even though not many readers seemed to understand her. I think part of the problem was that readers wanted her to be more likable than I ever had any intention of making her. I wouldn't even necessarily say that she was a good guy, and she certainly wasn't meant to be a long-term match for Dick. That people accuse her of being a Mary Sue kills me—other than being brunette and thinking Dick Grayson's pretty awesome, I can't think of a single thing she and I have in common.

Your *Nightwing* run ended up being cut short by *One Year Later*—are there any storylines you were planning that never got to see the light of day? Is there anything you would've written differently had you had more time?

Totally. The whole last two years, really. I had a lot of fun with the "Crutches" story arc, but all of that was editorially driven. I was told Dick had to be out of costume for a year (which is a very strange limitation to put on a superhero), I was told I had to use Rose, etc., etc. … and it's not like you get all of those edicts at once, either. You start a storyline, get given a weird, impossible note like that your superhero has to be out of his costume for a year, you adjust to try to make a story work around that and then two issues into that you're told to take out a certain character and start using another and it just keeps going like that. It's actually a miracle that any series makes any sense ever. DC was going through a huge cultural shift at that time, too, and the entire way arc approval and editorial notes and crossover events and even continuity between existing titles worked was changing and we were all just doing our best to keep up with the changes. I can't even say how different the stories would have been because they would have started from completely different premises. But that's part of this particular job. You jump through the hoops as best you can.

Speaking of your run on *Nightwing*. You left the book, and DC, in 2006. Any particular reason why?

I was fired. Well, I guess the correct phrasing would be that I was dismissed from that title, because technically I was under an exclusive contract with DC at the time. I was working on issue 115 of *Nightwing* when I was told that 116 would be my last. No explanation was ever given and no other proposal I tried to get through was ever accepted, with the brief exception of the Batwoman series, which they assigned to me and had me working on before announcing to *The New York Times* that they had no plans of publishing a Batwoman series. It was all really weird and confusing, and now I have to try to factor in the new information I have about the company's internal response to *Inheritance* as well. Clearly there was a lot going on of which I wasn't made aware. But I did not leave the book, or the company, voluntarily.

We saw Dick take the mantle of the Bat when Bruce had apparently died. Do you feel that taking on the role of Batman is Dick's right and/or responsibility? Do you see this as Dick's future?

This is hard, because I think Dick would, and I think it would be crazy and wrong for Bruce to ask anyone else, at least initially, but I also think it would be unhealthy for Dick psychologically. It's just not who he is. At the same time, though, I think it would be easier for Dick to be Batman than to be in a world without Batman.

But I'm a purist, and to me, Batman is Bruce Wayne, period. Having other people fill in from time to time is fine—those can be great stories—but I have a six-year-old son, and for us, Batman sounds like Kevin Conroy and is named, in his civilian life, Bruce Wayne. We're not very flexible on that.

Your writing of Dick often emphasizes his recklessness, to the point of portraying him as someone with no regard for his own safety (and even someone who enjoys danger/pain). This element is arguably far more present in your writing than in the way other writers have portrayed Dick. Do you see Dick as an essentially incautious character?

I see him as someone who is fairly fearless, but someone for whom that lack of fear is based in a lot of precedence. He can do things we can't. And many of the things he does, which look incredibly risky and reckless to us, are actually fairly safe, practiced moves for him. I see him as being impulsive, but that impulsivity is grounded in so much experience that it wouldn't exactly be fair to call it reckless. There's no question that Bruce grilled him on personal safety—probably to a nearly absurd extent, really, since Bruce would both recognize any tendency Dick might have toward physical impulsiveness and hold himself personally responsible for any harm that might come from it (such harm being, of course, "UNACCEPTABLE."). So it's not like Dick's the guy who throws himself off a building and laughs off the injury. He's the guy who throws himself off a building and has to decide which of the eight ways to safety he identifies in that one quarter of one second on the way down he's gonna use. And of course, the more you do that, the more it takes to really scare you or, I suppose, give you a genuine thrill. So yeah, there's some adrenaline junky in him for sure. But again, it's not so much a matter of being someone who has to push the limit to feel anything as being someone who has to maintain a very high level of adrenaline just to get through their day.

If it's true that that element of his personality is more prevalent in my work than elsewhere, I'm going to guess that it's due, at least in small part, to my own physical limitations. I've had Type 1 diabetes since I was fourteen … basically my body has always been a liability to me. So I love the characters that are physical as well as cerebral, and I love thinking about what people might do when they have confidence in their own strength and agility and health.

At his most basic core, how would you describe Dick's character? What do you consider his greatest strength? His biggest flaw?

The word I generally use to describe Dick is "loyal." Not just that he is loyal, but that he represents the quality of loyalty. He's a difficult character to sum up, though. For the first half of his career he's the ultimate sidekick and for the second half he's nearly the opposite (independent, a strong leader, etc.,). The qualities that don't change are his competence, his trustworthiness, his insatiable curiosity and the extent to which he's dutiful and devoted. That loyalty is what he derives his strength from, but it can also be a weakness or a liability—it can blind him to someone's faults or make him push himself further than he should before he's even fully considered why he's doing so. His brain and body are so fast—he's deeply thoughtful but he's not a contemplative person. It's kind of what we were talking about before with the concept of safe recklessness—he does have a tendency to throw himself into (or off of) things. He's at his best right in the middle of the action—he has an ability to thrive there that is very rare. I guess you could think of it in terms of stress; stress hobbles most of us, but it propels him. What you or I would find stressful Dick would find effortless. But ask him to stand still and wait … that's not something he tolerates well.

What do you think about Dick's rogues gallery? Who was his greatest foe in your opinion and who was his biggest challenge?

I think the dynamic between Dick and Slade—Deathstroke—is very interesting. What Nightwing can do because of natural talent and years of training, Deathstroke can do because of meta-human enhancements, so they're a good match. And Dick respects Slade at some level, and also acknowledges him as the father of someone who was once a close friend. Respecting someone pulls on that loyalty response I keep talking about, and one of the things I like about pitting Dick against Slade is that in addition to fighting Slade—who is an exceedingly formidable opponent in his own right—Dick ends up having to fight himself and his own instincts a little bit. That's far more interesting to me than pitting Dick against someone he just has to kick into submission.

You worked with many different artists at DC, in different styles. Did you adopt different working methods for different pencilers? What did different styles bring out in the character or adventures of Dick Grayson?

Holy crap, yeah, I've had the privilege of working with so many amazing people. I write very detailed scripts with lot of notes about moods and motivations, but I think when I first started out I didn't know how to tailor scripts to individual artists. But it probably didn't really matter, because I got to work with some astonishingly brilliant artists like Rodolpho Damaggio, Greg Land and Duncan Fegredo straight out of the gate. Later, by the time I was truly collaborating with people like Brian Stelfreeze and John Bolton, I had a better understanding of how to shift stories and scripts to play to the strengths of individual artists (not that artists like that have any weaknesses to speak of, mind you!). But most of the time it's the editor putting together the team, and good editors are very aware of who to hire for a kinetic story and who to hire for a moody story and who to hire for a romantic story. In the end, it's not at all just the writer and the penciler influencing how the character is perceived—in addition to the publisher and the editor and the inker and the colorist and the letterer and everyone else involved with the actual creation of the book in question, the reader is ultimately the person imbuing the story with the greatest share of subtext and resonance.

Overall, how do you feel about your contribution to the Dick Grayson mythos? What are you particularly proud of? Is there anything you wish you could change?

Obviously, as we've been discussing, I'd change a lot about how the end of my run on *Nightwing* played out, and even though I don't know how much difference it's made (in terms of whether or not it's even canon) I am proud of having made his adoption official, because I feel strongly that that was the right thing to do for his contemporary iteration. I wish I had been more explicit, on the page, about who I think the character is and what he means to me—by which I guess I mean I wish I had had the skill and time to tell more stories *about* him as opposed to stories *with* him. But overall, I'm mostly at peace with what I created with and for Dick.

Did any writers or stories (comics or otherwise) particularly influence how you wrote Dick?

I really loved Marv Wolfman's *Teen Titans* Dick, and also Chuck Dixon's solo-Dick (that does not sound good out loud AT ALL), and I think mostly I was really intrigued by how different those two characters were and committed to bridging that distance. Wolfman's Nightwing is really cerebral and Dixon's Nightwing is really physical and of course both things are true of the character, so how do you wed that in a way that feels truly authentic? I also gleaned a lot of inspirations from my editors, particularly Scott Peterson and Michael Wright, both of whom cared about the character as much as I did and were willing to share their passion for and understanding of him.

At times, you have been known to role-play Dick Grayson.[10] How did that technique help you generate stories? What enabled you to identify so strongly with Nightwing? Did this tactic leave you feeling emotionally drained at times? Uplifted? Invigorated?

Uplifted and invigorated, definitely! I have been a role player (and/or role play gamer) longer than I've been a writer and the two activities are nearly inseparable to me. I don't know how other writers go about "getting into the heads" of their characters but that's how I do it, role play, I let them take over. Actually, to be fair, it's the other way around. Characters come to me, I find venues in which to play them (pencil and dice role playing games, massive multiplayer online role playing games, live action role plays with friends, creative play in the bedroom, etc.) and then the obsession to explore their story starts to build until I have to write it down. Maybe it's because of my early training in acting—I was doing plays and studying theater from first grade through college—or maybe it's just because I never got tired of playing "let's pretend," but if there was a way to get paid to be a role player, that would be my ideal job. And writing is actually pretty damn close.

With Dick specifically I think I relate to his circumstantial loyalty and his competence and his desire to make meaningful connections with difficult people, all of which have very clear correlations in my life. And then I'm really attracted to and excited by his grace and physicality and his indefatigable energy, all of which are very outside my personal experience. The best characters to role play are the ones who reflect some essential truth about you but express it in an entirely foreign way. I explore this a little in *USER*, a Vertigo miniseries I did that's about online role playing. The main character, Meg, supplies all of the poetic and romantic devotion of the character she plays online, Guilliame, but within the game he then commits to actions and relationships she is not yet capable of in the real world.

According to Comic Vine, you were supposed to write the new Batwoman series.[11] However, you were apparently fired without being notified—you found out through the newspaper. Is this true? If so, can you shed a little light on how such a strange, unprofessional situation came to pass?

I wish I could, but it is true, and that's pretty much as much as I know about the situation. I had turned in a six or maybe twelve-month outline, which had been approved, and although we did not yet have an artist in place I began working on the scripts. I was halfway through the third when someone showed me an interview in *The New York Times* in which the company publisher stated that DC had no plans to publish an ongoing Batwoman series. I spoke to my editor on the phone and he confirmed it but could not offer any additional information or insight, and then literally ten years went by before anyone from DC ever contacted me about anything again. It was so bizarre and I was so confused and unhappy. That was not long after being dismissed from *Nightwing*, so when my exclusive finally ran out, I went ahead and assumed that DC was no longer interested in working with me. And very recently I found out that it all may have been related to that scene we discussed with Ollie in *Inheritance*, but since no one ever actually contacted me about any of it, it's all conjecture on my part.

As an openly bisexual female I think there was a lot I could have brought to *Batwoman* and I was sad to lose the chance to contribute to her mythos, but I am glad that DC eventually went ahead and published a monthly series for her.

Finally, what are you up to these days? Any chance you might write Dick Grayson again?

In addition to the radio play I mentioned, I recently wrote a short story for Onyx Path Publishing and am currently working on an original YA novel as well as my second graphic novelization project for Random House; I'm adapting one of Tamora Pierce's *New York Times* bestselling fantasy series for a graphic novel. I finally have a website up again, so you can keep track of my published work at DevinGraysonCentral.com.

As for writing Dick Grayson again, I am absolutely up for it, but suspect that I am not a great cultural fit for DC at this particularly moment in history. If I'm wrong or if that changes, though, I can't imagine a time in my life that I wouldn't be happy to share with the fans and denizens of Gotham.

Notes

1. The questions asked herein were solicited from online fans. Geaman compiled and edited them, presenting them in a written format to the interviewee for their answers.

2. Yes, this is her real name. Although born with another name, Devin Grayson has been her legal name for over two decades and predates her acquaintance with Dick Grayson by several years. It's just a humorous coincidence (or fate) that the two have the same initials.

3. In this story, Hugo Strange has uncovered Batman's secret identity. To throw Strange off, Bruce Wayne hypnotizes himself to forget that he is Batman.

4. Lauren Davis, "Paul Dini: Superhero Cartoon Execs Don't Want Largely Female Audiences," *io9*, 15 December 2013, http://io9.com/paul-dini-superhero-cartoon-execs-dont-want-largely-f-1483758317.

5. The 2005 *Shameless Magazine* interview in which Grayson discussed this has been taken offline.

6. The editor apologizes for uncritically accepting that term and thereby perpetuating the assumed whiteness of fictional characters.

7. In *Batman: Gotham Knights* #17 and #20–21 (2001).

8. In this issue, Tarantula (Catalina Flores) raped a guilt-ridden, comatose Dick after Nightwing had failed to stop her from shooting the super-villain Blockbuster.

9. Interview with Randy Burtis; http://www.comicboards.com/devin.php.

10. See http://www.thecomicfanatic.com/modules.php?op=modload&name=News&file=articles&sid=301 and http://gailsimone.tumblr.com/post/10718077837/deathlyillandalway sbusy-thehappysorceress.

11. http://www.comicvine.com/devin-grayson/4040-42845/

Interview with Kyle Higgins

Kristen L. Geaman[1]

Kyle Higgins is a comic book writer, most famous for his run on DC's New 52 *Nightwing*. Higgins got his start through film; his college thesis was a movie about a superhero union in 1960s Chicago, entitled *The League*. Higgins wrote several issues for Marvel before moving over to DC in 2010, where he penned stories about Nightrunner, a French-Algerian member of Batman Incorporated, and the limited series *Batman: Gates of Gotham*, which featured Dick Grayson as Batman. Although his popular run on *Nightwing* is over, Higgins currently still writes *Batman Beyond 2.0*. He is also co-writer, with Alec Siegel, of the new series *C.O.W.L*, a series about Chicago superheroes that had its genesis in his thesis film.

Why is Nightwing your favorite character? Is it specifically Nightwing or Dick Grayson more generally?

It's Dick Grayson, but Nightwing is my favorite iteration of him. When I first discovered the character, the idea of Robin getting out from under Batman's shadow was what I really responded to. That, and his costume. At the time, he was in the black and robin's-egg-blue suit. It looked so elegant, and it felt distinct. I was also a Carolina Panthers' fan for like, three years mostly because of the colors. So, it was a little bit of a perfect visual storm for me. Comics are a visual medium, and I'd be lying if I didn't say the Nightwing visual was the first thing that really struck me.

I grew up a Marvel fan, except for Batman. Through the Burton film and *Batman: The Animated Series*, I really fell in love with Gotham. And, it was that interpretation of the mythos—where Dick Grayson was wearing a more grounded, Tim Drake–version of the Robin suit, while also being old enough that he was attending college—where I really started to gravitate towards the character. A few years later, I picked up issue #2 of *Marvel VS DC* and read a short scene where a guy named Nightwing fought Gambit. The caption boxes described Nightwing as being a former Robin, and then called him out later as being Dick Grayson. I remember having a lot of questions—Dick Grayson was no longer Robin? Why? What happened between him and Bruce? Did Dick quit? Or was he fired? And why the name Nightwing?

I reread that comic a lot over the next couple months, and at some point about a year later I was in the grocery store and *Nightwing* #16 or 17 was on the shelf. To be honest, I can't remember which I bought first. I want to say it was #17, with the Man-Bat cover, but I'm not sure anymore. Whichever it was, my mom bought me the other one a day or two later. Anyway, I'd had questions about the character since reading the *Marvel VS DC* issue, and the numbering on the Nightwing series was low enough that it felt accessible to me. So, that became my first read-it-every-month comic.

But, getting back to your question about the actual character, it's funny—a lot of my favorites have always been what you might consider "second tier" heroes. Nightwing, The Scarlet Spider, Havok ... in later years, the Winter Soldier. It wasn't something I was really conscious of, but a person trying to get out from under a shadow and make their own path in life always resonated with me. Hell, I remember reading a Spider-Man story with a one-off called the Steel Spider and thinking he was really cool. Whenever I talk about this people usually ask if I'm the youngest child. I'm not, though. I'm the oldest. I think a big part of the appeal was that these characters always felt more accessible—like, I couldn't be Spider-Man, but I could be someone like the Steel Spider. If that makes sense. Dick Grayson was the epitome of that. Plus, he was the coolest.

The more Grayson stories I read, the more I fell in love with him. He was Batman without the brooding. He was visually more akin to Spider-Man. He was respected by all the heroes of the DC universe. He was a lady's man. And, he was funny. As a kid, he was the total package. That said, I think a lot of that stuff is just surface level. It took a long time, but the more I got to know him, the more I got to the core of who he was and what I really loved about him: Dick Grayson is about people.

When you think of Batman and why he does what he does, you zero in on his parents—guilt over what happened and the desire to keep it from happening to anyone else. Bruce is driven by the memory of his parents' deaths. To me, Dick is driven by the memory of his parents' lives. It's a subtle difference, but it's substantial. Dick is an eternal optimist. He does what he does the way he does it because in a lot of ways, it's a performance. A celebration. He soars over rooftops, smiles, and—often times—is fine operating during the day when people can see him. He's a guy who grew up in a circus, under the spotlight, making people happy. That, to me, is what's so fantastic about him. He'll save you from a mugger, tie your shoe, and buy you a beer. In all my time writing the New 52 series, and through all the ups and downs on the title, I have to say—the thing I am the most proud of and will always stand by is the final narration of the series:

> *When you get down to it, my life isn't about the costumes or the bad guys.*
> *It's not about cities or symbols.*
> *It's way simpler than that.*
> *I mean, I grew up in a circus.*
> *It's **always** been about catching people when they fall.*

That, to me, is who Dick Grayson is. And it's why I love him.

What is Dick's special place in the DCU? The DCNU?

I've heard a lot of people describe him as the heart and soul of the DCU, and I think that's true. He knew, and was respected by, *everyone*. He was the leader of the Titans, had strong ties to the Justice League, was a mentor to Tim Drake and the younger sidekicks ... he was both the prodigal son and the cool uncle. But, all of that is dependent on the relationships he had. In the DCNU, he doesn't really have those relationships ... which was something I struggled with on the book. Wally West, his best friend, didn't exist. Donna Troy didn't exist. Kori wasn't recognizable. So, to be honest, I'm not really sure what his "special place" is. I think that's still a bit up in the air.

What is your favorite storyline or issue featuring Dick Grayson that you did not write? That you did?

I'd say it's the first twenty-nine issues of the Dixon/McDaniel series. That was my first real interaction with the character, and also the series that shaped me the most as a writer. After that, I'd point to the episode "Old Wounds" of *The New Batman Adventures*. As far as the stuff that I wrote, I'd probably point to the first three issues of the Chicago/Tony Zucco story, the Night of the Owls two-parter, and my final issue with Russell Dauterman.

Since you were a fan even before you were a writer, have there ever been issues or storylines which you thought mischaracterized Dick? Which ones and why?

Man, that's a tough one. The short answer is, yes. But ... I try not to talk about things I don't like. I don't think it's fair to the creators who worked on the stories. I mean, no one enters into a project with the goal of doing crappy work.

How would you define the relationship between Bruce and Dick? The New 52 has been a little murky on whether or not Dick is Bruce's ward and/or adopted son as he was previously.

Well, I can tell you first hand, he was *not* adopted by Bruce in the New 52. Their relationship was actually something that I was asked to augment a bit. The feeling was that in the year 2012, becoming the ward of a billionaire playboy didn't seem right. So, that's where the Wayne Foster Center, or whatever we called it, came into play. The idea was that Dick would live there, and have a "part time job" at Wayne manor ... which is where he trained with Bruce. This all happened in our issue #0, which is also where DC asked that Dick be the one to figure out who Batman really was. Later, when I wrote the *Secret Origins* issue, they changed their minds and asked to revert it back so that Bruce was the one who revealed his identity to Dick. So, I think that's where it stands now.

As far as their personal relationship, I'd still characterize it as a father-son dynamic. That's how I wrote it, anyway. The other thing I'll say about it, though, is that at a certain point, I tried to steer the series away from the Bruce/Dick relationship. As a fan, I really enjoy that stuff, but as a writer ... it puts a glass ceiling on DG. If you spend too much time on stories that feature the Bruce/Dick relationship, then you run the risk of it becoming the emotional core of your series. Once that happens, it means Dick is dependent on Bruce for any sort of emotional arc. That's not healthy for the character. And, it's not sustainable for an ongoing series. Plus, it puts him right back under that shadow that he long-ago escaped.

We had a lot of crossovers in my first year and half—Court of Owls, Death of the Family, the Death of Damian ... by the end of issue #18 I felt like we'd done enough with Bruce/Dick. That's where the focus on moving the series to Chicago came from.

How would you characterize Dick's relationship with his Bat-siblings? What are the differences in these relationships between the DCU and the rebooted universe?

I think the biggest differences are in the relationships with Tim and Jason. And to be honest ... I'm not sure what their relationships even are. Scott (Lobdell) did a lot of work redefining Tim and Jason for the New 52. Since they were pretty firmly in Scott's sandbox, I never brought them into my series.

The other big difference would be between Dick and Barbara. In the New 52, I'm pretty sure they've never *actually* been in a relationship. There was always a "will-they-won't-they" dynamic, but I'm pretty sure that's as far as their relationship ever went.

Speaking of relationships, *Nightwing Annual #1* (and other books) dropped some hints about a possible relationship, at some point, between Dick and Barbara. Would you like to see Dick and Babs as a couple again or do you think it's time for Dick (and his fans) to move on?

I'd like to see them together for a while, sure. But ... I don't think you'll ever see them wind up together. At least, not in any current-timeline-continuity. But, to be fair, I don't think you'll see Dick settle down with anyone permanently. I'm not saying that with any insider knowledge, but just a general feel for the types of stories we tend to see with characters who have been around as long as Dick has been.

What does the "Gray Son of Gotham" angle add to Dick's history and place in the rebooted DCU?

I think it adds to his legacy and place in Gotham City, but beyond that, I don't think it has much of an effect on him or his place in the wider DCU. The idea behind the Gray Son angle was essentially to acknowledge that, yes, Dick has roots in Gotham ... and they're not the kind you expect. That said, becoming a Talon for the Court of Owls never happened. It's a fate he escaped. So, I'm not sure there's too much about it that's applicable going forward, unless the Court comes back. Which, you know, is certainly possible.

All that said, the issue is still one of my favorites. I'd definitely put it in the top two or three of my run.

You were writing *Nightwing* and *Deathstroke* simultaneously. Would you have liked to have used Deathstroke as a Grayson adversary? Out of all the currently existing DC characters, who do you think is the best nemesis for Dick? The Joker to his Batman?

Oh, yeah. One hundred percent. But, I was only on Deathstroke for eight issues and I had a certain story I was trying to tell in the first arc. Plus, I wasn't sure if Slade and Dick even knew each other. That was something I was hoping to get into in my second arc on Deathstroke, figuring out if Nightwing and Deathstroke would be meeting for the first time or if they had a history. Sadly though, I never got the chance.

I don't think Dick really has a Joker. Something like that takes time to develop. I know there was a desire to turn the Prankster into his Joker, but I never really felt like their dynamic was built for that. At least, not after one story. I had wanted to do more with Zucco and building him up and his place in Chicago after my first story with him, but it didn't really fly.

I think the character who has the most potential as a Joker to Dick's Nightwing is James Jr. The way Scott (Snyder) built James Jr. during his Black Mirror story, James suffers from a complete lack of empathy. Contrast that with Dick, whose greatest asset is his empathy, and you have a pretty compelling dynamic. I'd be shocked if someone didn't explore that further in future stories.

Some Nightwing fans felt the frequent cross-overs with the Batman books hampered Dick's growth as a character and restricted you as a writer. Thoughts? Would you have liked to move Dick to Chicago even sooner? What was the benefit of having Dick move to an existing city rather than a fictional one such as Blüdhaven?

I'd agree with that, sure. Maybe not the "hampering me as a writer" portion, if only because crossovers are an understood part of writing in a shared universe, but yeah. I would have loved to move him to Chicago sooner. I had a big mythology planned out for Chicago and … we came really close to being able to execute it. I'm proud of the issues I did there—especially the first couple—but there will always be a "what could have been" feeling to that stuff for me. And as far as Chicago goes, I hate fictional cities. I feel pretty strongly that real cities help to make stories relatable, which in turn helps to ground the fantastic elements that superhero sagas feature. And with Chicago specifically, no one had really explored it in the DCU. I felt like there was a pretty fantastic opportunity to make it Dick's city. Where as a place like New York is kind of defined by its skyscrapers—at least in Marvel books—Chicago could be much more neighborhood based, with a heavy focus on the L trains as a way for Nightwing to get around. I felt like it really played into his parkour and rooftop running style, much in the way that Blüdhaven did.

Since you also write *Batman Beyond*, what do you see as the major differences between regular continuity Dick and the animated continuity (DCAU) Dick?

That's a really good question. I think animated Dick was—at least initially—a darker version of Nightwing. He was dealing with a lot more emotional baggage with Bruce. But, as the stories went on, he lightened up a bit. And, by the time you see him in the *Batman Beyond* era of his timeline, he's older and been through the wringer a bit. But, I still wrote him with optimism and quips. Even old, Dick Grayson should still be cool.

Why do you think DCAU Dick and Bruce have a more distant relationship than they do in regular continuity?

It's more dramatic, for starters. Plus, the DCAU is so Batman-centric, that most of the other characters are seen through the lens of their relationship with Batman. Like I was saying before, when you define a character that way ... there are only so many things you can do with them. Pushing the relationship to the brink is the most dynamic, and gets you the most mileage.

Like most Batman fans who are in their twenties and thirties, I imagine you watched *Batman: The Animated Series* as a child. What are your favorite episodes? Why?

I have a ton. No joke, I could do an entire interview just on *Batman: The Animated Series*. I guess if I have to narrow it down, and for the sake of this interview, I'll go with *Fear of Victory*. It was an early Robin-centric episode that showed Dick overcoming crippling fear and ultimately saving the day. Plus, FOX showed it in reruns all the time. So, I definitely watched it a lot.

As a viewer and writer, how do you feel about the changes that took place between B:TAS and *The New Batman Adventures*?

I was so happy we were getting more Batman that I was cool with the changes. Plus, they said they were bringing in Nightwing ... which put me over the moon. I remember I used to set our VCR to record episodes when my family and I would go to church, and every week I would come home and check the tape and hope it'd finally be a Nightwing episode.

The one thing I didn't love early on was the redesign to the characters and the animation style ... but I eventually came around to it.

How has Dick Grayson influenced your idea of what a superhero should be?

I think in an era where dark—especially in film and TV—is in vogue, Dick Grayson is one of the great examples of a character that doesn't need to be dark in order to work.

You are currently writing an original series, C.O.W.L. Can we see any traces of Dick Grayson in it?

Oh yeah, totally. There's a former sidekick—Sparrow—who hasn't come into the book in a big way yet, but when he shows up again as an older hero ... there's a lot of Dick Grayson about him. But, the biggest Dick Grayson influence on *C.O.W.L.* is actually the effect that Dick has had on me. I've talked about this in interviews before, but it's true. Dick Grayson made me a better writer. Very few people get to have the type of relationship with their favorite character that I've been able to have. Do I love everything I did with him? No, of course not. But the great thing is that he's an incredible character who has stood the test of time and is as strong now as he was seventy-five years ago. You can't break him.

Note

1. The questions asked herein were solicited from online fans. Geaman compiled and edited them, presenting them in a written format to the interviewee for their answers.

Conclusion
Dick Grayson: Becoming a Man
Dan Grayson Cordero

> Dick: "It wasn't rocket science. Not even long division. Just simple arithmetic. Little Robin grows up to be big, bad Nightwing."[1]

Dick Grayson was the Robin who left the nest (or cave, rather) and became Nightwing. This sole action defined Dick as a true agent of change. The turbulent transition from young squire to the Dark Knight into an independent hero set Dick on a journey that required an in-depth search of himself. His shedding of the Robin mantle and rebirth as Nightwing is, at its core, a story about growing up and discovering and developing one's identity. The impact of this journey has stood the test of time with its numerous retellings over the thirty years since Nightwing's initial debut into the DC Comic's universe.

Part of what makes Dick and his transformation into Nightwing so significant is its ability to impact readers. Watching the trying process through which Dick forged an identity that could stand firmly on its own, while acknowledging the impact and influence of his past, mirrored the same journey I underwent during a period of my life during which, for the most part, I was lost. His story gave me a way to process what I was trying so hard to understand, ultimately showing me someone I could look to for guidance as I worked through severe sensations of misplacement in my own body. Growing up, I took an incredible amount of solace and comfort in Dick Grayson's character and history, looking to him in my darkest hours, not only from the perspective of a child facing adulthood, but as a young trans[2] boy grappling with issues of gender and identity.

Following Dick Grayson's passage into maturity and his role as Nightwing allowed me to embark on both my inward and outward transitions. Having used Dick's moral character and how he relates himself to his past as a guide for so long, I can say without a doubt I wouldn't be the man I am today without his influence.

Dick's departure from the Dynamic Duo and the Robin mantle was all but amicable—Bruce cruelly fired Dick. Until that point, Robin (a title that was originally an homage to the nickname his mother had given him in his youth) had been the defining aspect of Dick's many relationships. Prior to his ejection from the cave, Dick had always lived his life as part of a team. The Flying Graysons. The Dynamic Duo. The Teen Titans. It was through these relationships that he had always been able to define himself. Son. Partner. Leader. The loss of Robin subsequently left him without the ability to continue to define himself by those relationships. Dick was left stripped of his past, present, and what he had pictured as his future.

> SUPERMAN: Have you thought of simply *pitching* it all? Just living the *rest* of your life as Dick Grayson?
> DICK: That seemed like a really sane thing to do for about five *seconds*. But I dedicated my *life* to being Robin. And I always thought—
> SUPERMAN: That someday *you'd* be Batman.
> DICK: I never *told* anyone that before.[3]

Dick's temporary falling out with Bruce and misplacement he endured afterwards unfortunately echoes the reality of transgender youth all over America, and a legitimate fear that lingered in the back of my head in anticipation of the day I was to come out to my parents. According to the National Transgender Discrimination survey conducted in 2011 by the National Center for Transgender Equality and National Gay and Lesbian Task Force, 57 percent of transgender participants surveyed experienced significant family rejection, and 26 percent experienced homelessness.[4]

Stripped of his identity as Robin and his relationship to Bruce Wayne and Batman, Dick existed in a state of limbo. It was the former acrobat's new mission to find a new means of making his way through the world, beginning with figuring out exactly who he was behind the mask. Proving a task that was easier said than done, Dick shared some of his concerns with Wally West, who around the same time had shed his identity as Kid Flash. As the two leave Titan's Tower, Dick (rather than think about his freedom) admits to Wally, "Without Robin I have no family."[5]

Disoriented and left wandering without a clear sense of purpose or direction, this portion of Dick's life closely paralleled my own as I finally began my transition from female to male. I began the physical portion of my transition in middle school, which meant a lot of visits to doctors and gender specialists in the hopes of quickly getting myself on testosterone hormone therapy. To my everlasting gratitude, I was lucky enough to have my parent's full support all throughout the process, although that isn't to say I still didn't face my fair share of difficulties.

Despite feeling more than ready to finally embark on my physical transition, doing so left me with a similar sensation of being lost. While I had been openly trans to my family and closest friends for over a year by the time I started testosterone therapy, nothing had felt so real until I began to present myself as male in my everyday life. Beginning to finally live as outwardly identifying as male meant having to rediscover myself and my relationships with the people that were taking this journey with me. That meant having to explore what it meant to be a son, brother, and nephew to those in my family. Likewise, I also had to learn how I was going to relate to society's ideas of men and masculinity.

I felt lost in facing such a daunting task. It was like the slate had been wiped clean on my life, and it was a sensation that was just as scary as it was exciting.

Like Dick, the first thing I had to do when I finally began my transition in middle school was to learn to let go and say goodbye to a huge part of who I'd been up to that point. While part of me was ecstatic at shedding my identity as a female, it was also especially terrifying. As much as I'd come to resent that part of myself, and everything it had prevented me from experiencing, it had still been part of me. Regardless of the future, my experiences and time spent presenting as female were going to play a huge role in influencing who I was supposed to become. The entire matter, in essence, was the struggle of coming to terms with how to think of and treat my time as "Daniela" now that I was finally being given the chance to become "Dan."

Dick has a similar realization just before donning the Nightwing suit for the first time, remembering that it took the support of those closest to him to keep him from rejecting his history as the Boy Wonder. He admits, "Kory, it's *so* funny. I spent the better part of last *year* fighting to forget what made me me. I almost *alienated* everyone, but you stuck by me and I *love* you for that."[6]

So much can be said about the importance Dick's friendships played during that tumultuous period. Despite his estranged relationship with Bruce, Dick was able to successfully navigate his evolution into Nightwing largely because of the support of Alfred, Superman, the Titans, Barbara and James Gordon, and more. They served as the safety net Dick needed in order for him to properly mourn what he lost, help him get back on his feet, and transition successfully into the next stage of his life. Even a similarly situated Wally West made sure to let Dick know that he was available to help his friend whenever need be.

> WALLY: You need to talk?
> DICK: You've got places to go.
> WALLY: I can stay if you need me. Just 'cause I'm leaving the Titans doesn't mean....
> DICK (Dick pats Wally's shoulder reassuringly): You take off, Wally. I know who to talk to.[7]

While I was lucky enough to have an extremely supportive network of people surrounding me, there were certain strains my transition put on some of my relationships, similar to the strain that was endured by Dick with Bruce. With Bruce Wayne being the closest thing Dick knew to a father after losing his parents, the two supported and relied on each other, and as the scourge of Gotham they seemed like an unbeatable team. Although their partnership was a "well-oiled machine,"[8] Dick also notes the tension in their relationship: "He [Alfred] always had faith that the Dynamic Duo could survive anything. Except maybe each other."[9]

My transition never endangered the relationship I had with either of my parents, but it did play a significant role in the loss of the first best friend I'd ever known. Funny enough, they had also been a big fan of comic books during our friendship, which resulted in the use of "Robin" and "Cyborg" as nicknames for each other. You can guess which one I was. I came out to him one afternoon in early middle school while hanging out at his home. He never spoke to me much at all after that.

The abandonment of my oldest friend at the time impaired my ability to trust others, even those that I had no reason to doubt, for the longest time. Even with their unwavering support, there have been several moments along the way where I wondered if my parents would ever truly be able to accept me as their son, and not just this kid who replaced their daughter. Those fleeting doubts aside, my parents and I have come out of this transition process stronger and better people for it. What a lot of people forget in regards to any type of transition is that it's a huge adjustment for everyone involved, not just the person undergoing whatever changes may be at hand.

I was lucky enough to find I had completely supportive parents when I came out. However, in preparing for the worst possible scenario, I admittedly looked to comics once again for guidance. It ended up being a passage in *Hush* that gave me tremendous hope to help combat the initial fear and hesitation I had in regards to coming out to my parents. The moment is brief, and takes place as Nightwing assists Batman in taking down The

Riddler and his crew. As he watches the aerialist in combat, Bruce notes, "... While, at the time the transition from Robin to *Nightwing* was ... difficult for us both—it was a day I had long prepared myself for because ... *Dick was born to be in the center ring.*"[10]

Reading that passage helped calm a lot of my fears at the time, and I was able to take comfort in knowing that even though it took time for Bruce to accept Dick's new identity, he was eventually able to. Beyond that, Dick, as Nightwing, continues to be one of the few people that Bruce trusts and respects completely.

Dick left behind his identity as Robin, and along with it, his partnership with Batman. There is just as much that could be said in the realizations Bruce had to make during the extreme adjustment from seeing Dick as the young boy who had once served as both the literal and metaphoric light in direct contrast to his darkness, to the man who was embracing his heritage as a performer and stepping out to boldly face the world on his own.

However, even while trying to step out from Bruce's shadow, Dick found it extremely difficult to separate himself from the ideals and standards of his mentor, who, whatever the task, constantly pushed Dick to "do it *better*."[11] Naturally, that level of impossible, self-imposed standards based off his former mentor's ideals built Dick into a person who strives for perfection and is the first to take responsibility in any situation, regardless of whether he has any actual involvement. Because of this, Dick also has the tendency to blame himself the minute things go wrong, as he did when he found out his landlord, Bridget Clancy, was nearly electrocuted as she attempted to fix a fan in their apartment complex.[12] Although his absence was irrelevant (Clancy had knowingly left the power on while fixing the fan), Dick still berated himself, insisting he shouldn't have strayed from his usual schedule and so been home when the accident occurred.

Though the years under Bruce's wing left Dick striving tirelessly for perfection, the aerialist also inherited an unflinching sense of altruism from his former mentor. In the wake of a series of chemical bombs that leave Blüdhaven devastated, Nightwing leaps into action without hesitation, determined to not let any additional lives be lost. Launching himself off a building, he is temporarily stopped by Superman, who tries to thwart Dick's well-intentioned, but dangerous actions. Although Dick agrees with Superman's assessment that he might die, he soldiers on because Blüdhaven is "My *responsibility*. I've lived there, protected it.... Promised Bruce I'd make it *better*.... Please. I don't want to defy you [Superman], not now. But you can't keep me out."[13]

Like Dick, life dealt me a very specific, albeit unique hand. With the cards I was dealt originally, the first half of my own life was spent playing a certain role I was socialized and groomed to fit, and it wasn't as a naturally gifted acrobat or Batman's partner. I remember the frustrations I endured as a child whenever I was faced with the fact that I couldn't do everything that all my friends could do. I was constantly reminded that there was this big, blaring difference whenever there was a sleepover or cub scouts meeting I had to miss out on. I cringed at every reminder, because it just reinforced what I was trying so hard to forget each day.

For so long there was this sense of suffocation in the way I existed because of these constant occurrences. Like feeling another wave crash over you just as you've made it back to the surface for a breath of fresh air. Relentlessly frustrating, I was able to endure until middle school, where the differences between the genders seemed to reign supreme. That was the point at which it started to become unbearable to try to continue in the same façade day after day.

My more masculine presentation was often met with snide remarks or blatant cruelty. I felt claustrophobic within the confines of my own body and the box my gender had been bound to. This box that defined me as a daughter and a sister. I knew neither of those were right. They didn't feel right. The world and my own truth had me pulled in two opposite directions, and it was like I was fighting a losing battle every time I tried to get any closer to who I knew I was inside—a boy. For a while, I allowed bitterness and anger to seep in, and even began alienating some of the people I loved most.

This was the point in my life during which I took the greatest solace in comic books. There was a sense of immense relief when I escaped into those fictional worlds, and I was inspired when I read stories of self-sacrificing heroes who, despite whatever difficult circumstances they endured, refused to succumb to them, fighting instead to be better people who could help shape a better, brighter world.

I think this is part of what makes comics such amazing art forms, and I'm lucky that I've been able to appreciate them as both a fan and practicing artist. Above anything else, I love how they can touch people emotionally and a lot of characters can influence readers as if they were real, living, breathing, people. That's what Nightwing has done for me. As I began to struggle with figuring out who the hell I was, he was there to guide me through it all, and take that journey with me.

Dick has come a long way over the years. Despite the time it took, and all the struggles he encountered, he has persevered and grown from all those experiences into his own hero, a man with an identity that is shaped from the influences of those who have made their impact on him. Dick's roots lie firmly in the foundation he was given as an acrobat and his years as Robin, fighting along Batman to keep Gotham City safe, and he no longer shies away from the collection of influences that have left their mark on him. In preparation for Nightwing's debut, the aerialist pays tribute to the figures that have made the biggest differences in his life.

> The *Batman* taught me, guided me, trained me. What I am I *owe* to him. What more can I say? And *Superman*. I grew up in *your* shadow, too. You taught me honor, selflessness, and the *true* meaning of the word *"hero"*! A long time ago, you used the name I've been thinking of. It was a name from your *Kryptonian* heritage. I'm the *sum* of so many people who have influenced me, shaped my thinking, and given me love.[14]

As Dick credits each important figure, a list which includes those such as Starfire and his parents John and Mary Grayson, he goes on to say, "…I gave up being Robin because that tied me to Batman. But now I become someone *new* who commemorates all those who made me someone *special*."[15]

This particular scene always deeply resonated with me because it's a moment in which Dick is finally able to make peace with his past and move forward. He realizes that his previous identity and experiences don't have to dictate who he is, but instead all of these individual pieces become different parts of who he is to become. It's finally during this moment that Dick is able to use his ties to the past to help move forward and solidify his new identity, and he emerges a self-made man ready to step out from the shadows of his mentors and face the world as his own hero. As Nightwing.

After reading that passage, I knew that kind of acceptance was my goal. Alongside my desire to be seen as the man I knew I was on the inside, as just another guy, above all else, I wanted to feel that sense of peace with my own past, just as Dick had found with his. Identifying with Dick and relating my experiences to his has helped with that tremendously.

There are days where I still struggle with refusing to let my perception of the past dictate the kind of person I'm to become in the future, and place limits on myself based on my biology. But when that happens, I think about this exact moment. I picture Dick reflecting on all those important people in his life, and I'm able to make the connection to those who have supported and loved me during this long, seemingly endless journey. It's thanks to them, and Dick Grayson, that I've been able to make it this far, and I know that he'll always be there to serve as the perfect reminder whenever I need it.

In all honesty, Dick has guided and influenced me more than any other person or professional in my life has, and I'll readily admit that. I'm proud of that fact. I'm proud to know that I've undergone similar trials as a character who, to me, has become the embodiment of hope, perseverance, and change. Using Dick as a role model has kept me on course, reminding me through his own reflections that it's how we rise to meet our challenges that define us as people, not our circumstances. As Dick tells Bruce, "We are who we choose to be, Bruce. Not the role the past says we should play."[16]

Dick Grayson's journey to become Nightwing gave me the strength I needed to finally push forward and begin the pursuit of my own happiness by taking the plunge into transitioning from female to male. It's thanks to him, and the pathway that he initially forged, that I was able to come to terms with my past; he helped me move forward and shaped the man I am today and the one I continue to strive towards being. Dick has been my biggest source of inspiration and writing this essay is probably the closest I'll ever get to being able to tell him so. I'm the man I am today because of Dick Grayson.

When I look at this character, I don't just see the first Robin. I see an acrobat, a son, a brother, a cop, a leader, a friend, a hero, and I see Nightwing. I see everything he's gone through and in that I see a reflection of my life and my own struggles that I've been able to get through in part because of him. Ultimately, when I look at Dick Grayson, I see myself.

I see the 4'11" Latino transman who just hopes and dreams that one day his art can positively impact someone else in the same positive way that Dick Grayson affected him.

Dick Grayson is one of the greatest characters I've ever had the privilege of getting to know. He's been a role model, a source of inspiration and guidance. He's also provided a source of escapism and company when I needed it most. When I was given the opportunity to write about him for this spectacular project alongside so many people that love him just as much as I do, I leapt at the chance.

And now, collectively with everyone else who's written about this fantastic character, from the bottom of my heart I want to say,

> Thank you, Dick Grayson, and thank you to all artists and writers and editors who made this character so amazing for these last seventy five years.

Notes

1. Chuck Dixon, et al., "Yesterday Never Dies," *Nightwing* #57 (New York: DC Comics, July 2001), 1.

2. A shortened version of "transgender," a word used as an umbrella term for people whose gender identity and/or gender expression differs from what is typically associated with the sex they were assigned at birth.

3. Dixon et al., "Year One, Chapter Two: Friends in High Places," *Nightwing* #102 (Late March 2005), [14].

4. Jaime M. Grant, Lisa A. Mottet, Justin Tanis, Jack Harrison, Jody L. Herman, Mara Keisling, *Injustice at Every Turn: A Report of the National Transgender Discrimination Survey* (Washington: National Center for Transgender Equality and National Gay and Lesbian Task Force, 2011).

5. Chuck Dixon and Scott McDaniel, "Taking Wing," in *Nightwing Secret Files and Origins* (October 1999), 14.

6. Marv Wolfman et al., "The Judas Contract Book 3—There Shall Come a Titan," *Tales of the Teen Titans* #44 (New York: DC Comics, July 1984), 21.

7. Dixon and McDaniel, "Taking Wing," 14.

8. Chuck Dixon, Scott McDaniel, and Karl Story, "The Visitor," *Nightwing* #6 (March 1997), 12.

9. Dixon et al., "Nightwing: Year One, Chapter One: Only Robins Have Wings," *Nightwing* #101 (Early March 2005), [19].

10. Jeph Loeb, Jim Lee, and Scott Williams, "Hush (Part VIII of XII)—The Dead," *Batman* #615 (New York: DC Comics, July 2003), [15].

11. Dixon et al., *Nightwing* #101, [7].

12. Chuck Dixon, Greg Land, and Drew Geraci, "In the Middle of the Cold, Cold Night," *Nightwing* #54 (April 2001), 19.

13. Devin Grayson, Wellington Alves, and Eddie Wagner, "Marathon," *Nightwing* #116 (March 2006), [6].

14. Wolfman et al., *Tales of the Teen Titans* #44, 21.

15. Wolfman et al., *Tales of the Teen Titans* #44, 21.

16. Kyle Higgins et al., "Turning Points," *Nightwing* #7 (New York: DC Comics, May 2012), [18].

Bibliography

Comic Books

All comics published by DC Comics in New York unless otherwise noted.

This bibliography lists creators named only on the cover of the issue, and they are credited in the order they appear. If no one is listed on the cover, credit is given in the order of writer (w), artist (a), penciler (p), inker (i).

Batman, Volume 1 (1940–2011)

16—Cameron, Don (w), Jack Burnley (p), and Jerry Robinson (i) with George Roussos (i). "Here Comes Alfred," in *Batman* #16. April–May 1943.

23—Cameron, Don (w), and Dick Sprang (a). "Damsel in Distress!" in *Batman* #23. June–July 1944.

32—Finger, Bill (w) and Dick Sprang (a). "Dick Grayson, Boy Wonder!" in *Batman* #32. December 1945–January 1946.

50—Writer unknown, Bob Kane (p), Lew Sayre Schwartz (p), and Charles Paris (i). "The Second Boy Wonder!" in *Batman* #50. December 1948–January 1949.

57—Finger, Bill (w), Dick Sprang (p), and Charles Paris (i). "The Trial of Bruce Wayne!" in *Batman* #57. February–March 1950.

62—Finger, Bill (w), Bob Kane (p), Lew Sayre Schwartz (p), and Charles Paris (i). "The Secret Life of the Catwoman!" in *Batman* #62. December 1950–January 1951.

65—Finger, Bill (w), Bob Kane (p), Lew Sayre Schwartz (p), and Charles Paris (i). "A Partner for Batman!" in *Batman* #65. June–July 1951.

66—Finger, Bill (w), Bob Kane (p), and Charles Paris (i). "Batman II and Robin, Junior!" in *Batman* #66. August 1951.

67—Vern, David (w), Bob Kane (p), Lew Sayre Schwartz (p), and Charles Paris (i). "The Man who Wrote the Joker's Jokes!" in *Batman* #67. October–November 1951.

81—Vern, David (w), Sheldon Moldoff (p), and Stan Kaye (i). "The Boy Wonder Confesses!" in *Batman* #81 February 1954.

105—Herron, France (w), Sheldon Moldoff (p, i), and Charles Paris (i). "The Second Boy Wonder," in *Batman* #105. February 1957.

107—Finger, Bill (w), Sheldon Moldoff (p), and Charles Paris (i). "Robin Falls in Love," and Finger (w), Moldoff (p), and Stan Kaye (i), "The Grown-Up Boy Wonder," both in *Batman* #107. April 1957.

129—Finger, Bill (w), and Sheldon Moldoff (a). "The Man from Robin's Past," in *Batman* #129. February 1960.

139—Finger, Bill (w), Sheldon Moldoff (p), and Charles Paris (i). "Bat-Girl!" in *Batman* #139. April 1961.

153—Finger, Bill (w), Sheldon Moldoff (p), and Charles Paris (i). "Prisoners of Three Worlds," in *Batman* #153. February 1963.

156—Finger, Bill (w), Sheldon Moldoff (p), and Charles Paris (i). "Robin Dies at Dawn." *Batman* #156. June 1963.

159—Finger, Bill (w), Sheldon Moldoff (p), and Charles Paris (i). "The Great Clayface-Joker Feud," in *Batman* #159. November 1963.

164—Herron, France (w), Sheldon Moldoff (p), and Joe Giella (i). "Two-Way Gem Caper!" *Batman* #164. June 1964.

184—Fox, Gardner (w), Chic Stone (p),

and Sid Greene (i). "The Boy Wonder's Boo-Boo Patrol" in *Batman* #184. September 1966.

213—Bridwell, E Nelson (w), Ross Andru (p), and Mike Esposito (i). "The Origin of Robin!" *Batman* #213. July–August 1969.

217—Robbins, Frank (w), Irv Novick (p), and Dick Giordano (i). "One Bullet Too Many!" *Batman* #217. December 1969.

312—Wein, Len (w), Walter Simonson (p), and Dick Giordano (i). "A Caper a Day Keeps the Batman at Bay." *Batman* #312. June 1979.

316—Wein, Len (w), Irv Novick (p), and Frank McLaughlin (i). "Color Me Deadly!" *Batman* #316. October 1979.

330—Wolfman, Marv (w), Irv Novick (a), and Vince Colletta (a). "Target." *Batman* #330. December 1980. Cover by Ross Andru (p) and Dick Giordano (i).

344—Conway, Gerry (w), Gene Colan (a), and Klaus Janson (a). "Monster My Sweet!" *Batman* #344. February 1982.

356—Conway, Gerry (w), Don Newton (p), and Dick Giordano (i). "The Double Life of Hugo Strange." *Batman* #356. February 1983.

358—Conway, Gerry (w), Curt Swan (a), and Rodin Rodriguez (a). "Don't Mess with Killer Croc!" *Batman* #358. April 1983.

368—Moench, Doug (w), Don Newton (a), and Alfredo Alcala (a). "A Revenge of Rainbows." *Batman* #368. February 1984.

408—Collins, Max Allan (w), Chris Warner (p), and Mike DeCarlo (i). "Did Robin Die Tonight?" *Batman* #408. June 1987.

409—Collins, Max Allan (w), Ross Andru (p), and Dick Giordano (i). "Just Another Kid in Crime Alley!" *Batman* #409. July 1987.

416—Starlin, Jim (w), Jim Aparo (p), and Mike DeCarlo (i). "White Gold and Truth." *Batman* #416. February 1988.

424—Starlin, Jim (w), Mark Bright (p), and Steve Mitchell (i). "The Diplomat's Son." *Batman* #424. October 1988.

441—Wolfman, Marv (w), Jim Aparo (p), and Mike DeCarlo (i). "A Lonely Place of Dying (Part III)—Parallel Lines." *Batman* #441. November 1989.

442—Wolfman, Marv (w), George Pérez (w), Jim Aparo (p), and Mike DeCarlo (i). "A Lonely Place of Dying (Part V)—Rebirth." *Batman* #442. December 1989.

500—Moench Doug (w), Jim Aparo (p), Terry Austin (i), and Mike Manley (i). "Dark Angel." *Batman* #500. October 1993.

512—Moench, Doug (w), Mike Gustovich (p), and Romeo Tanghal (i). "Prodigal Part 1: Robin and Batman." *Batman* #512. November 1994.

513—Moench, Doug (w), Mike Gustovich (p), and Romeo Tanghal (i). "Double Deuce." *Batman* #513. December 1994.

514—Moench, Doug (w), Ron Wagner (p), and Joe Rubinstein (i). "One Night in the War Zone." *Batman* #514. January 1995.

600—Brubaker, Ed (w), Scott McDaniel (p), and Andy Owens (i). "The Scene of the Crime." *Batman* #600. April 2002.

615—Loeb, Jeph (w), Jim Lee (p), and Scott Williams (i). "Hush (Part VIII of XII)—The Dead." *Batman* #615. July 2003.

631—Willingham, Bill (w), Kinsun Loh (p), and Aaron Sowd (i). "Last Stand at Alamo High." *Batman* #631. October 2004.

636—Winick, Judd (w), Doug Mahnke (p), and Tom Nguyen (i). "Under the Hood, Part 2: First Strike." *Batman* #636. March 2005.

637—Winick, Judd (w), Doug Mahnke (p), and Tom Nguyen (i). "Under the Hood Part 3: Overnight Deliveries." *Batman* #637. April 2005.

656—Morrison, Grant (w), Andy Kubert (p), and Jesse Delperdang (i). "Batman & Son, Part 2: Man-Bats of London." *Batman* #656. October 2006.

657—Morrison, Grant (w), Andy Kubert (p), and Jesse Delperdang (i). "Batman & Son, Part 3: Wonderboys." *Batman* #657. November 2006.

687—Winick, Judd (w), Ed Benes (p), and Rob Hunter (i). "A Battle Within." *Batman* #687. August 2009.

688—Winick, Judd (w), Mark Bagley (p), and Rob Hunter (i). "Long Shadows, Part One: Old Sins Cast Long Shadows." *Batman* #688. September 2009.

703—Nicieza, Fabian (w) and Cliff Richards (a). "The Great Escape." *Batman* #703. November 2010.

713—Nicieza, Fabian (w), Steve Scott (p), Daniel Sampere (p), Andrei Bressan (a), Walden Wong (i), Rich Perrotta (i), and Rodney Ramos (i). "In Storybook Endings." *Batman* #713. August 2011.

Batman and Robin, Volume 1 (2009–2011)

1—Morrison, Grant (w), and Frank Quitely (a). "Batman Reborn, Part One: Domino Effect." *Batman and Robin* #1. August 2009.

2—Morrison, Grant (w), and Frank Quitely (a). "Batman Reborn, Part Two: The Circus of Strange." *Batman and Robin* #2. September 2009.

3—Morrison, Grant (w), and Frank Quitely (a). "Batman Reborn, Part 3: Mommy Made of Nails." *Batman and Robin* #3. October 2009.

6—Morrison, Grant (w), Philip Tan (p), and Jonathan Glapion (i). "Revenge of the Red Hood Part Three: Flamingo is Here." *Batman and Robin* #6. January 2010.

7—Morrison, Grant (w), and Cameron Steward (a). "Blackest Night, Part One: Pearly and the Pit." *Batman and Robin* #7. March 2010.

12—Morrison, Grant (a), and Andy Clarke (p). "Batman vs Robin, Part 3: Mexican Train." *Batman and Robin* #12. July 2010.

13—Morrison, Grant (w), and Frazer Irving (a). "Batman and Robin Must Die, Part 1: The Garden of Death." *Batman and Robin* #13. August 2010.

15—Morrison, Grant (w), and Frazer Irving (a). "Batman and Robin Must Die, Part 3: The Knight, Death and the Devil." *Batman and Robin* #15. December 2010.

16—Morrison, Grant (w), Cameron Stewart (a), and Frazer Irving (a). "Black Mass." *Batman and Robin* #16. Early January 2011.

17—Cornell, Paul (w), Scott McDaniel (p), and Rob Hunter (i). "The Sum of Her Parts, Part 1 of 3." *Batman and Robin* #17. January 2011.

19—Cornell, Paul (w), Scott McDaniel (p), and Rob Hunter (i). "The Sum of Her Parts, Part 3 of 3." *Batman and Robin* #19. March 2011.

20—Tomasi, Peter J. (w), Patrick Gleason (p), and Mick Gray (i). "Dark Knight vs White Knight, Part 1 of 3: Tree of Blood." *Batman and Robin* #20. April 2011.

22—Tomasi, Peter J. (w), Patrick Gleason (p), and Mick Gray (i). "Dark Knight vs White Knight: Tree of Blood, Conclusion." *Batman and Robin* #22. June 2011.

23—Winick, Judd (w), Guillem March (a), and Andrei Bresson (a). "The Streets Run Red: Ins and Outs." *Batman and Robin* #23. July 2011.

25—Winick, Judd (w), Greg Tocchini (a), and Andy Smith (a). "The Streets Run Red, Part 3 of 3: Boys Night Out. *Batman and Robin* #25. September 2011.

Batman Family, Volume 1 (1975–1978)

1—Maggin, Elliot S! (w) and Mike Grell (a). "The Invader from Hell." *Batman Family* #1. September–October 1975.

3—Maggin, Elliot S! (w), J.L. Garcia Lopez (a), and Vince Colletta (a). "Isle of a Thousand Thrills." *Batman Family* #3. January–February 1976.

5—Maggin, Elliot S! (w), Cary Bates (w), Curt Swan (a), and Vince Colletta (a). "The Princess and the Vagabond." *Batman Family* #5. May–June 1976.

7—Maggin, Elliot S! (w), Curt Swan (a), and Vince Colletta (a). "Thirteen Points to a Dead End." *Batman Family* #7. September–October 1976.

8—Rozakis, Bob (w), Irv Novick (a), and Vince Colletta (a). "The Copycatgirl Capers." *Batman Family* #8. November–December 1976.

9—Rozakis, Bob (w), Irv Novick (a), and

Vince Colletta (a). "Startling Secret of the Devilish Daughters." *Batman Family* #9. January–February 1977.

11—Rozakis, Bob (w), Curt Swan (a), and Vince Colletta (a). "Till Death Do Us Part!" *Batman Family* #11. May–June 1977.

12—Rozakis, Bob (w), Irv Novick (a), and Vince Colletta (a). "Rally Round Robin." *Batman Family* #12. July–August 1977.

13—Rozakis, Bob (w), Don Newton (a), Marshall Rogers (a), and Bob Wiacek (a). "The Man who Melted Manhattan." *Batman Family* #13. September 1977.

14—Rozakis, Bob (w), Don Heck (a), and Bob Wiacek (a). "Old Super-Heroines Never Die—They Just Fade Away!" *Batman Family* #14. October 1977.

Batman: Gotham Knights (2000–2006)

1—Grayson, Devin (w), Dale Eaglesham (p), and John Floyd (i). "Constants." *Batman: Gotham Knights* #1. March 2000.

8–11—Grayson, Devin (w), Roger Robinson (p), and John Floyd (i). "Transference." *Batman: Gotham Knights* #8–11. October, November, December, 2000 and January 2001.

14—Grayson, Devin (w), Roger Robinson (p), and John Floyd (i). "Sibling Rivalry." *Batman: Gotham Knights* #14. April 2001.

17—Grayson, Devin (w), Roger Robinson (p), and John Floyd (i). "Matatoa, Part 2 of 2: A Moment in the Light." *Batman: Gotham Knights* #17. July 2001.

20–21—Grayson, Devin (w), Roger Robinson (p), and John Floyd (i). "Retribution." *Batman: Gotham Knights* #20–21. October–November 2001.

Detective Comics, Volume 1 (1937–2011)

38—Finger, Bill (w), Bob Kane (p, i), and Jerry Robinson (i). "Introducing Robin, The Boy Wonder." *Detective Comics* #38. April 1940.

177—Finger, Bill (probable writer), Dick Sprang (p), and Charles Paris (i). "The Robberies in the Bat-Cave." *Detective Comics* #177. November 1951.

190—Finger, Bill (probable writer), Bob Kane (p), Lew Sayre Schwartz (p), and Stan Kaye (i). "How to be Batman!" *Detective Comics* #190. December 1952.

215—Hamilton, Edmond (w), Sheldon Moldoff (a), and Charles Paris (i). "The Batmen of All Nations." *Detective Comics* #215. January 1955.

218—Finger, Bill (w) Sheldon Moldoff (p), and Stan Kaye (i). "Batman Junior and Robin Senior." *Detective Comics* #218. April 1955.

226—Samachson, Joe (w), Dick Sprang (a), and Joe Certa (p). "When Batman was Robin." *Detective Comics* #226. December 1955.

233—Hamilton, Edmond (w), Sheldon Moldoff (p), and Stan Kaye (i). "The Bat-Woman." *Detective Comics* #233. July 1956.

235—Finger, Bill (w), Sheldon Moldoff (p), and Joe Certa (p). "The First Batman." *Detective Comics* #235. September 1956.

327—Broome, John (w), Carmine Infantino (p), and Joe Giella (i). "The Mystery of the Menacing Mask!" *Detective Comics* #327. May 1964.

351—Fox, Gardner (w), Carmine Infantino (p), and Sid Greene (i). "The Cluemaster's Topsy-Turvy Crimes!" *Detective Comics* #351. May 1966.

386—Friedrich, Mike (w), Ross Andru (p), and Mike Esposito (i). "The Teen-Age Gap." *Detective Comics* #386. April 1969.

390—Friedrich, Mike (w), Gil Kane (p), and Murphy Anderson (i). "Countdown to Chaos!" *Detective Comics* #390. August 1969.

391—Friedrich, Mike (w), Gil Kane (p), and Murphy Anderson (i). "Strike!" *Detective Comics* #391. September 1969.

393—Robbins, Frank (w), Bob Brown (a), and Joe Giella (a). "The Combo Caper!"

Detective Comics #393. November 1969. Cover by Irv Novick.
398—Robbins, Frank (w), Gil Kane (p), and Vince Colletta (i). "Moon-Struck." *Detective Comics* #398. April 1970.
481—Rozakis, Bob (w). "Does the costume make the hero?" *Detective Comics* #481. December–January 1978–79.
482—Rozakis, Bob (w) and Juan Ortiz (a). "The League of Crime!" *Detective Comics* #482. February–March 1979.
486—Harris, Jack C. (w), Kurt Schaffenberger (a), and Jack Abel (a). "Fear times four." *Detective Comics* #486. October–November 1979.
495—Harris, Jack C. (w), Charles Nicholas (a), and Vince Colletta (a). "The Gotham Connection." *Detective Comics* #495. October 1980.
523—Conway, Gerry (w), Gene Colan (a), and Tony DeZuñiga (a). "Inferno." *Batman* #523. February 1983.
524—Conway, Gerry (w), Don Newton (a), and Ed Hannigan (p). "Deathgrip." *Detective Comics* #524. March 1983.
526—Conway, Gerry (w), Bob Kane (a), and Don Newton (a). "All My Enemies Against Me." *Detective Comics* #526. May 1983.
680—Dixon, Chuck (w), Lee Weeks (I, p), Graham Nolan (p), and Joe Rubinstein (i). "Prodigal Seven: A Twice Told Tale." *Detective Comics* #680. December 1994.
696—Dixon, Chuck (w), Graham Nolan (p), and Scott Hanna (i). "Contagion, Part 8: Babylon Falls." *Detective Comics* #696. April 1996.
698—Dixon, Chuck (w), Graham Nolan (p), and Scott Hanna (i). "The Tomb." *Batman* #698. July 1996.
725—Dixon, Chuck (w), William Rosado (p), and Tom Palmer (i). "At the End of the Day." *Detective Comics* #725. September 1998.

The New Teen Titans (Volume 1) and *Tales of the Teen Titans*

1—Wolfman, Marv (w), George Pérez (p), and Romeo Tanghal (i). "The Birth of the Titans." *The New Teen Titans* #1. November 1980.
2—Wolfman, Marv (w), George Pérez (p), and Romeo Tanghal (i). "The Terminator." *The New Teen Titans* #2. December 1980.
3—Wolfman, Marv (w), George Pérez (p), and Frank Chiaramonte (i). "The Fearsome Five!" *The New Teen Titans* #3. January 1981.
10—Wolfman, Marv (w), George Pérez (p), and Romeo Tanghal (i). "Promethium: Unbound!" *The New Teen Titans* #10. August 1981.
7—Wolfman, Marv (w), George Pérez (p), and Romeo Tanghal (i). "Assault on Titans' Tower." *The New Teen Titans* #7. May 1981.
16—Wolfman, Marv (w), George Pérez (p), and Romeo Tanghal (i). "Starfire Unleashed!" *The New Teen Titans* #16. February 1982.
20—Wolfman, Marv (w), George Pérez (p), and Romeo Tanghal (i). "Dear Mom and Dad." *The New Teen Titans* #20. June 1982.
26—Wolfman, Marv (w), George Pérez (p), and Romeo Tanghal (i). "Runaways Part 1." *The New Teen Titans* #26. December 1982.
28—Wolfman, Marv (w), George Pérez (p), and Romeo Tanghal (i). "Terra in the Night." *The New Teen Titans* #28. February 1983.
37—Wolfman, Marv (w), George Pérez (p), and Romeo Tanghal (i). "Lights, Out, Everyone!" *The New Teen Titans* #37. December 1983.
38—Wolfman, Marv (w), and George Pérez (p, i). "Who is Donna Troy?" *The New Teen Titans* #38. January 1984.
39—Wolfman, Marv (w), and George Pérez (p, i). "Crossroads." *The New Teen Titans* #39. February 1984.
42—Wolfman, Marv (w), George Pérez (p), and Dick Giordano (i). "The Judas Contact Book One: The Eyes of Tara Markov!" *Tales of the Teen Titans* #42. May 1984.
44—Wolfman, Marv (w), George Pérez (p), Dick Giordano (i), and Mike De-

Carlo (i). "The Judas Contract Book 3—There Shall Come a Titan!" *Tales of the Teen Titans* #44. July 1984.

50—Wolfman, Marv (w), George Pérez (p), Mark DeCarlo (i), and Dick Giordano (i). "We are Gathered Here Today..." *Tales of the Teen Titans* #50. February 1985.

56—Wolfman, Marv (w), Chuck Patton (p), Mike DeCarlo (i). "Fearsome Five Minus One!" *Tales of the Teen Titans* #56. August 1985.

Wolfman, Marv (w), George Pérez (p), and Gene Day (i). "The Changeling." *Tales of the New Teen Titans* #3. August 1982.

The New Teen Titans (Volume 2) and *The New Titans*

6—Wolfman, Marv (w), George Pérez (p), Dan Jurgens (layouts), and Romeo Tanghal (finishes). "Titansmania." *The New Teen Titans* #6. March 1985.

13—Wolfman, Marv (w), Eduardo Barreto (p), and Romeo Tanghal (i). "Crisis." *The New Teen Titans* #13. October 1985.

16—Wolfman, Marv (w), Chuck Patton (p), and Romeo Tanghal (i). "The Night Before." *The New Teen Titans* #16. January 1986.

18—Wolfman, Marv (w), Eduardo Barreto (p), and Romeo Tanghal (i). "Homecoming." *The New Teen Titans* #18. March 1986.

19—Wolfman, Marv (w), Eduardo Barreto (p), and Romeo Tanghal (i). "Breaking Up is Hard to Do." *The New Teen Titans* #19. April 1986.

23—Wolfman, Marv (w), Eduardo Barreto (p), and Romeo Tanghal (i). "Loser Take All!" *The New Teen Titans* #23. August 1986.

31—Wolfman, Marv (w), Paul Levitz (w), Eduardo Barreto (p), and Romeo Tanghal (i). "Resolution." *The New Teen Titans* #31. May 1987.

32—Levitz, Paul (w), Eduardo Barreto (p), and Pablo Marcos (i). "Trivial Pursuits." *The New Teen Titans* #32. June 1987.

34—Wolfman, Marv (w), Eduardo Barreto (p), and Romeo Tanghal (i). "Non Compos Mento: Epilogue." *The New Teen Titans* #34. August 1987.

48—Wolfman, Marv (w), Eduardo Barreto (p), and Romeo Tanghal (i). "Crimes and Punishment!" *The New Teen Titans* #48. October 1988.

52—Wolfman, Marv (w), George Pérez (w, p, i), and Bob McLeod (i). "Who Is Wonder Girl? (Part III of V)—Trackdown." *The New Titans* #52. January 1989.

55—Wolfman, Marv (w), George Pérez (w, p), and Romeo Tanghal (i). "Transitions." *The New Titans* #55. June 1989.

57—Wolfman, Marv (w), George Pérez (w, p), and Bob McLeod (i). "Study in Steel." *The New Titans* #57. August 1989.

60—Wolfman, Marv (w), George Pérez (p), and Bob McLeod (i). "A Lonely Place of Dying (Part II)—Roots." *The New Titans* #60. November 1989.

61—Pérez, George (w, p), Marv Wolfman (w), Tom Grummett (a), Bob McLeod (i). "A Lonely Place of Dying, Part 4." *The New Titans* #61. December 1989.

65—Wolfman, Marv (w), Tom Grummett (p), and Al Vey (i). "Dejavu." *The New Titans* #65. April 1990.

71—Wolfman, Marv (w), Tom Grummett (p), and Al Vey (i). "Beginnings... Endings ... and (we promise) New Beginnings!" *The New Titans* #71. November 1990.

89—Wolfman, Marv (w), June Brigman (p), Mike DeCarlo (i), Steve Montana (i), and Andrew Pepoy (i). "With Every Little Step We Take." *The New Titans* #89. August 1992.

97—Wolfman, Marv (w), Tom Grummett (p), and Al Vey (i). "The Darkening Part One: An Unholy Pact." *The New Titans* #97. May 1993.

99—Wolfman, Marv (w), Tom Grummett (p), and Al Vey (i). "The Darkening Part Three: The Brotherhood." *The New Titans* #99. July 1993.

100—Wolfman, Marv (w), Tom Grummett (p), and Al Vey (i). "The Darkening Chapter Four: Something Old, Something New, Something Borrowed, Something ... DEAD." *The New Titans* #100. August 1993.

Spotlight 14—Reaves, Michael (w), Stan Woch (p), and Rodin Rodriguez (i). "Night of the Dragon." *Teen Titans Spotlight* #14. September 1987.

Nightwing (1996–2009)

6—Dixon, Chuck (w), Scott McDaniel (p), and Karl Story (i). "The Visitor." *Nightwing* #6. March 1997.
15—Dixon, Chuck (w), Scott McDaniel (a), and Karl Story (c). "Warriors Two." *Nightwing* #15. December 1997.
25—Dixon, Chuck (w), Scott McDaniel (p), and Karl Story (i). "The Boys." *Nightwing* #25. October 1998.
29—Dixon, Chuck (w), Scott McDaniel (p), and Karl Story (i). "Back to Back to Back." *Nightwing* #29. March 1999.
54—Dixon, Chuck (w), Greg Land (p), and Drew Geraci (i). "In the Middle of the Cold, Cold Night." *Nightwing* #54. April 2001.
57—Dixon, Chuck (w), Rick Leonardi (p), Jesse Delperdang (i), and Mark Farmer (i). "Yesterday Never Dies." *Nightwing* #57. July 2001.
63—Dixon, Chuck (w), Trevor McCarthy (p), and Karl Kesel (i). "Red, Fright and Blue." *Nightwing* #63. January 2002.
65—Dixon, Chuck (w), Trevor McCarthy (p), Robert Stull (i), and Rodney Ramos (i). "Bruce Wayne: Murderer? Part Three: Bustout!" *Nightwing* #65. March 2002.
68—Dixon, Chuck (w), Trevor McCarthy (p), Robert Campanella (i), and Rob Stull (i). "Bruce Wayne, Fugitive: Time & Motion." *Nightwing* #68. June 2002.
80—Grayson, Devin (w), Rick Leonardi (p), Jesse Delperdang (i). "Venn Diagram, Part 1: Close Encounters." *Nightwing* #80. June 2003.
87—Grayson, Devin (w), Patrick Zircher (p), and Andy Owens (i). "Snowball." *Nightwing* #87. January 2004.
93—Grayson, Devin (w), Patrick Zircher (p), and Andy Owens (i). "Slow Burn." *Nightwing* #93. July 2004.
94—Grayson, Devin (w), Mike Lilly (p), and Andy Owens (i). "Road to Nowhere, Part 1." *Nightwing* #94. August 2004.
95—Grayson, Devin (w), Mike Lilly (p), and Andy Owens (i). "Road to Nowhere, Part 2." *Nightwing* #95. September 2004.
96—Grayson, Devin (w), Mike Lilly (p), and Andy Owens (i). "War Games: Act 1 Part 3: A Sort of Homecoming." *Nightwing* #96. October 2004.
99—Grayson, Devin (w), Zach Howard (p), and Andy Owens (i). "Back to the Life." *Nightwing* #99. January 2005.
100—Grayson, Devin (w), Mike Lilly (p), and Andy Owens (i). "The Ride's Over." *Nightwing* #100. February 2005.
101—Dixon (w), Chuck, Scott Beatty (w), Scott McDaniel (p), and Andy Owens (i). "Nightwing: Year One, Chapter One: Only Robins Have Wings." *Nightwing* #101. Early March 2005.
102—Dixon (w), Chuck, Scott Beatty (w), Scott McDaniel (p), and Andy Owens (i). "Year One, Chapter Two: Friends in High Places." *Nightwing* #102. Late March 2005.
103—Dixon (w), Chuck, Scott Beatty (w), Scott McDaniel (p), and Andy Owens (i). "Nightwing: Year One, Chapter Three: Deadman Talking." *Nightwing* #103. Early April 2005.
104—Dixon (w), Chuck, Scott Beatty (w), Scott McDaniel (p), and Andy Owens (i). "Year One, Chapter Four: Night in the City." *Nightwing* #104. Late April 2005.
105—Dixon (w), Chuck, Scott Beatty (w), Scott McDaniel (p), and Andy Owens (i). "Year One, Chapter Five: Like Killing Two Birds …" *Nightwing* #105. Early May 2005.
106—Dixon (w), Chuck, Scott Beatty (w), Scott McDaniel (p), and Andy Owens (i). "Year One, Chapter Six: First Flight." *Nightwing* #106. Late May 2005.
107—Grayson, Devin (w), Phil Hester (p), and Ande Parks (i). "Criminal." *Nightwing* #107. June 2005.
110—Grayson, Devin (w), Phil Hester (p), and Ande Parks (i). "Incorporation." *Nightwing* #110. September 2005.
112—Grayson, Devin (w), Phil Hester (p), and Ande Parks (i). "The Devil You Know." *Nightwing* #112. November 2005.

114—Grayson, Devin (w), Phil Hester (p), and Ande Parks (i). "Cowboys and Indians." *Nightwing* #114. January 2006.
116—Grayson, Devin (w), Wellington Alves (p), and Eddie Wagner (i). "Marathon." *Nightwing* #116. March 2006.
119—Jones, Bruce (w), Joe Dodd (p), and Bit (i). "Pleased to Meet You—Hope You Guess My Name!" *Nightwing* #119. June 2006.
120—Jones Bruce (w), Paco Diaz (p), and Bit (i). "Yours, Mine, and Ours." *Nightwing* #120. July 2006.
121—Jones, Bruce (w), Paco Diaz (p), and Bit (i). "Sorry I Brought That Up." *Nightwing* #121. August 2006.
122—Jones, Bruce (w), Paco Diaz (p), and Bit (i). "Odd Couples." *Nightwing* #122. September 2006.
138—Nicieza, Fabian (w), Don Kramer (p), and Wayne Faucher (i). "The Resurrection of Ra's al Ghul, Part 2: The Lesser of Two Evils." *Nightwing* #138. January 2008.
139—Nicieza, Fabian (w), Don Kramer (p), and Wayne Faucher (i). "The Resurrection of Ra's al Ghul, Part 6: Living Proof." *Nightwing* #139. February 2008.
141—Tomasi, Peter J. (w), Rags Morales (p), and Michael Bair (i). "Nightwing: Freefall Chapter Two." *Nightwing* #141. April 2008.
Secret Files—Dixon, Chuck (w) and Scott McDaniel (p). "Taking Wing," in *Nightwing: Secret Files and Origins*. October 1999.

Outsiders, Volume 3 (2003–2007)

1—Winick, Judd (w), Tom Raney (p), and Scott Hanna (i). "Role Call, Part One: Opening Offers." *Outsiders* #1. August 2003.
2—Winick, Judd (w), Tom Raney (p), and Scott Hanna (i). "Roll Call, Part Two: Lawyers, Guns and Monkeys." *Outsiders* #2. September 2003.
4—Winick, Judd (w), ChrissCross (p), and Sean Parsons (i). "Brothers in Blood, Part One: Small Potatoes." *Outsiders* #4. November 2003.
6—Winick, Judd (w), ChrissCross (p), and Sean Parsons (i). "Brothers in Blood, Part 3: Pandora's Box." *Outsiders* #6. January 2004.
8—Winick, Judd (w), Tom Raney (p, i), and Sean Parsons (i). "Devil's Work, Part 1: Sacrifice." *Outsiders* #8. March 2004.
11—Winick, Judd (w), Will Conrad (p), and Sean Parsons (i). "Scream Without Raising Your Voice." *Outsiders* #11. 2004.
16—Winick, Judd (w), Dan Jurgens (p), and Nelson (i). "A Change of Plans." *Outsiders* #16. November 2004.
17—Winick, Judd (w) and Carlos D'Anda (a). "Most Wanted, Part 1." *Outsiders* #17. December 2004.
23—Winick, Judd (w), Sean Moll (p), and Kevin Conrad (i). "Lockdown." *Outsiders* #23. June 2005.
31—Winick, Judd (w), Matthew Clark (p), and Art Thibert (i). "Out-of-Town Work." *Outsiders* #31. February 2006.
44—Winick, Judd (w), Carlo Barberi (p), and Art Thibert (i). "Pay as You Go Part One: The Skeleton Crew." *Outsiders* #44. March 2007.

Red Robin (2009–2011)

1—Yost, Chris (w) and Ramon Bachs (p). "The Grail, Part 1." *Red Robin* #1. August 2009.
4—Yost, Chris (w) and Ramon Bachs (p). "The Grail, Part 4." *Red Robin* #4. November 2009.
11—Yost, Chris (w), Marcus To (p), and Ray McCarthy (i). "Collision, Part 3." *Red Robin* #11. June 2010.
12—Yost, Chris (w), Marcus To (p), and Ray McCarthy (i). "Collision, Part 4." *Red Robin* #12. July 2010.
13—Nicieza, Fabian (w), Marcus To (p), and Ray McCarthy (i). "The Hit List, Part 1: The Domino Effect." *Red Robin* #13. August 2010.
23—Nicieza, Fabian (w), Marcus To (p), and Ray McCarthy (i). "7 Days of Death, Part One: Little Triggers." *Red Robin* #23. July 2011.

Robin (1993–2009)

0—Dixon, Chuck (w), Tom Grummett (p), and Ray Kryssing (i). "Brothers in Arms." *Robin* #0. October 1994.

13—Dixon, Chuck (w), Chuck Cleary (p), Phil Jiminez (p, i), and Ray Kryssing (i). "Prodigal Conclusion: Wings over Gotham." *Robin* #13. January 1995.

28—Dixon, Chuck (w), Mike Wieringo (p), and Stan Woch (i). "Contagion, Part 11: Bitter Dregs." *Robin* #28. April 1996.

71—Dixon, Chuck (w), Staz Johnson (p), and Wayne Faucher (i). "The Lizard King." *Robin* #71. December 1999.

74—Dixon, Chuck (w), Pete Woods (p), and Jesse Delperdang (i). "The Worst is Yet to Come." *Robin* #74. March 2000.

156—Beechen, Adam (w) and Freddie E. Williams II (p, i). "The High Dive." *Robin* #156. January 2007.

175—Nicieza, Fabian (w), Joe Bennett (p), and Jack Jadson (i). "Scattered Pieces." *Robin* #175. August 2008.

Teen Titans, Volume 3 (2003–2011)

6—Johns, Geoff (w), Mike McKone (p), and Mario Alquiza (i). "War and Peace." *Teen Titans* #6. February 2004.

7—Johns, Geoff (w), Tom Grummett (p), Kevin Conrad (i), and Nelson (i). "Wednesday." *Teen Titans* #7. February 2004.

17—Johns, Geoff (w), Mike McKone (p), and Mario Alquiza (i). "Titans Tomorrow (Part I of III)—Big Brothers and Sisters." *Teen Titans* #17. December 2004.

20—Johns, Geoff (w), Tom Grummett (p), and Nelson (i). "Hiding," *Teen Titans* #20. December 2005.

33—Johns, Geoff (w), Marv Wolfman (w), Todd Nauck (p), and Sean Parsons (i). "The Brave and the Bold." *Teen Titans* #33. April 2006.

The Titans, Volume 1 (1999–2003)

1—Grayson, Devin (w), Mark Buckingham (p), Wade Von Grawbadger (i). "That Strange Buzzing Sound." *The Titans* #1. March 1999.

12—Grayson, Devin (w), Mark Buckingham (p), Wade Von Grawbadger (i). "The Immortal Coil, Part 3." *The Titans* #12. February 2000.

13—Grayson, Devin (w), Jay Faerber (w), Patrick Zircher (p), Andrew Robinson (i), and Mark Propst (i). "Fallout." *The Titans* #13. March 2000.

16—Grayson, Devin (w), Mark Buckingham (P), and Marlo Alquiza (I). "Gargoyle's Revenge." *The Titans* #16. June 2000.

19—Grayson, Devin (w), Jay Faerber (w), Adam DeKraker (a), and Andy Lanning (a). "The Price of Victory." *The Titans* #19. September 2000.

28—Faerber, Jay (w), Paul Pelletier (p), and Bud LaRosa (i). "The All-Nighter." *The Titans* #28. June 2001.

29—Faerber, Jay (w), Paul Pelletier (p), and Bud LaRosa (i). "Kid Stuff." *The Titans* #29. July 2001.

42—Peyer, Tom (w), Barry Kitson (p), and Rich Faber (i). "Chemical World Part One." *The Titans* #42. August 2002.

Secret Files—Faerber, Jay (w), Paul Pelletier (p), and Bud LaRosa (i). "Interludes," in *The Titans Secret Files and Origins* #2. October 2000.

Titans, Volume 2 (2008–2011)

3—Winick, Judd (w), Joe Benitez (p), Victor Llamas (i), and Sandra Hope (i). "Family Affair (Part II)—Sins of the Father." *Titans* #3. August 2008.

5—Winick, Judd (w), Julian Lopez (p), Prentis Rollins (i), and Bit (i). "I Know Your Heart Because I Know Mine." *Titans* #5. October 2008.

21—Krul, J.T. (w), Angel Unzueta (p), and Wayne Faucher (i). "Fractured, Part 1." *Titans* #21. March 2010.

23—Berganza, Eddie (w), Scott Clark (p), Ardian Syaf (p), David Beaty (i), and Vicente Cifuentes (i). "The Way Things Were." *Titans* #23. May 2010.

30—Wallace, Eric (w), Fabrizio Fiorentino (a), and Cliff Richards (a). "Family Re-

World's Finest Comics (1941–1986)

30—Finger, Bill (w), Bob Kane (p), and Ray Burnley (i). "The Penny Plunderers," in *World's Finest Comics* #30. September–October 1947.

44—Schwartz, Alvin (probable writer) and Jim Mooney (a). "The Confession of Batman," in *World's Finest Comics* #44. February–March 1950.

71—Schwartz, Alvin (w), Curt Swan (p), and Stan Kaye (i). "Batman—Double for Superman!" in *World's Finest Comics* #71. July 1954.

75—Finger, Bill (w), Curt Swan (p), and Stan Kaye (i). "Superman, Batman and Robin!" in *World's Finest Comics* #75. March–April 1955.

128—Coleman, Jerry (w) and Jim Mooney (a). "The Power that Transformed Batman," in *World's Finest Comics* #128. September 1962.

141—Hamilton, Edmond (w), Curt Swan (p), and George Klein (i). "The Olsen-Robin Team vs. 'The Superman-Batman Team.'" *World's Finest Comics* #141. May 1964.

153—Hamilton, Edmond (w), Curt Swan (p), and George Klein (i). "The Clash of Cape and Cowl." *World's Finest Comics* #153. New York: DC Comics, November 1965.

New 52: *Nightwing* (2011–2014)

0—DeFalco, Tom (w), Kyle Higgins (w), Eddy Barrows (p), and Eber Ferreira (i). "Perpetual Motion." *Nightwing* #0. November 2012.

1—Higgins, Kyle (w), Eddy Barrows (p), and J.P. Mayer (i). "Welcome to Gotham." *Nightwing* #1. November 2011

2—Higgins, Kyle (w), Eddy Barrows (p), J.P. Mayer (i), and Paulo Sisqueira (i). "Haly's Wish." *Nightwing* #2. December 2011.

3—Higgins, Kyle (w), Eddy Barrows (p), and Eduardo Pansica (p). "Past and Present." *Nightwing* #3. January 2012.

7—Higgins, Kyle (w), Eddy Barrows (p), Geraldo Borges (p), Eber Ferreira (i), and Paulo Siqueira (i). "Turning Points." *Nightwing* #7. May 2012.

9—Higgins, Kyle (w), Eddy Barrows (p), and Andres Guinaldo (p). "The Gray Son." *Nightwing* #9. July 2012.

10—Higgins, Kyle (w), Eddy Barrows (p), Geraldo Borges (p), Ruy José (i), and Eber Ferreira (i). "The Tomorrow People." *Nightwing* #10. August 2012

15—Higgins, Kyle (w), Eddy Barrows (p), and Eber Ferreira (i). "Cleaning House." *Nightwing* #15. February 2013.

16—Higgins, Kyle (w), Eddy Barrows (p), and Eber Ferreira (i). "Turning Point." *Nightwing* #16. March 2013.

17—Higgins, Kyle (w), Juan Jose Ryp (p), and Roger Bonet (i). "The Long Week." *Nightwing* #17. April 2013.

18—Higgins, Kyle (w), Juan Jose Ryp (p), Roger Bonet (i), and Juan Albarran (i). "Slow Burn." *Nightwing* #18. May 2013.

24—Higgins, Kyle (w) and Will Conrad (a). "Buyer's Remorse." *Nightwing* #24. December 2013.

27—Higgins, Kyle (w), Will Conrad (a), and Cliff Richards (a). "Curiouser and Curiouser. *Nightwing* #27. March 2014.

28—Higgins, Kyle (w) and Russell Dauterman (a). "Butterfly Effects." *Nightwing* #28. April 2014.

29—Higgins, Kyle (w) and Russell Dauterman (a). "Safety Net." *Nightwing* #29. May 2014.

30—Seeley, Tim (w), Tom King (w), Javier Garrón (a), Jorge Lucas (a), Mikel Janín (p), and Guillermo Ortego (i). "Setting Son" *Nightwing* #30. July 2014.

Annual—Higgins, Kyle (w), Jason Masters (a), Daniel Sampere (p), and Vicente Cifuenetes (i). "Embers." *Nightwing Annual* #1. December 2013.

Other New 52 Comics

Johns, Geoff (w), David Finch (p), and Richard Friend (i). "Nightfall." *Forever Evil* #1. November 2013.

King, Tom (w), and Stephen Mooney (a).

"Only a Place for Dying." *Grayson: Future's End* #1. November 2014.

Lobdell, Scott (w), and Kenneth Rocafort (a). "Who are You?—Hoo Hoo?" *Red Hood and the Outlaws* #9. May 2012.

Seeley, Tim (w), Tom King (w), and Mikel Janin (a). "Grayson." *Grayson* #1. September 2014.

Seeley, Tim (w), Tom King (w), Mikel Janín (a), and Jeromy Cox (colorist). "The Gun Goes Off." *Grayson* #3. December 2014.

Seeley, Tim (w), Tom King (w), Mikel Janín (a), and Jeromy Cox (colorist). "Gut Feelings." *Grayson* #2. October 2014.

Snyder, Scott (w), Greg Capullo (p), and Jonathan Glapion (i). "Face the Court." *Batman* #4–5. February 2012 and March 2012.

Snyder, Scott (w), Greg Capullo (p), and Jonathan Glapion (i). "The Talons Strike!" *Batman* #7. May 2012.

Snyder, Scott (w), James Tynion IV (w), and Rafael Albuquerque (a). "The Call," in *Batman* #8. June 2012.

Tomasi, Peter J. (w), Patrick Gleason (p), and Mick Gray (i). "Born to Kill." *Batman and Robin* #1. November 2011.

Tomasi, Peter J. (w), Patrick Gleason (p), and Mick Gray (i). "Terminus Last Gasp." *Batman and Robin* #12. October 2012.

Tomasi, Peter J. (w), Patrick Gleason (p), and Mick Gray (i). "Terminus, Scar of the Bat." *Batman and Robin* #10. August 2012.

Tomasi, Peter J. (w), Patrick Gleason (p), Mick Gray (i), and Mark Irwin (i). "Acceptance." *Batman and Robin* #23. October 2013.

Other DC Comics

Barr, Mike W. (w), and Jim Aparo (a). "Psimon Says...." *Batman and the Outsiders* #5. December 1983.

Beechen, Adam (w), Darryl Banks (p), and Sean Parsons (i). "I am Donna Troy," in *Teen Titans/Outsiders Secret Files and Origins Vol. 1* #2. October 2005.

Daniel, Tony (w), and Sandu Florea (a). "Hostile Takeover." *Batman: Battle for the Cowl* #1. May 2009.

Daniel, Tony (w), and Sandu Florea (a). "Army of One." *Batman: Battle for the Cowl* #2. June 2009.

Daniel, Tony (w), and Sandu Florea (a). "Last Man Standing." *Batman: Battle for the Cowl* #3. July 2009.

Dixon, Chuck (w), Jason Armstrong (p), and Robert Campanella (i). "Year One." *Robin Annual* #4. 1995.

Dixon, Chuck (w), Scott Beatty (w), Javier Pulido (p), Robert Campanella (i), and Lee Loughridge (colorist). "Robin: Year One, Book 2." *Robin: Year One* #2. November 2000.

Dixon, Chuck (w), Scott Beatty (w), Javier Pulido (p), Robert Campanella (i), and Lee Loughridge (colorist). "Book Three." *Robin: Year One* #3. December 2000.

Dixon, Chuck (w), Scott Beatty (w), Rick Burchett (p), Mark Lipka (i), and Dan Davis (i). "Part Six: You Only Laugh Twice." *Joker: Last Laugh* #6. January 2002.

Finger, Bill (w), Jack Kirby (w), and Roz Kirby (w). "The Green Arrows of the World." *Adventure Comics* #250. July 1958.

Grant, Alan (w), and Brett Blevins (a). "Prodigal Part Two." *Batman: Shadow of the Bat* #32. November 1994.

Grant, Alan (w), Dave Taylor (p), and Stan Woch (i). "Hobson's Choice." *Batman: Shadow of the Bat* #53. August 1996.

Grant, Alan (w), Scott McDaniel (p), and Ray McCarthy (i). "Of Mice and Men" in *The Batman Chronicles* #5. June 1996.

Grant, Alan (w), Vince Giarrano (p), and Ray McCarthy (i). "Contagion, Part 7: Angel of Death." *Batman: Shadow of the Bat* #49. April 1996.

Grayson, Devin (w), Greg Land (p), and Bill Sienkiewicz (i). "Cosa Nostra Part One: Familia." *Nightwing and Huntress* #1. May 1998.

Grayson, Devin (w), Greg Land (p), and Bill Sienkiewicz (i). "Cosa Nostra Part Three: Black Sheep." *Nightwing and Huntress* #3. July 1998.

Grayson, Devin (w), Rick Mays (p, i), Jason Martin (i), and Karl Story (i). "Six Degrees, Part 1—Next of Kin." *Arsenal* #1. October 1998.

Grayson, Devin (w), and Rodolfo Damaggio (a). "Like Riding A Bike," in *The Batman Chronicles* #7. December 1997.

Haney, Bob (w), and Bruno Premiani (a). "The Thousand-and-One Dooms of Mr. Twister." *The Brave and the Bold* #54. June–July 1964.

Haney, Bob (w), Lee Elias (p), and Nick Cardy (i). "Captain Rumble Blasts the Scene!" *Teen Titans* #15. May–June 1968.

Haney, Bob (w), and Nick Cardy (a). "The Return of the Teen Titans." *Showcase* #59. November–December 1965.

Jimenez, Phil (w), José Luis García-López (p), and George Pérez (i). "The Return of Donna Troy, Chapter 2: Stark Contrast." *DC Special: Return of Donna Troy Vol. 1* #2. September 2005.

Kelly, Joe (w), Yvel Guichet (p), and Mark Propst (i). "New Blood." *JLA* #69. Early October 2002.

Kelly, Joe (w), Yvel Guichet (p), and Mark Propst (i). "Transition." *JLA* #71. Early November 2002.

Kirby, Jack (w, p) and Joe Simon (i). "Dreams of Doom," in *Adventure Comics* #77. August 1942.

Krul, J.T. (w), Geraldo Borges (p), Kevin Sharpe (p), Sergio Arino (p), Marlo Alquiza (i), and John Dell (i). "Domestic Disturbance." *Justice League: The Rise of Arsenal* #3. July 2010.

Loeb, Jeph (w), and Tim Sale (a). "Peace." *Batman: Dark Victory* #13. December, 2000.

Meltzer, Brad (w), Rags Morales (p), and M.R Bair (i). "Chapter Six: Husbands and Wives." *Identity Crisis* #6. January 2005.

Mishkin, Dan (w), Erik Larsen (p), and Mike DeCarlo (i). "The Secret Origin of Nightwing," in *Secret Origins* #13. April 1987.

Moench, Doug (w), and Bob McLeod (a). "Robin and Nightwing: Partners." *Showcase '93* #12. December 1993.

Morrison, Grant (w), Chris Burnham (a), and Jason Masters (a). "The Boy Wonder Returns." *Batman Incorporated* (2012–2013) #8. April 2013.

Morrison, Grant (w), Chris Burnham (a), and Jason Masters (a). "Fallen Son." *Batman Incorporated* (2012–2013) #9. May 2013.

Morrison, Grant (w), David Finch (p), Batt (i), and Ryan Winn (i). "Planet Gotham." *Batman: The Return*. January 2011.

Morrison, Grant (w), J.G. Jones (p), Marco Rudy (p), Carlos Pacheco (p), and Jesus Marino (p). "How to Murder the Earth." *Final Crisis* #6. January 2009.

O'Neil, Dennis (w), Greg Land (i), and Mike Sellers (a). *Nightwing mini-series* #1 and 4. September and December 1995.

Robinson, James (w), Mark Bagley (p), and Rob Hunter (i). "Team History." *Justice League of America* (2) #42. April 2010.

Robinson, James (w), Mark Bagley (p), Rob Hunter (i), and Norm Rapmund (i). "JLA: Omega Part 1—Worlds Collide." *Justice League of America* (2) #50. December 2010.

Samachson, Joe (probable writer), Cliff Young (p), and Steve Brodie (i). "Birth of the Battling Bowman," in *More Fun Comics* #89. March 1943.

Simone, Gail (w), Nicola Scott (p), and Doug Hazelwood (i). "A Debt of Significant Blood." *Secret Six* (3) #9. July 2009.

Smith, Kevin (w), Walter Flanagan (p), and Art Thibert (i). "Part Two: The Falconer." *Batman: The Widening Gyre* #2. November 2009.

Waid, Mark (w), and Scott Kolins (a). "Wings and Arrows." *The Brave and the Bold* (3) #15. September 2008.

Winick, Judd (w), Alé Garza (p), Trevor Scott (i), and Lary Stucker (i). "Part Three: Recessional." *Titans/Young Justice: Graduation Day* #3. August 2003.

Winick, Judd (w), Geoff Johns (w), Ivan Reis (p), Carlo Barberi (p), Marc Campos (i), and Norm Rapmund (i). "A Day After," in *Teen Titans/Outsiders Secret Files and Origins Vol. 1* #1. December 2003.

Wolfman, Marv (w), Chuck Patton (p), and Tom Poston (i). "First Blood," in *Action Comics Weekly* #614. August 23, 1988.

Graphic Novels and Trade Paperbacks

The Batman Chronicles 1 (May 1939–Spring 1940). New York: DC Comics, 2005.

The Batman Chronicles 2 (Spring 1940–November 1940). New York: DC Comics, 2006.

The Batman Chronicles 3 (December 1940–Spring 1941). New York: DC Comics, 2007.

The Batman Chronicles 4 (May 1941–November 1941). New York: DC Comics, 2007.

The Batman Chronicles 5 (November 1941–March 1942). New York: DC Comics, 2008.

The Batman Chronicles 6 (Spring 1942–July 1942). New York: DC Comics, 2008.

The Batman Chronicles 7 (August 1942–December 1942). New York: DC Comics, 2009.

The Batman Chronicles 10 (August 1943–November 1943). New York: DC Comics, 2010.

The Batman Chronicles 11 (December 1943–March 1944). New York: DC Comics, 2012.

Batman from the 30's to the 70's. New York: Crown Publishers, [1960] 1971.

DC's Greatest Imaginary Stories, Vol. 2: Batman and Robin. New York: DC Comics, 2010.

Dixon, Chuck (w), Scott Beatty (w), Javier Pulido (p), Marcos Martin (p), and Robert Campanella (i). *Robin: Year One.* New York: DC Comics, 2000, 2002.

Dixon, Chuck (w), Scott McDaniel (p), and Karl Story (i). *Nightwing: A Knight in Blüdhaven.* New York: DC Comics, 1998.

Dixon, Chuck (w), Scott Beatty (w), Scott McDaniel (p), and Andy Owens (i). *Nightwing: Year One.* New York: DC Comics, 2005.

Jimenez, Phil (w), Judd Winick (w), Luis Garcia-Lopez (a), Alé Garza (a), George Pérez (a). *Teen Titans/Outsiders: The Death and Return of Donna Troy.* New York: DC Comics, 2006.

Johns, Geoff (w), Phil Jimenez (p), George Pérez (p), Jerry Ordway (p), Ivan Reis (p), and Andy Lanning (i). *Infinite Crisis.* New York: DC Comics, 2006.

Kelly, Joe (w), Doug Mahnke (p), Yvel Guichet (p), and Lewis LaRosa (i). *JLA: The Obsidian Age Book 2.* New York: DC Comics, 2003.

Kelly, Joe (w), Doug Mahnke (p), Yvel Guichet (p), and Tom Nguyen (i). *JLA: The Obsidian Age Book 1.* New York: DC Comics, 2003.

Loeb, Jeph (w), Jim Lee (p), and Scott Williams (i). *Batman: Hush, Vol. 1.* New York: DC Comics, 2003.

Loeb, Jeph (w) and Tim Sale (a). *Batman: The Long Halloween.* New York: DC Comics, 2011.

Loeb, Jeph (w) and Tim Sale (a). *Batman: Dark Victory.* New York: DC Comics, 1999, 2000.

Miller, Frank (w) and David Mazzucchelli (p). *Batman: Year One.* New York: DC Comics, 1988.

Miller, Frank (w) and Jim Lee (a). *Absolute All Star Batman and Robin, the Boy Wonder.* New York: DC Comics, 2014.

Miller, Frank (w), Klaus Janson (i), and Lynn Varley (colorist). *The Dark Knight Returns.* New York: Warner Books, 1986.

Miller, Frank (w), Klaus Janson (i), and Lynn Varley (colorist). *The Dark Knight Returns.* Tenth Anniversary Edition. New York: DC Comics, 1996.

Miller, Frank (w, a) and Lynn Varley (colorist). *The Dark Knight Strikes Again.* New York: DC Comics, 2002.

The Robin Archives, Volume 1. New York: DC Comics, 2005.

The Robin Archives, Volume 2. New York: DC Comics, 2010.

Snyder, Scott (w), Greg Capullo (a), Jonathan Glapion (a), James Tynion IV (w), Rafael Albuquerque (a), and Jason Fabok (a). *Batman Vol. 2: The City of Owls.* The New 52. New York: DC Comics, 2013.

Tomasi, Peter (w), Patrick Gleason (p), Lee Garbett (p), Andy Clarke (p), Tomas Giorello (p), Mick Gray (i), Ray McCarthy (i), Keith Champagne (i), Tom Nguyen (i), Tomas Giorello (i), John Kalisz (c), Allen Passalaqua (c), and Hi-Fi (c). *Batman and Robin, Vol. 2: Pearl.* The New 52. New York: DC Comics, 2013.

Tomasi, Peter (w), Patrick Gleason (p), and Mick Gray (i). *Batman and Robin, Vol. 1: Born to Kill.* The New 52. New York: DC Comics, 2012.

Waid, Mark (w), Dan Curtis Johnson (w), Howard Porter (p), and Drew Geraci (i). *JLA: Tower of Babel.* New York: DC Comics, 2001.

Winick, Judd (w), Doug Mahnke (p), Shane Davis (p), and Eric Battle (p). *Batman: Under the Hood, Vol. 2.* New York: DC Comics, 2006.

Winick, Judd (w), Doug Mahnke (p), Tom Nguyen (i), Paul Lee (p), and Cam Smith (i). *Batman: Under the Hood, Vol. I.* New York: DC Comics, 2005.

Wolfman, Marv (w), Cherie Wilkerson (w), Erik Larsen (a), Mike DeCarlo (a), and Tom Mandrake (a). *Nightwing: Old Friends, New Enemies.* New York: DC Comics, 2013.

Wolfman, Marv (w), George Pérez (w, p), Jim Aparo (p), Tom Gummett (p), Mike DeCarlo (i), and Bob McLeod (i). *Batman: A Lonely Place of Dying.* New York, DC Comics 1990.

Wolfman, Marv (w), Jamal Igle (p), Jon Bosco (p), with Marc Andreyko (w), Joe Bennett (p), Keith Champagne (i), Alex Silva (i), and Jack Jadson (i). *Nightwing: The Lost Year.* New York: DC Comics, 2008.

Wolfman, Marv (w), George Pérez, and Romeo Tanghal (i). *The New Teen Titans Omnibus. Vol. I.* New York: DC Comics, 2011.

Other Sources

Arnold, C.F. "Nightwing Is the Centre of the (DC) Universe." *Comics Are Dead.* 24 March 2010. http://comicsaredead. yolasite.com/reviews-news/nightwing-is-the-centre-of-the-dc-universe.

Backer, Dan. "A Brief History of Political Cartoons." *Uniting Mugwumps and the Masses*, Part 1. University of Virginia (Aug. 1996) http://xroads.virginia.edu/~MA96/PUCK/part1.html#christi.

The Batman Universe. 2008–present. thebatmanuniverse.net.

The Batman Vault: A Museum-in-a-Book with Rare Collectibles from the Batcave. Philadelphia, PA: Running Press, 2006.

Bechdel, Alison. *Are You My Mother?* Boston: Houghton Mifflin, 2012.

Bedore, Pamela. *Dime Novels and the Roots of American Detective Fiction.* New York: Palgrave Macmillan, 2013.

Berger, Asa. *Manufacturing Desire: Media, Popular Culture, and Everyday Life.* New Brunswick, N.J.: Transaction Publishers, 1996.

Black, J. "Robin: Innocent Bystander," in *Batman Unauthorized.* Dallas: BenBella Books, 2008.

Bleeding Cool Forums. www.bleedingcool.com/forums/.

Bloom, Sandra L. "Trauma Theory Abbreviated." *Final Action Plan: A Coordinated Community-Based Response to Family Violence.* CommunityWorks, 1999. 1–14.

Bongco, Mila. *Reading Comics: Language, Culture, and the Concept of the Superhero in Comic Books.* New York: Garland Publishing, Inc., 2000.

Brady, Matt. "Marv Wolfman on Nightwing." *Newsarama.* 20 Nov. 2006. http://www.titanstower.com/marv-wolfman-on-nightwing-2/.

Brick, Scott. "Out of the Shadow of the Bat, Dick Grayson Flies on His Own as Nightwing." *Wizard #72.* Oct. 1997.

Brooker, Will. *Batman Unmasked: Analyzing a Cultural Icon.* New York: Continuum, 2005.

Buckley, Jerome Hamilton. *Seasons of Youth: The Bildungsroman from Dickens to Golding.* Cambridge, MA: Harvard University Press, 1974.

Burtis, Randy. "An Interview with Devin Grayson." *Comic Boards.* 9 Aug. 2004.

http://www.comicboards.com/devin.php.
Butler, Judith. *Gender Trouble: Feminism and the Subversion of Identity*. London: Routledge, 1989.
Cadigan, Glen. *Titans Companion*. Raleigh, NC: TwoMorrows Publishing, 2005.
Caruth, Cathy. *Unclaimed Experience: Trauma, Narrative and History*. Baltimore: Johns Hopkins University Press, 1996.
Chandler, Alfred. *The Visible Hand: The Managerial Revolution in American Business*. Cambridge, MA: Belknap Press, 1977.
Cochran, John D. "Batman and Robin were Lovers ..." *The Realist* #57 (March 1965).
Comic Vine. 2014. www.comicvine.com.
Contino, Jennifer M. "Marv Wolfman: From ROBIN to NIGHTWING: Chronicling the Adventures of Dick Grayson" *mania.com*. 19 Oct. 2006. http://www.mania.com/marv-wolfman-from-robin-to-nightwing-chronicling-adventures-dick-grayson_article_52561.html.
Daniels, Les. *Batman: The Complete History*. San Francisco: Chronicle, 1999, 2004.
The Dark Knight Rises. Directed by Christopher Nolan. 2012. Los Angeles: Warner Brothers. 2012. Blu Ray.
Davis, Lauren. "Paul Dini: Superhero Cartoon Execs Don't Want Largely Female Audiences." *io9*. 15 December 2013. http://io9.com/paul-dini-superhero-cartoon-execs-dont-want-largely-f-1483758317.
DC Editorial. "What's Next for Frank Miller and Jim Lee?" 2 April 2010. http://www.dccomics.com/blog/2010/04/02/whats-next-for-frank-miller-and-jim-lee.
Dessner, Lawrence Jay. "The Ghost of a Man's Own Father." *MLA* 91, no. 3 (May 1976): 436–49.
"Devin Grayson." *Comic Vine*. Last modified 22 September 2013. http://www.comicvine.com/devin-grayson/4040-42845/.
Disney's Hercules. Performed by Rip Torn, Tate Donovan, Susan Egan, James Woods, Danny DeVito. United States: Walt Disney Pictures, 1997. DVD.
Donald, Alan. "Is Batman Gay?" *The Panel: Silver Bullet Comic Books*. http://www.comicsbulletin.com/panel/106070953757230.htm.
Doyle, A.C. *The Case-book of Sherlock Holmes*. Oxford: Oxford University Press, 2009.
Duncan, Randy, and Matthew J. Smith. *Icons of the American Comic Book: From Captain America to Wonder Woman*. 1 1. Santa Barbara, CA [u.a.]: Greenwood, 2013.
Edrington, Don. "Comic Books, Milton Berle, and Holloway Milk Duds." www.pcdon.com/page451.html.
Faderman, L. *Surpassing the Love of Men*. London: HarperCollins, 1998.
Fantuzzi, M. *Achilles in Love*. Oxford: Oxford University Press, 2012.
Feiffer, Jules. *The Great Comic Book Heroes*. New York: Dial Press, 1965.
Finger, Dwight (compiler). "Bill Finger." *Fingar and Finger Family Genealogy*. http://www.fingerfamily.com/html/bio-finger-bill-12367.html.
Fingeroth, Danny. *Disguised as Clark Kent: Jews, Comics, and the Creation of the Superhero*. New York: Continuum, 2007.
Fisher, Will. "The Renaissance Beard: Masculinity in Early Modern England." *Renaissance Quarterly* 54, no. 1 (2001): 155–187.
Fleisher, Michael L. *The Encyclopedia of Comic Book Heroes: Volume 1, Batman*. New York: Collier Books, 1976.
François, Anne-Lise. "Fashion as Compulsive Artifice," in *The Seventies: The Age of Glitter in Popular Culture*. Edited by Shelton Waldrep. New York: Routledge, 2000.
Frye, N. *Anatomy of Criticism*. Princeton: Princeton University Press, 2000.
"Gabbing with the Dynamic Devin Grayson." *TheComicFanatic.com*. Last modified 21 November 2003. http://www.thecomicfanatic.com/modules.php?op=modload&name=News&file=article&sid=301&mode=thread&order=0&thold=0.
"The Gathering Storm." *Shadows of the Bat: The Cinematic Saga of the Dark Knight Part 2*. Directed by Constantine

Nadr. 2005. Burbank: Warner Brothers, 2005. DVD.

Gohlman, Susan Ashley. *Starting Over: The Task of the Protagonist in the Contemporary Bildungsroman.* New York: Garland Publishing, 1990.

The Grand Comics Database. www.comics.org.

Grant, Donovan. "Devin Grayson on Her Batman Universe Work." *The Batman Universe.* 20 May 2014. http://thebatmanuniverse.net/tbu-exclusive-3/.

Grant, Jaime M., Lisa A. Mottet, Justin Tanis, Jack Harrison, Jody L. Herman, and Mara Keisling. *Injustice at Every Turn: A Report of the National Transgender Discrimination Survey.* Washington: National Center for Transgender Equality and National Gay and Lesbian Task Force, 2011.

Groth, Gary. "Jerry Robinson: Been There, Done That." *The Comics Journal,* 271 (2004): 72–111.

Gurian, Michael. *Nurture the Nature: Understanding and Supporting Your Child's Unique Core Personality.* San Francisco: Jossey-Bass, 2007.

Gustaveson, Rob. "Gary Conway Talks Back to The Comics Journal." *The Comics Journal No. 69.* Dec. 1981.

Hadju, David. *The Ten-Cent Plague: The Great Comic-Book Scare and How It Changed America.* New York: Macmillan, 2009.

Hamerlinck, P.C., editor. *The Fawcett Companion: The Best of FCA.* Raleigh: TwoMorrows, 2001.

Hamilton, Neil. *The 1970s.* New York: Infobase, 2006.

Hardin, James, ed. *Reflection and Action: Essays on the Bildungsroman.* Columbia: University of South Carolina Press, 1991.

Haubold, J. *Homer's People: Epic Poetry and Social Formation.* Cambridge: Cambridge University Press, 2000.

Hine, Thomas. *The Great Funk: Styles of the Shaggy, Sexy, Shameless 1970s.* New York: Sarah Crichton Books, 2007.

Homans, Margaret. "Adoption Narratives, Trauma, and Origins." *Narrative* 14, no. 1 (January 2006): 4–26.

Homer. *The Iliad.* Oxford: Oxford University Press, 2008.

Hopkins, Michael F. "Subtlety and Power: The George Pérez Interview." *Amazing Heroes* #50. 1 July 1984.

Hughes, Jonathan, and Louis P. Cain. *American Economic History*, 8th edition. Upper Saddle River, NJ: Prentice Hall, 2010.

Iversen, Anniken Telnes. *Change and Continuity: The Bildungsroman in English.* PhD Dissertation. University of Tromsø, 2009.

Jacobs, Dale. *Graphic Encounters: Comics and the Sponsorship of Multimodal Literacy.* New York: Bloomsbury, 2013.

Johnston, Rich. "The Entire Meghan Hetrick Art From Nightwing #30—Before It Was Binned." *Bleeding Cool.* 2 June 2014. http://www.bleedingcool.com/2014/06/02/the-entire-art-from-nightwing-20-by-before-it-was-binned/.

_____. "Wash Your Mouth out with Batsoap." *Lying in the Gutters*, 9 September 2008, http://www.comicbookresources.com/?page=article&id=17985.

Jones, Gerard. *Men of Tomorrow: Geeks, Gangsters, and the Birth of the Comic Book.* New York: Basic Books, 2004.

Kane, Bob, and Tom Andrae. *Batman & Me.* Forestville: Eclipse, 1989.

Kohn, Alfie. *Unconditional Parenting: Moving from Rewards and Punishment to Love and Reason.* New York: Atria Books, 2005.

Langley, Travis. *Batman and Psychology: A Dark and Stormy Knight.* Hoboken, NJ: Wiley, 2012.

Lehman, Christopher. *American Animated Cartoons of the Vietnam Era: A Study of Social Commentary in Films and Television Programs, 1961–1973.* Jefferson, NC: McFarland, 2007.

Leverenz, David. "The Last Real Man in America: From Natty Bumppo to Batman." *American Literary History* 3, no. 4 (Winter 1991): 753–781.

"List of Comic Book Sidekicks." *Wikipedia.* http://en.wikipedia.org/wiki/List_of_comic_book_sidekicks.

Medhurst, Andy. "Batman, Deviance, and

Camp." In *The Many Lives of Batman: Critical Approaches to a Superhero and his Media.* Ed. Roberta Pearson and William Uricchio. New York: Routledge, 1991: 149–163.

Miedzian, Myriam. *Boys Will Be Boys: Breaking the Link Between Masculinity and Violence.* New York: Lantern Books, [1991] 2002.

Miller, John Jackson. *The Comics Chronicles.* www.comicchron.com.

Miller, Stephen. *The Seventies Now: Culture as Surveillance.* Durham: Duke University Press, 1999.

Mitchell, W.J.T. *Picture Theory.* Chicago: University of Chicago Press, 1994.

Morris, Jon. "The Year in Tights: the Best (and Worst) Superhero Comics of 2006." *Potlatch.* 2006. http://www.thehighhat.com/Potlatch/007/top10_morris.html

Morton, J.L.. "Color Matters." Last Modified 2011. http://www.colormatters.com.

Nagy, G. *The Best of the Achaeans: Concepts of the Hero in Archaic Greek Poetry.* Baltimore: Johns Hopkins, 1998.

_____. *Homer the Classic.* New York: Harvard, 1979.

Nancy, Jean-Luc. *The Ground of the Image.* New York: Fordham University Press, 2005.

Nielsen, Carsten Fogh. "Leaving the Shadow of the Bat: Aristotle, Kant, and Dick Grayson on Moral Education," in *Batman and Philosophy: The Dark Knight of the Soul.* Ed. by Mark D. White and Robert Arp. Hoboken, NJ: John Wiley & Sons, 2008: 254–268.

Nobleman, Marc Tyler. "Interview with Co-Author of Bob Kane's Autobiography." *Noblemania.* 30 March 2014. http://noblemania.blogspot.com/2014/03/interview-with-co-author-of-bob-kanes.html.

North, Sterling. "A National Disgrace." *Chicago Daily News.* 8 May 1940.

Oulton, C. *Romantic Friendship in Victorian Literature.* Hampshire: Ashgate, 2007.

Pangborn, Joshua R. "Speculative Nostalgia and Its Role in Shakespeare and Renaissance Literature." DA diss, St. John's University, 2014.

Parker, Kim, and Wendy Wang. "Modern Parenthood: Roles of Moms and Dads Converge as They Balance Work and Family." Pew Research Center. March 13, 2013. http://www.pewsocialtrends.org/2013/03/14/modern-parenthood-roles-of-moms-and-dads-converge-as-they-balance-work-and-family/

Pearson, Roberta E., and William Uricchio (eds). *The Many Lives of the Batman: Critical Approaches to a Superhero and His Media.* New York: Routledge, 1991.

_____. "Notes from the Batcave: An Interview with Dennis O'Neil." In *The Many Lives of the Batman: Critical Approaches to a Superhero and His Media.* New York: Routledge, 1991: 18–32.

Pittman, David J. "Mass Media and Juvenile Deliquency," in *Juvenile Delinquency.* Ed. by Joseph S. Roucek. New York: Philosophical Library, 1958.

Polce-Lynch, Mary. *Boy Talk: How You Can Help Your Son Express His Emotions.* Oakland, CA: New Harbringer, 2002.

Pustz, Matthew. *Comic Book Culture: Fanboys and True Believers.* Jackson: University of Mississippi, 1999.

Roberts, Garyn G. *Dick Tracy and American Culture: Morality and Mythology, Text and Content.* Jefferson, NC: McFarland, 1993.

Robinson, Iann. "All Star Batman and Robin the Boy Wonder." 17 December 2007. http://www.craveonline.com/comics/articles/154736-all-star-batman-and-robin.

Rollin, R. "Beowulf to Batman: The Epic Hero and Pop Culture." *College English*, Vol 31, No. 5 (February 1970): 431–449.

Sabin, Roger. *Comics, Comix and Graphic Novels.* London: Phaidon Press Limited, 1996.

Sagert, Kelly Boyer. *The 1970s.* Westport, CT: Greenwood Press, 2007.

Sanderson, Peter. "Comics in Context #34—Knight Makes Right." 16 April 2004. http://www.ign.com/articles/2004/04/17/comics-in-context-34-knight-makes-right.

Schechter, Daniel S., and M. Cevdet

Tosyali. "Posttraumatic Stress Disorder." In *Anxiety Disorders in Children and Adolescents: Epidemiology, Risk Factors and Treatment*, edited by Cecelia A. Essau and Franz Peterman, 285–322. London: Routledge, 2002.

Schramm, Wilbur. *Television in the Lives of Our Children*. Palo Alto, CA: Stanford University Press, 1961.

"Secret Origins of the Batman TV Show, Part One: Batman Begins!" *Dial B for Bats*. dialbforblog.com/archives/204/.

Sedgwick, Eve Kosofsky. *Between Men: English Literature and Male Homosocial Desire*. New York: Columbia University Press, 1985.

———. *Epistemology of the Closet*. Berkeley: University of California Press, 1990.

Sharrett, Christopher. "Batman and the Twilight of the Idols: An Interview with Frank Miller." In *The Many Lives of the Batman*. Edited by Roberta E. Pearson and William Uricchio. New York: Routledge, Chapman and Hall, 1991: 33–46.

Siegel, Daniel J., and Mary Hartzell. *Parenting from the Inside Out: How a Deeper Self-Understanding Can Help You Raise Children Who Thrive*. New York: Jeremy P. Tarcher/Penguin, 2004.

Simone, Gail. [Untitled Post]. *Tumblr*. 27 September 2011. http://gailsimone.tumblr.com/post/10718077837/deathly-illandalwaysbusy-thehappysorceress.

Sinos, D. *Achilles, Patroklos and the Meaning of Philos*. Washington: H. Kowatsch, 1980.

Smith, Kevin. "Episode #22–#23: Kyle Higgins." Fat Man on Batman Podcast. 2012. http://smodcast.com/episodes/kyle-higgins-master-of-dick/.

SpinMedia. "Batman Bale Says No to Robin." *Starpulse*. July 2, 2008. http://www.starpulse.com/news/index.php/2008/07/02/batman_bale_says_no_to_robin_.

Steranko, Jim. *The Steranko History of Comics*. Reading, PA: Supergraphics, 1970.

Taylor, Shelley. *The Tending Instinct: How Nurturing Is Essential to Who We Are and How We Live*. New York: Times Books, 2002.

Terr, Lenore. *Too Scared to Cry: Psychic Trauma in Childhood*. New York: Harper & Row, 1990.

Tilley, Carol L. "Seducing the Innocent: Fredric Wertham and the Falsifications That Helped Condemn Comics." *Information & Culture* 47:4 (2012): 383–413.

Trachtenberg, Alan. *The Incorporation of America: Culture and Society in the Gilded Age*. New York: Hill and Wang, 1982.

Tramountanas, George A. "Devin Grayson—The 'Nightwing' Crisis." *Comic Book Resources*. 10 November 2005. http://www.comicbookresources.com/?page=article&id=5934.

Under the Red Hood. Directed by Brandon Vietti. 2010. Burbank, CA: Warner Home Video, 2010. DVD.

Van Nortwick, T. *Imagining Men: Ideals of Masculinity in Ancient Greek Culture*. Stanford: Praeger Publishers, 2008.

Warshow, Robert S. *The Immediate Experience: Movies, Comics, Theatre & Other Aspects of Popular Culture*. Cambridge, MA: Harvard University Press, 2001.

Wertham, Fredric. *Seduction of the Innocent*. New York: Rinehart, 1954.

White, Mark D., Robert Arp, and William Irwin, eds. *Batman and Philosophy*. Hoboken, NJ: Wiley, 2008.

Williams, Bronwyn T. "Action Heroes and Literate Sidekicks: Literacy and Identity in Popular Culture." *Journal of Adolescent and Adult Literacy* 50, no. 8 (2007): 680–685.

Williamson, Catherine. "'Draped Crusaders': Disrobing Gender in *The Mask of Zorro*." *Cinema Journal* 36, no. 2 (Winter 1997): 3–16.

Worden, Daniel. *Masculine Style: The American West and Literary Modernism*. New York: Palgrave Macmillan, 2011.

Wright, Bradford W. *Comic Book Nation: The Transformation of Youth Culture in America*. Baltimore, MD: The Johns Hopkins University Press, 2001.

Zanker, G. *The Heart of Achilles*. Ann Arbor: University of Michigan Press, 1997.

About the Contributors

As a historian, J.L. **Bell** focuses on the American Revolution in New England. He is an assistant editor of the anthology *Colonial Comics* and has scripted stories for the collections *Minimum Paige, Hellbound, The Greatest of All Time Comics Anthology* and *In a Single Bound*.

Bethany F. **Brengan** is a freelance writer and editor living on Washington's Olympic Peninsula. By day, she abolishes dangling participles; by night, she toils over the next Great American Novel. Her work has been published in *The Sow's Ear Poetry Review* and *Cicada*.

Dan Grayson **Cordero** is a sequential art major at Southwestern Community College, where he often presents as a guest speaker on transgender-related topics and also works as one of the cartoonists for the award-winning paper *The Sun*. He plans to transfer to an art school and learn more about animation and comic books.

Kristen L. **Geaman** has a doctorate in medieval history from the University of Southern California. She teaches pre-modern world history and historical methods at the University of Toledo in Ohio. Her research interests include medieval England and her writing has appeared in *The English Historical Review* and *Social History of Medicine*.

Jordan **Hass** is a Los Angeles–based writer, comedian, and host of assorted internet shows and blogs. His website, JordanHass.com, is constantly updated with dissections of the week's current events and personal pieces. He can be followed on social media @jordha.

Mollie **Herlocker** has a BA in history and American studies from California Lutheran University. She is currently exploring pathways for bringing historical education to a more accessible and entertaining medium for young people.

Tini **Howard** is a writer of comics and other pop culture miscellanea. Her award-winning debut comic, *Magdalena: Seventh Sacrament* was published in 2014 by Image/Top Cow Comics. Her commentary and musings have also been featured on Gawker and io9. She writes about comics and culture on her blog, tinihoward.tumblr.com.

About the Contributors

Kalina **Keester** is a business major at Murray State College in Oklahoma. She is relatively new to comics, with the first series that she read being *Batman and Robin* (2009–2011), but she grew up watching the *Teen Titans* cartoon show.

David **Kingsley** has an MA in English literature and teaches high school English; he also works as a university supervisor at Northern Arizona University. Publications include essays in collections on incest in Wes Craven's 1984 *Nightmare* and the effect of horror comics on the fiction of Stephen King.

Yasmin **Lysaker** works in patient administration in a small European hospital. She first started reading *Batman*, *Detective Comics* and *The New Teen Titans/Tales of the Teen Titans* in the 1980s. After a 20-year break, she took up reading comics again in 2011.

Cara L. **MacNeil-Donoghue** is a graduate student at the College of New Jersey who writes about gender and feminist theories. She is a contributing writer for *The California Journal of Women Writers* and also is a high school teacher.

César Alfonso **Marino** is a graduate of the Universidad de Buenos Aires (UBA) and has published about popular culture in a number of books and international journals. He has an essay in a collection about the comics of Joss Whedon.

Christopher **McKittrick** is an instructor and administrator at St. John's University in Queens, New York. His published work on comics include an essay on Superman creators Jerry Siegel and Joe Shuster and an essay on graphic novelist Harvey Pekar. He is a regular contributor to MovieBuzzers.com and DailyActor.com.

Fernando Gabriel **Pagnoni Berns** teaches at Universidad de Buenos Aires (UBA), where he gives seminars on American horror cinema and Euro horror. He has published essays in collections ranging from *Undead in the West*, to *Reading Richard Matheson*.

Joshua R. **Pangborn** is an educator and award-winning playwright living in New York City. He is the artistic director and playwright-in-residence for the theatre company SideKick Productions (www.sidekickproductionsny.com) and has a doctorate in English literature from St. John's University.

Star **Schneider** is an English and history buff who lives in Los Angeles. She likes going to comic book stores for the new releases, but her collection mainly consists of older and less polished treasures that she has sourced out of various store bins, comic conventions and friends' garages.

Alexandra **Schulz** is a freelance writer and translator with a degree in screenwriting from the Konrad Wolff Academy for Film and Television. Professionally she has developed web shows, worked in advertising and penned an award-winning motion comic "Forever Mine." She is the translator of the Cartoon Network show "Steven Universe."

Pamela **Shah** was born in the prairies and grew up in Calgary, Alberta. She has obtained her bachelor's degree in history at the University of Calgary where she also discovered a passion for politics, archeology and literature. She plans to further her studies in early-modern European history.

Shelly **Sposato** is a student in the computer engineering department at Cal Poly Pomona where she works as an on-campus writing tutor. She has been reading comic books since she was fifteen and aspires to work in the industry.

Catherine M. **Vale** is a doctoral candidate at Arizona State University, where she studies the changing depictions of technology and progress in science museums. She has served as an intern at a wide range of institutions, including the Children's Museum of Phoenix, the Arizona Popular Culture Museum and the International Association of Amusement Parks and Attractions.

Emily **Zinkin** studied history at the University of Nottingham, where she was introduced to comics through her professors, who proved to be supportive when she decided to integrate Batman and Robin into her dissertation on the *Iliad*. She has just completed an MA in creative writing.

Index

al Ghul, Ra's 204, 205, 211, 265, 268
al Ghul, Talia 211, 217, 218
All-Star Batman and Robin 244, 245, 250–259
Arsenal *see* Harper, Roy
Azrael *see* Valley, Jean-Paul

Batman 60–61, 74–76; successor 152, 268, 276, 302; *see also* Wayne, Bruce
Batman: Dark Victory 42, 44, 180, 186, 187
Batman Family 28–37
Beatty, Scott 280
Bechdel, Alison 170
Bertinelli, Helena (New 52) 165, 166, 167, 171, 172, 173; *see also* Huntress
bildungsroman 112, 120–121, 122, 123, 127n39, 128n41
Blockbuster 137–138, 139, 140, 280, 303, 304, 305
Blüdhaven 135, 136, 141, 275, 279, 319
boy hostage 13, 102, 248
Butler, Judith 54

Clancy, Bridget 199–200, 326
Court of Owls 58, 157–158, 159, 317, 318
Crisis on Infinite Earths 4

*The Dark Knight Return*s 245, 246, 258
The Dark Knight Strikes Again 245, 246–250, 258
Dark Victory see *Batman: Dark Victory*
Deadman (Boston Brand) 150, 279
Deathstroke 140, 236, 272, 309, 318
Detective Comics #38 1, 8
Didio, Dan 141, 287
dime novels 96–97, 98, 99
Dixon, Chuck 45, 134, 135–136, 138, 140, 142, 266, 274–283, 311
Drake, Tim 42, 43, 45–46, 48, 74, 140, 148, 151, 164, 191, 196, 201–207, 209n43, 212, 214, 215, 217, 231, 275, 276, 278, 281, 282, 314, 316

Ellsworth, Whitney 8, 9
Elton, Lori 34

female gaze 169, 170, 171
feminism 171, 173–174, 269
Finger, Bill 8, 9, 10, 69, 94, 96, 99, 147

Flores, Catalina (Tarantula) 137, 138–140, 173, 313n8, 304–305, 306

Gordon, Barbara 28, 30, 31, 32, 124, 125, 136, 137, 141, 161, 164, 167n8, 244, 278, 317, 318, 324
Grayson, Devin 137, 138–139, 140, 141, 142, 173, 284–313
Grayson, John 156, 179
Grayson, Mary 49, 156, 179–180
Green Arrow (Oliver Queen) 150, 151, 264, 265, 299, 300

Harper, Roy (Speedy, Arsenal, Red Arrow) 47, 140, 224–225, 226–232, 237, 242n44, 264, 265, 293
heroic friendship 81, 87, 88, 89, 91–92
Higgins, Kyle 142, 156, 157, 164, 314–321
homoeroticism 248, 259n13, 260n35, 300
homosociality 95, 101, 103, 105, 106n30
Hudson University 35, 71, 132
Huntress (Helena Bertinelli) 137, 172, 279, 280, 281, 303

Jiminez, Phil 75, 145
Joker 58, 59, 73, 159–160, 163, 198, 217, 231, 248, 257, 264, 280
Joker's Daughter 35
Justice League 79n35, 149, 151, 152

Kane, Bob 8, 69, 94, 96, 99, 103
Kane, Kathy (Batwoman) 20, 26n58
Kelley, Carrie 246–247, 248, 260n21
Kent, Clark 73, 96, 122, 146, 147, 149, 277, 323, 326
Kent, Connor (Superboy) 148
Koriand'r (Starfire) 68, 72, 114, 116, 117, 133, 134, 141, 148, 223, 224, 232–240, 278
Kyle, Selina (Catwoman) 16, 103–104

Land, Greg 282
leadership 31–32, 37, 115, 294

masculinity 97–98, 100, 105
McDaniel, Scott 280, 282
Miller, Frank 13, 56, 68, 77, 137, 192n4, 244–259, 269
Morrison, Grant 142

353

New 52 2, 5, 142, 156, 172, 207, 317
New Look 21, 131
New Teen Titans 113, 114, 115, 116, 117, 125, 132, 133, 189, 197, 235, 271, 272
Nightwing: costume 157, 267; origins of name 73, 122, 134, 147, 328
Nightwing: Year One 120–125, 184, 189, 280
Nolan, Christopher 49, 68, 77, 165

O'Neil, Dennis 264–270, 275, 277–279

Pennyworth, Alfred 15, 42, 43, 44, 78n7, 121, 123, 124, 125, 146–147, 164, 178–192, 204, 212, 213, 217, 234, 265, 302
Pérez, George 37, 48, 117, 133, 134, 147, 271, 272
performance theory 54–55, 61
Peterson, Scott 275, 311
pictorial turn 40, 41
pulp fiction 97, 98, 99

Queen, Oliver *see* Green Arrow

rape 138–139, 173, 303–306
reader stand-in 11, 66, 99, 102, 130, 265
reasons for Robin 10, 11, 12, 13, 78, 83, 90, 102, 104–105, 147, 274
reboot *see* New 52
Red Arrow *see* Harper, Roy
Robin costume 28, 33–34, 40, 45, 48, 51, 52n18, 70, 145
Robin Hood 41, 48, 100, 255
Robin Rooters 29, 33, 36
Robin: Year One 42, 44, 183, 281
Robinson, Jerry 8, 11, 41
Romani heritage 3, 140, 175n9, 296
romantic friendship 84, 92

Seduction of the Innocent see Wertham, Fredric
sidekick 1, 9, 44, 51n2, 87, 107n38, 133, 145
speculative nostalgia 49–50, 53n37
Speedy *see* Harper, Roy

Starfire *see* Koriand'r
Superman *see* Kent, Clark

Tarantula *see* Flores, Catalina
Teen Titans 131, 147–148, 222
Teen Titans (television cartoon) 48
theatricality 49
therapon/hetairos relationship 82, 86, 92
Todd, Jason 57, 58–59, 61, 88, 116, 119, 123–125, 133, 148, 151, 164, 184, 191, 196–200, 207, 212, 215, 246, 259n3, 266, 269, 270, 317
trauma theory 66–67, 69–70, 71–72, 74, 75–76
Troy, Donna 114, 125, 148, 152, 156, 222–225, 228, 236, 237–238
Two-Face 74, 124, 183, 281

Valley, Jean-Paul (Azrael) 61, 134, 201, 202, 270

Wayne, Bruce (Batman) 14–15, 16, 42–43, 44, 45, 46, 47, 50, 67, 69, 70, 71–73, 75–76, 78, 83, 85, 86, 88, 89, 91–92, 96, 98, 100, 102, 104, 113, 114, 115, 116, 118–119, 121, 123, 124, 125, 132, 133, 134, 135, 136, 139, 146, 150, 158, 164, 165, 171, 178–192, 195n65, 196, 197, 198, 201, 205, 206, 216, 217, 218, 219, 223, 224, 233, 234, 236, 237, 240, 245–249, 251–258, 277–278, 285, 292–294, 297–299, 302, 317, 319, 323, 325, 326
Wayne, Damian 151, 152, 160–161, 180, 182, 184, 191, 192, 200, 205, 206, 211–220
Wayne, Thomas 79n26, 186, 187, 188, 189
Wertham, Fredric 17–20, 26n48, 103, 146, 251
West, Wally 148, 149, 150, 294, 303, 323, 325
Winick, Judd 141
Wolfman, Marv 37, 48, 72–73, 113, 127n28, 132, 133, 134, 135, 138, 139, 142, 147, 266, 271–272, 311

Zucco, Sonia 159
Zucco, Tony 67, 70, 156, 161, 162, 166

www.ingramcontent.com/pod-product-compliance
Ingram Content Group UK Ltd.
Pitfield, Milton Keynes, MK11 3LW, UK
UKHW041922140426
5217IPUK00014B/266